Trübner's Oriental Series

THE ECONOMIC HISTORY OF INDIA UNDER EARLY BRITISH RULE

Trübner's Oriental Series

INDIA: HISTORY, ECONOMY AND SOCIETY
In 11 Volumes

THE ECONOMIC HISTORY OF INDIA UNDER EARLY BRITISH RULE

FROM THE RISE OF THE BRITISH POWER IN 1757 TO THE ACCESSION OF QUEEN VICTORIA IN 1837

ROMESH CHUNDER DUTT

ROUTLEDGE
Taylor & Francis Group

First published in 1950 by
Routledge &Kegan Paul Ltd

Reprinted in 2000, 2002 by
Routledge
11 New Fetter Lane, London EC4P 4EE

Routledge is an imprint of the Taylor & Francis Group

Printed and Bound in Great Britain

British Library Cataloguing in Publication Data
A CIP catalogue record for this book
is available from the British Library

The Economic History of India Under Early British Rule
ISBN 0-415-24493-5
India: History, Economy and Society: 11 Volumes
ISBN 0-415-24288-6
Trübner's Oriental Series
ISBN 0-415-23188-4

THE ECONOMIC HISTORY OF INDIA UNDER EARLY BRITISH RULE

FROM THE RISE OF THE BRITISH POWER IN 1757 TO THE ACCESSION OF QUEEN VICTORIA IN 1837

BY

ROMESH DUTT, C.I.E.

LECTURER IN INDIAN HISTORY AT UNIVERSITY COLLEGE, LONDON
LATE COMMISSIONER OF ORISSA AND MEMBER OF THE
BENGAL LEGISLATIVE COUNCIL

SEVENTH EDITION

LONDON
ROUTLEDGE & KEGAN PAUL LTD
BROADWAY HOUSE, 68-74 CARTER LANE, E.C.4
1950

PREFACE

EXCELLENT works on the military and political transactions of the British in India have been written by eminent historians. No history of the people of India, of their trades, industries, and agriculture, and of their economic condition under British administration, has yet been compiled.

Recent famines in India have attracted attention to this very important subject, and there is a general and widespread desire to understand the condition of the Indian people—the sources of their wealth and the causes of their poverty. A brief Economic History of British India is therefore needed at the present time.

Englishmen can look back on their work in India, if not with unalloyed satisfaction, at least with some legitimate pride. They have conferred on the people of India what is the greatest human blessing—Peace. They have introduced Western Education, bringing an ancient and civilised nation in touch with modern thought, modern sciences, modern institutions and life. They have built up an Administration which, though it requires reform with the progress of the times, is yet strong and efficacious. They have framed wise laws, and have established Courts of Justice, the purity of which is as absolute as in any country on the face of the earth. These are results which no honest critic of British work in India regards without high admiration.

On the other hand, no open-minded Englishman contemplates the material condition of the people of

India under British rule with equal satisfaction. The poverty of the Indian population at the present day is unparalleled in any civilised country; the famines which have desolated India within the last quarter of the nineteenth century are unexampled in their extent and intensity in the history of ancient or modern times. By a moderate calculation, the famines of 1877 and 1878, of 1889 and 1892, of 1897 and 1900, have carried off fifteen millions of people. The population of a faired-sized European country has been swept away from India within twenty-five years. A population equal to half of that of England has perished in India within a period which men and women, still in middle age, can remember.

What are the causes of this intense poverty and these repeated famines in India? Superficial explanations have been offered one after another, and have been rejected on close examination. It was said that the population increased rapidly in India, and that such increase must necessarily lead to famines; it is found on inquiry that the population has never increased in India at the rate of England, and that during the last ten years it has altogether ceased to increase. It was said that the Indian cultivators were careless and improvident, and that those who did not know how to save when there was plenty, must perish when there was want; but it is known to men who have lived all their lives among these cultivators, that there is not a more abstemious, a more thrifty, a more frugal race of peasantry on earth. It was said that the Indian money-lender was the bane of India, and by his fraud and extortion kept the tillers of the soil in a chronic state of indebtedness; but the inquiries of the latest Famine Commission have revealed that the cultivators of India are forced under the thraldom of money-lenders by the rigidity of the Government revenue demand. It was said that in a country where the people depended almost entirely on their crops, they must starve when the crops failed in years of drought; but the crops in India, as a whole, have never failed, there has never been a single year when the food supply of the country was insufficient for the people, and there must be something wrong, when failure in a single province brings on a famine, and the people are unable to buy their supplies from neighbouring provinces rich in harvests.

Deep down under all these superficial explanations we must seek for the true causes of Indian poverty and Indian famines. The economic laws which operate in India are the same as in other countries of the world; the causes which lead to wealth among other nations lead to prosperity in India; the causes which impoverish other nations impoverish the people of India. Therefore, the line of inquiry which the economist will pursue in respect of India is the same which he adopts in inquiring into the wealth or poverty of other nations. Does agriculture flourish? Are industries and manufactures in a prosperous condition? Are the finances properly administered, so as to bring back to the people an adequate return for the taxes paid by them? Are the sources of national wealth widened by a Government anxious for the material welfare of the people? These are questions which the average Englishman asks himself when inquiring into the economic condition of any country in the world; these are questions which he will ask himself in order to ascertain the truth about India.

It is, unfortunately, a fact which no well-informed Indian official will ignore, that, in many ways, the sources of national wealth in India have been narrowed under British rule. India in the eighteenth century was a great manufacturing as well as a great agricultural country, and the products of the Indian loom supplied the markets of Asia and of Europe. It is, unfortunately, true that the East Indian Company and the British Parliament, following the selfish commercial policy of a hundred years ago, discouraged Indian manufacturers in the early years of British rule in order to encourage the rising manufactures of England. Their fixed policy, pursued during the last decades of the eighteenth century and the first decades of the nineteenth, was to make India subservient to the industries of Great Britain, and to make the Indian people grow raw produce only, in order to supply material for the looms and manufactories of Great Britain. This policy was pursued with unwavering resolution and with fatal success; orders were sent out, to force Indian artisans to work in the Company's factories; commercial residents were legally vested with extensive powers over villages and communities of Indian weavers; prohibitive tariffs excluded Indian silk and cotton goods from England; English goods were admitted into India free of duty or on payment of a nominal duty.

The British manufacturer, in the words of the historian, H. H. Wilson, "employed the arm of political injustice to keep down and ultimately strangle a competitor with whom he could not have contended on equal terms;" millions of Indian artisans lost their earnings; the population of India lost one great source of their wealth. It is a painful episode in the history of British rule in India; but it is a story which has to be told to explain the economic condition of the Indian people, and their present helpless dependence on agriculture. The invention of the power-loom in Europe completed the decline of the Indian industries; and when in recent years the power-loom was set up in India, England once more acted towards India with unfair jealousy. An excise duty has been imposed on the production of cotton fabrics in India which disables the Indian manufacturer from competing with the manufacturer of Japan and China, and which stifles the new steam-mills of India.

Agriculture is now virtually the only remaining source of national wealth in India, and four-fifths of the Indian people depend on agriculture. But the Land Tax levied by the British Government is not only excessive, but, what is worse, it is fluctuating and uncertain in many provinces. In England, the Land Tax was between one shilling and four shillings in the pound, *i.e.*, between 5 and 20 per cent. of the rental, during a hundred years before 1798, when it was made perpetual and redeemable by William Pitt. In Bengal the Land Tax was fixed at over 90 per cent. of the rental, and in Northern India at over 80 per cent. of the rental, between 1793 and 1822. It is true that the British Government only followed the precedent of the previous Mahomedan rulers, who also claimed an enormous Land Tax. But the difference was this, that what the Mahomedan rulers claimed they could never fully realise; what the British rulers claimed they realised with rigour. The last Mahomedan ruler of Bengal, in the last year of his administration (1764), realised a land revenue of £817,553; within thirty years the British rulers realised a land revenue of £2,680,000 in the same Province. In 1802 the Nawab of Oudh ceded Allahabad and some other rich districts in Northern India to the British Government. The land revenue which had been claimed by the Nawab in these ceded districts was £1,352,347; the land revenue which was claimed by the British rulers within three years of the cession was £1,682,306. In Madras, the Land Tax first imposed by the East India Company was one-half the gross produce of the land! In Bombay, the land revenue of the territory conquered from the Mahrattas in 1817 was £800,000 in the year of the conquest; it was raised to £1,500,000 within a few years of British rule; and it has been continuously raised since. "No Native Prince demands the rent which we do," wrote Bishop Heber in 1826, after travelling all through India, and visiting British and Native States. "A Land Tax like that which now exists in India," wrote Colonel Briggs in 1830, "professing to absorb the whole of the landlord's rent, was never known under any Government in Europe or Asia."

The people of Bengal and of Northern India gradually obtained some relief from the heavy land assessment of the early years of British rule. In Bengal the assessment was made permanent; and as it has not been raised with the extension of cultivation, it now bears (including Road and Public Work cesses, which have been since imposed on the rental) a ratio of about 35 per cent. on the rental. In Northern India the assessment was not made permanent, but it was reduced to slightly over 50 per cent., including all cesses, in 1855. But new cesses were added; calculations were made, not on the current, but on the prospective rental, until the tax rose to close upon 60 per cent. on the rental.

In Madras and Bombay things are worse. There the Land Tax is paid generally by the cultivators of the soil, there being, in most parts of those provinces, no intervening landlords. The British Government declared its intention in 1864 of realising as Land Tax about one-half of the economic rent. But what the British Government does take as Land Tax at the present day sometimes approximates to the whole of the economic rent, leaving the cultivators little beyond the wages of their labour and the profits of their agricultural stock. The Land Tax is revised once every thirty years; the cultivator does not know on what grounds it is enhanced; he has to submit to each renewed assessment, or to leave his ancestral fields and perish. This uncertainty of the Land Tax paralyses agriculture, prevents saving, and keeps the tiller of the soil in a state of poverty and indebtedness.

It will appear from the facts stated above that the Land Tax in India is not only heavy and uncertain, but that the very principle on which it is raised is different from the principle of taxation in all well-administered countries. In such countries the State promotes the accumulation of wealth, helps the people to put money into their pockets, likes to see them prosperous and rich, and then demands a small share of their earnings for the expenses of the State. In India the State virtually interferes with the accumulation of wealth from the soil, intercepts the incomes and gains of the tillers, and generally adds to its land revenue demand at each recurring settlement, leaving the cultivators permanently poor. In England, in Germany, in the United States, in France and other countries, the State widens the income of the people, extends their markets, opens out new sources of wealth, identifies itself with the nation, grows richer with the nation. In India, the State has fostered no new industries and revived no old industries for the people; on the other hand, it intervenes at each recurring land settlement to take what it considers its share out of the produce of the soil. Each new settlement in Bombay and in Madras is regarded by the people as a wrangle between them and the State as to how much the former will keep and how much the latter will take. It is a wrangle decided without any clear limits fixed by the law—a wrangle in which the opinion of the revenue officials is final, and there is no appeal to judges or Land Courts. The revenue increases and the people remain destitute.

Taxation raised by a king, says the Indian poet, is like the moisture of the earth sucked up by the sun, to be returned to the earth as fertilising rain; but the moisture raised from the Indian soil now descends as fertilising rain largely on other lands, not on India. Every nation reasonably expects that the proceeds of taxes raised in the country should be mainly spent in the country. Under the worst governments that India had in former times, this was the case. The vast sums which Afghan and Moghal Emperors spent on their armies went to support great and princely houses, as well as hundreds of thousands of soldiers and their families. The gorgeous palaces and monuments they built, as well as the luxuries and displays in which they indulged, fed and encouraged the manufacturers and artisans of India. Nobles and Commanders of the army, Subadars, Dewans, and Kazis, and a host of inferior officers in every province and every district, followed the example of the Court; and mosques and temples, roads, canals and reservoirs, attested to their wide liberality, or even to their vanity. Under wise rulers as under foolish kings, the proceeds of taxation flowed back to the people and fructified their trade and industries.

But a change came over India under the rule of the East India Company. They considered India as a vast estate or plantation, the profits of which were to be withdrawn from India and deposited in Europe. They reserved all the high appointments in India for their own nominees seeking a lucrative career in the East. They bought their merchandise out of the revenues of India, and sold it in Europe for their own profit. They vigorously exacted from India a high interest on their stock-in-trade. In one shape or another all that could be raised in India by an excessive taxation flowed to Europe, after paying for a starved administration.

The East India Company's trade was abolished

in 1833, and the Company was abolished in 1858, but their policy remains. Their capital was paid off by loans which were made into an Indian Debt, on which interest is paid from Indian taxes. The empire was transferred from the Company to the Crown, but the people of India paid the purchase-money The Indian Debt, which was £51,000,000 in 1857, rose to £97,000,000 in 1862. Within the forty years of peace which have succeeded, the Indian Debt has increased continuously, and now (1901) amounts to £200,000,000. The "Home Charges" remitted annually out of the Indian revenues to Great Britain have increased to sixteen millions. The pay of European officers in India, virtually monopolising all the higher services, comes to ten millions. One-half of the nett revenues of India, which are now forty-four millions sterling, flows annually out of India. Verily the moisture of India blesses and fertilises other lands.

For one who has himself spent the best and happiest years of his life in the work of Indian administration, it is an ungracious and a painful task to dwell on the weak side of that administration, the financial and economic policy of the Indian Government. I have undertaken this duty because at the present moment the economic story of British India has to be told, and the deep-seated cause of the poverty of the Indian people has to be explained. Place any other country under the same condition, with crippled industries, with agriculture subject to a heavy and uncertain Land Tax, and with financial arrangements requiring one-half of its revenues to be annually remitted out of the country, and the most prosperous nation on earth will soon know the horrors of famine. A nation prospers if the sources of its wealth are widened, and if the proceeds of taxation are spent among the people, and for the people. A nation is impoverished if the sources of its wealth are narrowed, and the proceeds of taxation are largely remitted out of the country. These are plain, self-evident economic laws, which operate in India, as in every other country, and the Indian statesman and administrator must feel that the poverty of India cannot be removed until Indian industries are revived, until a fixed and intelligible limit is placed on the Indian Land Tax, and until the Indian revenues are more largely spent in India.

The statesman and administrator in India labours under peculiar difficulties. Three successive Governors-General, Lord Wellesley, Lord Minto, and Lord Hastings,, desired to place a permanent limit to the Land Tax of India, but the East India Company overruled them, and would consent to no limit to their demands. Three Viceroys under the Crown, Lord Canning, Lord Lawrence, and Lord Ripon, pressed again for some limitation of the Land Tax, but the Secretary of State for India rejected their proposals. Three times within the present generation have the Indian tariffs been altered, under the dictation of British manufacturers, against the interests of India, and sometimes against the opinions of the majority of the Viceroy's Council. Three times within this period have endeavours been made to grant adequate protection to Indian labourers, recruited for the tea-gardens of Assam, who cease to be free men and free women after they have once signed their contracts, sometimes under misapprehension or fraud. The penal laws which chain them to the gardens still remain on the Statute Book, the proposals recently made by the Honourable Mr. Cotton, Chief Commissioner of Assam, to assure them adequate pay, were whittled down in the Viceroy's Council, and their operation was then suspended for two years by Lord Curzon, because British shareholders in the tea concerns objected to them. Administrators in India are helpless on such occasions. Remedial measures, placing equitable limits on the taxes of India, have been vetoed by the Home Authorities, and protective measures needed for the welfare of the people of India have been sacrificed, when they were supposed to touch the interests of any class of capitalists or manufacturers commanding votes in Parliament.

Nor are Indian administrators strong in the support of the Indian people. The Indian Government means the Viceroy and the Members of the Executive Council, viz., the Commander-in-Chief, the Military Member, the Public Works Member, the Finance Member, and the Legal Member. The people are not represented in this Council; their agriculture, their landed interests, their trades and industries, are not represented; there is not, and never has been, a single Indian Member in the Council. All the Members of the Council are heads of spending departments, as was lately explained by Sir Auckland Colvin and Sir David Barbour before the Royal Commission on Indian expenditure. The Members are high English officials, undoubtedly interested in the welfare of the people, but driven by the duties of their office to seek for more money for the working of their departments; there are no Indian Members to represent the interests of the people. The forces are all arrayed on the side of expenditure, there are none on the side of retrenchment. "The tendency is," said Sir David Barbour, "ordinarily for pressure to be put on the Financial Department to incur expenditure. It is practically pressure. The other departments are always pressing to spend more money; their demands are persistent and continuous." There is no counter-pressure to reduce expenditure, to moderate taxation, to safeguard the agricultural interests of the people, to encourage their industries and manufactures. Thus the constitution of the Indian Government makes an alien rule still more isolated and weak. Every grave question is virtually decided *ex parte.* The Members of the Council are able, wise, experienced, and conscientious men; but the wisest judges will fail to decide cases rightly if they hear the evidence of one party only. And the Indian Government, with every honest desire to do its duty, is unable to secure the material welfare of the people, because it is not in touch with the people, does not accept the co-operation of the people, cannot by its constitution act in the interests of the people.

"The government of a people by itself," said John Stuart Mill, "has a meaning and a reality; but such a thing as government of one people by another does not, and cannot exist. One people may keep another for its own use, a place to make money in, a human cattle-farm to be worked for the profits of its own inhabitants."

There is more truth in this strongly worded statement than appears at first sight. History does not record a single instance of one people ruling another in the interests of the subject nation. Mankind has not yet discovered any method for safeguarding the interests of a subject nation without conceding to that nation some voice in controlling the administration of their own concerns. What is more, such an exclusive and absolute rule does not benefit the ruling nation. England's trade, which is her greatest interest in India, is practically at a standstill during these ten years. The average annual import of merchandise to India (largely but not wholly British) has, during the last ten or twelve years, remained stationary at somewhat under fifty millions sterling. It means a consumption of three shillings per head of the population of India. It might increase to five or six shillings per head if India was prosperous; it is likely to decrease with the poverty and the famines of India. Thus, British trade, which is a legitimate and invigorating source of wealth both to India and to Great Britain, languishes with the poverty of India; the money drawn from the revenues of India, "without a direct equivalent," as Lord Salisbury described it, impoverishes India; and it does not add to the strength of England or to the freedom of her institutions. The manufacturing, the working, and the progressive capacities of a nation, do not increase by the accession of wealth received "without a direct equivalent." It is with nations as with individuals. The bread which we earn by our labour nourishes and invigorates; the food that we consume without toil is poison to our system. And the history of past times and past nations has been recorded in vain if it does not teach us that large tributes from subject empires have led to luxury and decay in ancient as in modern times.

The Empire of India was won by England before her present colonies rose to importance. And it is possible to conceive, though it may be a heresy to say it in these days, that the Empire of India will last after the British Colonies have ceased to owe allegiance to the British Crown. Colonies have been described as fruits, which ripen only to fall from the parent tree; and he will be a bold prophet who will assert that, with some addition to their present population, power, and resources, Australasia and Canada will remain under the sovereignty of Great Britain, even to the middle of the twentieth century. In India, the people honestly desire a longer connection with Great Britain, not through sentimental loyalty, but, as Lord Dufferin once said, through a sense of self-interest. They still believe that they have much to gain by being in close touch with the West, through the rule of a Western Power. They have cast in their lot with Great Britain; they have identified themselves with British rule; they honestly desire that rule to last. But they do not desire the administration to last in its present absolute and exclusive form. This form of administration, shaped by Warren Hastings and Cornwallis, and improved by Munro, Elphinstone, and Bentinck, requires some change after seventy years. Education has spread within these seventy years; educated men are a growing power in India. They demand a fair share in the higher services of their own country; they desire to have a voice in the highest Councils of the Empire. It is easy to disregard this demand, to alienate the educated and influential sections of the Indian population, to increase discontent and dissatisfaction in the country, and to weaken the Empire by continuing an exclusive rule. It would be wiser, on the other hand, to array the rising forces on the side of the Government, to make educated and influential men in India partakers in the control of the administration, to make them represent their own interests, industries, and agriculture, and to make them responsible for improving the material condition of their countrymen and the prevention of famines. To quote once more from John Stuart Mill: "It is an inherent condition of human affairs that no intention, however sincere, of protecting the interests of others, can make it safe or salutary to tie up their own hands. By their own hands only can any positive and durable improvement of their circumstances in life be worked out."

The people of India are not fond of sudden changes and revolutions. They do not ask for new constitutions, issuing like armed Minervas from the heads of legislative Jupiters. They prefer to work on lines which have already been laid down. They desire to strengthen the present Government, and to bring it more in touch with the people. They desire to see some Indian members in the Secretary of State's Council, and in the Viceroy's Executive Council, representing Indian agriculture and industries. They wish to see Indian members in an Executive Council for each Province. They wish to represent the interests of the people in the discussion of every important administrative question. They seek that the administration of the Empire and its great provinces should be conducted with the co-operation of the people.

There is a Legislative Council in each large Indian Province, and some of the members of these Councils are elected under the Act of 1892. The experiment has proved a success, and some expansion of these Legislative Councils would strengthen administration and bring it more in touch with the people. Each Indian Province is divided into twenty or thirty or more Districts, corresponding to English counties, and each District has a population of a million or more. The time has come when each District might elect its own member for the Legislative Council of the Province. A Province with thirty Districts and a population of thirty millions may fairly have thirty elected members on its Legislative Council. Each District should feel that it has some voice in the administration of the Province.

The higher services in India, which were theoretically declared open to the people in 1833, in 1853, and by Queen Victoria's famous proclamation of 1858, should be practically opened to the people, and not reserved for English boys seeking a career in the East. In the great Indian Civil Service, as well as in the Education, Engineering, Postal, Telegraph, Police, and Medical departments, Indians should find it possible to obtain high employment. We want Englishmen in all these departments, we welcome them to help us, but we do not wish them to monopolise all the higher services to the virtual exclusion of the children of the soil.

In each Indian District there is a District Officer

who is the head Executive and Police Officer as well as the Magistrate. These duties should now be separated. Administration would be purer, as well as more popular, in India if the Chief Executive and Police Officer ceased to be a Magistrate.

In each Indian District again there is a District Board, and Village Unions are being formed. These Unions are the modern counterparts of those ancient Village Communities which have been described repeatedly in the following pages, and which were self-governing little republics all over India under Hindu and Mahomedan Governments. They have been swept away, somewhat hastily and unwisely, under British rule; but it is possible to revive them under modern conditions with some care and foresight. Some degree of trust and confidence should be reposed in them; some practical and useful work should be entrusted to them. Above all, the whole mass of civil and criminal village disputes should be sent to them, not for adjudication, but for amicable settlement. They could decide and settle such matters better on the spot than our courts at a distance of twenty or thirty miles. Millions of witnesses would thus be saved the trouble and expense of attendance at distant courts; millions of simple villagers would be saved the baneful lessons of litigation and perjury which are learned in law courts. More than this, the Village Unions and their members would form a link between the people and the rulers, which does not at present exist.

These are a few of the measures which could wisely be adopted to bring the Indian Government more in touch with the people, and to make it more popular and more efficacious for the good of the people. Isolation does not strengthen the Empire; it leads to ill-judged, unwise, and hasty measures of legislation, and spreads dissatisfaction and discontent among the people. It leads to sudden and bewildering changes in the policy of the Indian Government as a result of party government in Great Britain. It leads to increasing expenditure, and not to retrenchment, which can only be secured, as it has been secured in other countries, through the watchfulness of those who pay the taxes. It renders the administration incapable of improving the economic condition of the people, which can be improved only through the co-operation of the people themselves. It alienates the best educated, the most moderate, and the most influential sections of the Indian people, instead of making them partakers in the work of administration and responsible for the welfare of their countrymen. It impoverishes the nation and weakens the Empire.

The wisest administrators in the past, like Munro, Elphinstone, and Bentinck, whose work has been narrated in the following pages, sought to promote the welfare of the people by accepting the co-operation of the people, as far as was possible, in their day. What is needed to-day is a continuance and development of the same policy, not a policy of exclusiveness and distrust. What is needed to-day is that British rulers, who know less of India to-day than their predecessors did fifty years ago, should descend from their dizzy isolation, and should stand amidst the people, work with the people, make the people their comrades and collaborators, and hold the people responsible for good administration. The co-operation of the people is essential to successful administration in every civilised country; the co-operation of the people is more needful in India than anywhere else on earth.

The dawn of a new century finds India deeper in distress and discontent than any preceding period of history. A famine, wider in the extent of country affected than any previous famine, has desolated the country. In parts of India, not affected by this famine, large classes of people attest to semi-starvation by their poor physique; numbers of them suffer from a daily insufficiency of food; and the poorer classes are trained by life-long hunger to live on less food than is needed for proper nourishment. In the presence of facts like these, party controversy is silenced; and every Englishman and every Indian, experienced in administration and faithful to the British Empire, feel it their duty to suggest methods for the removal of the gravest danger which has ever threatened the Empire of India.

ROMESH DUTT.

LONDON, *December* 1901.

PREFACE TO THE SECOND EDITION

A FEW alterations and corrections have been made in preparing this second edition; and some subjects, which have been dealt with in *India in the Victorian Age,* have been omitted in the present work. The two works, taken together, cover the entire period of British rule in India,—from the battle of Plassy in 1757 to the commencement of the present century and the present reign.

ROMESH DUTT.

LONDON, *August* 1906.

CONTENTS

THE ECONOMIC HISTORY OF BRITISH INDIA

CHAPTER I

GROWTH OF THE EMPIRE

"I AM sure that I can save the country, and that no one else can." So spoke the great William Pitt, afterwards Lord Chatham, not boastfully, but with that consciousness of power, and that clear prevision of great events, which sometimes come to men inspired by a lofty mission. William Pitt more than redeemed his pledge. He directed the administration of his country from 1757 to 1761, and, singularly enough, these five years mark the rise of the modern British Empire. England's ally, Frederick the Great, won the battle of Rossbach in 1757, made Prussia, and humbled France. Wolfe took Quebec in 1759, and the whole of Canada was conquered from the French in 1760. Clive won the battle of Plassy in 1757, and Eyre Coote crushed the French power in India in 1761. Within five years England's greatness as a world-power was assured; France was humbled in Europe, and effaced in Asia and in America.

Our story concerns itself with the growth of the British Empire in India, or rather with the economic condition of the people under that Empire. And it will enable us to trace the economic history of the people more clearly if we briefly review in this preliminary chapter those great political events which led to the steady rise and expansion of the British power during the period of eighty years which forms the subject of this volume, from the battle of Plassy in 1757 to the accession of Queen Victoria in 1837.

Three generations of British statesmen and administrators laboured to extend and consolidate the Indian Empire within these eighty years, and each generation had a distinct and characteristic policy of its own. The first was the age of Clive and Warren Hastings, an age of bold adventures and arduous struggles, which made a Company of traders a great territorial power in India. This age ended with Pitt's India Act of 1784 and the retirement of Warren Hastings from India in the following year. The second age was the age of Cornwallis, Wellesley, and Lord Hastings, the age of the final wars with Mysore and the Mahrattas, which made the Company the supreme power in India. This age ended with the annexation of the province of Bombay in 1817, and the capture of the last of the Peshwas in the following year. The third age was an age of peace, retrenchment, and administrative reforms, the age of Munro, Elphinstone, and Bentinck, whose names are more gratefully cherished in India to the present day than the names of warriors and conquerors. This age ended with the arrival of Lord Auckland in India in 1836, and the accession of Queen Victoria in the following year.

I.—The Period of Clive and Warren Hastings, ending 1785.

The East India Company was founded in 1600 with a capital of £70,000. The Company built Fort St. George in Madras in 1639; bought the island of Bombay from King Charles II., and removed their factories to that place in 1687; and made their Bengal headquarters in Calcutta in 1700. The French had a settlement at Pondicherry, south of Madras, and another at Chandranagar, north of Calcutta.

The wars of Frederick the Great found the English and the French opposed to each other in the battlefields of Europe, Asia, and America, for well nigh twenty years, from 1744 to 1763. The servants of the English and the French Companies eagerly took up the contest in India, made alliances with Indian princes, besieged each other's commercial settlements, and evinced in the East those bitter jealousies which divided them in the West. The three wars between the English and the French, which were carried on in India within these twenty years, are known as the Karnatic wars.

In the first Karnatic war the French had decidedly the advantage. They took Madras from the English, and they beat back the army of the Nawab of the Karnatic which came to retake the town. Madras was, however, restored to the British by the Peace of Aix-la-Chapelle in 1748.

Dupleix, the Director-General of the French Company, was, however, fired by a lofty ambition to make his countrymen supreme in India; and for a time his success was complete. He helped an Indian ally to become Nizam of the Deccan, and he enabled another ally to become Nawab of the Karnatic. He was thus the most powerful "king-maker" in Southern India, and the influence of the British seemed completely annihilated. The genius of Robert Clive now turned the scales. He first distinguished himself by recovering and holding Arcot, the capital of the Karnatic, for a rival Nawab, an ally of the British. The second Karnatic war was at last concluded; the ally of the British remained Nawab of the Karnatic, and the ally of the French remained Nizam of the Deccan. There was thus a balance of power between the two European nations in Southern India, and the French obtained the whole of the eastern seaboard, called the Northern Circars, from the Nizam.

The third Karnatic war ended in the complete destruction of the French power. Lally, the patriotic but impulsive leader of the French, besieged the fort of Madras, but failed to take it. He was then beaten by Eyre Coote in the battle of Wandewash in 1761, and the French settlement of Pondicherry was taken by the British after an obstinate defence. Pondicherry was restored by the Peace of Paris in 1763, but the power of the French in India had been irrevocably extinguished. After 1763, the British had no European rivals in India.

Great events had in the meantime taken place in Bengal. Suraj-ud-Dawla, Nawab of Bengal, had taken Calcutta in 1756 from the English, and most of the English prisoners died in one hot summer night in a small and ill-ventilated prison-room, known as the Black Hole. Clive, on his return from Europe, recovered Calcutta in the following year; made peace with the Nawab; and then entered into a secret conspiracy against him. When everything was ready, he marched against the Nawab; defeated him in the battle of Plassy in 1757; and thus virtually conquered Bengal. Clive also conquered the Northern Circars from the French; and thus made the East India Company a great territorial power in India before he sailed for Europe in 1760.

The Nawabs of Bengal had now become mere puppets in the hands of the Company's servants. Mir Jafar was set up as Nawab after the battle of Plassy, and was deposed in 1760, when Mir Kasim was made

Nawab. This last was a strong ruler, and tried to check the abuses of the Company's servants in the inland trade of Bengal. A war followed; Mir Kasim was beaten and fled; and Mir Jafar was once more made Nawab. The feeble old man died shortly after, and his illegitimate son was then hastily set up as the nominal ruler of Bengal. The administration of Bengal was in the utmost disorder; the people were grievously oppressed.

Clive came to India for the third and last time in 1765, and initiated a new and a memorable policy. The feeble descendant of the Emperor of Delhi was now a homeless wanderer, but was still recognised as the titular Sovereign of India. All the kings and chiefs in the vast continent still owned nominal allegiance to him; all pretended to derive from him their power in the kingdoms and provinces which they conquered by force of arms. Clive imitated this example. He had conquered Bengal by force of arms in 1757; in 1765 he obtained from the Emperor of Delhi a charter making the East India Company the Dewan or administrators of that province. The East India Company thus obtained a legal status, and also formally took upon themselves the responsibility of administering the province which they had conquered eight years before. Lord Clive effected some other reforms in civil and military administration, and finally left India in 1767.

His scheme of administration did not succeed. The people of Bengal were grievously oppressed under the dual government of the Nawab and the Company; the revenues failed; and a serious famine carried off one-third of the population of Bengal in 1770–71.

In Madras the British authorities had got themselves involved in a war with Haidar Ali, the most capable military commander that India produced in the latter half of the eighteenth century. Haidar Ali devastated the Karnatic, and appeared within a few miles of Madras. The Council was struck with panic, and made peace with the terrible invader in 1769.

The British Parliament passed a measure called the Regulating Act of 1773 to improve the state of affairs in India. This Act gave a parliamentary title to the Company's administration in India, and created the post of a Governor-General for all the Company's possessions in that country. Warren Hastings, who was then Governor of Bengal, became the first Governor-General in 1774.

There was no abler Englishman in India at that time than Warren Hastings, and none who knew the country and its people more intimately. He had come out to India, almost as a boy, in 1750; he had protested against the abuse of power by his own countrymen both in Bengal and in Madras; and he was animated by a sincere desire, as he was now invested with the power, to improve the administration. But his financial difficulties, the opposition in his own Council led by Philip Francis, his frequent wars, and his own despotic instincts, led him to arbitrary acts which formed the subjects of his subsequent impeachment in the British Parliament.

Hastings stopped the stipulated tribute to the Emperor of Delhi; he took away the Emperor's possessions at Kora and Allahabad, and sold them to the Nawab of Oudh for £500,000; and he lent an English brigade to the same Nawab to crush the Rohillas for another sum of £400,000.

The Bombay Government had got themselves involved in difficulties with the Mahrattas, then the greatest power in India. There were two claimants to the post of Peshwa or the head of the Mahratta confederacy; the Bombay Government entered into a treaty to help one of them, and thus began the first Mahratta war. The British troops distinguished themselves by capturing Amadabad and Gwalior, but the war failed in its object. The ally of the British retired on a pension, but Salsette and some other islands were added to the British possessions by the peace of 1782.

A second war with Mysore had broken out with the great Haidar Ali of Mysore. He was defeated in four engagements by Sir Eyre Coote, who had, twenty years before, beaten the French at Wandewash; but Haidar Ali succeeded in safely withdrawing his troops from each battlefield, and his strength was not broken. On the other hand, by his excellent manœuvres, he surrounded two British detachments, commanded by Colonel Baillie and Colonel Brathwaite, and completely destroyed them. But Haidar Ali died in 1782, and the war ended in a peace with his son, Tipu Sultan, in 1783.

On the death of the Nawab of Oudh in 1775, Warren Hastings had obtained a cession of the state of Benares from his successor; and the Raja of Benares thus became a British vassal. Hastings demanded large contributions from the Raja in addition to the stipulated tribute; imposed a heavy fine; arrested and confined him; and drove his subjects to rebellion. The Raja was deposed, and a relation of his was made Raja on condition of paying an enhanced tribute.

The new Nawab of Oudh was also called upon to pay the arrears due from him; and as he pleaded inability, he was helped to rob his mother and his grandmother of their treasures, until over a million sterling was obtained to pay the debt. Assignments of the land revenue to British creditors, both in Oudh and in Madras, caused much hardship to the people; and in Bengal, Warren Hastings disregarded the hereditary rights of Zemindars or landlords, and sold their estates by auction to get an enhanced revenue for the Company.

All these acts cast a shadow over the administration

of Warren Hastings. Pitt's India Act was passed in 1784, and for the first time placed the Company's administration in India under the control of the Crown. Warren Hastings left India in the following year.

Such is, briefly, the history of the rise of British power in India down to 1785. The three wars with the French which made the British nation supreme in the Karnatic, the two wars with Suraj-ud-Dawla and Mir Kasim which made them masters of Bengal, and the first struggles with Mysore and the Mahrattas, were the leading military transactions which engaged the generation of Clive and Hastings in India. Bengal, the Northern Circars, and Benares, together with small tracts of country round Madras and Bombay, were the extent of the Company's actual possessions in India when Warren Hastings left the country in 1785.

II.—The Period of Cornwallis, Wellesley, and Lord Hastings, 1785–1817.

Pitt's India Act was passed on the 13th August 1784. All civil, military, and revenue affairs of the Company were placed under the superintendence of six Commissioners appointed by the Crown. There was a sincere desire to improve the administration of India, and to relieve the people from that oppression and misgovernment under which they had suffered during the first period of British rule. The Directors of the Company themselves wished to put their house in order. They sent out Lord Cornwallis, a nobleman of high character and generous instincts, as Governor-General after Warren Hastings, and they gave him definite instructions to permanently fix the State demand from the land, so as to leave the people a motive for making agricultural improvements and to better their own condition.

There was a gleam of sunshine in India after an

age of darkness and storms. Lord Cornwallis did not belie the expectations that had been formed of him. He improved the administration; he forced the Company to give adequate pay to their servants, and made them honest officers; he founded the Civil Service of India as it exists to this day. He was involved in one war only—with Tipu Sultan of Mysore; he captured the capital of the Sultan, and then made peace after annexing some of his territory and reducing his power. Before he left India in 1793, Cornwallis made a *Permanent Zemindari Settlement* of the land revenues of Bengal, a measure which has done more to secure the prosperity and happiness of British subjects in India than any other single measure of the British Government.

The East India Company's charter was renewed in 1793. Indian affairs were discussed in Parliament, and all the principal provisions of Pitt's India Act of 1784 were maintained. But the East India Company were now required to provide 3000 tons of shipping to other merchants trading in the East. This was the first breach made in the Company's monopoly. Sir John Shore, afterwards Lord Teignmouth, succeeded Lord Cornwallis as Governor-General, and pursued the peaceful policy of his predecessor. And he extended to Benares the Permanent Settlement of the land revenues which Cornwallis had granted to Bengal.

Lord Mornington, afterwards Marquis of Wellesley, succeeded Sir John Shore, and arrived in India in 1798. The wars of Napoleon Bonaparte now influenced British policy in India, as the wars of Frederick the Great had done in the previous generation. William Pitt was subsidising the great Powers of Europe to maintain armies against Napoleon. Wellesley was a friend of Pitt and an apt pupil. He introduced the policy of subsidies in India, but with an important variation. It would be useless to pay subsidies to the Indian princes to maintain their inefficient armies; Wellesley, therefore, obtained subsidies from them to maintain contingents of the British army in their dominions. This at once brought money to the Company, and kept the Indian princes under British control; and this policy is known as the policy of "subsidiary alliances."

The restless Tipu Sultan of Mysore had opened negotiations with the French and must be crushed. A fourth war was therefore undertaken against Mysore, and Tipu fell in the defence of his capital in 1799. Portions of Mysore were annexed by the conquerors. A portion was offered to the Mahrattas if they would form a subsidiary alliance, but they declined. Another portion was given to the Nizam of the Deccan, but was subsequently taken over by Wellesley in lieu of the annual subsidy which the Nizam was to pay for the British contingent. What remained of Mysore was formed into a little kingdom, and the old Hindu house was restored.

Weaker States were dealt with more summarily, and Wellesley was not very particular in his methods. The Nawab of Surat died in 1799; Wellesley made his brother retire on pension, and annexed his State. The Rajah of Tanjore was set aside; his brother resigned his powers to the British, and retired on pension. The Nawab of the Karnatic died in 1801, and his successor declined to abdicate; another prince was set up in his place, gave his kingdom to the British, and retired on pension. The boy-Nawab of Farakkabad was about to attain his majority; he was made to transfer the State to the British, and retired on pension. The Nawab of Oudh was asked either to make over the civil and military administration of his kingdom to the British, or to enter into a subsidiary alliance ceding one-half of his kingdom for the maintenance of the British contingent. He was compelled to accept the latter proposal, and ceded Allahabad and other districts to the British in 1801.

One great power in India still remained—the Mahrattas. Fortunately for Lord Wellesley, the Peshwa, or head of the Mahratta confederacy, was hard pressed by other Mahratta chiefs, and was compelled to seek British aid. A subsidiary alliance was concluded in 1802, and the Peshwa was placed on his throne by the help of British troops. The other Mahratta chiefs, Sindia, Holkar, and Bhonsla, were taken aback by this introduction of British power in their dominions, and then followed what is known as the second Mahratta war. General Wellesley, afterwards the famous Duke of Wellington, crushed the armies of Sindia and Bhonsla in the battles of Assye and Argaon in 1803, and Lord Lake triumphantly entered Delhi in the same year, and defeated Sindia's troops at Laswari. But Holkar, who was playing a waiting game, now joined in; and the interminable war with the many-headed Mahratta confederacy was still going on, when the alarmed Directors of the Company recalled their too warlike Governor-General, and once more sent out Lord Cornwallis to restore peace in India.

The great Pro-Consul of the East hastened to pay a visit to the great Commoner of England, whose European policy had so much shaped his own in India. And Wellesley arrived only in time to see William Pitt on his death-bed. Pitt had failed to conclude the European wars, as Wellesley had failed to end the Indian wars. "Roll up that map," Pitt had said, pointing to a map of Europe, "it will not be wanted these ten years." There was a touching meeting between the bed-ridden Prime Minister and the recalled Governor-General; it was the last interview which Pitt gave any one before his death. The wars had a further course to run; in Europe they were concluded in 1815; in India, in 1817.

Meanwhile, there was temporary peace in India. Cornwallis died in India shortly after his arrival, and his successors, Sir John Barlow and Lord Minto, left the Mahrattas alone. The East India Company's charter was renewed once more in 1813, but their monopoly of trade with India was abolished. Trade with the East, which had been granted to the Company by the charter of Elizabeth in 1600, was now opened to all British traders, except only with regard to China tea.

When Lord Moira, afterwards Marquis of Hastings, succeeded Lord Minto in 1813, the time had come for a final contest with the Mahrattas. A war with Nepal brought in some Himalayan territory to the Company, and a war was undertaken to crush the Pindarees—swarms of Afghan, Jat, and Mahratta condottieri—who offered their services to any chief who paid them, and often plundered villages on their own account. Last came the third and conclusive war with the Mahrattas. The Peshwa had formed a subsidiary alliance with the British in 1802, but chafed under the restraint. At last he threw off all disguise, and other Mahratta chiefs joined him. But the Peshwa was beaten at Khirki, Bhonsla's army was defeated at Sitabaldi, and Holkar's army was crushed by Sir John Malcolm at Mehidpur. The Peshwa's dominions were annexed in 1817 and formed into the province of Bombay; and he himself was captured in the following year, and retired on a pension. Minor Mahratta chiefs, Sindia and Holkar, Bhonsla and the Gaekwar, were allowed to rule in their own States under the imperial power of England.

Such is briefly the history of the political and military transactions of the second period of British rule in India. The Permanent Settlement of the land revenues, which was concluded in Bengal in 1793, and extended to Benares in 1795, and to the Northern

Circars and other tracts between 1802 and 1805, stands out as the most notable and the most beneficent act of civil administration within this period. The final quelling of the power of Mysore and the Mahrattas is the leading political achievement of the same period.

III.—Period of Munro, Elphinstone, and Bentinck, 1817–1837.

We now enter upon a period of peace, retrenchment, and reform, in Europe and in India. The nations of Europe were tired of the Napoleonic wars, and enjoyed a long term of peace after the battle of Waterloo. Everywhere there was an endeavour to effect reforms and to secure civil rights for the people. In France this continual struggle ended in the Revolution of 1830. In England it secured the Reform Act of 1832. Belgium separated itself from Holland and formed its own national government. In Germany and in Italy there were movements after national unity and national independence. Greece became independent in 1830. Slavery was abolished in 1833. The spirit of the times was for reforms and for bettering the condition of the people everywhere, and this spirit inspired the policy of the administrators in India.

Lord Hastings established the Hindu College of Calcutta in 1817, and was succeeded by Lord Amherst in 1823 as Governor-General. A short Burmese war brought in Assam, Arracan, and Tenasserim to the Company's dominions in 1826, and two years after Lord William Bentinck arrived in Calcutta as Governor-General. He, too, made some additions to the British territory, by annexing Coorg and taking over the administration of Mysore in 1830. But these few annexations were the least important features of the period we are now describing; the great civil reforms connected with the names of Munro, Elphinstone, and Bentinck, characterise the age.

The system of judicial administration organised by Warren Hastings and Cornwallis had failed, because the people of the country had been excluded from any real share in the administrative work. Judicial work fell into arrear; the delay in the disposal of cases by British judges amounted to a failure of justice. Crimes multiplied in the Company's dominions, and the measures adopted for employing secret informers and arresting men on suspicion aggravated the evil. Lord Minto wrote in 1810 that robbery, accompanied by murder, was prevailing in every part of Bengal. It was then that the ablest servants of the Company perceived the necessity of entrusting a larger share of administrative work in India to the people themselves. "In a civilised, populous country like India," wrote Sir Henry Strachey, Judge of Calcutta, "justice can be well dispensed only through the natives themselves."

Thomas Munro was the first Englishman in India who reduced this principle into practice, and who initiated a policy of trust and confidence in the people. He had come out to India as a young soldier in 1780; he had fought in the wars with Haidar Ali, and had distinguished himself in the revenue settlements made in the tracts of country acquired from Mysore and from the Deccan in 1793, 1799, and 1800. He bad come to India a second time in 1814 as the head of a Commission to revise and improve the judicial system of Madras, and had passed those famous Regulations which gave a wider employment to the people of India in responsible administrative work. Munro came out to India for the third and last time as Governor of Madras in 1820; he effected the *Ryotwari Land Settlement* of Madras; and he died in India in

July 1827, loved and lamented by the people for whom he had worked all his life.

What Sir Thomas Munro did in Madras, Mountstuart Elphinstone did in Bombay. Younger than Munro by eighteen years, he too came to India in early life in 1796, distinguished himself in his work, and was a sort of political secretary to the Duke of Wellington when he won the battle of Assye in 1803. He was selected by Lord Minto for a mission to Afghanistan in 1808, and wrote the first and perhaps the only standard work on the Afghans and their country. Returning to Poona as Resident in the Peshwa's court in 1811, he took an important part in the last Mahratta war of 1817; and his great experience in Mahratta affairs led to his appointment as Governor of Bombay in 1819, after the Mahratta dominions had been annexed. For eight years he performed the duties of this high office; he codified the Regulations of Bombay, gave a wider employment to the people of India in administrative work, and spread education in the province. He retired from Bombay in November 1827, a few months after the death of Sir Thomas Munro in Madras.

Therefore, when Bentinck arrived in India in 1828 as Governor-General, the work of reform had been more than half done. Bentinck's early career was eventful. He had gone out as Governor of Madras early in the nineteenth century, but had been recalled on the occurrence of a mutiny. Plunging into European politics, he had captured Genoa in 1814, restored to it its old constitution, and conceived the idea of a free and united Italy. Fourteen years after he came to India as Governor-General at the mature age of fifty-four

The Regulations recommended by Munro had been passed in Madras, and had virtually transferred the administration of civil justice to Indian judges; and

Elphinstone had effected similar reforms in Bombay. Lord William Bentinck entrusted the administration of civil justice in Bengal to Indian judges, fixing their powers and emoluments on a liberal and comprehensive scale, and appointed Indian deputy-collectors to assist European collectors in revenue administration. The more extended employment of the people of India in the work of administration enabled Lord William Bentinck to change an annual deficit of a million to a surplus of two millions. A reformed *Mahalwari Settlement* in Northern India was begun in 1833, and a *Ryotwari Settlement* in Bombay in 1835.

The East India Company's charter was renewed in 1833 on the condition that they should give up trade altogether, and should henceforth be only administrators and rulers of India. And it was provided at the same time that no native of India "shall by reason only of his religion, place of birth, descent, colour, or any of them, be disabled from holding any place, office, or employment."

Sir Charles Metcalfe acted as Governor-General after Bentinck, and was succeeded by Lord Auckland, who arrived in 1836; and in the following year Queen Victoria ascended the throne of the British Empire.

The date of the accession of the Great Queen is a memorable and convenient historical date for all countries forming the British Empire. But in India, as will appear from the foregoing narrative, it really marks the end of one historical epoch, and the commencement of another. Before 1837, the provinces of Bengal, Madras, Bombay, and the fairest tracts of Northern India, had passed under British rule. The great Civil Service of India had been organised. After many failures and unsuccessful experiments, the judicial administration of the country had been formed on a satisfactory basis. The still more difficult problem of land revenue administration had been settled, wisely or unwisely, in Bengal in 1793, in Madras in 1820, in Northern India in 1833, in Bombay in 1835. Peace had been secured all over the country. The Company had ceased to be traders in 1833, and stood forth as rulers and administrators of India. English colleges had been opened in Calcutta in 1817, and in Bombay in 1834; the liberty of the press had been granted in 1836. Communication by steam had been opened between Europe and India; retrenchment in expenditure had been effected; an annual surplus had been secured: a wider field of administrative work had been opened out for the people. The good of the people of India was recognised, at least in principle, as the great aim of the British Government. The people responded to this desire; there was an intellectual awakening among them; there were signs of progress and advancement. There is, therefore, a natural pause in the history of India about 1837, and with that date closes our present narrative of eighty years' British work in India.

CHAPTER II

INLAND TRADE OF BENGAL (1757–1765)

IN the eighteenth century, the transit of goods by roads and navigable rivers was subject to inland duties in India, as in other parts of the world. The East India Company had, however, obtained a Firman, or royal order, exempting their export and import trade from these payments. The goods which the Company imported from Europe, and those which they purchased in India for export to Europe, were thus permitted to pass through the country without duties. A Dustuck, or certificate, signed by the English President or by chiefs of English factories, was shown at the toll-houses, and protected the Company's merchandise from all duties.

The victory of Plassy in 1757 raised the prestige of the British nation in Bengal; and the servants of the East India Company, engaged in the inland trade of Bengal on their own account, now claimed as private traders that exemption from duties which had been granted only for the import and export trade of the Company. It is necessary to understand this point clearly, because it underlies the economic, commercial, and political history of Bengal during the succeeding years.

The Nawabs of Bengal recognised the right granted to the Company to carry on the Company's *import and export trade* duty-free; but the servants of the Company, who had taken to private trade on their own account, conveyed goods from one part of Bengal to another, and claimed exemption from duties for this *private inland trade.*

After the battle of Plassy, Clive had made Mir Jafar Nawab of Bengal in 1757. Mir Jafar made an incompetent ruler, and was unable to fulfil his engagements to the British. He was accordingly set aside in 1760, and Mir Kasim was set up as Nawab. The new Nawab agreed to assign the revenues of three districts—Burdwan, Midnapur, and Chittagong—to the East India Company; and he also agreed to pay the balance which Mir Jafar had left unpaid, and to make a present of five lakhs of Rupees (£50,000) as a contribution towards the Company's wars in Southern India. Mir Kasim faithfully fulfilled these engagements, and in less than two years discharged all his pecuniary obligations to the British.

But the difficulty about the inland trade increased from year to year. The Company's servants conveyed their goods from place to place duty-free, while the goods of the country merchants were heavily taxed in the transit. The country traders were ruined; the Nawab's revenues declined; and the servants of the Company monopolised the trade and reared colossal fortunes.

Henry Vansittart, who succeeded Clive as Governor in 1760, marked the growing evil and described its causes.

"With respect to trade, no new privileges were asked of Meer Jaffier; none indeed were wanted by the Company, who were contented with the terms granted them in 1716, and only wished to be relieved from the impositions to which they had been exposed from the arbitrary power of the Nabob. However, our influence over the country was no sooner felt than many innovations were practised by some of the Company's servants, or the people employed under their authority. They began to trade in the articles which were before prohibited, and to interfere in the affairs of the country."[1]

Mr. Verelst, who afterwards succeeded as Governor, also wrote to the same effect.

"A trade was carried on without payment of duties, in the prosecution of which infinite oppressions were committed. English agents or Gomastahs, not contented with injuring the people, trampled on the authority of government, binding and punishing the Nabob's officers whenever they presumed to interfere. This was the immediate cause of the war with Meer Cossim."[2]

The Nawab Mir Kasim himself presented a strong remonstrance to the English Governor against the oppressions of the Company's servants.

"From the factory of Calcutta to Cossim Bazar, Patna, and Dacca, all the English chiefs, with their Gomastahs, officers, and agents, in every district of the government, act as Collectors, Renters, Zemindars, and Taalookdars, and setting up the Company's colours, allow no power to my officers. And besides this, the Gomastahs and other servants in every district, in every Gunge, Perganah, and Village, carry on a trade in oil, fish, straw, bamboos, rice, paddy, betel-nut, and other things; and every man with a Company's Dustuck in his hand regards himself as not less than the Company."[3]

Mir Kasim's complaints were not unfounded; and Ellis, the Company's agent at Patna, made himself specially obnoxious to the Nawab by his hostile attitude. An Armenian merchant had been accused of purchasing a small quantity of saltpetre for the use of the Nawab; this was deemed an infringement of the Company's rights, and Ellis had him seized and sent

[1] *A Narrative of the Transactions in Bengal*, vol. i. p. 24.
[2] *View of Bengal*, p. 48.
[3] Mir Kasim's Letter, dated 26th March 1762.

in irons to Calcutta. Two deserters from the British army were supposed to have taken shelter in the Nawab's fort of Monghyr. Ellis sent his soldiers to search the fort, but no deserters were found. Warren Hastings, then a member of the Governor's Council, felt the impropriety of such defiance of the Nawab's authority, and foresaw an open rupture.

"With regard to Mr. Ellis, I am at a loss to act; his behaviour, in my opinion, has been so imprudent and his disaffection to the Nabob so manifestly inveterate, that a proper representation of it cannot fail to draw upon it the severest resentment of the Company. . . . The world, judging only from facts, sees the Nabob's authority publicly insulted, his officers imprisoned, Sepoys sent against his forts, and is told that the Chief of the English in these parts disavows the Nabob's right to the Subahship. The obvious end of such symptoms is an open rapture." [1]

It is to the credit of Warren Hastings that he consistently protested against the claims of the Company's servants to carry on their private trade duty-free, and deplored the ruin which was thus caused to the trade of the people of Bengal. His eyes were not blinded by self-interest, and his natural leaning towards his own countrymen did not prevent him from condemning in the strongest terms the injustice done to the people of Bengal.

"I beg leave to lay before you a grievance which loudly calls for redress, and will, unless duly attended to, render ineffectual any endeavours to create a firm and lasting harmony between the Nabob and the Company. I mean the oppression committed under the sanction of the English name. . . . I have been surprised to meet with several English flags flying in places which I have passed, and on the river I do not believe I passed a boat without one. By whatever

[1] Letters of Hastings to the Governor, dated 13th and 26th May 1762.

title they have been assumed (for I could trust to the information of my eyes without stopping to ask questions), I am sure their frequency can bode no good to the Nabob's revenues, the quiet of the country, or the honour of our nation, but evidently tends to lessen each of them. A party of Sepoys who were on the march before us afforded sufficient proofs of the rapacious and insolent spirit of those people where they are left to their own discretion. Many complaints against them were made me on the road, and most of the petty towns and Serais were deserted at our approach and the shops shut up from the apprehensions of the same treatment from us. You are sensible, sir, that it is from such little irregularities, too trivial perhaps for public complaint and continually repeated, that the country people are habituated to entertain the most unfavourable notions of our government."[1]

Hastings had been long in India, and was not mistaken in speaking of the unfavourable opinion entertained by the people of the administration of the Company's servants. The writer of the well-known chronicle known as *Siyar Mutakharin*, while admiring the conduct of the British troops on the field of battle, gives us a lamentable picture of their civil administration.

"They [the English] join the most resolute courage to the most cautious prudence; nor have they their equals in the art of ranging themselves in battle array and in fighting order. If to so many military qualifications they knew how to join the arts of government; if they showed a concern for the circumstances of the husbandman and the gentleman, and exerted as much ingenuity and solicitude in the relieving and easing the people of God as they do in whatever concerns their military affairs, no nation in the world would be

[1] Hastings' Letter, dated 25th April 1762.

preferable to them, or prove worthier of command. But such is the little regard which they show to the people of these kingdoms, and such their apathy and indifference for their welfare, that the people under their dominion groan everywhere, and are reduced to poverty and distress. O God! come to the assistance of thine afflicted servants, and deliver them from the oppressions they suffer."[1]

The Nawab of Bengal continued to make just but futile complaints to the English Governor.

"In every Perganah, every village, and every factory, they [the Company's Gomastahs] buy and sell salt, betel-nut, ghee, rice, straw, bamboos, fish, gunnies, ginger, sugar, tobacco, opium, and many other things, more than I can write, and which I think it needless to mention. They forcibly take away the goods and commodities of the Reiats, merchants, &c., for a fourth part of their value; and by ways of violence and oppressions they oblige the Reiats, &c., to give five rupees for goods which are worth but one rupee. . . . The officers of every district have desisted from the exercise of their functions; so that by means of these oppressions, and my being deprived of my duties, I suffer a yearly loss of nearly twenty-five lakhs of Rupees. . . . By the grace of God, I neither have transgressed, nor do, nor will transgress the treaty and agreement which I have made; why then do the chiefs of the Englishmen render my government contemptible and employ themselves in bringing a loss upon me?"[2]

A still more detailed account of the doings of the Company's Gomastahs is to be found in the letter of Sergeant Brego.

"A gentleman sends a Gomastah here to buy or sell; he immediately looks upon himself as sufficient

[1] *Siyar Mutakharin*, vol. ii. p. 101. Quoted in Mill's *History of British India*.

[2] Nawab's Letter, written May 1762.

to force every inhabitant either to buy his goods or sell him theirs; and on refusal (in case of non-capacity) a flogging or confinement immediately ensues. This is not sufficient even when willing, but a second force is made use of, which is to engross the different branches of trade to themselves, and not to suffer any person to buy or sell the articles they trade in; and if the country people do it, then a repetition of their authority is put in practice; and again, what things they purchase, they think the least they can do is to take them for a considerable deal less than another merchant, and oftentimes refuse paying that; and my interfering occasions an immediate complaint. These, and many other oppressions more than can be related, which are daily used by the Bengal Gomastahs, is the reason that this place [Backerjunj, a prosperous Bengal district] is growing destitute of inhabitants; every day numbers leave the town to seek a residence more safe, and the very markets, which before afforded plenty, do hardly now produce anything of use, their peons being allowed to force poor people; and if the Zemindar offers to prevent it, he is threatened to be used in the same manner. Before, justice was given in the public Catcheree, but now every Gomastah is become a judge, and every one's house a Catcheree; they even pass sentences on the Zemindars themselves, and draw money from them by pretended injuries, such as a quarrel with some of the peons, or their having, as they assert, stole something, which is more likely to have been taken by their own people."[1]

A similar detailed account is given in the letter of Mahomed Ali, Collector of Dacca, to the English Governor at Calcutta.

"In the first place, a number of merchants have made interest with the people of the factory, hoist English colours on their boats, and carry away their

[1] Letter dated 26th May 1762.

goods under the pretence of their being English property, by which means the Shah-bunder and other customs are greatly determined. Secondly, the Gomastahs of Luckypoor and Dacca factories oblige the merchants, &c., to take tobacco, cotton, iron, and sundry other things, at a price exceeding that of the bazaar, and then extort the money from them by force; besides which they take diet money for the peons, and make them pay a fine for breaking their agreement. By these proceedings the Aurungs and other places are ruined. Thirdly, the Gomastahs of Luckypoor factory have taken the Talookdars' talooks [the farmers' farms] from the Tahsildar by force for their own use, and will not pay the rent. At the instigation of some people, they, on a matter of complaint, send Europeans and Sepoys, with a Dustuck, into the country, and there create disturbances. They station chowkeys [toll-houses] at different places, and whatever they find in poor people's houses they cause to be sold, and take the money. By these disturbances the country is ruined, and the Reiats cannot stay in their own houses, nor pay the malguzaree [rents]. In many places Mr. Chevalier has, by force, established new markets and new factories, and has made false Sepoys on his own part, and they seize whom they want and fine them. By his forcible proceedings many hants, gauts, and perganas [markets, landing-places, and fiscal divisions] have been ruined."[1]

While the entire inland trade of Bengal was thus disorganised by the Company's servants and their agents in every important district, the methods by which they secured the manufactures to themselves were equally oppressive. These are fully described by William Bolts, an English merchant who saw things with his own eyes.

"It may with truth be now said that the whole inland trade of the country, as at present conducted, and that of the Company's investment for Europe in a

[1] Letter received in October 1762.

more peculiar degree, has been one continued scene of oppression; the baneful effects of which are severely felt by every weaver and manufacturer in the country, every article produced being made a monopoly; in which the English, with their Banyans and black Gomastahs, arbitrarily decide what quantities of goods each manufacturer shall deliver, and the prices he shall receive for them. . . . Upon the Gomastah's arrival at the Aurung, or manufacturing town, he fixes upon a habitation which he calls his Catcherry; to which, by his peons and hircarahs, he summons the brokers, called dallals and pykars, together with the weavers, whom, after receipt of the money despatched by his masters, he makes to sign a bond for the delivery of a certain quantity of goods, at a certain time and price, and pays them a certain part of the money in advance. The assent of the poor weaver is in general not deemed necessary; for the Gomastahs, when employed on the Company's investment, frequently make them sign what they please; and upon the weavers refusing to take the money offered, it has been known they have had it tied in their girdles, and they have been sent away with a flogging. . . . A number of these weavers are generally also registered in the books of the Company's Gomastahs, and not permitted to work for any others, being transferred from one to another as so many slaves, subject to the tyranny and roguery of each succeeding Gomastah. . . . The roguery practised in this department is beyond imagination; but all terminates in the defrauding of the poor weaver; for the prices which the Company's Gomastahs, and in confederacy with them the Jachendars [examiners of fabrics] fix upon the goods, are in all places at least 15 per cent., and some even 40 per cent. less than the goods so manufactured would sell in the public bazaar or market upon free sale. . . . Weavers, also, upon their inability to perform such agreements as have been forced upon them by the Company's agents, universally known in Bengal by the name of Mutchulcahs, have had their goods seized and sold on the spot to make good the deficiency; and the winders of raw silk, called Nagoads, have been treated also with such injustice, that instances have been known of their cutting off their thumbs to prevent their being forced to wind silk." [1]

Not the industries alone, but agriculture also declined in Bengal under this system; for the manufacturers of the country were largely peasants as well.

"For the Ryots, who are generally both landholders and manufacturers, by the oppressions of Gomastahs in harassing them for goods are frequently rendered incapable of improving their lands, and even of paying their rents; for which, on the other hand, they are again chastised by the officers of the revenue, and not unfrequently have by those harpies been necessitated to sell their children in order to pay their rents, or otherwise obliged to fly the country." [2]

These extracts are enough. They have been made from different sources,—from the letters and writings of an English Governor, an English Member of Council, and an English merchant, as well as from the complaints of the Nawab himself, the report of a Mahomedan collector, and the chronicles of a Mahomedan historian. And all these records tell the same melancholy tale. The people of Bengal had been used to tyranny, but had never lived under an oppression so far reaching in its effects, extending to every village market and every manufacturer's loom. They had been used to arbitrary acts from men in power, but had never suffered from a system which touched their trades, their occupations, their lives so closely. The springs of their industry were stopped, the sources of their wealth were dried up.

[1] *Considerations on India Affairs* (London, 1772), p. 191 to 194.

[2] *Ibid.*

There were two Englishmen in Bengal who endeavoured to put a stop to this state of things; they were Henry Vansittart and Warren Hastings. They came to Monghyr to see the Nawab Mir Kasim, and to settle matters amicably. Mir Kasim was a despot, but he was clear-sighted. He had proved himself strong and self-willed, but he knew himself powerless against the Company, and he felt that Vansittart and Hastings were his only friends. He made concessions where concessions were demanded, and the three came to an agreement.

The terms of the agreement were recorded under nine heads,[1] the first three being most important. They were that—

(1) For all trade, import or export, by shipping, the Company's Dustuck should be granted, and it should pass unmolested and free of the customs.

(2) For all trade from one place within the country to another, in commodities produced in the country, the Company's Dustuck should be granted.

(3) That duties should be paid on such commodities according to rates which shall be particularly settled and annexed to the agreement.

Nothing could be more equitable than this agreement, but it aroused an outburst of indignation in Calcutta. Amyatt, Hay, and Watts recorded on the 17th January 1763, "that the regulations proposed by him [Vansittart] are dishonourable to us as Englishmen, and tend to the ruin of all public and private trade." The General Council met on the 15th February. A solemn consultation was held on the 1st March. It was determined (Vansittart and Hastings dissenting) that the Company's servants had the right to carry on the internal trade duty-free; and that, as an

[1] See *Mongheer Treaty* in the Third Report of the House of Commons Committee on the Nature, &c., of the East India Company, 1773, Appendix, p. 361.

acknowledgment to the Nawab, a duty of 2½ per cent. would be paid on salt alone, instead of 9 per cent. on all articles, to which Vansittart had agreed.

This was the decision of selfish men fighting for their selfish interests. The dissentient opinion of Warren Hastings was that of a just man pleading for justice. One passage from Hastings' long statement should be quoted and remembered.

"As I have formerly lived among the country people, in a very inferior station, and at a time when we were subject to the most slavish dependence in the Government, and met with the greatest indulgence, and even respect, from the Zemindars and officers of the Government, I can with the greatest confidence deny the justice of this opinion; and add further, from repeated experience, that if our people, instead of erecting themselves into lords and oppressors of the country, confine themselves to an honest and fair trade, and submit themselves to the lawful authority of the Government, they will be everywhere courted and respected, and the English name, instead of becoming a reproach, will be universally revered; the country will reap a benefit from our commerce; and the power of the English, instead of being made a bugbear to frighten the poor inhabitants into submission to injury and oppression, will be regarded by them as the greatest blessing and protection." [1]

Nawab Mir Kasim heard of the rejection of the Agreement by the Calcutta Council, and of the resistance offered to his officers in the execution of his orders in accordance with the Agreement. In his noble indignation, Mir Kasim did one of the best and most benevolent acts which have ever been done by

[1] Fourth Report of the House of Commons Committee, 1773, Appendix, p. 486.

any king or ruler in the East. He sacrificed his revenues and abolished all inland duties, so that his subjects might at least trade on equal terms with the servants of the East India Company.

It is scarcely possible to believe, but it is nevertheless the fact, that the Calcutta Council, with the exception of Vansittart and Hastings, protested against this repeal of all duties as a breach of faith towards the English nation! "The conduct of the Company's servants upon this occasion," says James Mill in his History of British India, "furnishes one of the most remarkable instances upon record of the power of interest to extinguish all sense of justice, and even of shame." "There can be no difference of opinion," adds H. H. Wilson in his note, "on the proceedings. The narrow-sighted selfishness of commercial cupidity had rendered all Members of the Council, with the two honourable exceptions of Vansittart and Hastings, obstinately inaccessible to the plainest dictates of reason, justice, and policy."

The dissentients, Vansittart and Hastings, recorded their opinion pointedly, and argued that "although it may be for our interests to determine that we will have all the trade in our hands, that we will employ all our own people to make salt, take every article of produce of the country off the ground . . . yet it is not to be expected that the Nabob will join us in endeavouring to deprive every merchant of the country of the means of carrying on their business." This puts before us clearly the issues which were involved. The Company's servants, in order to make private fortunes for themselves, desired to deprive the population of a rich and civilised country of those sources of wealth which they had hitherto enjoyed under good and bad government alike, and those rights of free production and free barter which belong to all civilised communities on earth. The Company's servants desired not for a monopoly in one or two commodities, but for a distinction between their trade and the trade of the country merchants in all commodities, such as would eventually deprive the people of Bengal of one of the commonest rights of all human societies. History, perhaps, does not record another instance of foreign merchants asserting such far-reaching claims by the force of arms, in order to divert into their own hands virtually the entire trade of a great and populous country. Nawab Mir Kasim resisted the claims, and the result was war.

Henry Vansittart, who was Governor in Calcutta from 1760 to 1765, covering the entire period of Mir Kasim's administration of Bengal, thus sums up his opinion of that administration:

"He [Mir Kasim] discharged the Company's debt and the heavy arrears of his army, retrenched the expenses of his court, which had consumed the income of his predecessors, and secured his own authority over the country by reducing the power of the Zemindars, who were before continual disturbers of the peace of the province. All this I saw with pleasure, well knowing that the less need he had of our assistance, the less would be the Company's expenses, and the better able they would be to attend to the care of their own possessions; at the same time that we might depend upon him as a sure and useful ally against any common enemy. I was convinced that whilst we did not encroach upon the Nabob's rights or disturb his government he would never wish to quarrel with us; and, in effect, so cautious was he of giving occasion for dispute, that not one instance can be produced of his sending a man into any of the lands ceded to us, or molesting us in a single article of our commerce, till the contention which he was drawn into by the usurpation of our Gomastahs and our new claims with respect to our private trade, and even to the breaking out of the war during the height of our disputes, the Company's business, in every part, went on without the least interruption, excepting one or two aggravated complaints of Mr. Ellis's concerning the saltpetre business. How different was the conduct of the gentlemen who had formed themselves into a party against him! From the time of his advancement to the Subahship, scarce a day passed but occasion was taken from the most trifling pretences to trample on his government, to seize his officers, and to insult them with threats and invectives. I need not point out instances of this, they will be seen in every page of this narrative."[1]

It is not the purpose of the present work to narrate the military transactions of the East India Company. The issue of the war with Mir Kasim in 1763 was never doubtful for a moment. Mir Kasim fought better than any Indian prince or army had ever fought in Bengal against the English, but was beaten at Gheria and then at Uday-Nala. In a fit of fury he caused the English prisoners at Patna to be massacred, and then left his dominions for ever. Old Mir Jafar, who had been set aside in 1760, was now set up again as Nawab. But he died shortly after; and his illegitimate son, Najim-ud-Daula, was hastily created Nawab in 1765.

Every occasion for setting up a new Nawab was considered a suitable opportunity for shaking the proverbial pagoda-tree of the East. When Mir Jafar was first made Nawab after the battle of Plassy in 1757, the British officers and troops had received a bonus of £1,238,575, out of which Clive himself had taken £31,500 besides a rich jaigir or estate in Bengal. When Mir Kasim was made Nawab in 1760, the presents to the British officers came to £200,269, out of which Vansittart had taken £58,333. When Mir

[1] *Narrative*, vol. iii. p. 381.

Jafar was made Nawab a second time in 1763, the presents amounted to £500,165. And now, when Najim-ud-Daula was set up in 1765, further presents came in to the extent of £230,356. Besides these sums received in presents, amounting within eight years to £2,169,665, further sums were claimed and obtained as restitution within this period amounting to £3,770,833.[1]

The receipt of these sums was proved or acknowledged before the House of Commons Committee which inquired into the condition of the East India Company in 1772–73. Clive justified his own conduct.

"I never sought to conceal it, but declared publicly in my letters to the Secret Committee of the India Directors that the Nabob's generosity had made my fortune easy, and that the Company's welfare was now my only motive for staying in India. . . . What pretence could the Company have to expect, that I, after having risked my life so often in their service, should deny myself the only opportunity ever offered of acquiring a fortune without prejudice to them, who it is evident would not have had more for my having had less?"[2]

It never struck Clive that the treasure belonged neither to the Company nor to him, but to the country, and should have been devoted to the good of the people.

It is due, however, to the East India Company to state that they set their face against these exactions recovered under the name of presents, and condemned also the internal trade carried on by their servants in Bengal. In 1765 they sent out orders against the receipt of presents, and despatched Clive once more to put a stop to the internal trade of their servants,

[1] House of Commons Committee's Third Report, 1773, p. 311.
[2] House of Commons Committee's First Report, 1772, p. 148.

which they had already prohibited. The orders had arrived in Bengal, and the covenants to be signed by the Company's servants were shortly expected. There was no time to lose, so the Calcutta Council hastily set up Najim-ud-Daula, and reaped their last harvest of presents.

CHAPTER III

LORD CLIVE AND HIS SUCCESSORS IN BENGAL (1765-1772)

THE year 1765 marks a new epoch in the history of British India.

Lord Clive returned to India in that year for the third and last time, and obtained from the Great Moghal a charter making the East India Company the DEWAN or the administrators of Bengal. Though the Great Moghal had no real power, he was still the titular sovereign of India, and his charter gave the East India Company a legal status in the country.

Lord Clive had an arduous duty to perform. The Company's affairs were in a bad way; their servants were corrupt; their subjects were oppressed. It was Clive's endeavour to rectify all this within the brief period of his stay in India, and his letter to the Court of Directors from Calcutta, dated 30th September 1765, is one of the most memorable documents contained in the published volumes on Indian affairs. In this letter Lord Clive described the state of affairs as he found them on his last arrival in India, and also the measures he adopted to put things into order. It is necessary to describe Clive's work in Clive's own words.

"2. Upon my arrival, I am sorry to say, I found your affairs in a condition so nearly desperate as would have alarmed any set of men whose sense of honour and duty to their employers had not been estranged by the too eager pursuit of their own advantage. The sudden, and, among many, the unwarrantable acquisition of riches, had introduced luxury in every shape and in the most pernicious excess. These two enormous evils went hand in hand together through the whole Presidency, infecting almost every member of each Department; every inferior seemed to have grasped at wealth that he might be able to assume that spirit of profusion which was now the only distinction between him and his superior. . . . It is no wonder that the lust of riches should readily embrace the proffered means of its gratification, or that the instruments of your power should avail themselves of their authority, and proceed even to extortion in those cases where simple corruption could not keep pace with their rapacity. Examples of this sort, set by superiors, could not fail of being followed in proportionable degree by inferiors; the evil was contagious, and spread among the civil and military, down to the writer, the ensign, and the free merchant. . . .

"9. Two paths were evidently open to me; the smooth one, and strewed with abundance of rich advantages that might be easily picked up; the other untrodden, and every step opposed with obstacles. I might have taken charge of the government upon the same footing on which I found it; that is, I might have enjoyed the name of Governor, and have suffered the honour, importance, and dignity of the post to continue in their state of annihilation. . . . An honourable alternative, however, lay before me; I had the power within my own breast to fulfil the duty of my station, by remaining incorruptible in the midst of numberless temptations artfully thrown in my way; by exposing my character to every attack which malice or resentment are apt to invent against any man who attempts reformation; and by encountering, of course, the odium of the settlement. I hesitated not a moment which choice to make; I took upon my shoulders a burden which requires resolution, perseverance, and constitution to support. Having chosen my part, I was determined to exert myself in the attempt, happy in the reflexion that the honour of the nation, and the very being of the Company would be maintained by the success. . . .

"12. The sources of tyranny and oppression, which have been opened by the European agents acting under the authority of the Company's servants, and the numberless black agents and sub-agents acting also under them, will, I fear, be a lasting reproach to the English name in this country. . . . I have at last, however, the happiness to see the completion of an event, which, in this respect as well as in many others, must be productive of advantages hitherto unknown, and at the same time prevent abuses that have hitherto had no remedy: I mean the Dewanee, which is the superintendency of all the lands and the collection of all the revenues of the Provinces of Bengal, Behar, and Orissa. The assistance which the Great Moghal had received from our arms and treasury made him readily bestow this grant upon the Company; and it is done in the most effectual manner you can desire. The allowance for the support of the Nabob's dignity and power, and the tribute to His Majesty [the Great Moghal] must be regularly paid; the remainder belongs to the Company. . . .

"13. Your revenues, by means of this acquisition, will, as near as I can judge, not fall far short for the ensuing year of 250 lacks of Sicca Rupees, including your former possessions of Burdwan, &c. Hereafter they will at least amount to twenty or thirty lacks more. Your civil and military expenses in time of peace can never exceed sixty lacks of Rupees; the Nabob's allowances are already reduced to forty-two lacks, and the tribute to the King [the Great Moghal] at twenty-six; so that there will be remaining a clear gain to the Company of 122 lack of Sicca Rupees, or £1,650,900 sterling. . . .

"16. A competency ought to be allowed to all your servants from the time of their arrival in India, and advantages should gradually increase to each in proportion to his station. . . . This certainty would arise from the freight-ships, from the privileges of trade (the advantages of which you are not unacquainted with), and also upon the profits upon salt, betel, and tobacco, agreeable to the new regulation which we have made in order to rectify the abuses that have been so long committed. . . .

"19. Having now fully submitted to you my sentiments on the Civil Department, permit me to trouble you with a few observations on the Military. . . . The evil I mean to apprise you is of the encroachment of the military upon the civil jurisdiction, and an attempt to be independent of their authority. . . . The whole Army should in like manner be subordinate to the Civil Power. If at any time they should struggle for superiority, the Governor and Council must strenuously exert themselves, ever mindful that they are the trustees of the Company in this settlement, and the guardians of public property under a civil institution. . . .

"26. Permit me now to remind you that I have a large family who stand in need of a father's protection, that I sacrifice my health and hazard my fortune with my life by continuing in this climate. . . . I now only wait to be informed whether my conduct thus far be approved of, and whether the whole or part of the regulations I have had the honour to lay before you are conformable to your ideas of the reformation necessary to be established. If they meet with your approbation, I doubt not you will immediately empower me, in conjunction with the Select Committee, to finish the business so successfully begun, which may easily be effected before the end of the ensuing year; when I am determined to return to

Europe, and hope to acquaint you in person with the accomplishment of every wish you can form for the prosperity of your affairs in Bengal."[1]

We have here in Clive's own language an account of a transaction which marks an important step in the rise of British power in India. Hitherto the British had appeared only as traders in India, and though they had virtually been the masters of Bengal since the battle of Plassy in 1757, nevertheless it was the concession of the Dewani by the titular Emperor of Delhi in 1765 which gave the East India Company a legal status in India, and formally imposed upon them the duties of the administration of Bengal. How Lord Clive proposed to perform those duties has been described in his own words. His endeavours to introduce reforms both in the civil and military administration deserve all the praise that has been bestowed upon them by historians; but when we examine the essential features of his scheme, we find that it was framed—as so many schemes have since been framed in India—mainly in the interests of the British rulers, and not in the interests of the people. The whole of Bengal was considered as an estate, a source of profit to the East India Company.

The taxes raised from thirty milions of people were, after deduction of expenses and allowances, not to be spent in the country and for the benefit of the country, but to be sent to England as profits of the Company. An annual remittance of over a million and a half sterling was to be made from a subject country to the shareholders in England. A stream of gold was to flow perennially from the revenues of a poor nation to add to the wealth of the richest nation on the face of the earth.

We thus find that the very first scheme which

[1] House of Commons Committee's Third Report, 1773, Appendix, p. 391–398.

was framed by British rulers for the administration of India involved that fatal Economic Drain which has now swelled to an annual remittance of many millions sterling. The victory of British arms in India, the organised rule introduced into that country by the British, the maintenance of peace, the dispensation of justice, and the spread of western education, deserve all the praise which has been bestowed upon them. But the financial relations between India and England have always from the very commencement been unfair; and India, with her vast resources, her fertile soil, and her industrious population, is now the poorest country on earth after a century and a half of British rule.

Not content with securing an annual profit of over a million and a half for the Company, Lord Clive insisted on keeping up the inland trade of Bengal for the profit of the Company's servants. He devised measures to do away with the oppression incident to this private trade; but the trade itself had been lucrative to Englishmen in Bengal, and Lord Clive would not give it up. Indeed, so determined was Lord Clive to continue the inland trade in salt, betel-nut, and tobacco, in spite of the known opposition of his masters, the East India Company, that on the 18th September 1765 he executed an indenture, jointly with other servants of the Company, to carry on the trade regardless of the orders of the Company. The following passage from the indenture is significant:

"Provided any order should issue or be made by the said Court of Directors in England, thereby ordering and directing the said joint trade and merchandise to be dissolved or put to an end, or that may hinder and stop the carrying on of the same, or any part thereof, or contain anything contrary to the covenants, clauses, grants, articles, or agreements in the said hereinbefore recited deed mentioned and contained, or any of them, so that the same may thereby become void and of no effect; then, and in that case, they, the said Robert Lord Clive, as President, William Brightwell Sumner, &c., as Council of Fort-William aforesaid, shall and will, well and truly save harmless and keep indemnified, them, the said William Brightwell Sumner, Harry Verelst, Ralph Leycester, and George Grey, and all the proprietors entitled, or to be entitled, to the said exclusive joint trade, and their successors, their executors, and administrators; and shall and will, notwithstanding any order or direction to be issued to the contrary as aforesaid, keep up, continue, and enforce, or cause to be kept up, continued, and enforced, the said exclusive joint trade for the term of one year." [1]

On receipt of Lord Clive's important letter of the 30th September, the Court of Directors sent a reply to the Calcutta Committee, dated the 17th May 1766, and also a separate letter to Lord Clive, bearing the same date. The Directors thanked Lord Clive in warm terms for the great services rendered by him, and intimated their acceptance of the Dewani, or the administration of Bengal, Behar, and Orissa. But it is greatly to the credit of the Directors that they declined to approve of that scheme of inland trade which had been drawn up by Clive.

"Our letter to the Select Committee expresses our sentiments of what has been obtained by way of donations; and to that we must add, that we think vast fortunes acquired in the inland trade have been obtained by a scene of the most tyrannic and oppressive conduct that was ever known in any age or country. We have been uniform in our sentiments and orders on this subject, from the first knowledge we had of it; and your Lordship will not therefore wonder that, after the fatal experience we had of the violent abuses com-

[1] House of Commons Committee's Fourth Report, 1773, Appendix p. 534.

mitted in this trade, that we could not be brought to approve of it, even in the limited and regulated manner with which it comes to us in the plan laid down in the Committee's proceedings."[1]

The Directors had never spoken ambiguously on the subject of the inland trade carried on by the Company's servants. In their letter of the 8th February 1764 they had prohibited such inland trade; and in their letter of the 15th February 1765 they had repeated their prohibition in the strongest manner; but their orders had been disregarded by their servants in India. Now, in their letter of 17th May 1766, they refused to sanction Clive's scheme for continuing the trade under the regulations framed by him. But this order too was disregarded, and under the pretence of contracts formed and advances made, the inland trade was continued for two years more.

Lord Clive left India in 1767, and was succeeded as Governor by Verelst, who ruled until 1770; and he was succeeded by Cartier, who was Governor until 1772. The five years' administration of Verelst and Cartier was a continuation of the misgovernment from which Bengal had suffered during the preceding years. The scheme of administration introduced by Clive was a sort of dual government. The collection of revenues was still made for the Nawab's exchequer; justice was still administered by the Nawab's officers; and all transactions were covered by the mask of the Nawab's authority. But the East India Company, the real masters of the country, derived all the profits; and the Company's servants practised unbounded tyranny for their own gain, overawing the Nawab's servants, and converting his tribunals of justice into instruments for the prosecution of their own purposes. The English Governor saw this and condemned it, but was unable to remedy the state of affairs.

[1] House of Commons Committee's Third Report, 1773, Appendix, p. 400.

"We insensibly broke down the barrier betwixt us and Government, and the native grew uncertain where his obedience was due. Such a divided and complicated authority gave rise to oppressions and intrigues unknown at any other period; the Officers of Government caught the infection, and being removed from any immediate control, proceeded with still greater audacity." [1]

Agriculture had always been the main source of the subsistence of the people of Bengal; but it declined under the new system of land settlements introduced by the Company's servants. From very ancient times the soil of Bengal was held by Zemindars or hereditary landlords, armed with quasi-feudal powers, paying revenues and rendering military service to the Nawab in times of need, and virtually ruling the people within their own estates. They were recognised as Rajas by their subjects and tenants; they maintained order, settled disputes, and punished crimes; they encouraged religion and rewarded piety; they fostered arts and learning, and were the patrons of letters. Arbitrary Nawabs, like Murshed Kuli in the seventeenth century and Mir Kasim in the eighteenth century, had "squeezed" the Zemindars with an iron hand, but had seldom ousted them from the estates which were considered hereditary by custom. The Company's servants, however, introduced a new system in Burdwan and Midnapur soon after they had acquired those districts from Mir Kasim in 1760; they disregarded the customary rights of the Zemindars, and sold their estates by public auction to increase the revenue, with the most lamentable results.

"In the provinces of Burwan and Midnapur, of which both the property and jurisdiction were ceded to the Company by Mir Kasim in the year 1760, those evils

[1] Governor Verelst's Letter to the Directors, dated 16th December 1769.

which necessarily flowed from the bad policy of the Moorish Government had in no sort decreased. On the contrary, a plan was adopted in 1762 productive of certain ruin to the province. The lands were let by public auction for the short term of three years. Men without fortune or character became bidders at the sale; and while some of the former farmers, unwilling to relinquish their habitations, exceeded perhaps the real value in their offers, those who had nothing to lose advanced yet further, wishing at all events to obtain an immediate possession. Thus numberless harpies were let loose to plunder, whom the spoil of a miserable people enabled to complete their first year's payment."[1]

We shall see farther on that this new and oppressive system was subsequently extended all over Bengal by Warren Hastings, and caused the greatest discontent, disorder, and suffering. Throughout the administration of Verelst and Cartier the land revenue was exacted with the utmost rigour in order to meet the East India Company's demands.

"It was therefore to be wished," wrote Governor Verelst to the Court of Directors, "and was more than once proposed, that when their lands came under our management, we had lowered for a time the stated rents of most districts, as an incitement to cultivation and improvement, rather than have made the smallest attempt to increase. . . . Permit me to give you my most serious opinion, founded on almost nineteen years' experience in the various branches of your revenues, and in various districts of your possessions, that it is totally beyond the power of your administration to make any material addition to your rents."[2]

Trade and manufacture declined under a system of

[1] *View of the Rise, &c., of the English Government in Bengal*, by Harry Verelst, Esq., Late Governor of Bengal, London, 1772, p. 70.
[2] Letter to the Court of Directors, dated 26th September 1768.

monopoly and coercion. The Directors of the East India Company had tried to check their servants, but they themselves now perpetrated a greater offence. British weavers had begun to be jealous of the Bengal weavers, whose silk fabrics were imported into England, and a deliberate endeavour was now made to use the political power obtained by the Company to discourage the manufactures of Bengal in order to promote the manufactures of England. In their general letter to Bengal, dated 17th March 1769, the Company desired that the manufacture of raw silk should be encouraged in Bengal, and that of manufactured silk fabrics should be discouraged. And they also recommended that the silk-winders should be forced to work in the Company's factories, and prohibited from working in their own homes.

"This regulation seems to have been productive of very good effects, particularly in bringing over the winders, who were formerly so employed, to work in the factories. Should this practice [the winders working in their own homes] through inattention have been suffered to take place again, it will be proper to put a stop to it, which may now be more effectually done, by an absolute prohibition under severe penalties, by the authority of the Government."[1]

"This letter," as the Select Committee justly remarked, "contains a perfect plan of policy, both of compulsion and encouragement, which must in a very considerable degree operate destructively to the manufactures of Bengal. Its effects must be (so far as it could operate without being eluded) to change the whole face of that industrial country, in order to render it a field of the produce of crude materials subservient to the manufactures of Great Britain."[2]

[1] Ninth Report of the House of Commons Select Committee on Administration of Justice in India, 1783, Appendix, 37.

[2] Ninth Report, 1783, p. 64.

We shall see, as we proceed farther, that this continued to be the settled policy of England towards India for fifty years and more; that it was openly avowed before the House of Commons and vigorously pursued till 1833 and later; and that it effectually stamped out many of the national industries of India for the benefit of English manufactures.

But perhaps the greatest evil from which the country suffered was the continuous Economic Drain from Bengal, which went on year after year for the profit of the Company, or for their expenses in other parts of the world. A statement of the revenues and expenses of Bengal during the first six years after the grant of the Dewani to the East India Company is given in the Fourth Report of the House of Commons, 1773, from which the following figures are compiled:[1]

Year.	Gross collection.	Nett revenues after deducting tribute to the Great Moghal, allowance to the Nawab, charges of collection, salaries, commissions, &c.	Total expenses, civil, military, buildings, fortifications, &c.	Nett annual balance.
May April	£	£	£	£
1765 to 1766	2,258,227	1,681,427	1,210,360	471,067
1766 „ 1767	3,805,817	2,527,594	1,274,093	1,253,501
1767 „ 1768	3,608,009	2,359,005	1,487,383	871,622
1768 „ 1769	3,787,207	2,402,191	1,573,129	829,062
1769 „ 1707	3,341,976	2,089,368	1,752,556	336,812
1707 „ 1771	3,332,343	2,007,176	1,732,088	275,088
Total . .	20,133,579	13,066,761	9,027,609	4,037,152

These figures show that nearly one-third of the nett revenues of Bengal was annually remitted out of the country. But the actual drain from the country was

[1] Fourth Report, 1773, p. 535.

much larger. A large portion of the civil and military expenses consisted in the pay of European officials who sent all their savings out of India. And the vast fortunes reared by those who had excluded the country merchants from their legitimate trades and industries were annually sent out of India. The actual drain from Bengal is perhaps more correctly represented in the figures for imports and exports for the years 1766, 1767, and 1768, compiled by Governor Harry Verelst.[1]

Imports.	Exports.
£624,375	£6,311,250

In other words, the country sent out about ten times what it imported. Mr. Verelst himself saw the magnitude of the evil, and was never tired of describing its lamentable consequences on the material condition of the people of Bengal.

"Whatever sums had formerly been remitted to Delhi were amply reimbursed by the returns made to the immense commerce of Bengal. . . . How widely different from these are the present circumstances of the Nabob's dominions! . . . Each of the European Companies, by means of money taken up in the country, have greatly enlarged their annual Investments, without adding a rupee to the riches of the province." [2]

"The great demands which have been made on this Presidency for supplies of money from every quarter have reduced your treasury to a very low state, and alarm us for the consequences which must inevitably attend such a vast exportation from this country." [3]

"It will hardly be asserted that any country, how-

[1] *View of the Rise, &c., of the English Government in Bengal*, Appendix, p. 117.

[2] Letter dated 26th September 1767.

[3] Letter dated 24th March 1768.

ever opulent, could long maintain itself, much less flourish, when it received no material supplies, and when a balance against it, of above one-third of its whole yearly value, was yearly incurred. But besides this, there are other concomitant circumstances, which have contributed to diminish the riches of the country and must, if not remedied, soon exhaust them. I have observed that one great advantage the country formerly reaped was the diffusion of its revenues by large grants to different families, and by the expensive luxury of its governors. But now the whole amount of the lands is swallowed up in one gulf—your treasury; nor does any part of it return into the circulation, except the sum issued from our Investment and necessary expenses."[1]

What the *Investment* was, was fully explained by the Select Committee of the House of Commons in their Ninth Report of 1783.

"A certain portion of the revenues of Bengal has been, for many years, set apart in the purchase of goods for exportation to England, and this is called the Investment. The greatness of this Investment has been the standard by which the merit of the Company's principal servants has been too generally estimated; and this main cause of the impoverishment of India has been generally taken as a measure of its wealth and prosperity. Numerous fleets of large ships, loaded with the most valuable commodities of the East, annually arriving in England in a constant and increasing succession, imposed upon the public eye, and naturally gave rise to an opinion of the happy condition and growing opulence of a country whose surplus productions occupied so vast a space in the commercial world. This export from India seemed to imply also a reciprocal supply, by which the trading capital employed in those productions was continually strengthened and

[1] Letter, dated 5th April 1769.

enlarged. But the payment of a tribute, and not a beneficial commerce, to that country, wore this specious and delusive appearance."[1]

The evils of a perpetual Economic Drain from India, pointed out so clearly by Governor Verelst and by the Select Committee of the House of Commons, was also condemned by the greatest political philosopher of England in words which will be read as long as the English tongue is understood. In his speech on Fox's East India Bill, made in 1783, Edmund Burke described the desolating effects of the perpetual drain from India; and it is doubtful if even that great orator ever spoke anything more forcible, more eloquent, and more true, within the whole course of his brilliant parliamentary career.

"The Asiatic conquerors very soon abated of their ferocity, because they made the conquered country their own. They rose or fell with the rise and fall of the territory they lived in. Fathers there deposited the hopes of their posterity; the children there beheld the monuments of their fathers. Here their lot was finally cast; and it is the normal wish of all that their lot should not be cast in bad land. Poverty, sterility, and desolation are not a recreating prospect to the eye of man, and there are very few who can bear to grow old among the curses of a whole people. If their passion or avarice drove the Tartar lords to acts of rapacity or tyranny, there was time enough, even in the short life of man, to bring round the ill effects of the abuse of power upon the power itself. If hoards were made by violence and tyranny, they were still domestic hoards, and domestic profusion, or the rapine of a more powerful and prodigal hand, restored them to the people. With many disorders, and with few political checks upon power, nature had still fair play, the sources of

[1] Ninth Report, 1783, p. 54.

acquisition were not dried up, and therefore the trade, the manufactures, and the commerce of the country flourished. Even avarice and usury itself operated both for the preservation and the employment of national wealth. The husbandman and manufacturer paid heavy interest, but then they augmented the fund from whence they were again to borrow. Their resources were dearly bought, but they were sure, and the general stock of the community grew by the general effect.

"But under the English Government all this order is reversed. The Tartar invasion was mischievous, but it is our protection that destroys India. It was their enmity, but it is our friendship. Our conquest there, after twenty years, is as crude as it was the first day. The natives scarcely know what it is to see the grey head of an Englishman; young men, boys almost, govern there, without society, and without sympathy with the natives. They have no more social habits with the people than if they still resided in England; nor, indeed, any species of intercourse but that which is necessary to making a sudden fortune, with a view to a remote settlement. Animated with all the avarice of age, and all the impetuosity of youth, they roll in one after another; wave after wave, and there is nothing before the eyes of the natives but an endless, hopeless prospect of new flights of birds of prey and passage, with appetites continually renewing for a food that is continually wasting. Every rupee of profit made by an Englishman is lost for ever to India."

The administration of India has vastly improved since the days of Governor Verelst and Edmund Burke. The whole continent of India has enjoyed unbroken peace for half-a-century, such as was unknown in the eighteenth century. Trade and commerce have been freed from invidious and prohibitive duties.

The administration of justice and the protection of life and property have been more complete. And the spread of education has awakened a new life among the people, and befitted them for higher work and greater responsibilities. But nevertheless the evil of a perpetual Economic Drain from India, of which Verelst and Burke complained in their day, continues to this day in an ever-swelling current, and makes India a land of poverty and of famines.

Famines in India are directly due to a deficiency in the annual rainfall; but the intensity of such famines and the loss of lives caused by them are largely due to the chronic poverty of the people. If the people were generally in a prosperous condition, they could make up for local failure of crops by purchases from neighbouring provinces, and there would be no loss of life. But when the people are absolutely resourceless, they cannot buy from surrounding tracts, and they perish in hundreds of thousands, or in millions, whenever there is a local failure of crops.

Early in 1769 high prices gave an indication of an approaching famine, but the land-tax was more rigorously collected than ever. "The revenues were never so closely collected before."[1] Late in the year the periodical rains ceased prematurely, and the Calcutta Council in their letter of the 23rd November to the Court of Directors anticipated a falling off of the revenues, but specified no relief measures to be undertaken. On the 9th May 1770 they wrote: "The famine which has ensued, the mortality, the beggary, exceed all description. Above one-third of the inhabitants have perished in the once plentiful province of Purneah, and in other parts the misery is equal." On the 11th September they wrote: "It is scarcely possible that any description could be an exaggeration of the

[1] Resident at the Durbar, 7th February 1769. India Office Records, quoted in Hunter's *Annals of Rural Bengal*, London, 1868, p. 21, *note*.

misery the inhabitants . . . have encountered with. It is not then to be wondered that this calamity has had its influence on the collections; but we are happy to remark they have fallen less short than we supposed they would." On the 12th February 1771 they wrote: "Notwithstanding the great severity of the late famine and the great reduction of people thereby, some increase has been made in the settlements both of the Bengal and the Behar provinces for the present year." On the 10th January 1772 they wrote: "The collections in each department of revenue are as successfully carried on for the present year as we could have wished."[1]

It is painful to read of this rigorous collection of the land-tax during years of human sufferings and deaths perhaps unexampled in the history of mankind. It was officially estimated by the members of the Council, after they had made a circuit through the country to ascertain the effects of the famine, that about one-third of the population of Bengal, or about *ten millions of people*, had died of this famine. And while no systematic measures were undertaken for the relief of the sufferers perishing in every village, roadside, and bazaar, the mortality was heightened by the action of the Company's servants. Their Gomashtas not only monopolised the grain in order to make high profits from the distress of the people, but they compelled the cultivators to sell even the seed requisite for the next harvest. The Court of Directors were indignant on receiving this information, and hoped that "the most exemplary punishment had been inflicted upon all offenders who could dare to counteract the benevolence of the Company and entertain a thought of profiting by the universal distress."[2]

[1] Extracts from India Office Records, quoted in Hunter's *Annals of Rural Bengal*, 1868, pp. 399–404.

[2] *Ibid.*, p. 420.

But the "benevolence of the Company" was less conspicuous when their own interests were touched, and we find no indication of an abatement of the land-tax of Bengal after a third of its population had been swept away and a third of the lands had returned to waste. Warren Hastings wrote thus to the Court of Directors on the 3rd November 1772:

"Notwithstanding the loss of at least one-third of the inhabitants of the province, and the consequent decrease of the cultivation, the nett collections of the year 1771 exceeded even those of 1768. . . . It was naturally to be expected that the diminution of the revenue should have kept an equal pace with the other consequences of so great a calamity. That it did not was owing to its being violently kept up to its former standard."[1]

In the language of modern Indian administration this violently keeping up the land revenue would be described as the Recuperative Power of India!

[1] Extracts from India Office Records, quoted in Hunter's *Annals of Rural Bengal*, 1868, p. 381.

CHAPTER IV

WARREN HASTINGS IN BENGAL (1772–1785)

THE British Parliament passed the Regulating Act in 1773. Warren Hastings, who had succeeded as Governor of Bengal in 1772, became the first Governor-General in 1774 under the new Act. Three members of his Council, including Philip Francis, were appointed from England, and two other members were chosen from among the servants of the Company. A Supreme Court was established in Calcutta. It was hoped that the administration of India would be improved under these new arrangements.

The name of Warren Hastings recalls memorable events in Indian history, which formed the subjects of long debates in the Houses of Parliament. It brings back to mind the story of the Begams of Oudh, the Raja of Benares, and the war with the Rohillas. Less dramatic but far more important events connected with the administration of Hastings were the great struggles of the British with the Mahrattas in the west and with Haidar Ali in the south. And the conduct of Warren Hastings in respect of all these events has formed the subject of controversies which have not yet closed, after more than a century since the close of his administration.

It gives us unspeakable relief to be able to sweep aside all these controversies from the present narrative. In accordance with the scope of this work, we will confine our attention strictly to those measures of Warren Hastings which affected the material well-being of the million, the economic condition of the nation. In the present volume we will only review the civil and revenue administration of Warren Hastings, leaving out those controversial matters which have engaged the tongue of the orator and the pen of the historian for over a hundred years.

We have met Warren Hastings before as a strong and able man, as a just and honourable man, striving manfully but in vain to save the clear rights of Mir Kasim against the usurpations of the Company's servants, to save the inland trade of the people of Bengal from the privileged rapacity of their new rulers. But the land system of Bengal was entirely a new problem to Hastings, as it was to all Englishmen of his time; and the continuous demands of the Directors of the Company for an increasing revenue from the land left him little opportunity to master the problem correctly or to deal with it fairly.

Englishmen in the eighteenth century were familiar only with the English land system, under which the soil belonged to landlords, was let to farmers, and was tilled by labourers. The Bengal system was entirely different; and the contending claims put forward from time to time by the State, by the landlords or Zemindars, and by the cultivators or Ryots, obscured for a long time the real features of the institution. The State was in no sense the proprietor, but was only entitled to a *revenue* from the soil. The Zemindars held their estates from generation to generation; were virtually feudal lords armed with civil and criminal powers; and were entitled to customary *rents* from the cultivators. The cultivators or Ryots were not mere labourers, but had rights to their holdings, which they transmitted from father to son, paying the customary rents to the landlords. Occasionally the Nawabs of Bengal re-surveyed the estates and enhanced the revenues; occasionally Zemindars increased their rents;

but, nevertheless, through long centuries the arrangements remained unchanged in their main features. The State was entitled to a revenue; the Zemindars were entitled to customary rents, paying a revenue to the State; the Ryots had a hereditary right to their holdings, subject to payment of customary rents to landlords.

In 1765, when the East India Company became the Dewan or administrators of Bengal under the Imperial grant, the Company's servants did not immediately take upon themselves either the management of the revenues or the administration of justice. The Mahomedan officer at Murshedabad continued to make revenue collections in Bengal under the superintendence of the Company's Resident at the Nawab's court; and Sitab Roy, a Hindu chief, continued to make revenue collections in Behar under the superintendence of the Company's Agent at Patna.[1] Only the Twenty-four Perganas, Burdwan, Midnapur, and Chittagong districts, which were the Company's old possessions, were managed by the Covenanted Servants of the Company.

In 1769, Supervisors were appointed by the Company, with powers to superintend the collection of revenue and the administration of justice. The "Dual Government" had not worked well. The real rulers of the land, screening themselves behind Hindu and Mahomedan revenue collectors, took over the collections, but did not feel the responsibilities of rulers. The Hindu and Mahomedan revenue collectors felt themselves as agents for the Company, and therefore failed to realise the responsibilities of rulers. The people were oppressed by both and protected by neither. The inquiries made by the Supervisors appointed in 1769 showed that the administration was in the utmost disorder. The collecting officers "exacted what they could from the Zemindars and great farmers

[1] Select Committee's Fifth Report, 1812, p. 5.

of revenue, whom they left at liberty to plunder all below, reserving to themselves the prerogative of plundering them in their turn." And with regard to the administration of justice, "the regular course was everywhere suspended; but every man exercised it who had the power of compelling others to submit to his decisions."[1]

In 1772 it was decided to place the administration of the country in the hands of British officers. The Governor, Warren Hastings, and four members of his Council, formed a committee, and adopted measures for the management of the revenues and the administration of justice. The exchequer and the treasury were removed from Murshedabad to Calcutta, and were placed under a Board of Revenue composed of the Governor and his Council. In the provinces the European Supervisors, now called Collectors, were empowered to collect the revenues; a settlement of the land revenues for five years was adopted; and four junior members of the committee went on a circuit to carry this plan into execution. For the administration of justice a civil court and a criminal court were formed in each district; the Collector presided over the civil court, and he also attended the criminal court, where a Mahomedan Kazi, with the help of two Maulvies, dispensed justice. Appeals from these civil and criminal courts were allowed to two superior courts in Calcutta. A new system of police was organised; native police officers, called Fauzdars, were appointed in the fourteen districts into which Bengal was then divided; and regulations, framed for the guidance of the revenue and judicial officers, were printed and promulgated in the languages of the country. All these various administrative reforms bear testimony to the ability and capacity of Warren

[1] Letter from the President and Council, dated 3rd November 1772.

Hastings; but they also reveal that defect in British administration which has continued down to the present day—a want of trust and confidence in the people. Hindu and Mahomedan officers in the eighteenth century were corrupt and rapacious, as the Company's servants were corrupt and rapacious. Endeavours were made by Hastings, and by his successor Cornwallis, to make the British servants honest, by placing them in positions of trust and responsibility, and giving them adequate remuneration for their work. No endeavour was made to place Hindu and Mahomedan officers in positions of trust and responsibility, to pay them adequately, and to accept their co-operation in the work of administration.

In 1774 Warren Hastings became Governor-General under the Regulating Act. The settlement of the lands for five years had proved a failure. The rights of the Zemindars, who were hereditary landlords, had been ignored, and the settlement had been made by auction. Bidders at the auction had been led by the eagerness of competition to make high offers, had squeezed the cultivators of the soil, and had yet failed to pay the promised revenue. The land system of Bengal had been misunderstood, the ancient landed families had been ruined, the cultivating population had been grievously oppressed. In 1774 the European Collectors were recalled, the superintendence of collections was vested in Provincial Councils at Calcutta, Burdwan, Dacca, Murshedabad, Dinajpur, and Patna; and native Amils were appointed in districts to perform an impossible duty.

In 1776 the policy of an equitable land settlement was discussed at Calcutta. Warren Hastings and Barwell proposed that estates should be sold by public auction or farmed out on leases, and settlements should be made with purchasers or lessees *for life.* A wiser statesman, who is known to English literature as the author of the "Letters of Junius," took a broader and juster view of the situation. Philip Francis was then a member of the Council of the Governor-General, and in one of the ablest minutes recorded in India, recommended that the land revenue demand of the State should be *permanently fixed.*

"The greater part of the Zemindars were ruined and dispossessed of the management of their lands, and there were few people of rank and family left, or of those who had formerly held high employments; such as there were, looked for large profits, which the country could not afford them and pay the rents also. People of lower rank were therefore of necessity employed as Amils or collectors on the part of the Government. These people executed a contract for a stipulated sum for the district to which they were appointed, and in effect they may be considered as farmers of revenue. They then proceeded from the Sudder, or seat of government, to the districts, to settle with the Zemindars or tenants for the revenue they had engaged to pay."

Having described the evils of this farming system, and its disastrous effects on the country, Philip Francis recommended a perpetual settlement of the land revenue as calculated to promote the prosperity of the people.

"The Jumma [assessment] once fixed, must be a matter of public record. It must be permanent and unalterable; and the people must, if possible, be convinced that it is so. This condition must be fixed to the lands themselves, independent of any consideration of who may be the immediate or future proprietors. If there be any hidden wealth still existing, it will then be brought forth and employed in improving the land, because the proprietor will be satisfied that he is labouring for himself." [1]

[1] Philip Francis' Minute of 1776, published in London in 1782.

When these proposals came before the Directors in London, they hesitated to take a final step. With a policy of drift, truly British, they replied that, "having considered the different circumstances of letting the land on leases for lives or in perpetuity, we do not, for many weighty reasons, think it at present advisable to adopt either of these methods." This was the very worst decision which the Directors could come to; for it negatived the life-leases proposed by Warren Hastings and the perpetual leases proposed by Philip Francis, and it permitted those short leases by auction which had already half ruined the Province of Bengal. The merchant rulers of India were keenly alive, "for many weighty reasons," to the constant and frequent increase of their revenue, and Bengal continued to be afflicted by the auction system, the short leases, and the imprisonment of defaulting Zemindars, for ten years more.

In 1777 the five-years' settlement made in 1772 came to an end. The auction system was somewhat modified, and preference was now given to hereditary Zemindars. But the harshness of the system was greatly exaggerated when it was declared that the estates would be let, not for five years, but annually. Lands were thus let annually to Zemindars in 1778, 1779, and 1780. The country groaned under this economic tyranny, the revenues failed once more.

In 1781 great changes were introduced. Thirteen Articles and Regulations were prepared for the guidance of civil courts, which were afterwards incorporated in the Civil Code of ninety-five Articles of Regulations, which were printed with translations in the Persian and Bengali languages. Civil Judges and Collectors were entrusted with the powers of magistrates to grapple with the increase of crime in the province. A Committee of Revenue was formed at Calcutta, and submitted a plan for a new settlement of the land revenue for one year only, preference being given to Zemindars. The settlement was effected, and the land revenue was increased by twenty-six lakhs, or about £260,000.

All the great Zemindars of Bengal, all the ancient landed families, suffered under this system of annual settlements, frequent enhancements, and harsh methods of realisation, such as they had never known before. Descendants of old houses found their estates pass into the hands of money-lenders and speculators from Calcutta; widows and minor proprietors saw their peaceful subjects oppressed by rapacious agents appointed from Calcutta. It so happened that the three largest estates in Bengal, each paying a revenue of over a hundred thousand pounds sterling, were then under the administration of three distinguished ladies, who have left their names engraved in the memories of their countrymen. Burdwan, with its revenue of over £350,000, was held by the widow of the celebrated Tilak Chand, and mother of the equally celebrated Tej Chand. Rajshahi, with its revenue of over £260,000, was held by the venerable Rani Bhavani, whose name is cherished in India to this day for her high rank and abilities, as well as for her pious life and munificent charities. And Dinajpur, with its revenue of over £140,000, lost its Raja in 1780, and his widow was the guardian of the heir, then five years old. The history of these three estates will illustrate to some extent the sufferings of the people under the harsh and ever-changing revenue policy of Warren Hastings.

Dinajpur suffered most. An unscrupulous and rapacious agent, Debi Sing, was appointed from Calcutta to manage this estate during the minority. Debi Sing had been guilty of tyranny in Purnea and in Rungpur, and had been removed from his previous employment, and branded in the Company's records; but he was chosen as a proper agent when the object was to screw up the revenues of Dinajpur during a minority. Debi Sing proved himself equal to the task. With a cruelty perhaps unparalleled even in Bengal in the eighteenth century, he imprisoned the Zemindars and flogged the cultivators in order to raise the revenue. Women were not exempted from his tyranny, and insult and indecent outrage were added to the tortures of the stake and the lash.

The oppression of Debi Sing drove the suffering cultivators of Dinajpur from their homes and villages. They attempted to leave the district, but bands of armed soldiers drove them back. Many fled into the jungles, and large numbers of the most passive and submissive race of cultivators on earth were goaded to rebellion. The insurrection spread through Dinajpur and Rungpur; soldiers were called in, and then followed punishments and cruel executions. Mr. Goodlad, the English chief of the district, described the rising as the greatest and most serious disturbance which had ever happened in Bengal; the cruel severity by which it was suppressed was also perhaps unexampled in Bengal.

The story of Burdwan is less tragic, because the great wrong done fell on the territorial house, and not to any great extent on the people. Maharaja Tilak Chand had died in 1767, and the succession of the minor son, Tej Chand, had been allowed and confirmed. Lalla Umi Chand, a friend of the family, had been appointed administrator of the estate by the deceased Zemindar; but John Graham, the British chief of the district, forced on the widow Rani a rapacious and unscrupulous manager in Braj Kisor. The Rani, as far as a woman could, endeavoured to stop his dishonesty, and refused him the great seal of the estate.

"My son's seal," she said in a petition to Warren

Hastings in 1774, "was in my own possession; and as I affixed it to no paper without first perusing it, Braj endeavoured by every method to get it into his own hands, which I constantly persisted in refusing him. Upon this, in the Bengal year 1179 [A.D. 1772], Braj Kisor, having prevailed upon Mr. Graham to come to Burdwan, took from me my son Tej Chand, then nine years of age, and confined him in a separate place under a guard. In this situation, through affliction and apprehension, having remained more than seven days without sustenance to the absolute endangering my life, and finding no resource, I gave up the seal."[1]

The letter went on to say, that after thus obtaining the seal of the estate, Braj Kisor wasted the wealth of the estate, embezzled a large sum of money, and refused to submit any accounts. The Rani with her son was in dread of her life, and prayed to be allowed to proceed to Calcutta to reside in safety.

Clavering, Monson, and Francis, members of the Governor-General's Council, asked for an inquiry into the charge of embezzlement against Braj Kisor and John Graham. "We do not enter into the truth or falsehood," they wrote on 11th January 1775, "of the charge against Mr. Graham and the Dewan of Burdwan of an embezzlement of above eleven lakhs of rupees [£110,000], alleged to be the property of her infant son. It will be her business to make good the truth of her allegations. We are not so unjust as to give credit to charges against the honour or innocence of any man before the proofs are produced; neither does the Rani's petition require it of us. Let the prayer of the petition be granted."[2]

The dissensions in the Council, however, prevented a proper inquiry, and Warren Hastings defended John Graham. "Such inconsiderable presents," wrote Claver-

[1] Select Committee's Eleventh Report, 1783, Appendix O.
[2] *Ibid.*

ing, Monson, and Francis, "as the Governor-General says Mr. Graham received, could never have created the immoderate fortune he is known to possess." "I am totally unacquainted," replied Hastings, "with Mr. Graham's fortune; I know not on what foundation the majority style it immoderate. I thought it incumbent to vindicate him from the calumnies of the Burdwan Rani."

For the rest, the Burdwan estate was heavily assessed. Ganga Govind Sing, the Dewan of the Revenue Board, was no friend of the Burdwan house, and he fixed the assessment higher than in any other old zemindari in Bengal. For many decades Burdwan suffered from this; and the descendants of the feudal lords, who had been virtual rulers in their own estate, and had helped the old Nawabs of Bengal against the invasions of the Mahrattas, found themselves unable to meet the heavy pecuniary demands of the new masters of Bengal. The house was saved from utter ruin by the creation of a new order of permanent lessees who shared the responsibilities of the Zemindar; but to the present day the Burdwan estate pays a larger proportion of its collections as Government revenue than any other of the great estates in Bengal.

But the venerable lady whose misfortunes were regarded with the greatest commiseration in the eighteenth century, and whose name is cherished with almost religious respect by millions of men and women in Bengal to this day, was Rani Bhavani of Rajshahi. Her great estates had virtually embraced the whole of Northern Bengal before Lord Clive won the battle of Plassy. She had witnessed the greatness and decadence of the Mahomedan power and the rise and extension of the British power. Her talents and abilities stood forth as a signal example of the capacity of Hindu women in administration. And her pious life and unbounded benevolence made her name cherished as a household word in Bengal. To the present day her story is read by Hindu girls and boys as one of the nine women in history and fiction who are the models of Indian womanhood.

The new revenue system introduced by Warren Hastings, and the five-years' settlements made in 1772, affected Rajshahi as they affected every other estate in Bengal. The Governor and Council, in their letter of the 31st December 1773, remarked that "Rani Bhavani, the zemindar of Rajshahi, proves very backward in her payments." And on the 15th March 1774 they determined to make "a declaration to the Rani, that if she did not pay up the revenue due from her to the end of the Bengal month of Magh [10th February] by the 20th Phalgun [1st March], we should be under the necessity of depriving her of her zemindari, and putting it into the possession of those who would be more punctual in fulfilling their engagements with Government." In another letter, dated 18th October 1774, the Governor-General "resolved to dispossess her both of her farm and her zemindari, and of all property in the land, and to grant her a monthly pension of 4000 rupees (£400) during life, for her subsistence." [1]

Among the many petitions which the aged Rani submitted to avert this disgrace and humiliation, there are some which are of more than usual interest. In one of these petitions she recounted the history of her estate since the five-years' settlement of 1772, the oppressions committed by the farmer, Dulal Roy, who had been appointed, and the depopulation of the country in consequence.

"In the year 1179 [A.D. 1772], the English gentlemen of the Sircar [Government] did blend all the old rents of my land together, and did make the Ziladari Mathote [exactions on tenants] and other temporary rents perpetual. . . . I am an old Zemindar; and not

[1] Select Committee's Eleventh Report, 1783, Appendix O.

being able to see the griefs of my Ryots, I agreed to take the country as a farmer. I soon examined the country, and found there was not enough in it to pay the rents. . . .

"In Bhadra, or August 1773, the banks broke, and the Ryots' ground and their crops failed by being overflowed with water. I am a Zemindar, so was obliged to keep the Ryots from ruin, and gave what ease to them I could, by giving them time to make up their payments; and requested the gentlemen [English officials] would, in the same manner, give me time, when I would also pay up the revenue; but not crediting me, they were pleased to take the Cutchery [rent-collection office] from my house, and bring it away to Motijhil, and employed Dulal Roy as a servant and Sazawal, to collect the revenue from me and the country. . . .

"Then my house was surrounded, and all my property inquired into; what collections I had made as farmer and Zemindar were taken; what money I borrowed and my monthly allowances were all taken; and made together Rs.22,58,674 [£226,000].

"In the new year 1181 [A.D. 1774], for the amount of Rs.22,27,824 [£223,000] the country was given in farm to Dulal Roy, taking from me all authority Then Dulal Roy and Paran Bose, a low man, put on the country more taxes, viz., another Ziladari Mathote [exaction on tenants], and Assey Jzaffer, loss of Ryots' desertion taken from present Ryots, &c. These two men issued their orders, and took from Ryots all their effects, and even seed grain and ploughing bullocks, and have depopulated and destroyed the country. I am an old Zemindar; I hope I have committed no fault. The country is plundered, and the Ryots are full of complaints.

"For these reasons I make my petition now; that as Rs.22,27,817 [£223,000] is become the revenue which Dulal Roy is to pay for this year, I am ready, and will take care that the Sircar [Government] suffers no loss, and that this sum be paid."[1]

These extracts are valuable because they give us an insight into what was going on in most parts of Bengal. Old zemindars, if they failed to compete with auction bidders, were turned out from estates which their fathers had held for generations. If they kept their estates as farmers at an enhanced revenue, and failed in prompt payment, managers were forced on their estates, and they plundered the tillers of the soil and caused misery and depopulation. The land revenues failed, however, in spite of the utmost coercion; one-third of the cultivated lands in Bengal were overgrown with jungles.

Pran Krishna, son of Rani Bhavani, submitted other petitions, and there were many revenue consultations. Philip Francis protested against the practice of European servants holding farms in the names of their Banians or Indian agents. "The country," he said, "belongs to the natives. Former conquerors contented themselves with exacting a tribute from the land. . . . Every variation hitherto introduced from the ancient customs and establishments of the country appears to have been attended with fatal consequences, insomuch that I understand it to be the general opinion, that at least two-thirds of the whole surface of Bengal and Behar are in a state of total depopulation. The timid Hindoo flies from the tyranny which he dare not resist."[2]

In the end, the majority of the Council resolved in 1775 "to deprive Raja Dulal Roy of the farm of Rajshahi, and that the Rani be reinstated in possession of her lands in farm." Hastings never entirely approved of this decision; he never appreciated, like his successor Lord Cornwallis, the claims of the old hereditary

[1] Select Committee's Eleventh Report, 1783, Appendix O.
[2] *Ibid.*

families of Bengal; he never withdrew his support from the auction purchasers and farmers, who grew up under his harsh and unsympathetic system. Large slices of the old Rajshahi estates were carved out to create a flourishing estate for Kanta Babu, the Banyan of Warren Hastings.

The evils of an oppressive and ever-changing system of land administration were aggravated by the fact that virtually the whole of the revenues of the province were drained out of the country, and did not return in any shape to the people, to fructify their trades, industries, and agriculture.

"Notwithstanding the famine in 1770, which wasted Bengal in a manner dreadful beyond all example, the Investment, by a variety of successive expedients, many of them of the most dangerous nature and tendency, was forcibly kept up. . . . The goods from Bengal, purchased from the territorial revenues, from the sale of European goods, and from the produce of the monopolies . . . were never less than a million sterling, and commonly nearer £1,200,000. This million is the lowest value of the goods sent to Europe, for which no satisfaction is made. About £100,000 a year is also remitted from Bengal on the Company's account to China, and the whole of the product of that money flows into the direct trade from China to Europe. Besides this, Bengal sends a regular supply in time of peace to those Presidencies [in India] which are unequal to their own establishment. . . .

"When an account is taken of the intercourse, for it is not commerce, which is carried on between Bengal and England, the pernicious effects of the system of Investment from revenue will appear in the strongest point of view. In that view, the whole exported produce of the country, so far as the Company is concerned, is not exchanged in the course of barter, but it is taken away without any return or payment whatever. . . .

"But that the greatness of these drains and their effects may be rendered more visible, your Committee have turned their consideration to the employment of those parts of the Bengal revenue which are not employed in the Company's own Investments, for China and for Europe. . . . From the portion of that sum which goes to the support of civil government the natives are almost wholly excluded, as they are from the principal collections of revenue. With very few exceptions, they are only employed as servants and agents of Europeans, or in the inferior departments of collections, when it is absolutely impossible to proceed a step without their assistance."[1]

The following figures, showing the receipts and disbursements for Bengal for eight years, are taken from official records:[2]

Year.	Land revenue.	Total revenues.	Civil charges.	Military charges.	Total disbursements.
May to April	£	£	£	£	£
1771 „ 1772	2,341,941	3,259,564	206,781	1,164,348	2,884,192
1772 „ 1773	2,298,441	2,866,968	234,051	1,288,667	2,827,141
1773 „ 1774	2,438,405	3,160,186	213,237	1,304,883	2,727,975
1774 „ 1775	2,777,870	3,564,915	268,232	1,080,304	3,300,124
1775 „ 1776	2,818,071	4,198,017	335,968	1,051,969	3,438,480
1776 „ 1777	2,755,043	3,971,440	325,192	942,199	3,424,401
1777 „ 1778	2,530,042	3,688,088	477,293	1,184,708	3,353,029
1778 „ 1779	2,656,809	3,782,690	553,810	1,846,237	4,972,590

We have so far dwelt on the state of things in Bengal. If we travel out of Bengal, and briefly survey the condition of other provinces which came under the administration or the influence of Warren Hastings, we shall find that the first results of the extension of his power was not happy. Among the many little States into which Northern India was divided in the

[1] Select Committee's Ninth Report, 1783, p. 55.
[2] Volume ii. of the Six Reports of the Committee of Secrecy, 1782, p. 362.

eighteenth century, none was more flourishing and prosperous, according to the testimony of all eye-witnesses, than Benares. The people were industrious, agriculture and manufactures flourished, and Raja Balwant Sing had his capital in that sacred city which was revered by all Hindus in all parts of India.

Balwant Sing died in 1770, and his liege lord, the King of Oudh, known as the Vizir, confirmed his son, Chait Sing, in succession on receipt of a succession fee and on a slight increase of the revenue previously paid. The East India Company had interested themselves in this succession, and in a general letter to the Directors, dated 31st October 1770, the Governor of Bengal wrote that "the Vizir's readiness in complying with this our recommendation and request has offered us great satisfaction, and is a circumstance the most pleasing, as it must give strength to the opinions of the several Powers in Hindustan of the strict friendship subsisting between the English and him."[1]

The King of Oudh, Suja-ud-Daula, himself died in 1775, and Warren Hastings, then Governor-General, took advantage of the death of the old ally of the British to extend British dominion and power. In May 1775 a new treaty was ratified between his son and successor, Asof-ud-Daula, by which Benares was ceded to the East India Company, and Raja Chait Sing became a vassal of the British.

"The cession of Benares and the other territories of the Raja Chait Sing," wrote the Governor-General to the Directors in August 1775, "to the Company, we flatter ourselves, will prove perfectly agreeable to your ideas, as it conveys a valuable acquisition to the Company. . . . The revenue which accrues from this acquisition amounts to Rs.23,72,656 [£237,000], and will be paid by the Raja in monthly payments as a neat tribute, without rendering any account of his

[1] Select Committee's Second Report, 1782, p. 452.

collections, or being allowed to enter any claims for deduction."[1]

Three years after this the unfortunate Chait Sing comprehended the full import of the change of his masters. "War having been declared between the Courts of Great Britain and France," wrote Warren Hastings to Chait Sing in July 1778, "by the former on the 18th March . . . I am to request of you, in my own name and that of the Board, as a subject of the Company, bound to promote their interest on every occasion, to contribute your share of the burden of the present war."[2]

In justice to one honest Englishman, it is necessary to record that Philip Francis endeavoured to oppose the demands and exactions of Warren Hastings. He had been the foremost to bring the State of Benares under British supremacy; but he protested against arbitrary demands on the Raja, who was now a vassal of the Company.

"There is no question but the Raja must yield to the power of this Government, and I shall be as ready as any member of this Board to support its authority as long as its power is directed by justice. I did from the first express a doubt whether we had strictly a right to increase our demands upon the Raja beyond the terms which we originally agreed to give him, which he consented to, and which, as I have constantly understood it, were made the fundamental tenure by which he held his zemindari. If such demands can be increased upon him at the discretion of the superior Power, he has no right, he has no property, or at least he has no security for either. Instead of five lakhs let us demand fifty, or whether he refuses or is unable to pay the money, the forfeiture of his zemindari may be the immediate consequence of it."[3]

[1] Select Committee's Second Report, 1782, p. 460.
[2] *Ibid.*, p. 463.
[3] *Ibid.*, p. 465.

These protests were made in vain. A second year's contribution of five lakhs (£50,000) was demanded from Chait Sing, then a third year's contribution of five lakhs, and then a fourth year's contribution, besides expenses of troops. He was reprimanded for failure of payment and then arrested; and when his people attacked the Company's guards, his fate was sealed. He fled from his estate; his sister's son, Mahip Narayan, was seated in his place with a large increase of the revenue demand; and the administration was controlled by the Governor-General's own agents.

The administration was a ghastly failure—not because Warren Hastings was a less able administrator than Bulwant Sing and Chait Sing, under whom Benares had flourished—but because the increased revenue demand under the new administration crushed the agricultural industry of the State.

The first deputy whom Hastings appointed for the Raja was dismissed for the offence of not making punctual payments. The second accordingly acted upon the "avowed principle that the sum fixed as the revenue must be collected." Lands were over-assessed, collections were made with the utmost harshness, the population was plunged into misery, and the country was desolated by a terrible famine in 1784.

Hastings himself witnessed the effects of the desolation and the famine. "From the confines of Buxar," he wrote to the Council Board on the 2nd April 1784, "to Benares, I was followed and fatigued by the clamours of the discontented inhabitants. The distresses which were produced by the long-continued drought unavoidably tended to heighten the general discontent. Yet I have reason to fear that the cause existed principally in a defective, if not a corrupt and oppressive, administration. I am sorry to add, that from Buxar to the opposite boundary, I have seen nothing but traces of complete devastation in every village. I cannot help remarking that, except the city of Benares, the province is in effect without a government. The administration of the province is misconducted, and the people oppressed, trade discouraged, and the revenue in danger of a rapid decline from the evident appropriation of its means."[1]

Such was the condition of Benares nine years after it had passed from the dominions of Oudh to the dominions of the East India Company. We will now travel a step further and survey the condition of Oudh itself.

Suja-ud-Daula, the ally of the British, died in 1775, as has been stated before. He was cruel and relentless towards his enemies, but he left the population of his kingdom contented, prosperous, and happy; and English officers who visited Oudh during the last years of his administration bear testimony to the flourishing condition of the country and its people.

When Asof-ud-Daula ascended his father's throne, Warren Hastings extended the power of the East India Company in Oudh. The old treaty with Suja-ud-Daula was modified, and a new treaty was made with Asof-ud-Daula, "by which the latter eventually and necessarily became a vassal of the Company."[2]

This vassalage was the ruin of Oudh. Colonel Hanny, who was sent up to Oudh by Hastings in command of a brigade, shared with many of his countrymen of those days the desire to make the best of his opportunities, and to rear a rapid fortune in his new station. The practice of the assignment of the land revenues, which had proved so fatal in

[1] Quoted in Mill's *History of British India*, 1858, vol. iv. chapter vii.

[2] Select Committee's Tenth Report, 1783, Appendix 7.

Madras and elsewhere, was pursued in Oudh. Colonel Hanny exercised civil and military powers in Oudh, and became the farmer of the revenues of Barraich and Gorakpur. Rents were increased; collections were made with every circumstance of cruelty and coercion; the people fled from their fields and villages; the country became desolate.

Asof-ud-Daula saw the ruin he had brought on himself. In 1779 he wrote to the British Government: "From the great increase of expense, the revenues were necessarily farmed out at a high rate, and the deficiencies followed yearly. The country and cultivation is abandoned."[1] The Nawab accordingly protested against fresh assignments for the new brigade, declaring that the troops were quite useless to him, and were the cause of loss in the revenues and of confusion in the affairs of his government.

The Calcutta Council deliberated on this important communication. Philip Francis, with that instinct of justice which was natural to him, recorded a characteristic Minute.

"I have not been long enough in the habits of dominion to see anything offensive or alarming in the demand made by an independent prince to be relieved from the burden of maintaining a foreign army, which, it is notorious, have devoured his revenues and his country under colour of defending it. . . .

"The Court of Directors, in their letter of the 15th December 1775, approve of the keeping of a brigade in the service of the Soubah of Oudh, *provided it be done with the free consent of the Soubah, but by no means without it.*

"Concerning this part of the army, however, there is at present no dispute, since the Vizier does not desire to have it recalled; his demand goes solely to

[1] Select Committee's Tenth Report, 1783, Appendix 7.

the temporary brigade and independent battalions under Major Hanny and Captain Osborne; the former, he says, is not only quite useless to his government, but it is, moreover, the cause of much loss both in the revenues and customs; the latter, he asserts, bring nothing but confusion to the affairs of government, and are entirely their own masters. . . .

"The motion supposes not only a necessity of our compelling him to keep those troops in his pay, but that we ourselves should be collectors of the revenues which is to pay them; which, as things are now managed, is nearly equivalent to putting his country under military execution. Thus one necessity produces another, and will continue to do so as long as the Indian States possess anything that can tempt our avarice or gratify our ambitions, or until we ourselves are taught by experience that there is some self-wisdom in doing justice to others."[1]

In the eyes of Warren Hastings, the pecuniary loss which would be inflicted on the Company by withdrawing the battalions had greater weight than the miseries imposed on the people of Oudh. The Nawab, he said, was the vassal of the Company, and the troops "cannot be withdrawn without imposing on the Company the additional burden of their expense." "It was for a great convenience, then," remarks the historian of India, James Mill, "and for nothing else, that the English, without any claim of right, compelled the Nawab Vizir to maintain their troops, that is, treated as the vassal which Hastings described him, and substantially seized and exercised the rights of sovereign and master over both him and his country."[2]

The demands of the British Government in 1780 stood at £1,400,000. How the Governor-General recalled Bristow from Lucknow and sent Middleton as

[1] Select Committee's Tenth Report, 1783, Appendix 7.
[2] *History of British India*, 1858, vol. iv. chapter viii.

Resident; how the Nawab was helped to rob his mother and his grandmother, the Begams of Oudh, to meet the demands of the Company's government; and how a large sum of money was extorted from them with every circumstance of oppression and indignity, are matters of history which it is unnecessary to narrate in these pages. The condition of the cultivators of Oudh is of far greater importance for the purposes of the present work than the more dramatic story of the wrongs of the royal house.

The facts which were deposed to at the celebrated impeachment of Warren Hastings relating to the collection of rents from the impoverished tenantry are sufficiently dismal. It was stated that the defaulters were confined in open cages, and it was replied that confinement in such cages under the Indian sun was no torture. It was stated that fathers were compelled to sell their children, and it was replied that Colonel Hanny had issued orders against such unnatural sales. Large masses of the people left their villages and fled the country, and troops were employed to prevent their flight. At last a great rebellion broke out; farmers and cultivators rose against the unbearable exactions; and then followed horrors and executions with which the untrained tillers of the soil are put down by the infuriated soldiery.

Colonel Hanny was then recalled from Oudh, and the rebellion was quelled, but Oudh was in a state of desolation. Captain Edwards visited Oudh in 1774 and in 1783. In the former year he had found the country flourishing in manufactures, cultivation, and commerce. In the latter year he found it "forlorn and desolate." Mr. Holt, too, stated that Oudh had fallen from its former state, that whole towns and villages had been deserted, and that the country carried the marks of famine. A severe famine actually visited the province in 1784, and the horrors of starvation were added to the horrors of misgovernment and war.

The cruel exactions of the East India Company, the miseries inflicted upon the people in every new territory added to their dominions, and the failure of the Regulating Act of 1773 to effect any adequate reforms, were revealed to the British Parliament by the Six Reports of the Committee of Secrecy, and the Eleven Reports of the Select Committee, published in 1782 and 1783. A reform in the administration was loudly called for. Fox's India Bill, supported by Edmund Burke, was rejected by the House; but at last Mr. Pitt's Bill for the better government of India was passed into law in 1784, and for the first time placed the administration of the Company under the control of the Crown. All civil, military, and revenue affairs of the Company were placed under the superintendence of six Commissioners appointed by the Crown. Warren Hastings resigned his post in the following year, and Lord Cornwallis, a nobleman of high character and of a generous disposition, was sent out as Governor-General to India.

In this brief narrative of the administration of Warren Hastings, we have strictly confined our attention to the economic condition of the people, and we deplore, with all impartial historians, that, from this point of view, his administration was a failure. In justice, however, to Warren Hastings, it is necessary to quote what was so ably urged in 1789 in his defence by Mr. Shore, afterwards Lord Teignmouth.

"A period of twenty-eight years has now elapsed since the Company first acquired a right to the revenues of any considerable part of the provinces, and of twenty-four years only since the transfer of the whole in perpetuity was regularly made by the grant of the Dewani. When we consider the nature and magnitude of this acquisition, the character of the people placed under our dominion, their difference of language and dissimilarity of manners, that we entered upon the administration of the government ignorant of its former constitution and with little practical experience in Asiatic finance, it will not be deemed surprising that we should have fallen into errors, or if any should at this time require correction."[1]

There is a great deal of truth in these remarks; and yet they apply to Warren Hastings in a less degree than perhaps to any other Englishman of his time. Warren Hastings was not a stranger in India, and was not ignorant of the people. He had come to India almost as a boy. He had passed his early life in a humble capacity, had mixed with the people, and had studied and appreciated their character. "I affirm, by the oath that I have taken," he said before the British Parliament, twenty-eight years after his retirement from India, "that this description of them [that the people of India were in a state of moral turpitude] is untrue and wholly unfounded. . . . They are gentle, benevolent, more susceptible of gratitude for kindness shown them than prompted to vengeance for wrongs inflicted, and as exempt from the worst properties of human passion as any people on the face of the earth."[2] Such were the people whom Hastings knew, and among whom he worked, with brief intervals of absence, for thirty-five years of his life, from 1750 to 1785.

Nor were these sentiments of Warren Hastings towards the people altogether belied by his public acts in India. At a time when the Company's servants were engaged in acquiring sudden and large fortunes by robbing the people of Bengal of their inland trade, Warren Hastings stood forth alone by the side of his leader, Vansittart, to oppose the tyranny of his country-

[1] Select Committee's Fifth Report, 1812, p. 169.

[2] Minutes of Evidence taken before the Lords' Committees, 1813, p. 1.

men. And even during his own administration of thirteen years, from 1772 to 1785, he endeavoured to bring order out of chaos; he compiled and published the laws of the Hindus and the Mahomedans; he established courts to administer those laws; he shaped a system of administration which has been improved since, but of which he was the first great architect.

From a man so gifted with the power of organisation and so rich in the knowledge of the country and its people, a high degree of administrative success would naturally be expected. Yet, if the success of a government be judged by the happiness it confers on the people, the administration of Hastings was a ghastly failure. The extension of British power and influence did not ameliorate the economic condition of the people, but left behind it a dark trail of misery, insurrections, and famines, in Bengal, Benares, and Oudh.

It is possible for us, after the lapse of a century, to calmly inquire into the causes of this failure. Hastings shared with all other Englishmen of his age the ineradicable conviction that India was a great estate for the profit of the East India Company and its servants, and he applied the whole forces of his vigorous mind to make India pay. The good of the people was made subservient to this primary object of the Company's administration; the rights of princes and people, of Zemindars and Ryots, were sacrificed to this dominant idea of the commercial rulers of India. Land revenue was increased even after the famine of 1770 had swept away one-third of the population of Bengal; landed families who had owned their estates for centuries were made to bid for them as annual farmers against money-lenders and speculators; cultivators flying from their homes and villages or rising in insurrection were driven back by soldiers to their homes with cruel severity; and a great portion of the money so raised was annually sent in the shape of Investments to the gratified shareholders in England. No administrator however gifted, and no administration however perfect, could prevent national poverty and famines when the whole of their fiscal policy was to drain the resources of one country for the traders of another.

This was the main cause of the failure of the administration of Warren Hastings, and his harsh, despotic, and arbitrary measures deepened the evils. There is a verdict on the conduct of great rulers which is more true and more abiding than that of historians, and that verdict is the verdict of the people. The people of India look back with pain and horror on the administration of Hastings which impoverished the country, as they look back with feelings of gratitude on the administration of his successor, who had the sympathy to feel and the courage to act for the material well-being of the vast population entrusted to his charge.

CHAPTER V

LORD CORNWALLIS AND ZEMINDARI SETTLEMENT IN BENGAL (1785–1793)

PITT'S India Bill became law on the 13th August 1784. It placed the administration of the Company under the control of the Crown, and thus compelled some reforms. The Directors of the Company felt that they must put their house in order. They selected a nobleman of high character and broad sympathies to succeed Warren Hastings, and in their letter of the 12th April 1786 they gave the new Governor-General, Lord Cornwallis, full instructions for his guidance.

In this memorable letter the Directors expressed their disapprobation of the frequent changes in the revenue system of Bengal and their desire to pursue any one system under watchful superintendence. They condemned the endeavours which had been made to continually increase the land-tax, and to oust Zemindars in favour of farmers, Sazawals, and Amins, who had no permanent interest in the well-being of the cultivators. They expressed their opinion that the most likely means of avoiding defalcations would be to introduce a *Permanent Settlement* of the land revenue, estimated on reasonable principles, for the due payment of which the hereditary tenure of the possessor would be the best and the only necessary security. They directed that the settlement should be made in all practicable instances with the Zemindars, and they declared that "a moderate *jumma* or assessment, regularly and punctu-

F

ally collected, unites the consideration of our interests with the happiness of the natives and security of the landholders more rationally than any imperfect collection of any exaggerated *jumma* to be enforced with severity and vexation."[1] And while they intended the settlement to be ultimately made permanent, they desired that the first settlement should be concluded for ten years only. The reader will perceive from this brief summary of the Directors' letter of 1786 that the statesmanlike recommendations made by Philip Francis in 1776 had borne fruit in ten years. After a bitter experience of ten years—bitter in the miseries inflicted on the people of Bengal—the wisdom of the proposals of Philip Francis was vindicated, and the unwisdom of the harsh and varying schemes of Hastings was condemned.

The man who was chosen to give effect to the new scheme was worthy of his task. Without that minute knowledge of Indian affairs which Warren Hastings possessed, Lord Cornwallis was gifted with a real sympathy with the people over whom he was sent to rule. Not once or twice in the history of India has the administrator of strong and benevolent sympathies succeeded, where the administrator of larger local experience and narrower sympathies has failed. And hence the necessity which is felt to this day, as it was felt in the eighteenth century, of leavening Anglo-Indian administration by the wider statesmanship of Europe.

On his arrival in India, Lord Cornwallis found it impossible to conclude a ten years' settlement without some further inquiry into the question of usages, tenures, and rents, and he vigorously prosecuted these inquiries. The Committee of Revenue had already changed its name to that of Board of Revenue, and its authority and functions were continued. The

[1] Select Committee's Fifth Report, 1812, p. 13.

European civil servants were vested with the combined powers of collector, judge, and magistrate,[1] and the administration of criminal justice still remained vested in the Deputy-Nawab of Bengal, to whose courts the European magistrates committed all serious cases for trial.

A great change in administration was effected in 1790. The Governor-General in Council accepted the superintendence of criminal justice throughout the provinces.[2] The chief criminal court was removed from Murshedabad to Calcutta. Four courts of circuit, superintended respectively by two covenanted officers, conducted the trial of offences not triable by magistrates. Regulations in the civil, criminal, and revenue departments were revised and printed in the English and Indian languages.

Further administrative and judicial reforms were effected in 1793. A separation of the judicial and executive duties was effected. The Board of Revenue and the District Collectors were deprived of their judicial functions in revenue cases. The Collectors were also divested of their magisterial authority. A covenanted officer of higher official rank than the Collector was appointed Judge and Magistrate in each division, and this officer was entrusted with the superintendence of the police within his division. Four appellate courts were established at Calcutta, Patna, Dacca, and Murshedabad respectively.[3]

The war with Tipu Sultan of Mysore compelled Lord Cornwallis to undertake the operations personally. He forced his way to the capital of Mysore, and dictated terms of peace to the Sultan in 1792. The British obtained Calicut and Coorg in the west, as well

[1] Regulations of June 1787.

[2] Bengal Consultations, 3rd December 1790. Lord Cornwallis's Minute.

[3] Regulation V. of 1793. A fifth appellate court was established at Benares in 1795, and a sixth for the North-Western Provinces in 1803.

as the district of Baramahal in the east, and it was in the revenue settlement of Baramahal, on which Thomas Munro was employed from 1792 to 1799, that he gained that experience and success which ultimately made him the most distinguished revenue officer in Madras.

In Bengal the revenue inquiries were proceeding rapidly to a conclusion. The famous Minute of Mr. Shore, afterwards Lord Teignmouth, dated 18th June 1789, "respecting the Permanent Settlement of the lands in the Bengal provinces," laid the foundation of that settlement on which the East India Company and Lord Cornwallis were determined. It is impossible within our limits to give any summary of this able and exhaustive Minute, which, with its appendices and propositions, covers seventy closely printed folio pages of the celebrated fifth report,[1] but it is necessary to mention a few facts elicited by Mr. Shore's exhaustive inquiry.

Mr. Shore refers to the revenue settlements made by Todar Mall in 1582 and by Jaffar Khan in 1722.

"If we suppose the assessment of Todar Mall to have been moderate in the first instance, the stated increase will not be deemed extravagant. Between the two periods of Todar Mall and Jaffar Khan the country had considerably improved in opulence, as new sources of trade had been opened, and commerce in general had become more diffused; specie, comparatively scarce in Akbar's reign, was afterwards poured into the country through new channels. On the contrary, we invest [respect ?], acknowledge, and applaud that political wisdom which prescribed limits to exaction, and allowed the subjects of the State to enjoy the profits of their own industry and good management."[2]

[1] Fifth Report, 1812, pp. 169–238.
[2] Paragraph 14.

Mr. Shore then refers to the subsequent enhancements made by Suja Khan, Alivardi Khan, and Mir Kasim; an appendix[1] furnishes us with the following figures for the land revenues of Bengal on different dates:

	Rupees.	£
By Todar Mall's settlement, 1582 . .	10,693,152	[1,070,000]
By Sultan Suja's settlement, 1658 . .	13,115,907	[1,312,000]
By Jaffar Khan's settlement, 1722 . .	14,288,186	[1,429,000]
By Suja Khan's settlement, 1728 . .	14,245,561	[1,425,000]

It will be seen that the amount of the land revenue was not much altered to the close of the Mahomedan rule, although sundry other taxes were imposed between 1722 and 1763.

Referring to the collections just before the commencement of British administration, Mr. Shore gives us the figures of four years (1762–1765). "The first year of this period belongs to Cossim Ali [Mir Kasim]; the second and third to Nundcomar under the authority of Mir Jaffer; and the fourth to Mahomed Reza Khan, being the first year of the Dewani."[2]

	Actual collection in rupees.	Actual collection in £
1762–63	6,456,198	[646,000]
1763–64	7,618,407	[762,000]
1764–65	8,175,533	[818,000]
1765–66	14,704,875	[1,470,000]

The peculiar economic feature of the British rule, as distinguished from the preceding Mahomedan rule, was the annual Economic Drain from the country which was introduced by the foreign rulers. This did not escape the observation of Mr. Shore.

"The Company are merchants as well as sovereigns of the country. In the former capacity they engross its trade, whilst in the latter they appropriate the revenues. The remittances to Europe of revenues are

[1] Appendix I. to the Minute.

[2] Paragraph 68.

made in the commodities of the country which are purchased by them."

"Whatever allowance we may make for the increased industry of the subjects of the State, owing to the enhanced demand for the produce of it (supposing the demand to be enhanced), there is reason to conclude that the benefits are more than counterbalanced by evils inseparable from the system of the remote foreign dominion."

"Every information from the time of Bernier to the acquisition of the Dewani shows the internal trade of the country, as carried on between Bengal and the upper parts of Hindustan, the Gulf of Moro, the Persian Gulf, and the Malabar coast, to have been very considerable. Returns of specie and goods were made through these channels by that of the foreign European companies, and in gold dust for opium from the eastward."

"But from the year 1765 the reverse has taken place. The Company's trade produces no equivalent returns. Specie is rarely imported by the foreign companies, nor brought into Bengal from other parts of Hindustan in any considerable quantities."

"Upon the whole, I have no hesitation in concluding that since the Company's acquisition of the Dewani the current specie of the country has been greatly diminished in quantity, that the old channels of importation by which the drains were formerly replenished are now in a great measure closed, and that the necessity of supplying China, Madras, and Bombay with money, as well as the exportation of it by Europeans to England, will continue still further to exhaust the country of its silver."[1]

It will be seen that Mr. Shore specially dwells on the depletion of silver. Before the time of Adam Smith the precious metals were believed to represent

[1] Paragraphs 131, 132, 135, 136, 140.

the wealth of a country. But the real exhaustion, which he so forcibly describes, was the exhaustion of the wealth, the produce, the food of the people.

Discussing the three possible methods of land settlements in Bengal, viz., a settlement with Ryots, a settlement with farmers of the revenue, and a settlement with Zemindars, Mr. Shore proves conclusively that the last one was the only one consistent with good government and the improvement of the country.

"We have admitted the property in the soil to be vested in the Zemindars. . . . The mere admission of the right, unless followed by the measures that will give value to it, will operate but little towards the improvement of the country. The demands of a foreign dominion like ours ought certainly to be more moderate than the impositions of the native rulers; and to render the value of what we possess permanent, our demands ought to be fixed. Removed from the control of our own Government the distance of half the globe, every practicable restriction should be imposed upon the administration in India, without circumscribing the necessary power, and the property of the inhabitants be secured against the fluctuations of caprice or the license of unrestrained control."[1]

The State demand was fixed at nine-tenths of the actual rental, in the hope that Zemindars would succeed by the improvement of their estates to gradually increase the scanty one-tenth left to them.

"A proportion of nine-tenths of the zemindari receipts is surely as much as our Government ought to demand, if it means to regard the welfare of their subjects by zemindari receipts; I mean that proportion of the gross produce which comes to the Zemindar after deducting immediate profits and charges. I should hope that the profits of the Zemin-

1 Paragraph 264.

dars would in time exceed this proportion by a due attention to the improvements of their lands and the encouragement of their Ryots." [1]

Farther on, Mr. Shore describes clearly and forcibly what he understood to be the rights of the Zemindars of Bengal.

"I consider the Zemindars as the proprietors of the soil, to the property of which they succeed by right of inheritance, according to the laws of their own religion, and that the sovereign authority cannot justly exercise the power of depriving them of the succession, nor of altering it, when there are any legal heirs. The privilege of disposing of the land by sale or mortgage is derived from this fundamental right, and was exercised by the Zemindars before we acquired the Dewani."

'Despotism could extend its claims to the subversion of the rights of the Zemindars without an avowed and direct infringement of them, but its practice, generally speaking, has been in favour of them. The Zemindars of Bengal were opulent and numerous in the reign of Akbar, and they existed when Jaffer Khan was appointed to the administration under him and his successors. Their respective territorial jurisdictions appeared to have been greatly augmented; and when the English acquired the Dewani, the principal Zemindars exhibited the appearance of opulence and dignity." [2]

So far with regard to the Zemindars. With regard to the Ryots or cultivators, Mr. Shore is equally emphatic.

"In every district throughout Bengal, where the licence of exaction has not superseded all rule, the rents of the land are regulated by known rates called Nirik, and in some districts each village has its own. These rates are formed, with respect of the produce

[1] Paragraph 355. [2] Paragraphs 370 and 382.

of the land, at so much per bigha [a third of an acre]; some soil produces two crops in a year of different species, some three; the more profitable articles, such as mulberry plant, betel-leaf, tobacco, sugar-cane, and others, render the value of the land proportionably great."

"Pattahs [leases] to the Khod-Khast Ryots, or those who cultivate the land of the village where they reside, are generally given without any limitation of period, and express that they are to hold the land paying the rents from year to year. Hence the right of occupancy originates."

"Pykast Ryots, or those who cultivate the land of villages where they do not reside, hold their lands upon a more indefinite tenure. The Pattahs to them are generally granted with a limitation in point of time; where they deem the terms unfavourable, they repair to some other spot."[1]

Towards the conclusion of his Minute, Mr. Shore gives a summary of his proposals.

"The leading principles upon which I shall ground my propositions for the ensuing settlement are two."

"The security of Government with respect to its revenues, and the security and protection of its subjects."

"The former will be best established by concluding a Permanent Settlement with the Zemindars or proprietors of the soil, the land, their property, is the security of the Government."

"The second must be ensured by carrying into practice, as far as possible, an acknowledged maximum of taxation. The tax which each individual is bound to pay ought to be certain, not arbitrary. The time of payment, the manner of payment, the qnantity to be paid, ought all to be clear and plain to the contributor and every other person."

[1] Paragraphs 391, 406, 407.

"The settlement is then to be made for a period of ten years certain, but with a view to permanency." [1]

The above is a bare outline of the exhaustive Minute of Mr. Shore, in which he supported the proposal of a Permanent Settlement, first advocated by Philip Francis. In a second Minute, submitted in the same year, Mr. Shore, however, suggested the omission of the proposed notification to Zemindars that the settlement made for ten years would be eventually made permanent. Lord Cornwallis objected to this omission, which might indicate some uncertainty as to the policy of the Government; and some of the remarks recorded by his Lordship are so clear, so cogent, and so forcible, that it is impossible to omit them even in this brief narrative.

"Mr. Shore has most ably, and, in my opinion, most successfully, in his Minute delivered in June last, argued in favour of the rights of the Zemindars to the property of the soil. But if the value of permanency is now to be withdrawn from the settlement now in agitation, of what avail will the power of his arguments be to the Zemindars, for whose rights he has contended? . . .

"When the landlord of the soil himself, the rightful owner of the land, is only to become a farmer for a lease of ten years, and if he is then to be exposed to the demand of a new rent, which may perhaps be dictated by ignorance or rapacity, what hopes can there be—I will not say of improvement—but of preventing desolation? . . .

"I may safely assert that one-third of the Company's territory in Hindustan is now a jungle inhabited only by wild beasts. Will a ten-years' lease induce any proprietor to clear away that jungle, and encourage the Ryots to come and cultivate his lands, when at the end of that lease he must either submit to

[1] Paragraphs 457, 458, 459, 460, 462.

be taxed *ad libitum* for their newly cultivated lands, or lose all hopes of deriving any benefit from his labour, for which perhaps by that time he will hardly be repaid? . . .

"I cannot avoid declaring my firmest conviction that if those provinces are let upon lease for that period only, they will find, at the end of it, a ruined and impoverished country."[1]

In a subsequent Minute, Lord Cornwallis again recorded his statesmanlike views.

"If laws are enacted which secure to them [Zemindars] the fruits of industry and economy, and at the same time leave them to experience the consequence of idleness and extravagance, they must either render themselves capable of transacting their own business, or their necessities will oblige them to dispose of their lands to others, who will cultivate and improve them. This I conceive to be the only effectual mode which this or any other Government could adopt, to render the proprietors of the lands economical landlords and prudent trustees of the public interest. . . .

"Twenty years have been employed in collecting information. In 1769 Supervisors were appointed; in 1770 Provincial Councils were established; in 1772 a Committee of Circuit was deputed to make the settlement, armed with all the powers of the Presidency; in 1776 Amins were appointed to make a Hastbood [rent-roll] of the country; in 1781 the Provincial Councils of revenue were abolished, and Collectors were sent into the several districts, and the General Council and management of the revenues was lodged in a Committee of Revenue at Calcutta under the immediate inspection of Government. Like our predecessors, we set out with seeking for new information, and we have now been three years in collecting it.

[1] Lord Cornwallis's Minute, dated 18th September 1789.

Voluminous reports have been transmitted by the several Collectors on every point which was deemed of importance. . . .

"The consequences of the heavy drain of wealth from the above causes, with the addition of that which has been occasioned by the remittances of the private fortunes, have been for many years past, and are now, severely felt, by the diminution of the current specie, and by the languor which has thereby been thrown upon the cultivation and the general commerce of the country. . . .

"A very material alteration in the principles of our system of management has therefore become indispensably necessary, in order to restore this country to a state of prosperity, and to enable it to continue to be a solid support to the British interests and power in this part of the world. . . .

"We are, therefore, called upon to endeavour to remedy evils by which the public interests are essentially injured, and by granting perpetual leases of the lands at a fixed assessment we shall render our subjects the happiest people in India."[1]

In November 1791 an amended and complete Code of Regulations was promulgated by the Government for a settlement of ten years, and the settlement was concluded in every district in Bengal in 1793. The whole amount of land revenue[2] obtained from the provinces of Bengal, Behar, and Orissa for the year 1790–91 was Rs.26,800,989 (£2,680,000). The amount was nearly double the assessment of Jaffer Khan and of Suja Khan in the early part of the century; it was three times the collections of Maharaja Nandkumar in the last year of the rule of Mir Jafar (1764–65); and it was nearly double the collections made by Mahomed Reza Khan, under British super-

[1] Lord Cornwallis's Minute, dated 3rd February 1790.
[2] Fifth Report, 1812, p. 19.

vision, in the first year of the Company's Dewani (1765–66). The assessment was, therefore, as severe as it could possibly be made; and it was possible to raise it so high because it was declared to be final and permanent.

The Directors, in their letter of the 29th September 1792, expressed themselves in high terms of approbation of what had been done, and gave their assent to the settlement of the land revenue in perpetuity. On receipt of these orders, Lord Cornwallis issued a proclamation on the 22nd March 1793, announcing the permanency of the settlement which had just been concluded or was still in progress. The first three articles of the proclamation run thus:

Art. I. "In the original regulations for the decennial settlement of the public revenues of Bengal, Behar, and Orissa, passed for these provinces respectively on the 18th September 1789, the 25th November 1789, and the 10th February 1790, it was notified to the proprietors of land with or on behalf of whom a settlement might be concluded, that the jumma assessed upon the lands, under those regulations, would be continued after the expiration of the ten years, and remain unalterable for ever, provided such continuance should meet with the approbation of the Honourable Court of Directors for the affairs of the East India Company, and not otherwise."

Art. II. "The Marquis Cornwallis, Knight of the Most Noble Order of the Garter, Governor-General in Council, now notifies to all Zemindars, independent Talookdars, and other actual proprietors of land in the provinces of Bengal, Behar, and Orissa, that he has been empowered by the Honourable Court of Directors for the affairs of the East India Company to declare the jumma which has been or may be assessed upon their lands under the regulations above mentioned, fixed for ever."

Art. III. "The Governor-General in Council accordingly declares to the Zemindars, independent Talookdars, and other actual proprietors of land, with or on behalf of whom a settlement has been concluded under the regulations above mentioned, that at the expiration of the term of the settlement no alteration will be made in the assessment which they have respectively engaged to pay, but that they and their heirs and lawful successors will be allowed to hold their estates at such assessment for ever."[1]

Regulation I. of 1793, making the Permanent Settlement, was accordingly passed. It is the one act of the British nation within the century and a half of their rule in India which has most effectually safeguarded the economic welfare of the people. It is an act which is in consonance with the modern policy of civilised nations to permit the people to profit by their own industries, instead of paralysing their industries by an uncertain and increasing State demand. Agriculture has largely extended in Bengal within the last hundred years, and the land-tax of Bengal, which was fixed in 1793 at 90 per cent. of the rental, now bears a proportion of about 28 per cent. to the rental of landlords; and new taxes amounting to 6¼ per cent. on the rental have been added for roads and public works.

Since 1793 there has never been a famine in permanently settled Bengal which has caused any serious loss of life. In other parts of India, where the land-tax is still uncertain and excessive, it takes away all motives for agricultural improvements and prevents saving, and famines have been attended with the deaths of hundreds of thousands, and sometimes of millions. If the prosperity and happiness of a nation be the criterion of wisdom and success, Lord Cornwallis's Permanent Settlement of 1793 is the

[1] Fifth Report, 1812, p. 21.

wisest and most successful measure which the British nation has ever adopted in India.

We cannot conclude this account of the Permanent Settlement of the land-tax in Bengal without comparing it with the settlement of the land-tax which was made in England five years after, *i.e.* in 1798. The property-tax of William III., originally intended to bear on personal property and offices, was subsequently described as the annual land-tax, when personal property slipped out of the assessment. Raised for the war of the Spanish Succession to four shillings in the pound of annual value, *i.e.* 20 per cent. of the rental, it was reduced to two shillings, *i.e.* 10 per cent. of the rental, after the Peace of Utrecht in 1713. And down to the close of the eighteenth century it varied between four shillings and one shilling in the pound, *i.e.* between 20 per cent. and 5 per cent. of the rental.

Five years after the Permanent Settlement of Bengal, the great Minister, William Pitt, made the land-tax perpetual in England in the various districts specified in the Act, and landlords were enabled by this Act to redeem the tax altogether by the payment of a lump sum. £1,300,000 of the tax has been redeemed up to date, and over £1,000,000 remains yet unredeemed. This last is now regarded as a fixed charge upon estates, subject to which they are bought and sold.[1]

There may be some doubt as to the wisdom of Pitt's Permanent Settlement of the land-tax in England; there can be no doubt as to that of Cornwallis's Permanent Settlement in Bengal. In England the settlement benefited the landed classes only; in Bengal the settlement has benefited the whole agricultural community; the entire peasant population

[1] Stephen Dowell's *History of Taxation and Taxes in England*, 1884, vol. iii. pp. 97–101.

shares the benefit, and is more prosperous and resourceful on account of this measure. In England the settlement limited the tax on one out of the many sources of national income; in Bengal it has afforded a protection to agriculture which is virtually the only means of the nation's subsistence. In England it precluded the State from drawing a larger land-tax to be spent in the country for the benefit of the nation; in Bengal it has precluded the State from increasing the annual Economic Drain of wealth out of the country. In England it saved the landlord class from added taxation; in Bengal it has saved the nation from fatal and disastrous famines.

CHAPTER VI

FARMING OF REVENUES IN MADRAS (1763-1785)

IN the preceding chapters we have narrated the economic history of Bengal from 1757 to 1793; and we must now turn to the state of things in Madras, where the long wars between the British and the French were at last concluded by the Peace of Paris in 1763.

The eventful history of these wars has been often told. It was a momentous struggle for the possession of Southern India. It was a contest between Dupleix, who began the construction of a French empire, and Robert Clive, who demolished that unfinished structure. Later on, it was a patriotic and persevering endeavour made by the talented Bussy and the impetuous Lally for saving the power of France in the East, which was finally destroyed by Eyre Coote. The Treaty of Paris finally recognised the success of England; France was never after her rival in India.

It is a great relief to us to turn from the twice-told tale of these wars to the economic condition of the people. The history of India is not the history of the British and French wars, but of the people of India—their material and moral condition, their trades, industries, and agriculture. And it is because this true history of the people has hitherto received scant attention, that we devote the present work entirely to that instructive subject, leaving the more dramatic story of wars to more brilliant writers.

The twenty years' struggle between the French and the English ended, as has been stated before, in

1763. The settlement of Pondicherry and a few other places were restored to the French, but the English remained supreme in Southern India. Mahomed Ali, a creature of the British, was recognised as Nawab of the Karnatic, while the immediate possessions of the British extended over some territory round Madras, and over the whole of the eastern seaboard stretching northwards to Bengal.

The character of Mahomed Ali, Nawab of the Karnatic, was the very opposite of that of his contemporary, Mir Kasim, Nawab of Bengal. Mir Kasim was a determined man and a strong ruler; Mahomed Ali was a feeble man and a luxurious prince. Mir Kasim removed his seat of government to Monghyr in order to organise his own administration away from British influence; Mahomed Ali left his own capital, Arcot, to live amidst the luxuries of the British town of Madras. Mir Kasim was a stern economist, and paid off all his pecuniary obligations to the British in two years after he had ascended the throne; Mahomed Ali never could liquidate the claims of the Company, and drifted more and more into debt. Mir Kasim fought with the British in order to keep the inland trade of Bengal in the hands of his own subjects; Mahomed Ali made assignments of his land revenues to his British money-lenders, until virtually the whole of his territories passed into the hands of his creditors. Mir Kasim was driven out of his dominions and died an exile; Mahomed Ali lived in inglorious dependence, luxury, and debt, and died in ripe old age. A strong ruler had no place in the scheme of British dominion in the East; a weak ruler was permitted to live and to borrow, and to pay the interest out of the revenues of his kingdom.

Under the administration of this feeble potentate the Company found it easy to extend its influence and power. The Company did not stand forth as the

Dewan of the Karnatic, as they had done in Bengal in 1765. On the contrary, Mahomed Ali remained nominally the Dewan or revenue administrator, as well as the Nizam or military governor, while the Company virtually enjoyed all real power. The military defence of the country was undertaken by the Company, and a part of the Nawab's revenues was assigned for this purpose. The demands of the Company increased with their wars, and the Nawab came to adopt the strange method of borrowing from the servants of the Company in order to meet the demands of the Company.

What was still more significant and fatal was the security which the Nawab offered for these private debts. Unable or unwilling to draw from his own hoards, he readily delivered up to his private creditors the revenues of his territories. The cultivators of the Karnatic passed from the rule of the Nawab's agents to the rule of British money-lenders. The crops that grew in the fields were subject to the inalienable claims of British creditors. The collections which were made by the Nawab's servants, often under coercion and the use of the whip, were handed over to the British servants of the Company in order to be remitted to Europe. The whole of the Karnatic resembled an egg-shell with its contents taken out. The fields and villages of Southern India were converted into a vast farm, and the tillers tilled and the labourers toiled in order that all the value of the produce might be annually exported to Europe.

A double injury was thus done to the country and to the people. The Nawab's methods of collection, though always harsh and severe, were elastic; and his demands were suited to the produce of the soil from year to year. But when his creditors appeared on the scene, the harshness of the Nawab's method was combined with the strictness and inelasticity of the British procedure. The claims of the Nawab's creditors were strictly enforced, and the agriculturists felt a pressure which they had seldom known before. In the second place, so long as the revenues were enjoyed by the Nawab, they were spent in the country and flowed back to the people in one shape or another; but when the entire revenues of the assigned districts were claimed and obtained by the British money-lenders, they left the country once and for ever. The country became poorer, industries and trades declined.

We have evidence of this in the testimony of witnesses examined by the Select Committee of the House of Commons appointed in 1782 to inquire into the administration of justice in India.

"George Smith, Esquire, attending according to order, was asked how long he resided in India, where, and in what capacity? He said he arrived in India in the year 1764; he resided in Madras from 1767 to October 1779. Being asked what was the state of trade at Madras at the time when he first knew it, he said it was in a flourishing condition, and Madras one of the first marts in India. Being asked in what condition did he leave it with respect to trade, he replied at the time of his leaving it, there was little or no trade, and but one ship belonging to the place. Being asked in what state the interior country of the Karnatic was with regard to commerce and cultivation when he first knew it, he said at that period he understood the Karnatic to be in a well-cultivated and populous condition, and as such consuming a great many articles of merchandise and trade. Being asked in what condition it was when he left Madras with respect to cultivation, population, and internal commerce, he said in respect to cultivation, greatly on the decline, and also in respect of population; and as to commerce, exceedingly circumscribed."[1]

[1] Ninth Report, 1783, Appendix, p. 120.

The servants of the Company, comprising members of the Madras Council, were building up large fortunes from their loans to the Nawab, and were not anxious to keep the Court of Directors fully informed of their doings. Under the orders of the Court of Directors, however, they had consolidated their loans into one loan of 1767 at the moderate rate of 10 per cent. interest, and they even expressed a hope, from time to time, that the Nawab would pay off his loan. It was neither their interest, however, nor that of the effete and inefficient Nawab, to close the transaction; and it was never closed. And when the full official account of the transaction at last reached the Directors in 1769, their anger knew no bounds.

"As this whole transaction has, to your great reproach, been concealed from us, we cannot but suspect this debt to have had its weight in your proposed aggrandisement of Mahomed Ally; but whether it has or not, certain it is that you are guilty of a high breach of duty in concealing it from us."[1]

"Charged on our part with the recovery of a debt due from the Nawab, for supporting him in a war during almost twenty years, how can our servants, consistent with their duty and fidelity, neglect the discharge of so great a public trust, or suffer any interest of their own to come in competition with it? Or how can they dare to employ the forces, influence, and authority of the Company in collecting the revenues of the Nawab, mortgaged to themselves?"[2]

"The said Governor and Council have, in notorious

[1] Court of Directors to the President and Council at Fort St. George, dated 17th March 1769.

[2] Court of Directors to the Select Committee at Fort St. George, dated 17th March 1769. The reader will notice that the Directors represent the war of twenty years between the French and the English for the dominion of India, as a war waged for the Nawab, to be paid for by the Nawab.

violation of the trust reposed in them, manifestly preferred the interest of private persons to that of the Company, in permitting the assignment of the revenues of certain valuable districts to a very large amount from the Nawab to individuals which ought to have been applied towards the discharge of the Nawab's debt to the Company; the impropriety of which conduct is the more striking as those revenues, in a very great degree, owe their existence to the protection of the Company; and by such unnatural application of the said revenues, although the care and expense of protecting the Karnatic falls principally on the Company, the prospect of paying off the vast sums owing to us by the Nawab is postponed."[1]

Warren Hastings, who had protested against the claim of the Company's servants to a virtual monopoly of the inland trade in Bengal, was now a member of the Madras Council, and he made an honest endeavour to terminate the assignment of land revenues made by the Nawab of Arcot to the Company's servants in Madras. In a clear and forcible letter, which bears the impresss of his style, and which was signed by him and three other members of the Madras Council, the action taken at Madras on receipt of the Directors' letters is fully described.

"We understand the sense and spirit of your orders to us to be this: that whereas the Nawab having made an assignment, by deed under his hand and seal, to certain persons of the revenues of part of the Karnatic, in trust, that the same should be applied in discharge of his private debts in exclusion of the Company, you highly disapprove of, tell us that you will not suffer the idea of such an independent right to exist either

[1] Court of Directors to the Superintending Commissioners, dated 23rd March 1770. The assignment of revenues appeared "unnatural" to the Court, not because it impoverished the country, but because it postponed the prospect of the Nawab's repaying his debt to the Company.

in the Nawab or your servants, and enjoin us to demand a renunciation of the right they claim under that deed of assignment; that done, you command us to inform the Nawab that his first obligation is to discharge the debt to the Company, and that being done you authorise us to give the sanction of the Company's authority to such measures as we shall concert with the Nawab for the discharge of his debts to individuals. . . .

"The President and Mr. Du Pre made their formal renunciation of all pretentions under the deed of assignment, and put themselves under the Company's protection for the recovery of their debts, and the example was followed by several others after your orders had been publicly made known to them; but a very large majority having in effect refused to submit themselves to the Company's protection on the mode we had proposed, we thought it not advisable to enforce the demand by any act of compulsion." [1]

In another letter written in the same year, Warren Hastings indicated how the Nawab, who was a tool in the hands of his private creditors, was endeavouring to create influence in England against the Company, and in favour of his creditors.

"Till very lately the Nawab placed his dependence on the Court of Directors, and considered them as the Company; now he has been taught by ill-advisers that an interest out of doors may stand him in good stead; he has been made to believe that his private creditors have power and interest to overrule the Court of Directors; and what is worse than all, he seems to be strongly impressed with an opinion that the authority of Parliament and of the Crown will be exerted in his behalf against the Company." [2]

[1] Select Committee at Fort St. George to the Court of Directors, dated 31st January 1770.

[2] Select Committee at Fort St. George to the Court of Directors, dated 6th April 1770.

The Nawab had not been misinformed. His creditors, who amassed vast fortunes from the rents of the assigned districts, were soon able to qualify a large number of votes, and to make themselves masters of the Court of Directors; and, as we shall see farther on, all their claims were admitted eventually without inquiry.

In the meantime the Nawab had nearly exhausted the resources of his own kingdom by assignments to his creditors, and began to cast longing eyes on the rich state of the Raja of Tanjore. In the treaty which had been concluded between the British and Haidar Ali in 1769, the Raja of Tanjore had been recognised as an ally of the British. But even the Court of Directors became covetous of the wealth of their "ally," and gave a willing ear to the proposals of Mahomed Ali to rob Tanjore in order to repay his debts to the Company.

"It appears most unreasonable to us," wrote the Directors, "that the Raja of Tanjore should hold possession of the most fruitful part of the country, which can alone supply an army with subsistence, and not contribute to the defence of the Karnatic. . . . We therefore enjoin you to give the Nawab such support in his pretentions as may be effectual, and if the Raja refuses to contribute a just proportion to the expense of the war, you are then to pursue such measures as the Nawab may think consistent with the justice and dignity of his government. Whatever sums may, in consequence of the above orders, be obtained from the Raja of Tanjore, we expect shall be applied to the discharge of the Nawab's debt to the Company; and if more than sufficient for the purpose, to the discharge of his debts to individuals."[1]

This was a broad hint, and was acted upon. Tan-

[1] Court of Directors to the Select Committee at Fort St. George, dated 17th March 1769.

jore was besieged in 1771, and saved itself only by the payment of £400,000. But this only whetted the appetite of the Nawab, and his friends the British were easily led to think that "it is dangerous to have such a power in the heart of the province." Tanjore was besieged again and captured on the 16th September 1773; the unfortunate Raja and his family were taken prisoners in the fort; and his dominions were transferred to the Nawab.

Never was a flourishing and prosperous state so reduced within a few years of misgovernment as the State of Tanjore after it passed under the government of the Nawab. Regarding it as a hostile and conquered country, Mahomed Ali multiplied his exactions upon the people, made assignments of its revenues to his British creditors, and ruined its trade and industries; and within a few years Tanjore, the garden of Southern India, became one of the most desolate tracts on the eastern coast.

"Before I speak of the present state of Tanjore country," said Mr. Petrie in his evidence before the Committee of Secrecy in 1782, "it will be necessary to inform the Committee that not many years ago that province was considered as one of the most flourishing, best cultivated, populous districts in Hindustan. I first saw this country in 1768, when it presented a very different picture from its present situation. Tanjore was formerly a place of great foreign and inland trade; it imported cotton from Bombay and Surat, raw and worked silks from Bengal, sugar, spices, &c., from Sumatra, Malacca, and the eastern islands; gold, horses, elephants, and timber from Pegu, and various articles of trade from China. It was by means of Tanjore that a great part of Haidar Ali's dominions and the north-western parts of the Mahratta empire were supplied with many European commodities, and with a species of silk manufacture from Bengal, which is almost universally worn as a part of dress by the natives of Hindustan. The exports of Tanjore were muslins, chintz, handkerchiefs, ginghams, various sorts of long-cloths, and a coarse printed cloth, which last constitutes a material article in the investments of the Dutch and the Danes, being in great demand for the African, West Indian, and South American markets. Few countries have more natural advantages than Tanjore; it possesses a rich and fertile soil, singularly well supplied with water from the two great rivers Cavery and Coleroon, which, by means of reservoirs, sluices, and canals, are made to disperse their waters through almost every field in the country; to this latter cause we may chiefly attribute the uncommon fertility of Tanjore. The face of the country is beautifully diversified, and in its appearance approaches nearer to England than any other part of India that I have seen. Such was Tanjore not many years ago, but its decline has been so rapid, that in many districts it would be difficult to trace the remains of its former opulence. . . .

"At this period [1771], as I have been informed, the manufactures flourished, the country was populous and well cultivated, the inhabitants were wealthy and industrious. Since the year 1771, the era of the first siege, until the restoration of the Raja, the country having been during that period twice the seat of war, and having undergone revolutions in the government, trade, manufactures, and agriculture were neglected, and many thousands of inhabitants went in quest of a more secure abode."[1]

The time now came for the appointment of a new Governor of Madras. Mr. Pigot had been Governor of Madras at the time of the French wars, had returned to England in 1763, and had been successively raised to

1 Fourth Report of the Committee of Secrecy, 1782, Appendix, No. 22.

the dignity of a baronet and an Irish peer. Desirous of introducing reforms in the administration of the province, he was appointed Governor of Madras once more in 1775. The Directors had not altogether approved of the annexation of Tanjore by Mahomed Ali, and under their orders Lord Pigot resolved to restore the Raja. Mahomed Ali tried all his arts to prevent the restoration, but Lord Pigot was determined, and the Raja was seated on his throne once more on the 30th March 1776.

The Governor's difficulties now began. Among the many creditors of the Nawab of Arcot, one Paul Benfield had obtained an unenviable prominence. He had come out to India in 1763 in the Company's service as a civil architect, but had succeeded better as an architect of his own fortunes by usury. When the Raja of Tanjore was reseated on his throne, Benfield claimed that he had assignments upon the revenues of Tanjore to the amount of £162,000 for money lent to the Nawab, and that for money lent to individuals in Tanjore he had assignments upon the standing crops to the amount of £72,000. The incident throws a strong light on the times. Benfield was still a junior servant of the Company drawing a few hundred pounds a year, but he kept the finest carriages and horses in Madras, and he claimed a fabulous sum from the Nawab. The revenues of a rich state and the standing crops of a nation of agriculturists were supposed to be hypothecated for the satisfaction of his claim.

Lord Pigot laid Benfield's claims before the Board. Benfield was unable to produce vouchers, but urged that the Nawab would admit his debt. The Board resolved by a majority that Benfield's claims against individuals had not been sufficiently explained, and that the assignments of the Nawab on the revenues of Tanjore were not admissible. Benfield was not satisfied, and he had friends and resources. His claims were again brought before the Council, and admitted. Lord Pigot's proposal to send Russell as Resident to Tanjore did not satisfy the majority of members. Colonel Stuart, who was supposed to have agreed to manage Tanjore affairs in the interest of the creditors, was chosen. Lord Pigot resisted the majority, and on the 24th August 1776 he was arrested by Colonel Stuart and imprisoned.

"Colonel Stuart dined with me, and after dinner I invited him to supper at the Company's garden house. . . . Between seven and eight o'clock at night I went from the fort-house with Colonel Stuart to my chaise. On the island, between the two bridges, I saw Lieutenant-Colonel Edington, the Adjutant-General, come running aslant the road, from the southern side, towards the chaise. Supposing he wanted to speak to us, I reined in the horses; and when Edington got near their heads, he waved his naked sword and cried 'Sepoys;' whereupon a party of Sepoys came from behind the trees on the other side, and Captain Lysaught, with a pistol in his hand, came up to the chaise from that side, and said to me, '*You are my prisoner*.' . . . I was then conducted by Captain Lysaught to Mr. Benfield's post-chaise."[1]

The Court of Directors were staggered by this information, but there was a division of opinion among them. They ordered Lord Pigot to be restored to liberty, but they also ordered his recall. Before these orders could reach India, Lord Pigot had passed beyond the reach of honour or of disgrace. He died in confinement in 1777. Sir Thomas Rumbold succeeded as Governor of Madras in 1778.

The creditors of the Nawab, who had brought about the revolution of 1776, were not unmindful of their

[1] Lord Pigot's *Narrative of the Revolution in the Government of Madras*, dated 11th September 1776, p. 11 *et seq.*

own interests. We have spoken before of the first loan of 1767. A second loan was now contracted in 1777. The Nawab was persuaded to discharge his useless cavalry, but had no money to pay them. Taylor, Majendie, and Call offered to advance £160,000 if the Company's sanction were given to the debt, and this was done. Assignments of revenues were of course made, and the Nawab's manager complained to him two years after: "The entire revenue of those districts is by your Highness's order set apart to discharge the Tuncaws granted to the Europeans. The Gomastas of Mr. Taylor . . . are there in order to collect those Tuncaws, and as they receive all the revenue that is collected, your Highness's troops have seven or eight months' pay due which they cannot receive."

A third loan of over two million pounds sterling was also consolidated in this eventful year, 1777, and Sir Thomas Rumbold, on his arrival at Madras, wrote of this new loan with just indignation.

"How shall I paint to you my astonishment on my arrival here, when I was informed that, independent of this four lakhs of pagodas [£160,000, the cavalry loan], independent of the Nabob's debt to his old creditors and the money due to the Company, he had contracted a debt to the enormous amount of sixty-three lakhs of pagodas [£2,520,000]. I mention this circumstance to you with horror, for the creditors being in general servants of the Company, renders my task on the part of the Company difficult and invidious."[1]

From this miserable state of affairs in the Karnatic, Sir Thomas Rumbold turned his attention to the Northern Circars, the maritime country extending northwards which belonged to the British. The country was parcelled out among Zemindars, who were hereditary landlords as well as ruling chiefs within

[1] Letter to the Court of Directors, dated 15th March 1778.

their own estates. The Company's administration had been harsh towards these Zemindars, and their estates had been impoverished. Sir Thomas himself bears eloquent testimony to their former prosperity and their present decline.

"It will remain an eternal reproach to the Company's government in India, that it seems to have been a principle of their policy to drive every native of consequence out of their territories. Let any man who has traced the change from the happier days of Bengal and the Circars to their present desolate and deserted state, come forward and explain to the nation, whose name and honour are deeply concerned in the question, what is become of the train of princes, chiefs, and opulent landholders which once covered the face of these countries? . . .

"From the language which the Court of Directors have lately adopted, the public must be led to infer that the Company have not barely succeeded to some rights of sovereignty in this country, but they are become exclusive proprietors of the soil! And that these noble Zemindars, the real and sole holders of the lands, which they inherit from a line of ancestry that would appear fabulous in Europe, had on a sudden been converted into farmers, or rather peasants and labourers in the Company's fields. The *tribute*, not *rent*, paid by these chiefs to the Moghal invaders (who were never able entirely to subjugate their country) was a sort of ransom of their ancient independence. It was the price of a quiet possession of their property, privileges, customs, and habits. It was always assessed with moderation, and with a just regard to the immense establishments which the opinion of the country renders it necessary for persons of their consequence and distinction to keep on foot. The Soubah [the Great Moghal's Viceroy] settled with the Zemindars without ever attempting to interfere with the collection, It would have been happy for all parties, if the same wise maxims had continued to be respected after the cession of the Circars to the Company. The country would have flourished, and the Company would have prospered in the prosperity of their tributaries."[1]

It had been proposed to form a Committee of Circuit for settling the revenues payable by the Zemindars of the Northern Circars after local inquiries. Sir Thomas Rumbold suspended this Committee, and ordered the Zemindars to come down to Madras. This created much consternation among them; but eighteen of the thirty-one Zemindars summoned to Madras obeyed the order. Settlements were made for five years, and "the sum total of the additions made to the revenue at different times since the accession of the Company to the Circars amounts to above 50 per cent. upon the old establishment."[2]

But the Directors were not satisfied. They believed that the Committee of Circuit would have shown still more satisfactory results. They charged Sir Thomas Rumbold with violation of orders in suspending the Committee, and with harshness to the Zemindars in summoning them to Madras. They also charged him with corruption, and pointed out that he had remitted £164,000 to Europe within two years. They accordingly dismissed him from the Company's service in January 1781.

Lord Macartney, a nobleman of great urbanity and moderation, of political experience and undoubted talents, was appointed Governor of Madras, and arrived in June 1781. The Province was in the lowest

[1] *An Answer to the Charges exhibited against Sir Thomas Rumbold.* By himself, pp. 19 and 22.

[2] *Ibid.*, p. 32. For instance, the Zemindar of Peddapore paid £37,000 under the Moghals. The revenue was increased to £56,000 by Sir Thomas Rumbold. Similar enhancements were made in all zemindaris except one poor estate.

depths of misery and wretchedness. To the effects of long misrule were added the misfortunes of a great war with Haidar Ali, the ruler of Mysore. His cavalry overran the country, spread ruin and desolation within a circle of many miles round Madras, aud filled the Karnatic with dismay. The people fled to the woods, fields were left uncultivated, villages were burnt and destroyed. Alarm succeeded alarm, while the Council of Madras were vacillating in their plans for meeting this terrible enemy.

Into the events of this war it is not our purpose to enter. Warren Hastings, who was now Governor-General, sent the veteran commander, Sir Eyre Coote, to save Southern India once more. Sir Eyre fought four battles with Haidar Ali. Haidar Ali retreated, but was not crushed. In September 1872 Sir Eyre left Madras for Bengal, and in December 1782 Haidar Ali died. Peace was made with his son Tipu Sultan in 1783.

These accumulated misfortunes, coupled with the impoverishment of the people, brought on the widespread and terrible famine of Madras in 1783. The revenues of the Company generally showed a surplus, but their "Investments," *i.e.* commodities and merchandise purchased out of the revenues for sale in Europe, converted the surplus into a deficit. The following figures[1] are taken from official records:

---

[1] Fourth Report of the Committee of Secrecy, 1782, pp. 672 and 674.

Receipts and Expenditure for Twelve Years in Madras Presidency.

Year.	Total nett revenue.	Total charges, civil and military, defrayed by the Company.	Surplus.	Deficit.
May April	£	£	£	£
1767 to 1768	381,330	489,012	...	107,682
1768 „ 1769	369,720	691,471	...	321,751
1769 „ 1770	500,110	467,492	36,618	...
1770 „ 1771	562,359	434,393	127,960	...
1771 „ 1772	558,860	407,446	151,414	...
1772 „ 1773	529,233	309,138	220,095	...
1773 „ 1774	524,762	407,144	117,618	...
1774 „ 1775	503,629	454,589	49,040	...
1775 „ 1776	514,591	345,867	168,724	...
1776 „ 1777	563,349	533,182	30,167	...
1777 „ 1778	283,198	485,830	...	202,632
1778 „ 1779	494,208	803,924	...	309.716
Total . .	5,785,349	5,829,488	897,642	941,781

Surplus or deficit, the purchase of Investments never ceased; and the amount of cargoes to Europe valued at prime cost during this period exceeded two million sterling.

But the oppressiveness of the Company's exactions was exceeded tenfold by that of the British creditors who had received assignments of revenues for their loans. And when the matter came for final settlement in the House of Commons, the influence created by those creditors in the House was so great, that all the supposed claims, fraudulent or otherwise, were admitted without inquiry.

Paul Benfield, the greatest and most successful of the creditors, used the vast wealth he had accumulated in India in creating parliamentary influence in England. He returned eight members to Parliament including himself, and he was a powerful and influential man whom the Ministry did not care to offend. "It was to hold the corrupt benefit of a large parliamentary interest, created by the creditors and creatures, fraudulent and not fraudulent, of the Nawab of Arcot, that . . . the Ministry of 1784 decided that they should all, whether fraudulent or not fraudulent, receive their demands."[1]

The historian of British India, from whose work we have made the above extract, proceeds to quote from the ever-memorable speech in which Edmund Burke condemned this most discreditable episode of British parliamentary history.

"Paul Benfield is the grand parliamentary reformer. What region in the empire, what city, what borough, what county, what tribunal in this kingdom, is not full of his labours? In order to station a steady phalanx for all future reforms, the public-spirited usurer, amidst his charitable toils for the relief of India, did not forget the poor rotten constitution of his native country. For her he did not disdain to stoop to the trade of a wholesale upholsterer for this House, to furnish it, not with the faded tapestry figures of antiquated merit, such as decorate, and may reproach, some other Houses, but with real, solid, living patterns of true modern virtue. Paul Benfield made, reckoning himself, no fewer than eight members of the last Parliament. What copious streams of pure blood must he not have transfused into the veins of the present. . . .

"For your Minister, this worn-out veteran [Benfield's agent] submitted to enter into the dusty field of the London contest; and you will remember that in the same virtuous cause he submitted to keep a sort of public office or counting-house, where the whole business of the last general election was managed. It was openly managed by the direct agent and attorney of Benfield. It was managed upon Indian principles and for an Indian interest. This was the golden cup

[1] Mill's *History of British India*, book vi. chap. 1.

of abominations . . . which so many of the people, so many of the nobles of this land, had drained to the very dregs. Do you think that no reckoning was to follow this lewd debauch? That no payment was to be demanded for this riot of public drunkenness and national prostitution? Here you have it, here before you. The principal of the grand election manager must be indemnified. Accordingly the claims of Benfield and his crew must be put above all inquiry."[1]

The golden cup was drained by the people and the nobles of England, and the payment was demanded from India! An inquiry was not made into Benfield's claims because the cultivators of the Karnatic were to pay. The admission of all such claims without inquiry exaggerated the evil, and shoals of British money-lenders flocked to the Karnatic to make rapid fortunes in a similar way. New claims against the Nawab of the Karnatic amounting to £20,390,570 were preferred, and Commissioners were appointed to decide on these claims. The Karnatic had by that time been annexed by Lord Wellesley and was British territory. The claims, if admitted, would have to be paid, not by a Nawab, but by the Company's Government. Therefore an inquiry was made; and the result of the inquiry was that a sum of only £1,346,796 was admitted as valid, the remainder, exceeding nineteen millions sterling, was rejected as fraudulent and bad.

[1] Burke's speech on the Nawab of Arcot's debts.

CHAPTER VII

OLD AND NEW POSSESSIONS IN MADRAS (1785–1807)

PITT's India Bill became law in 1784, as has been stated before. The immediate possessions of the East India Company in the Province of Madras down to that date consisted of a small tract of country round the town of Madras, and the long strip of country along the sea known as the Northern Circars. The first land settlements in Madras were therefore made in these Circars or States.

As early as 1765, when Lord Clive obtained for the Company the Dewani of Bengal, he also obtained from the Great Moghal a grant of four of these Circars, viz. Cicacole, Rajamandri, Ellor, and Kondapily. After a period of native administration, these Circars were placed in 1769 under the charge of Provincial Chiefs and Councils, and the system of administration was similar to that of the Bengal Districts.

In 1775 the Court of Directors directed that a Committee of Circuit should be appointed to inquire into the state of the Northern Circars, in order to ascertain the population, the produce, and the state of manufactures, as well as the gross revenues of the States, and the customary rights of Zemindars and cultivators.[1] The Court also intimated their desire to secure to the Zemindars their annual incomes, and to save the cultivators from undue exactions; and they wished to ascertain if it was possible to introduce into the Circars such regulations as had been

[1] Second Report of the Committee of Secrecy, 1782, Appendix v.

established in Bengal. A Committee was accordingly appointed, but was abolished in 1778 by Sir Thomas Rumbold, as has been stated in the last chapter. It was revived in 1783, and continued its inquiries till 1788.

It appeared from the reports submitted by this Committee that lands in the Northern Circars were principally held by Zemindars. The Zemindars in the hill country, descended from the Rajas of the kingdom of Orissa, were virtually independent rulers within their States, and had only paid a fixed tribute to the Mahomedan Government. The Zemindars in the plains were more under the control of the Government, but had been allowed to appropriate to their uses the rents of their estates, so long as they paid a fixed revenue to the Government.

Besides these Zemindari lands, there were certain demesne or household lands of the Government, known as Haveli lands. They were tracts of country adjoining capital towns, and reserved for the supply of the garrisons and civil establishments of the Mahomedan rulers. "Since the establishment of the British Government they [the Haveli lands] may be correctly described as being portions of territory which were not in the hands of the Zemindars, but in those of the Government, and in which it was therefore optional to adopt any system of management for collecting the land revenues from the Ryots that might be preferred." The system which was actually adopted was not a wise one; the Haveli lands were farmed out to agents or large speculating renters, who were thus furnished with "the most ample means of oppression."[1]

Both in the Zemindari territories and in the Haveli territories there existed from time immemorial the Village Community system, a simple form of self-government which protected the cultivators of every

[1] Fifth Report, 1812, p. 83.

village from the oppression of the Zemindars and the Government. This ancient institution—ancient in the days of Manu—had survived the wreck of dynasties and the downfall of empires, had secured peace and order in villages in times of war, and struck the servants of the East India Company in the eighteenth century as a unique and excellent institution.

" A village, geographically considered, is a tract of country comprising some hundreds or thousands of acres of arable and waste land; politically viewed, it resembles a corporation or township. Its proper establishment of officers and servants consists of the following descriptions. The *potail*, or head inhabitant, who has the general superintendence of the affairs of the village, settles the disputes of the inhabitants, attends to the police, and performs the duty, already described, of collecting the revenues within his village, a duty which his personal influence and minute acquaintance with the situation and concerns of the people renders him best qualified to discharge; the *curnum*, who keeps the accounts of cultivation and registers everything concerned with it; the *talliar* and *totie*, the duty of the former appearing to consist in a wider and more enlarged sphere of action, in gaining information of crimes and offences, and in escorting and protecting persons travelling from one village to another, the province of the latter appearing to be more immediately confined to the village, consisting, among other duties, in guarding the crops and assisting in measuring them; the *boundary-man*, who preserves the limits of the village or gives evidence respecting them in case of dispute; the *superintendent of tanks and water-courses* distributes the water therefrom for the purpose of agriculture; the *Bramin*, who performs the village worship; the *schoolmaster*, who is seen teaching the children in the villages to read and write in the sand; the *calendar Bramin*, or astrologer, who proclaims the lucky or unpropitious periods for sowing and threshing; the *smith* and *carpenter*, who manufacture the implements of agriculture and build the dwelling of the Ryot; the *potman*, or potter; the *washerman;* the *barber;* the *cowkeeper*, who looks after the cattle; the *doctor;* the *dancing-girl*, who attends at rejoicings; the *musician*, and the *poet*. These officers and servants generally constitute the establishment of a village; but in some parts of the country it is of less extent, some of the duties and functions above described being united in the same person; in others it exceeds the number of individuals which have been described.

"Under this simple form of municipal government the inhabitants of the country have lived from time immemorial. The boundaries of villages have been but seldom altered, and though the villages themselves have been sometimes injured, and even desolated, by war, famine, and disease, the same name, the same limits, the same interests, and even the same families have continued for ages. The inhabitants give themselves no trouble about the breaking up and divisions of kingdoms; while the village remains entire, they care not to what power it is transferred or to what sovereign it devolves; its internal economy remains unchanged; the Potail is still the head inhabitant, and still acts as the petty judge and magistrate and collector or renter of the village."[1]

The above extract is of the utmost importance, as it gives us an insight into the constitution of self-governing Indian villages, not in the mystic days of ancient Hindu rule, but in the eighteenth century; not described in old Sanscrit works like Manu, but depicted by the servants of the East India Company in official documents from actual observation and inquiry. It shows us at a glance how the great agricultural population of India tilled

[1] Fifth Report, 1812, p. 85.

their lands and manufactured their commodities in their own self-contained little republics through thousands of years, while dynasty succeeded dynasty and empires rose and fell. Happy it were if the British administrators of India had preserved and fostered and reformed these ancient institutions, and thus continued to rule the people through their organised assemblies. Two causes, however, operated from the commencement of the British rule to weaken the old village communities. An extreme anxiety to enhance the land revenue to its very utmost limits induced the administrators to make direct arrangements with every individual cultivator.[1] An equally unreasonable anxiety to centralise all judicial and executive powers in their own hands led the modern rulers to virtually set aside those village functionaries who had so long exercised these powers within the limits of their own villages. Deprived of their functions, the village communities rapidly fell into decay, and the Indian administration of the present day, better organised in many respects than the administration of the past, suffers from this disadvantage, that it is more autocratic, and rests in a far less degree on the co-operation of the people themselves.

But we must return to our narrative of the administration of *Zemindari lands* in the Northern Circars. These lands were annually settled with Zemindars until 1778, when Sir Thomas Rumbold made a five-years' settlement, as has been stated in the last chapter. The oppressive practice of annual settlements was resumed in 1783 and continued till 1786, when a three-years' settlement was concluded on an increased revenue demand by the Board of Revenue. In 1789 a settlement for three, and eventually for five, years was con-

[1] An interesting controversy between Sir Thomas Munro and the Board of Revenue about the continuance of the village system will be referred to in the next chapter.

cluded, and the Zemindars were assessed at two-thirds of their gross collections. The new Circar or State of Guntoor, which had come into the Company's possession in 1788, was settled in the same way.

Lord Hobart, who was appointed Governor of Madras in 1794, effected a great reform in abolishing the Company's Chiefs and Councils, and in appointing Collectors in all districts for the administration of the land revenue under the control of the Board of Revenue. The settlement of Zemindari lands continued to be made on the same principles as before. Lord Clive, son of the victor of Plassey, succeeded Lord Hobart, and it was during Lord Clive's administration that a Permanent Settlement of the land revenues, such as had been made in Bengal in 1793, was extended generally into the Northern Circars between 1802 and 1805. The general standard by which the revenue demand was regulated appears to have been two-thirds of the gross collections from the cultivators.[1]

The *Haveli lands* of the Northern Circars have a somewhat different history. Collectors were first appointed in 1787, and they adopted two different methods for collecting the revenue in Haveli lands. In some places they collected it directly from the cultivators in kind, *i.e.* taking a share of the produce as the Government revenue; and in other places they farmed out the lands for stipulated sums. The general arrangement, however, was that the Collector made settlements with the head inhabitants of villages, and they made a separate arrangement with each individual cultivator.[2] When the Company's Chiefs and Councils were abolished in 1794, the Collectors became alone responsible for these settlements, subject to the control of the Board of Revenue; and when the Zemindari lands were permanently settled

[1] Fifth Report, 1812, p. 114. [2] *Ibid.*, pp. 93 and 98.

between 1812 and 1804, the Haveli lands were parcelled out into mootas or blocks of a convenient size, yielding generally from 1000 to 5000 Star Pagodas as the annual revenue, and were sold by public auction as permanent Zemindaris.[1] The Jaigir lands round the town of Madras were also settled permanently at the same time.

Such is the history of land administration from 1765 to 1805 in the oldest portions of the Company's territory in Madras, embracing the Northern Circars and the tract of land round the city of Madras. But in the meantime, other tracts of country had come into the Company's possession, and it is necessary now to refer to these new acquisitions.

Lord Cornwallis's war with Tipu Sultan, concluded by the Peace of Seringapatam in 1792, brought in the districts of Salem and Krishnagiri, comprising the Baramahal. Lord Wellesley's final war with Tipu Sultan in 1799 brought in Canara, Coimbatore, Balaghat, and some other places. Tanjore was annexed by Lord Wellesley in 1799, and the whole of the country between the Krishna and the Tumbhadra was taken over from the Nizam of the Deccan in 1800. Lord Wellesley made the Nawab of Arcot retire on pension, and the whole of the Karnatic was added to the Company's dominions. Thus within ten years, between 1792 and 1802, the East India Company acquired the richest and fairest portions of that great territory which now forms the Province of Madras, and a new system of land settlements grew up with the acquisition of this new territory.

When the Baramahal districts were acquired by the East India Company in 1792, Lord Cornwallis entrusted their administration to Captain Read and three other military officers, who were better acquainted with the languages and the habits of the people than

[1] Fifth Report, 1812, p. 113.

the civilians of those times. The principle on which Captain Read formed settlements with individual cultivators was the principle which was subsequently developed and introduced into other parts of the province by his assistant, Thomas Munro, afterwards Sir Thomas Munro, Governor of the province. His name is as intimately connected with the *Ryotwari settlement* of Madras as the name of Lord Cornwallis is connected with the *Zemindari settlement* of Bengal.

Thomas Munro had arrived as a young man of nineteen at Madras in 1780, and had taken his share in the wars against Haidar Ali and Tipu Sultan. Later in life he won his laurels in the wars with the Mahrattas, and received encomiums from the British Parliament for his courage, ability, and success. But it is not as a successful soldier that Munro is remembered in India. He was one of the few of the Company's servants who devoted his life to promote the welfare of the people, and his name, therefore, is gratefully remembered by the people of Madras to this day, as the name of Cornwallis is in Bengal, and the name of Elphinstone in Bombay.

Employed under Captain Read on settlement work in the Barmahal districts, his keen eye detected the defects of the Company's system of administration, and his sympathetic judgment suggested the true remedies.

About the Karnatic he wrote: "A great part of the Nawab's revenues are remitted through agents in Madras at 3 per cent. and 4 per cent. per month. The rents in some parts of the Karnatic are regulated by the grain sown, every kind paying a different rate, and in others they are levied in kind, and in all the leases are annual. When the rents are fixed according to the grain, the lands are measured every year. The surveyors in making their reports are guided by the bribes they receive, and a thousand frauds are practised both on the farmers and the Government; and where they are collected in kind, the produce of the land is either thrown upon the cultivator, at a price much above its value, or else a standard is fixed for the market below which no person can sell until the whole of the public grain has been disposed of. Such wretched management, one would think, must soon ruin the country."

Similarly of the British territory he wrote: "The Revenue Board made some time ago an application for an increase of salary to the Collectors, which Government rejected with great marks of displeasure; but in doing this, they showed little knowledge either of true policy or human nature, for when men are placed in situations where they can never become independent by their avowed emoluments, but where they may also, by robbing the public without any danger of discovery, become so on a sudden, the number of those who would balance which side to take is so small that it ought not to be brought into account. We see every day Collectors who have lived above their salary amassing great fortunes in a very few years. The operation by which this is accomplished is very simple. When rents are paid in money, by giving Government a rent roll below the real one; and when in kind, by diminishing the produce of the land or of the sales. It is vain to say that Collectors, being men of education and character, will not descend to such practices; the fact is against this conclusion."[1]

By 1798 the Ryotwari settlement of the newly acquired Baramahal districts was completed.

"The Baramahal has now been completely surveyed and the rents of it fixed. . . . The great number of farmers in the Baramahal necessarily occasions much detail in the management of the revenue; but there

[1] Letter dated 31st January 1795.

is no difficulty in it—nothing is required but constant attention, and where this is given, it is both better for the country and easier for the Collector to receive the rents directly from 60,000 farmers than by the medium of ten or twelve Zemindars or great landholders. The rent of the division of the country under my charge last year was 165,000 Pagodas, which was collected within the year without a single Rupee outstanding, and without any trouble, from about 20,000 farmers." [1]

In this letter we see the growing partiality of Thomas Munro for the Ryotwari system in tracts of country where there were no hereditary Zemindars. In places like Bengal and the Northern Circars, where the prevailing system was the possession of lands by great landlords, the Government had continued that system and made settlements with Zemindars. In other places, where the prevailing system was the payment of the revenues by the Ryots or cultivators direct to the State, Munro continued that system and made settlements direct with the Ryots. It was necessary and essential to give some permanency to the Government demand, in both cases, for the improvement of agriculture and the prosperity of the people. This was done by Lord Cornwallis in Bengal; and this was desired and recommended by Thomas Munro for Madras, but has never been done. Herein lies the fatal defect in the land settlements of Southern India.

From Baramahal, Munro was transferred to Canara, where he completed the settlement work with his usual ability and success within one year, and the settlement here was made with landlords.

"I came here," he wrote in 1800, "because, after having been named as a person qualified to ascertain the actual revenue of the country, I could not decline

[1] Letter dated 21st September 1798.

the task without seeming to desert my duty; but now that this is done, and that the collections, except where interrupted by invasion, are as regular as in the Baramahal, or even more so, I think my work is performed."[1]

"All my settlements were made with the landlords, or, in cases where there was no landlord, with the immediate occupant. . . . The produce was perfectly ascertained, because the accounts of it were brought forward by both parties. There was no instance in which the Sirkar's share [the Government's share] was more than one-third. In many it was not one-fifth or one-sixth, and in some not one-tenth of the gross produce."[2]

When the country between the Krishna and the Tumbhadra was ceded by the Nizam of the Deccan to the East India Company in 1800, Thomas Munro, who had settled Baramahal and Canara, was chosen to settle that country. The Ceded Districts were therefore the third field of Munro's civil administration. That Munro performed his work in the new field with his usual ability and knowledge of details is beyond question; that the pressing demands of the revenue authorities prevented him from showing that consideration for the people which his own judgment suggested is admitted by him with a candour which almost disarms criticism

"Were I sure that every succeeding Board of Revenue and Government would support the slow and gradual increase of assessment which has already been recommended, I would undoubtedly adhere to it; but it is not likely that I shall be permitted. The desire that men at the head of affairs usually have of seeing the country, or at least the public income, flourishing under their auspices, will most probably compel me to proceed too rapidly. . . . I may get nervous as I grow older, and become afraid of censure. If I leave room for my successor to

[1] Letter dated 13th July 1800. [2] Letter dated 7th October 1800.

raise the revenue, it would be said that I allowed the inhabitants to defraud Government. . . . I have no thoughts at present of precipitating matters, though I shall, for the sake of assisting the public want of money, press the ryots more than I ought to do."[1]

When Munro wrote this, he had in his mind the case of his friend G——, who was about to be removed from the service because he had made assessments in the Karnatic which the Board of Revenue had considered too low. It was by such undue pressure on its revenue officers that the Company's government raised the land revenues of their newly acquired territories to a point which was harsh and oppressive to the cultivators of the soil.

"The report is that the Board thinks that he was precipitate in his settlement of the Karnatic, that it was much too low, and that he trusted too much to his old friend, Lachman Row. G—— says, that he made it low on purpose, with the view of being better able to raise it hereafter. I shall be extremely concerned if he is removed, not only for my regard for him as an old friend, but because I am afraid that his marriage, after his long revenue life, has left him but little before the world. I think it hard, too, that a man should be removed merely for an error of judgment; censure would, I think, have been sufficient. You will observe, too, that his error is on the right side."[2]

After an administration of the Ceded Districts for seven years, Thomas Munro at last left India in 1807 for a well-earned rest. The authorities were highly pleased with the gradual increase of revenue which he showed, from £402,637 to £606,909, or an increase of 50 per cent. within seven years![3] It was by such results that the Company judged the work of its officers.

[1] Letter dated 5th September 1802.
[2] Letter dated 28th September 1802.
[3] Fifth Report, 1812, p. 124.

Other districts were in the meantime settled by other officers. Malabar came into the possession of the Company in 1792, and was for a time included in the Bombay Presidency. The Bombay Government made two annual settlements with the Rajas and Nair chiefs of Malabar, followed by a five-years' settlement. On the failure of the Rajas and the Nair chiefs to make punctual payments, their lands were taken from them, and they rose in rebellion. The Bombay Government having thus failed in their administration, Malabar was transferred to the Madras Presidency in 1800. Lord Clive, then Governor of Madras, appointed a Principal Collector and Subordinate Collectors for the administration of the country. Settlements were made partly with landlords and partly with the tenants themselves, but the system of revenue management generally adopted was the Ryotwari system, which was now finding favour with the authorities.[1] And thus the hereditary Rajas and Nair chiefs who had owned lands in Malabar before the time of the British rule were gradually got rid of, and finally disappeared from the scene. True statesmanship would have continued the old order of things, and reduced the Rajas and Nair chiefs into loyal subjects of the British Government and leaders of the people. But the desire to make settlements immediately with the cultivators, in order to get as much revenue as the land could yield, steadily influenced the policy of the Company's government more and more as years passed by.

Tanjore was annexed by Lord Wellesley in 1799. The cultivators in this State used to pay their rents to their Raja through head-ryots, called Pattakdars. A Pattakdar's circle included from one to 128 villages; and many of the Pattakdars were virtually Zemindars. The British Government made a clean

[1] Fifth Report, 1812, pp. 124–127.

sweep of these Pattakdars, introduced the Ryotwari system in 1804, and fixed the revenue with reference to the produce of an average number of years, not on a survey valuation of the lands.[1]

The administration of the Karnatic was transferred to the East India Company, firstly by the treaty concluded by Lord Cornwallis with the Nawab in 1792, and finally by the annexation of the Karnatic made by Lord Wellesley in 1801. A great portion of this territory had been for many generations, often for centuries, under the rule of the local military chiefs, known as the Polygars.

The Polygars were "head-men of villages, or public servants of other descriptions, whose actual condition had become changed to that of military rulers during the revolutions of power in the Deccan, which had everywhere contributed to the usurpation of authority, and in no part more than in the southern division of the Peninsula. Though their Sunnuds, where Sunnuds could be produced, did not particularly describe the terms on which they held their Pollums [estates], they all bore internal evidence of their dependence on the Emperor, and of their subjection to the Subadars of the Karnatic, to whom they yielded tribute, and whose camp they were bound to attend, whenever summoned, with a military force proportioned to the extent of their local jurisdictions."[2]

The condition of the Polygars had formed the subject of much correspondence from the time of Warren Hastings. The Nawab of the Karnatic had frequently sought the help of his British allies to extirpate these local chiefs, in order to extend his own power over the people, but the Court of Directors had marked with concern the employment of British

[1] Fifth Report, 1812, p. 127.
[2] *Ibid.*, p. 143.

troops in the disagreeable service of helping the Nawab against the Polygars. They had given precise orders that "the native princes, called Polygars, should not be extirpated." They had considered it "repugnant to humanity to force them [the Polygars] to such dreadful extremities." They had feared that the Nawab's government was "none of the mildest," and that there was "great oppression in collecting his revenues." And while they were aware that the people of the Karnatic had suffered from many distresses, they had held that the oppression of the Nawab of the Karnatic was "greater than all."

After the conclusion of Cornwallis's treaty of 1792 with the Nawab of the Karnatic, the Directors entered into a full discussion of the principles of that treaty in their despatch of the 10th June 1795. This was followed by discussions in India, and in 1797 Lord Hobart, Governor of Madras, recorded a minute suggesting the means of rendering the Polygars useful subjects and obedient tributaries of the British Government. The Directors replied in their despatch of the 5th June 1799, in which they insisted on the absolute suppression of the military power of the Polygars, and on the institution of a pecuniary tribute higher than the Polygars had paid before.

Armed with this despatch, the Madras authorities went beyond all just and reasonable limits. They concluded a settlement in 1799–1800, by which they retained all lands held by the Polygars outside their own villages, and demanded a revenue which exceeded the previous demand by no less than 117 per cent. The Southern Polygars rose in insurrection. The rising was soon put down, and the insurgents were deprived of their estates, and in some cases capitally punished. The revenue was declared to be progressive for several years, and afterwards to remain unalterable to an amount calculated to be equal to two-thirds of the gross collections. Finally, a Permanent Settlement was made in 1803 for the fourteen estates which still remained in the hands of the Southern Polygars, and the revenues fixed were more moderate than the exorbitant demands of 1799–1800, varying from 41 per cent. to 51 per cent. of the gross rental. These estates were principally situated in the Tinivelly district, and similar settlements were made with the Polygars in Sivaganga and Ramnad.[1]

Permanent Settlements were also made with the Western Polygars in 1802; but for the Polygars of Chitoor, who came under British rule with the annexation of the Karnatic, a worse fate was reserved. They resisted the British claims and were mostly driven from their fastnesses, and took refuge in the jungles. With a few exceptions, all the estates of the Chitoor Polygars were resumed, and settlements were made with the tenants direct.

Looking back to these transactions after the lapse of a century, one cannot but regret the harsh policy which led to the virtual extirpation of the Polygars in the Karnatic. The Directors of the East India Company were right in depriving them of all military power, for under the modern system of administration that power must necessarily belong to the State alone. But it was not a just or wise policy to deprive them of their estates outside their own villages, to demand from them a sudden and exorbitant increase in revenue, or to punish their insurrection by virtually stamping them out. They had preserved some sort of peace and order in their estates during the harassing and troublesome wars of Southern India in the

[1] Fifth Report, 1812, pp. 146–147.

seventeenth and eighteenth centuries; they had protected weavers and manufactures and shielded the cultivators when there was hardly any other constituted authority in the land; they had excavated great canals and reservoirs for irrigation all over Southern India; and they had given shelter to the British themselves when Madras was taken by the French in the early Karnatic wars. If the Polygars were guilty of turbulence and oppression, they shared their faults with almost all chiefs and nobles in the seventeenth and eighteenth centuries in Asia and in Europe, and a wise statesmanship would have attempted to reduce them to order instead of trying to "root out the Polygars." It is not a wise policy for any Government to change the old institutions of a land; it is not a humane policy for an alien Government to suppress a class, and to confiscate its proprietary rights, in order to add to its income by direct settlements with the tillers of the soil.

The policy of Lord Wellesley's Government in Madras appears in strong and unfavourable contrast with the policy of Lord Cornwallis in Bengal. Lord Cornwallis found the Bengal peasantry living under hereditary Zemindars, and strengthened and perpetuated the Zemindari institution. Lord Wellesley's government found a large part of the Karnatic under the power of the Polygars, and virtually rooted them out in order to bring the people under its direct control. Lord Cornwallis respected an ancient institution, and has thus preserved in Bengal a large, prosperous, and contented middle class. Lord Wellesley's policy denuded Madras of a similar class, and the loss has not been repaired after a century of British rule. Madras has no strong, influential, prosperous middle class, forming a natural link between the cultivators and an alien Government.

The policy of Lord Wellesley's Government in Madras bore a resemblance rather to the policy of the French Revolution, which a few years before had confiscated the rights of the territorial aristocracy of France. Yet what the barons lost in France was a gain to the French nation; what the Polygars lost in Madras was a gain to an alien trading company. The rents which the Polygars had obtained from the people under their jurisdictions had been spent among the people, had flowed back to them through various channels, and had fructified their trades, manufactures, and industries. The land revenues which the Company obtained — after the Polygars had been virtually extirpated—were, after defraying the cost of administration, withdrawn from the country as the profits of foreign traders. "It cannot be concealed or denied," said one of the ablest of the Directors of the Company, "that the object of this [Ryotwari] system is to obtain for Government the utmost that the land will yield in the shape of rent."[1]

We have in the foregoing pages given a brief but connected account of the land settlement in Madras down to 1807. We have reviewed the revenue arrangements in the Northern Circars, ending in the Permanent Settlement of 1802–1805. We have referred to the settlements of Thomas Munro in Baramahal, Canara, and the Ceded Districts. We have described the operations undertaken in Malabar and in Tanjore; and we have also described the transactions in the Karnatic, ending in Permanent Settlements with some of the remaining Polygars, while the greater portion of the province was settled with the cultivators direct.

[1] Henry St. John Tucker, *Memorials of Indian Government*. London, 1853, p. 113.

The results of all these settlements can be best shown in the form of the appended list:[1]

Permanently Settled

The Jaigir round Madras	1801–2
The Northern Circars	1802–5
Salem Western Polygars' estates Chitoor Polygars' estates Southern Polygars' estates . . .	1802–3
Ramnad	1803–4
Krishnagiri	1804–5
Dindigal	1804–5
Trevendapuram Jaigir villages	1806–7

Not Permanently Settled.

Mysore . .	Malabar. Canara. Coimbatur. Ceded Districts. Balaghat.
Karnatic . .	Palnad. Nellor and Ongole. Arcot. Sativad. Trichinopoly. Madura. Tinivelly.

It will appear from what has been stated before that, as the system of settlements with Zemindars, Polygars, and other head-men began to be looked upon with disfavour in Madras, direct settlements with Ryots or cultivators began to find favour. The story of the final acceptance of this Ryotwari system for the Province will be narrated in the two succeeding chapters.

[1] Fifth Report, 1812, p. 163.

CHAPTER VIII

VILLAGE COMMUNITIES OR INDIVIDUAL TENANTS?— A DEBATE IN MADRAS, 1807–1820

THE table given at the close of the last chapter shows the districts in Madras which were permanently settled, and those which had not been so settled in 1807. The question was then discussed, what durable arrangements should be made with regard to these last.

Would a *Permanent Zemindari Settlement*, similar to that introduced by Lord Cornwallis in Bengal, be extended to these places?

Would a *Permanent Ryotwari Settlement*, recommended by Thomas Munro, be adopted?

Or would a *Permanent Mauzawari Settlement*, *i.e.* a collective settlement with each Village Community, as recommended by the Madras Board of Revenue, be finally decided upon?

The economic history of India has no more interesting chapter than the debates on this momentous question.

On the eve of his departure for Europe in 1807, after his labour of seven years in the Ceded Districts, Thomas Munro recorded his famous report recommending a Permanent Ryotwari Settlement of those Districts. He described the exorbitant revenue he had raised, being 45 per cent. of the gross produce; he recommended a reduction of this revenue by a quarter; and he proposed that the assessment should then be made permanent.

"As one-third of the produce is, therefore, the highest point to which assessment can in general be carried without destroying landed property, and as it is also the point to which it must be lowered before persons who are not cultivators can occupy Circar lands without loss, it is obvious that unless the assessment is reduced to this rate, land can neither be occupied by all classes of inhabitants, nor ever become private property, nor can any Permanent Settlement be made, calculated to improve the condition of the Ryots or of the public revenue. I am, therefore, of opinion, that in a Permanent Settlement of the Ceded Districts, the rent of Government should be about one-third of the gross produce. The present assessment is about 45 per cent. To bring it to the proposed level would require a remission of 25 per cent., as may be seen from the following example:—

Total gross produce, say	100
Government share by the present assessment .	45
Deduct 25 per cent. of assessment . .	$11\frac{1}{4}$
Government's share by proposed permanent assessment	$33\frac{3}{4}$

. . . . . .

"I shall now proceed to state the manner in which I think a Permanent Ryotwari Settlement in the Ceded Districts may be made. . . .

"1st. The settlement shall be Ryotwari.

"2nd. The amount of the settlement shall increase and decrease annually, according to the extent of land in cultivation.

"3rd. A reduction of 25 per cent. on all land shall be made in the survey rate of assessment.

"4th. An additional reduction in the assessment of 8 per cent., or 33 per cent. in all, shall be allowed on all lands watered by wells, or by water raised by machinery from rivers and nullahs; provided the cultivators keep the wells or embankments (Dirroas) in repair at their own expense. A similar reduction shall be allowed on the lands watered by small tanks, wherever the cultivators agree to bear the expense of repairs.

"5th. Every Ryot shall be at liberty, at the end of every year, either to throw up a part of his land or to occupy more, according to his circumstances; but whether he throw up or occupy, he shall not be permitted to select, but shall take or reject proportional share of good and bad together.

"6th. Every Ryot, as long as he pays the rent of his land, shall be considered as the complete owner of the soil, and shall be at liberty to let it to a tenant without any limitation as to rent, and to sell it as he pleases.

"7th. No remission shall be made, on ordinary occasions, for bad crops or other accidents. Should failure occur which cannot be made good from the property or land of the defaulters, the village in which they happen shall be liable for them to the extent of 10 per cent. additional on the rent of the remaining Ryots, but no further.

"8th. All unoccupied land shall remain in the hands of the Government, and the rent or whatever part of it may be hereafter cultivated shall be added to the public revenue.

"9th. All taxes on houses, shops, and professions, all duties, licenses, &c., shall belong exclusively to Government. The Ryot on whose land houses or shops may be built shall not be entitled to receive a higher rent from them than the equivalent of the survey rent of the ground which they occupy.

"10th. The repairs of all tanks which are not rendered private property by an extra remission, or

Desivundum Enaum, shall be made at the expense of Government.

"11th. Tuccavie shall be gradually discontinued.

"12th. Potails, Curnums, and all other village servants shall remain as heretofore under the Collector.

"13th. Private creditors, who may distrain the property of Ryots, shall discharge the rent which may be due from such Ryots to Government, and shall give security for it before they begin the distraint."[1]

We have made this long extract because it is necessary to clearly understand the plan of a Ryotwari settlement as conceived by its real author. Thomas Munro desired a settlement with each individual Ryot, and desired it to be permanent, subject to increase or decrease of revenue as more or less land was taken under cultivation.

Lord William Bentinck, who succeeded Lord Clive as Governor of Madras in 1803, was precisely of the same opinion. In a minute recorded by him in 1806 he recorded that the Zemindari settlement suited Bengal, where there were hereditary Zemindars, but did not suit those parts of Madras where such landlords did not exist.

"I am satisfied that the creation of Zemindars is a measure incompatible with the true interests of the Government and of the community at large. . . . I am not at all at variance with the principles of the Permanent Settlement, which I admire, and which I believe to be applicable to this and to every part of the world."

And in a subsequent minute recorded in the same year the Governor said:

"If an annual settlement with the Ryots, founded upon fixed principles, the essential part of which was to secure to the Ryot for a year the fruits of his industry, had actually been productive of such decided advan-

[1] Report dated 15th August 1807.

tages, a Permanent Settlement founded upon the same principles, but carried to a greater extent with regard to the benefit of the Ryot, would produce the same effect in an increased ratio."[1]

It will appear from these extracts that a Permanent Settlement was the predominant idea both of Thomas Munro and of Lord William Bentinck when they advocated the Ryotwari system. Six years after he had left India, Thomas Munro was examined by the Committee of the House of Commons, on the eve of the renewal of the Company's charter in 1813, and he explained his ideas before the Committee as forcibly, as lucidly, and as unmistakably, as he was capable of doing it.

"Has any permanent revenue arrangement been extended to the Ceded Districts of which you were the Collector?"

"Until the period that I left India no Permanent Settlement had been made, but the Ryots were so far protected in the enjoyment of their property, that a fixed rent had been settled upon all the land, and every Ryot could retain his own farm for ever, provided he paid that rent; no increase could be made upon the land rent."

"Have the goodness to explain to the Committee what you understand by the Ryotwari system."

"I shall state what I understand to be the principle of the Ryotwari system, the details will perhaps be too extensive. The principle of the Ryotwari system is to fix an assessment upon the whole land of the country; this assessment is permanent; every Ryot who is likewise a cultivating proprietor of the land which he holds is permitted to hold that land at a fixed assessment as long as he pleases; he holds it for ever without any additional assessment; if he occupies any waste or additional land, he pays the assessment that

1 Minutes dated 29th April and 25th November 1806.

is fixed upon that land and no more; his rent undergoes no alteration."

"Is the Committee to understand that in respect to permanency there is no difference between the Ryotwari system and the Bengal Permanent Settlement?"

"With respect to permanency there is no difference between the two systems, but the Ryotwari leaves the Government an increasing revenue arising from the waste in proportion to its cultivation."[1]

If language has any meaning, then it is clear that the Ryotwari settlements which Munro had already made, and which he desired to introduce in other parts of Madras, were on the condition that every Ryot would hold his land *for ever without any additional assessment*, except for new lands reclaimed. If words have any definite significance, then it is clear that *there was no difference with respect to permanency* between Cornwallis's Zemindari settlement and Munro's Ryotwari settlement, except that waste lands brought under cultivation had to be paid for under the latter system. It is necessary to comprehend this clearly, because the right of the cultivators in Madras to a fixed, unchanging, unalterable revenue for the same lands has been ignored by the Madras Government in the recent years, and the first principle of Munro's Ryotwari settlement has been disregarded.

While the idea of a Permanent Zemindari Settlement began to be looked upon with disfavour, and that of a Permanent Ryotwari Settlement received Munro's favour, a third system was advocated by the Madras Board of Revenue—a scheme of a Permanent Mauzawari Settlement, or a settlement with each village community. Referring to Munro's proposal of the 15th August 1807 in favour of a reduction of 25 per cent.

[1] Minutes of Evidence taken before the Committee of the whole House and the Select Committee on the affairs of the East India Company, 1813, pp. 149, 170, and 173.

on the exorbitant revenue which had been fixed, the Board of Revenue made this new suggestion.

"29. This is the outline of Colonel Munro's plan, which is not less applicable to all the districts as yet unsettled than to the Ceded Districts; and if the exigencies of Government allowed of so great a sacrifice as a remission on the present standard rents to the extent of 25 per cent., or even of 15 per cent., we should consider the measure highly advisable and calculated to produce great ulterior advantages. Indeed, it would be idle to dispute that the less we take from the cultivator of the produce of his labour the more flourishing must be his condition.

"30. But if the exigencies of Government do not permit them to make so great a sacrifice, if they cannot at once confer the boon of private property, they must be content to establish a private interest in the soil as effectually as they can under the farming system; if they cannot afford to give up a share of the landlord's rent, they must be indulgent landlords.

"31. Under such circumstances the transition from Ryotwari to Village-rents, as suggested by Mr. Hogdson, appears to us best adapted to secure the revenue of the State and the prosperity of the country. . . .

"38. Every village with its twelve Agagandeas, as they are denominated, is a petty commonwealth, with its Mokuddum, Potail, Rapod, Reddy or chief inhabitant at the head of it, and India is a great assemblage of such commonwealths. The inhabitants, during war, look chiefly to their own head-inhabitants; they give themselves no trouble about the breaking up and division of kingdoms while the village remains entire: they care not to what power it is transferred, on whomsoever it devolves, the internal management remains unaltered; the head-inhabitant is still the collector, magistrate, and head-farmer.

"39. From the age of Manu to the present day the settlements have been made either with or through the head-inhabitants. When the revenue was thought to be high enough, and the head-inhabitant agreed to it, he was usually left to settle with the Ryots; if it was too low and the head-inhabitant objected to an increase, the Amaldar settled with the Ryots in his presence. This system has stood the test of time, and as under it whole provinces have often been in a highly cultivated state, it must certainly be well calculated for the great object of promoting agriculture." [1]

The Government of Madras, in their reply to the Board of Revenue, authorised the conclusion of triennial village settlements in many of the unsettled districts as a preparatory measure to the introduction of a Permanent Village Settlement.[2] And on the expiry of these triennial settlements they proposed in their letter to the Court of Directors the conclusion of a decennial settlement, to become permanent if approved by the Directors.[3]

The Directors were now alarmed at the idea of a Permanent Settlement, and they charged the Board of Revenue with having acted without orders in authorising the decennial settlement.

"In all the provinces that may be unsettled when the despatch shall reach you, the principle of the Ryotwari system, as it is termed, shall be acted upon, and that where the village rents upon any other principle shall have been established, the leases shall be declared terminable at the expiration of the period for which they may have been granted." [4]

The Government of Madras protested against this decision of the Directors.

"That agriculture was regarded as the basis of

[1] Letter dated 25th April 1808.
[2] Letter dated 25th May 1808.
[3] Letter dated 29th February 1812.
[4] Letter dated 16th December 1812.

national wealth and prosperity; that it was considered essential to the improvement and extension of agriculture to restrict the demands of Government upon landed property; that it was not supposed Government could lose by this restriction, since without it agriculture would never be improved and extended, nor the resources of the country increased. . . . In offering the foregoing remarks, we have considered the Permanent Settlement strictly as a question of fiscal policy. But it does not need to be shown that it is of vital importance also, as being calculated to give to the mass of the people, who are engaged in agriculture, a deep and permanent interest in the stability of our Government."[1]

In the following year, the Government of Madras made a still more eloquent appeal to the Court of Directors in favour of Permanent Village Settlements and against Permanent Ryotwari Settlements.

"If the primary object of a Permanent Settlement be to give the people the management of their own affairs, from the belief that their affairs will be indefinitely managed by themselves than by public officers, how little would that object be attained under such a system [the Ryotwari system]? How entirely would all management still remain in those hands from which it was meant to transfer it. It is singular that, under such a system, professedly designed to protect the rights and interests of landed proprietors, they are to forfeit all property in any land which, through general or peculiar calamity or indolence or mismanagement, they may any year fail to cultivate, and their property in it is, on every such occurrence, to escheat to the Government; assuredly a more violent encroachment on landed property, where it really exists, than ever was attempted under any other system. . . .

"He [the cultivator] is not secure against a fraudu-

[1] Letter dated 5th March 1813.

lent measurement on the estimation of the land he quits or the land he occupies; nay, if to escape from the mode of oppression he resolves not to alter his limits, the current business of agriculture, the means of irrigation, the distribution of Tuccavy, or of an abatement of rent on account of calamity, all must be regulated by men who have no interest in his property, no sympathy with his feelings. Surely it were better that confidence should be reposed where self-interest affords a security against its being abused, and that the people should be left to improve the country in their own way, without the encumbrance of useless and ill-judged aid from public officers, and without the dread of their oppression and rapacity. At any rate, we own that the Ryotwari system, proposed by Colonel Munro, seems to us in no respect to deserve the name of a Permanent Settlement of the land revenue, but, on the contrary, to leave land revenue and landed property as unsettled as ever, and the people liable to all that prying, meddling interference of public officers under which no private concern can prosper. . . .

"The grand difference between the view at present taken in England regarding Indian land revenue and that taken here, seems to be, that in England the fear is that the public demands upon the resources of India may not keep pace with its prosperity; while here the universal sentiment, we believe without any exception whatever, is, that the prosperity of the country is so much depressed by the public demands, that, without the most liberal and judicious management, there is more danger of its resources declining than room to hope for their speedy increase. This is a sentiment which we cannot too strongly convey to your Honourable Court. It is addressed to your wisdom, to your sense of justice, to your humanity; it concerns the successful administration of your Government no less than the welfare and happiness of a numerous population and the prosperity of an extensive country, favoured by nature, protected from internal commotion and foreign assault, and requiring only moderation in the demands of Government upon its resources to render it rich and flourishing. Compared with the attainment of these great ends, of how little value appears every sacrifice which can be made for them?"[1]

The decision of the question between Ryotwari settlements and Village settlements was delayed for a time, as judicial and administrative reforms claimed more immediate attention. Thomas Munro had passed seven years in England after his twenty-seven years' labours in India, when he was sent out again as the head of a Commission to revise the judicial system, and arrived at Madras on the 16th September 1814. How he laboured to improve the judicial system, and to admit the people of India to some responsible posts in the judicial service, will be narrated in another place; how he distinguished himself in the last Mahratta War by placing his confidence and trust in the people of India, as much as by his bravery in the field, is a subject which does not fall within the scope of this work.[2] On the con-

[1] Letter dated 12th August 1814.

[2] The admiration felt by Sir John Malcolm, himself a distinguished soldier and a friend of the people of India, for Munro's plan of operation is thus expressed in his letter of the 17th February 1818:—"I send you a copy of a public letter from *Tom Munro Sahib*, written for the information of Sir Thomas Hislop. If this letter makes the same impression upon you that it did upon me, we shall all recede as this extraordinary man comes forward. We use vulgar means, and go on zealously, and actively, and courageously enough; but how different is his part in the drama! Insulated in an enemy's country with no military means whatever (five disposable companies were nothing), he forms the plan of subduing the country, expelling the army by which it is occupied, and collecting the revenues that are due to the enemy, through the means of the inhabitants themselves, aided and supported by a few irregular infantry whom he invites from the neighbouring provinces for that purpose. His plan, which is at once simple and great, is successful in a degree that a mind like his could alone have anticipated. The country comes into his hands by the most legitimate of all modes, the zealous and spirited efforts of the

clusion of this war, Munro left once more for England in January 1819, and the question of land settlements now came up for decision.

The Board of Revenue at Madras were still in favour of the introduction of Village settlements, and in 1818 they recorded one of the most exhaustive and memorable minutes ever written in India.

Speaking of the Zemindari system, they said: "The increased facility and regularity with which this revenue had been collected, free from any extensive abuses on the part of the native revenue servants, and exempting the Government through its Collectors and Superintending Boards from the heavy duties inseparable from annual settlements, and from investigations into annual accusations of fraud and embezzlement in the collection of the revenue . . . forms a striking contrast with the former fruitless attempts of the Government to enforce the payment of their dues in the Circars, the evasion and subterfuges practised by the Zemindars and Polygars, the coercion and assistance of a military force, to which it was so often found necessary to resort for the purpose of realising the collections from the zemindari and pollam lands, and the numerous abuses of every description formerly so prevalent throughout the native establishments, and which still continue to disgrace the districts in which temporary settlements continue to prevail. . . .

"The ancient Zemindars and Polygars were, in fact, the nobility of the country, and though the origin of some of their tenures would not bear too minute a scrutiny, they were connected with the people by ties by which it was more politic, more liberal, and more just to strengthen than to dissolve.

natives to place themselves under his rule, and to enjoy the benefits of a Government which, when administered by a man like him, is one of the best in the world."

Had our power in the Circars been as strong on the acquisition of these provinces as it subsequently became at the period of the transfer of the Ceded Districts, the ancient Zemindars, like the Polygars of the latter country, might perhaps have been removed from their lands and reduced to the situation of mere pensioners on our bounty; but when the attachment of the people to their native chieftains and the local situation of many Zemindaris are considered, it may be greatly doubted whether such a policy would not have been as unwise as it would have been ungenerous."

Speaking of the Ryotwari system, they wrote: "The Ryotwari system had its origin in the Baramahal and Salem districts, ceded to the Company in 1792, and was first introduced by Colonel Read, the officer appointed to take charge of that country on its cession; Colonel Munro, Colonel Macleod, and Colonel Graham, then lieutenants, were assistants under Colonel Read. . . .

"In the Northern Division of Arcot, all these superiorities [special rights of Mirasdars or hereditary peasant proprietors] were also resumed and incorporated with the public revenue. In short, the survey assessment was raised so high as to absorb in the Government revenue any little rent remaining to the landholders. No intermediate person was acknowledged between the State and the actual cultivator. . . .

"The Ryotwari settlement, in fact, was made annually, frequently by the Tehsildars and Sheristadars [subordinate low-paid officers], and was not in general concluded until after the crop had been raised; the system then was to make as high a settlement as it was practicable to realise. If the crop was good, the demand was raised as high within the survey rates as the means of the Ryots would admit; if the crop was bad, the last farthing was notwithstanding demanded, and no remission was allowed unless the Ryot was totally unable to pay the rent. On this point the most severe scrutiny was instituted, for not only was the whole of the Collector's detailed establishment of servants employed in an investigation of his means, but each of his neighbours were converted into inquisitors by being themselves made liable for his failure, unless they could show that he was possessed of property. . . .

"He [the cultivator] was constrained to occupy all such fields as were allotted to him by the revenue officers, and whether he cultivated them or not, he was, as Mr. Thackeray emphatically terms it, saddled with the rent of each. To use the words of Mr. Chaplin, the Collector in Bellary, one of the most able of Colonel Munro's former assistants, and still one of the most strenuous advocates of the Ryotwari system, it was the custom under it, 'to exert in a great degree the authority, which is incompatible with the existing regulations, of compelling the inhabitants to cultivate a quantity of ground proportionate to their circumstances.' This he explains to have been done by 'the power to confine and punish them,' exercised by the Collector and his native revenue servants; and he expressly adds, that if the Ryot was driven by these oppressions from the fields which he tilled, it was the established practice 'to follow the fugitive wherever he went, and by assessing him at discretion, to deprive him of all advantage, he might expect to derive from a change of residence.' . . .

"Ignorant of the true resources of the newly-acquired countries, as of the precise nature of their landed tenures, we find a small band of foreign conquerors no sooner obtaining possession of a vast extent of territory, peopled by various nations, differing from each other in language, customs, and habits, than they attempt what would be called a Herculean task, or rather a visionary project even in the most civilised countries of Europe, of which every statistical information is possessed, and of which the Government are one with the people, viz., to fix a land-rent, not on each province, district, or country, not on each estate or farm, but on every separate field within their dominions. In pursuit of this supposed improvement, we find them unintentionally dissolving the ancient ties, the ancient usages which united the republic of each Hindu village, and by a kind of agrarian law, newly assessing and parcelling out the lands which from time immemorial had belonged to the Village Community collectively, not only among the individual members of the privileged order (Mirasdars and Kadeems), but even among the inferior tenantry (Pykaris), we observe them ignorantly denying, and by their denial abolishing private property in the land, resuming what belonged to a public body (the Gramamanium), and conferring in lieu of it a stipend in money on one individual; professing to limit their demand to each field, but in fact, by establishing such limit, an unattainable maximum, assessing the Ryot at discretion, and, like the Musalman Government which preceded them, binding the Ryot by force to the plough, compelling him to till land acknowledged to be over-assessed, dragging him back to it if he absconded, deferring their demand upon him until his crop came to maturity, then taking from him all that could be obtained, and leaving him nothing but his bullocks and seed grain, nay, perhaps obliged to supply him even with these, in order to renew his melancholy task of cultivating, not for himself, but for them."

Such was the state of cultivators under the Ryotwari system without the protection of a permanent and moderate assessment which Munro had recommended. A more forcible picture of a "human cattle-farm" has never been painted.

Lastly, with regard to the Village system the Board wrote: "Although this system has not been equally successful in every district, yet even where (as in Bellary) it has been the least so, the Collectors are unanimous in opinion that it has most materially improved the condition of the agricultural population of the country, and it is the great body of the Ryots, and not the mere parties with whom the settlement was concluded, who have chiefly benefited by the Village settlement. The Ryotwari Teerwas have nearly everywhere been greatly reduced, and instead of the head Ryots oppressing their inferiors, most of the Collectors have been obliged to prop their weakened authority by that of their Tehsildars. This, without any material exception, is the universal language of all their reports, and it is a result which may be confidently offered as conclusive evidence that the system has generally answered the expectations of those by whom it was introduced. But where the settlement has been best conducted, as in Cuddapah and the Northern Division of Arcot, a picture of prosperity is drawn of which the parallel may in vain be sought throughout the revenue records of this Presidency."[1]

This last appeal was made in vain. The great author of the Ryotwari system, now Sir Thomas Munro, K.C.B., returned to India, for the third and last time as Governor of Madras; and the Ryotwari system was finally accepted for the Province, except where Zemindari settlements had already been made with Zemindars and Polygars. Looking back, after a lapse of over eighty years, to these memorable debates, the student of Indian history still reflects on them with a melancholy interest, and his admiration for the high personal character of Sir Thomas Munro does not prevent him from feeling that in this controversy the

[1] Board's Minute dated 5th January 1818.

Board of Revenue was in the right. A wise Government tries to foster and improve, not to sweep aside, the ancient institutions of a country, when they are consistent with modern progress. It is undeniable that the internal concerns of villages in India could be managed more successfully, and more satisfactorily to themselves, by the villagers than by Tehsildars, Sheristadars, and policemen; and that it is a gain to the cause of humanity to let large classes of people manage their own concerns where possible. Munro himself, if he had seen village communities in a workable condition in the early scenes of his settlement work, in Baramahal, Canara, and the Ceded Districts, would have been the strongest advocate of that system. But having made settlements direct with the cultivators in those places, having advocated that system to the Government of Madras and before the House of Commons, having got the Directors of the Company to sanction that system in all the unsettled parts of the province, he was unable, late in his life, to change his opinion, and appreciate the more desirable form of land administration through the agency of village communities which the Board of Revenue had fostered between 1812 and 1818. As Governor of Madras, Sir Thomas Munro did all he could to foster the village institutions; he organised Panchyets, and conferred on them judicial powers, and he endeavoured to continue the village communities of India as living and organic institutions, such as they had been in the past. But all these endeavours failed. When all real power is taken away from old institutions, forms of authority will not keep them alive. And the villagers, harassed by every petty revenue officer and corrupt policeman, could no longer continue to work together as corporate bodies, as they had done before. Among the many changes which India has witnessed with the advent of the

British rule, many of them making for progress and advancement, and some of them deplorable, the saddest change is the virtual extinction of the old forms of self-government, and the disappearance of those ancient Village Communities of which India was the first home among all the countries of the earth.

The final rejection of the Village system advocated by the Board of Revenue has only an academical interest for the modern reader; what has more practical significance is that the Ryotwari system, advocated by Thomas Munro himself, has not been continued in its entirety. Thomas Munro had declared in 1807 and in 1813, as strongly and emphatically as it was possible to do it, that the essence of the Ryotwari system was the permanency of assessments, that the Ryotwari settlement was as permanent as the Zemindari settlement of Bengal except in regard to waste lands. The Ryotwari system was introduced finally in all unsettled tracts in Madras in 1820, but the permanency of the assessments, recognised and admitted by the Madras Government down to 1862, has since been ignored. The uncertainty of the State demand, now altered at each recurring settlement on grounds which are unintelligible to the people, leaves the agricultural population of Madras in a state of perpetual uncertainty and chronic poverty.

CHAPTER IX

MUNRO AND THE RYOTWARI SETTLEMENT IN MADRAS (1820–1827)

SIR THOMAS MUNRO came to Madras as Governor of that Province in May 1820, and the Ryotwari system was declared to be generally introduced in the same month. Every possible opportunity was taken of getting back, on occasions of lapses or by means of purchase, the Zemindaris and Mootahs, and all other tenures into which the Ryotwari system was now to be introduced, and village leases were rapidly got rid of. Collectors were encouraged to break up joint-tenure wherever it existed, and to enter into engagements with tenants separately. The high rate of assessment, by which the State demand was fixed at 45 per cent., or 50 or 55 per cent. of the field produce, caused endless oppression; and was generally reduced under the considerate administration of Sir Thomas Munro.

It is not our purpose in the present chapter to trace the history of the introduction of the Ryotwari system into every district in Madras. But from the voluminous State records of the period a few extracts will throw much side-light on the operations of these years, and the economic condition of the people of Madras.

NELLORE.

The Collector of Nellore had selected the village of Covoor for the experimental introduction of the Ryotwari system, after survey, classification, and assessments of lands, as early as 1818; and the proceedings of the Board of Revenue show how the assessment was originally made, and how it was subsequently modified.

Wet lands.—"The grain being valued at 20 rupees per Candy, being the average selling price, gives Rs.34,374, from which the usual Calavasum or 6¼ per cent., or Rs.2234, being deducted, there remains to be divided between the Circar [State] and the cultivators Rs.32,139."[1]

"The proportion allowed the cultivators being nine in twenty, or 45 per cent., comes to Rs.14,462; and consequently the sum which remains receivable by the Circar [State] is Rs.17,667."

Dry lands.—"The dry land and garden produce being estimated upon similar principles, and valued at 28 rupees per Candy, the share which remained to Government was for dry lands, Rs.768, for garden Rs.205."

The cultivators objected to the Collector's calculations and the selling prices of grain which he had assumed. Some deductions were allowed, and the Board came to the conclusion that "the estimated amount of the annual revenue of Covoor will be in round numbers about Rs.15,600." In other words, about one-half the estimated produce of the village was demanded by the State as its revenue under the new system.[2]

TRICHINOPOLY.

The village of Tertaloor was selected by the Collector of Trichinopoly, and was measured and assessed after a classification of soils. The estimated gross produce, after the usual deductions, was 5816 Cullums.[3]

[1] Fractions of Rupees have been omitted in these extracts.
[2] Proceedings of the Board of Revenue, dated 17th September 1818.
[3] Fractions are omitted.

"This being divided being the Circar [State] and the inhabitants at the usual rate of Warum, 50 per cent., leaves as the Circar's share 2908 Callums, which being commuted at the average price of the last three years, as recommended by the Collector, amounts to Rs.3,232."[1] Certain further deductions and additions were made, and the revenue fixed upon was Rs.3211. One-half the produce of the soil levied as land-tax, was an impoverishing taxation, but the Madras Board was slow to reduce their demand even to one-third, while they still professed moderation! "Although one-third of the gross produce," they said, "cannot be considered as a standard for a general assessment to be valued and paid in money, it may nevertheless serve as a guide to direct Collectors to moderation."

COIMBATORE.

In the District of Coimbatore the evils of a gross corruption were added to the evils of a cruelly excessive assessment. A Commission was appointed to inquire into these abuses, and they reported that the treasurer, Causy Chitty, from his first appearance upon the scene, "directed his attention constantly and anxiously to the converting of every person and everything in the country to the benefit of his private trade." The Collector, Mr. Garrow, was suspected to be equally corrupt, and the Court of Directors wrote indignantly in 1821 to Sir Thomas Munro, then Governor of Madras.

"Great as these abuses are in themselves, they excite the most painful considerations when they are contemplated as an evidence of defect in our institutions. We can see no ground of assurance that what has happened in Coimbatore should not happen

[1] Proceedings of the Board of Revenue, dated 26th November 1818.

in any other District; that a Collector should not obtain the confidence of the Board of Revenue, and becoming either the dupe or the accomplice of an artful and fraudulent native, render the whole Province subject to his mismanagement, the prey of a few men armed with the powers of Government. If either the weakness or the corruption of the Collector may produce such scenes as those which were exhibited in Coimbatore, and for seven years laid the property of the inhabitants, as well as the public revenue, at the mercy of the lowest agent of the Government, without exciting the attention of those whom we have appointed to superintend the details of government and to discover and prevent abuse, it is impossible not to dread the extensive existence of evil, and infer the necessity of more effectual securities. As the death of Mr. Garrow has rendered it unnecessary for us to decide upon the propriety of his being allowed to continue in our service, it is of less importance to determine the species and degree of his delinquency. It is certain, however, that the existence under a public officer of abuses of great extent and long duration, abuses which were attended with great profit to his immediate dependents, and which an ordinary degree of vigilance would have enabled him to prevent, is to a certain degree evidence of corrupt participation."[1]

In another letter, written in the subsequent year, the Court of Directors give us details of the over-assessment of Coimbatore, apart from its oppression from corrupt motives.

"A rent called a full rent was, according to custom, charged upon all the arable, not garden, *i.e.* upon the uncultivated and fallow as well as upon that under crop. A third or a fourth of the full rent was charged

[1] Revenue Letter from the Court of Directors to the Governor in Council at Madras, dated 31st October 1821.

for grass land, and something more than the full rent for the garden land. . . .

"In his letter dated 7th September 1816, he [the Collector, Mr. Sullivan] says: 'When a ryot has occupied and paid rent for land for two years, he is considered as its proprietor, and is, in fact, saddled with the rent of it as long as he can pay.' It hence appears that his character of proprietor was fixed upon him by the Government for its own advantage, and not for his, viz., that he might be made responsible for a certain amount of rent. . . .

"The additional tax upon land watered by wells, or cultivated with garden produce, is justly represented by the Collector as a tax upon improvement. He describes the formation of wells as by far the greatest improvement of which the land in that part of India is susceptible. A well places the crops of the land which it suffices to water beyond the accidents of season, so variable, and often so fatal, in India. Nothing, therefore, can be more useful than to give encouragement to the formation of wells. All the encouragement necessary would be to allow the people to reap the fruit of their own labour; for the Collector describes them as prone to the formation of wells, but deterred by the tax."[1]

The complaint of over-assessment runs through the whole of the correspondence of these years, and yet the Directors, while they were eloquent in condemning the sins of the deceased Mr. Garrow, were not very prompt or explicit in remedying their own. In a letter written only three weeks before the one quoted above, the Directors speak thus:

"'The same features,' he [the Collector of Trichinopoly] adds, 'of distress and poverty which must ever accompany a rack-rent, are but too visible in Trichino-

[1] Revenue Letter from the Court of Directors to Madras, dated 2nd January 1822.

poly, and the ruin of all agricultural improvements is evident in the depreciation of the value of landed property. Mirasdars who formerly farmed an extent of land amounting to some thousand Cawnies, now possess scarcely as many hundreds, and these will be sold in the course of this or the ensuing year, if either the assessment is not altered or the balance of arrears allowed to lay over. But what I chiefly wish to impress upon the Board is my conviction of the impossibility of continuing the present assessment.' . . .

"For a remedy of the immediately pressing evils, you [Madras Government] have thought proper, without dissolving the leases, to authorise remissions in proportion to what may, in each several instance, appear to the Collector to be required. This is, therefore, an annual settlement in fact; and it will require some pains on your part to prevent it from having the effects of an annual settlement without the accuracy; in other words, from pressing too heavily upon the renters in some instances, and sacrificing too much of the interests of Government in others—in accordance to the zeal or humanity, the negligence or severity of the Collectors."[1]

In other words, the assessment was to be maintained at an impossible rate, and as much of it was to be taken from the cultivators from year to year as they could possibly pay. And the Directors considered this compatible with the improvement of the condition of the people!

TANJORE.

The same story is repeated from the once flourishing State of Tanjore.

[1] Revenue Letter from the Court of Directors to Madras, dated 12th December 1821.

"The lease settlement of Tanjore expired with Fusly 1229 [1820], and the money value of produce having greatly fallen, and appearing likely to remain at a depressed level, the money assessment had become higher than was intended, and sufficient evidence was adduced of the necessity of an abatement. . . .

"It was, no doubt, expedient to adhere, as you [Madras Government] did, to the principle of the fixed money assessment, notwithstanding the predilection of the people for their old methods of a division of the produce. . . .

"The principle which you have laid down for such contingency we think a proper one, 'that no addition should be made to the assessment unless the price of grain should rise 10 per cent., but that a deduction should be allowed if it should fall 5 per cent.,' the degree of addition or deduction to correspond with the alteration in the price."[1]

ARCOT.

The same melancholy tale was told from Arcot.

"The Board, in conformity with the suggestion of the Collector, made, and as you say 'strenuously urge,' another proposal—a reduction of the assessment. This is a subject which peculiarly attracts our attention. The Collector and the Board of Revenue are unwilling to acknowledge our assessment. They declare the assessment to be 'as high as the exhausted state of the country could bear,' but express a confident expectation that it could be realised. They allege, however, that under such an assessment the country could not improve, and in order to afford it the means of improving, they propose a reduction from 7 to 10 per cent.

[1] Revenue Letter of the Court of Directors to Madras, dated 18th August 1824.

"Upon this you [Madras Government] express a very strong opinion with respect to the evils arising from over-assessment, and you add that it did not appear to you that there were any grounds for reducing the settlement in the Northern Division of Arcot which did not exist equally in other districts. In fact, you affirm that the same necessity exists in every part of the country. You then proceed to recommend a general reduction, and you propose that the standard upon which it should be regulated should be that of a third of the gross produce as the Government share. . . .

"We must, however, express a doubt whether a third, or any other proportion of the produce, can be assumed as an invariable standard of assessment."[1]

These extracts are enough. They will sufficiently indicate to every reader the distress and poverty from which the people of Southern India suffered during the first quarter of the nineteenth century through the harshness of local officers and the greed of the Court of Directors. It is to the credit of Sir Thomas Munro that he strove all through his seven years' administration to lower the assessments, and that he did succeed in lowering them throughout the Province. He has himself given us, in his own lucid and forcible style, an account of his aims and endeavours in his Minute recorded on the 31st December 1824, perhaps the most thoughtful and statesmanlike minute ever recorded in India since the time of Lord Cornwallis. It is a long document, and covers more than thirty folio pages of the East India Papers."[2]

It is impossible within our limits to give a full summary of this valuable document, and we can, therefore, only make a few extracts from those portions of the Minute which relate to the condition of the people.

[1] Revenue Letter from the Court of Directors to Madras, dated 12th December 1821.

[2] Vol. iii., London, 1826, pp. 602–632.

Fixed and Moderate Assessment of Land.

"In order to make the land saleable, to encourage the Ryots to improve it, and to regard it as a permanent property, the assessment must be fixed and more moderate in general than it is now; and above all, so clearly defined as not to be liable to increase from ignorance or caprice. . . .

"The Ryot is the real proprietor, for whatever land does not belong to the Sovereign belongs to him. The demand for public revenue, according as it is high or low in different places and at different times, affects his share; but whether it leaves him with only the bare profit of his stock, or a small surplus beyond it as landlord's rent, he is still the true proprietor, and possesses all that is not claimed by the Sovereign as revenue. . . .

"It is the ever-varying assessment which has prevented, and as long as it continues will prevent, land from becoming a valuable property; for even where the assessment is lowest, the knowledge that it may at any time be raised, hinders the land from acquiring such a value as to render it a saleable article. We cannot communicate to it the value which it ought to possess, or render it a private property capable of being easily sold or mortgaged, unless the public assessment upon every part of it be previously fixed. When it is fixed, all uncertainty is removed, and all land, which is not absolutely over-assessed, soon acquires a value which is every day increased by improvements, made in consequence of the certainty of reaping all the profit arising from them."

Employment of Indians in Administrative Work.

"With what grace can we talk of our paternal Government if we exclude them from every important office, and say, as we did till very lately, that in a country containing fifteen millions of inhabitants, no man but a European shall be entrusted with so much authority as to order the punishment of a single stroke of a rattan. Such an interdiction is to pass a sentence of degradation on a whole people for which no benefit can ever compensate. There is no instance in the world of so humiliating a sentence having ever been passed upon any nation. The weak and mistaken humanity which is the motive of it can never be viewed by the natives as any just excuse for the disgrace inflicted on them, by being pronounced to be unworthy of trust in deciding on the petty offences of their countrymen. We profess to seek their improvement, but propose means the most adverse to success. The advocates of improvement do not seem to have perceived the great springs on which it depends; they propose to place no confidence in the natives, to give them no authority, and to exclude them from all office as much as possible; but they are ardent in their zeal for enlightening them by the general diffusion of knowledge.

"No conceit more wild and absurd than this was ever engendered in the darkest ages, for what is in every age and every country the great stimulus to the pursuit of knowledge but the prospect of fame, or wealth, or power? or what is even the use of great attainments, if they are not to be devoted to their noblest purpose, the service of the community, by employing those who possess them, according to their respective qualification, in the various duties of the public administration of the country? . . .

"Our books alone will do little or nothing; dry simple literature will never improve the character of a nation. To produce this effect, it must open the road to wealth, and honour, and public employment. Without the prospect of such a reward, no attainments in science will ever raise the character of the people.

"This is true of every nation as well as India; it is true of our own. Let Britain be subjugated by a foreign power to-morrow, let the people be excluded from all share in the Government, from public honours, from every office of high trust or emolument, and let them in every situation be considered as unworthy of trust, and all their knowledge and all their literature, sacred and profane, would not save them from becoming, in another generation or two, a low-minded, deceitful, and dishonest race.

"Even if we could suppose that it were practicable without the aid of a single native to conduct the whole affairs of the country both in the higher and in all the subordinate offices, by means of Europeans, it ought not to be done, because it would be both politically and morally wrong. The great number of public offices in which the natives are employed is one of the strongest causes of their attachment to our Government. In proportion as we exclude them from these, we lose our hold on them, and were the exclusion entire, we should have their hatred in place of their attachment, their feelings would be communicated to the whole population, and to the native troops, and would excite a spirit of discontent too powerful for us to subdue or resist. But were it possible that they could submit silently and without opposition, the case would be worse, they would sink in character, they would lose with the hope of public office and distinction all laudable ambition, and would degenerate into an indolent and abject race, incapable of any higher pursuit than the mere gratification of their appetites. It would certainly be more desirable that we should be expelled from the country altogether, than that the result of our system of government should be such a debasement of a whole people."

TAXATION AND LEGISLATION.

"The right of the people to be taxed only by their own consent has always, in every free country, been esteemed amongst the most important of all privileges; it is that which has most exercised the minds of men, and which has oftenest been asserted by the defenders of liberty. Even in countries in which there is no freedom, taxation is the most important function of government, because it is that which most universally affects the comfort and happiness of the people, and that which has oftenest excited them to resistance, and hence both its utility and its danger have, under the most despotic governments, taught the necessity of employing in its administration the ablest men of the country. . . .

"In other countries, Government and its officers are part of the community, and are of course acquainted with the effect of every public measure and the opinion of the country regarding it, but here Government is deprived of this advantage, it makes laws for the people who have no voice in the matter, and of whom it knows very little, and it is therefore evident that it cannot adapt its laws to the circumstances of the people, unless it receive accurate information upon this subject from active and intelligent local officers, whose duty it is to investigate carefully the conditions and opinions of the inhabitants, and to report upon them. But these officers can acquire this information only through an establishment of experienced native servants, who have, beyond all other men, from the very nature of their official duties, the best means of obtaining it."

Advantages and Disadvantages of British Rule.

"If we make a summary comparison of the advantages and disadvantages which have occurred to the natives from our Government, the result, I fear, will hardly be so much in its favour as it ought to have been. They are more secure from the calamities both of foreign war and internal commotions; their persons and property are more secure from violence; they cannot be wantonly punished or their property seized by persons in power; and their taxation is, on the whole, lighter. But, on the other hand, they have no share in making laws for themselves, little in administering them, except in very subordinate offices; they can rise to no high station, civil or military; they are everywhere regarded as an inferior race, and often rather as vassals or servants than as the ancient owners and masters of the country.

"It is not enough that we confer on the natives the benefits of just laws and of moderate taxation, unless we endeavour to raise their character; but under a foreign government there are so many causes which tend to depress it that it is not easy to prevent it from sinking. It is an old observation that he who loses his liberty loses half his virtue. This is true of nations as well as of individuals. To have no property scarcely degrades more in the one case than in the other to have property at the disposal of a foreign government in which we have no share. The enslaved nation loses the privileges of a nation as the slave does those of a freeman; it loses the privilege of taxing itself, of making its own laws, of having any share in their administration, or in the general government of the country. British India has none of these privileges. . . .

"One of the greatest disadvantages of our Government in India is its tendency to lower or destroy the higher ranks of society, to bring them all too much to one level, and by depriving them of their former weight and influence to render them less useful instruments in the internal administration of the country. The native governments had a class of richer gentry, composed of Jageerdars and Enamdars and of all the higher civil and military officers. These, with the principal merchants and Ryots, formed a large body, wealthy or at least easy in their circumstances. The Jagheers and Enams of one prince were often resumed by another, and the civil and military officers were liable to frequent removal, but as they were replaced by others, and as new Jagheers and Enams were granted to new claimants, these changes had the effect of continually throwing into the country a supply of men whose wealth enabled them to encourage its cultivation and manufactories. These advantages have almost entirely ceased under our Government. All the civil and military offices of any importance are now held by Europeans, whose savings go to their own country."

Future of India.

"There is one great question to which we should look in all our arrangements; what is to be their final result on the character of the people? Is it to be raised or is it to be lowered? Are we to be satisfied with merely securing our power and protecting the inhabitants, leaving them to sink gradually in character, lower than at present, or are we to endeavour to raise their character, and to render them worthy of filling higher situations in the management of their country, and of devising plans for its improvement? It ought undoubtedly to be our aim to raise the minds of the natives, and to take care that whenever our connection with India might cease, it did not appear that the only fruit of our dominion there had been to leave the people more abject and less able to govern themselves than when we found them. Many different plans may be suggested for the improvement of their character, but none of them can be successful, unless it be first laid down as a main principle of our policy, that the improvement must be made. This principle, once established, we must trust to time and perseverance for realising the object of it. We have had too little experience, and are too little acquainted with the natives, to be able to determine without trial what means would be most likely to facilitate their improvements. Various measures might be suggested, which might all probably be more or less useful; but no one appears to me so well calculated to ensure success, as that of endeavouring to give them a higher opinion of themselves, by placing more confidence in them, by employing them in important situations, and perhaps by rendering them eligible to almost every office under the Government. It is not necessary to define at present the exact limit to which their eligibility should be carried, but there seems to be no reason why they should be excluded from any office for which they were qualified, without danger to the preservation of our own ascendancy. . . .

"When we reflect how much the character of nations has always been influenced by that of governments, and that some, once the most cultivated, have sunk into barbarism, while others, formerly the rudest, have attained the highest point of civilisation, we shall see no reason to doubt that, if we pursue steadily the proper measures, we shall in time so far improve the character of our Indian subjects, as to enable them to govern and protect themselves."

Three-quarters of a century have elapsed since the death of Sir Thomas Munro. Administrators of the stamp of Thomas Munro are rare, and the difficult task of realising an equitable land-tax from 150,000 tenants in each district in the Province of Madras has not been satisfactorily performed. Twenty-five years after the death of Munro, another eminent Scotchman, who rose to high distinction as an Indian administrator, wrote thus of the Madras system:

"Only imagine one Collector dealing with 150,000 tenants, not one of whom has a lease; but each pays according as he cultivates and gets a crop, and with reference to the number of his 'cattle, sheep, and children'; and each of whom gets a reduction if he can make out a sufficiently good case. What a cry of agricultural distress and large families there would be in England or any other country under such a system! Would any farmer ever admit that his farm had yielded anything, that his cattle had produced, or that his wife had not produced? If the Collector were one of the prophets, and remained in the same district to the age of Methuselah, he would not be fit for the duty; and as he is but an ordinary man and a foreigner, and continually changed, it would be strange if the native subordinates could not do as they liked, and, having the power, did not abuse it. Accordingly, it is generally agreed that the abuses of the whole system, and specially that of remissions, is something frightful; chicanery, and intrigue of all kinds, are unbounded; while the reliance of the Madras Collector on informers by no means mends the matter."[1]

Sir Thomas Munro had laboured all his life to obtain for the cultivator of Madras a fixity of rental, so that all improvements made by him might lead to his own profit. And though such a fixity of rental was not declared by any Act or Proclamation, it was accepted as a fact by the Madras Government forty years after the time of Thomas Munro. The Madras Ryot, said the Administration Report of 1855–56, "cannot be ejected by Government so long

[1] *Modern India*, by George Campbell, London, 1852.

as he pays the fixed assessment. . . . The Ryot under the system is virtually a proprietor on a simple and perfect title, and has all the benefits of a perpetual lease." "A Madras Ryot," said the Board of Revenue in 1857, "is able to retain his land perpetually without any increase of assessment." "There can be no question," said the Government of Madras in 1862 to the Government of India, "that one fundamental principle of the Ryotwari system is that the Government demand on the land is fixed for ever."[1]

These repeated assurances, as emphatic as words can make them, have now been ignored and set aside. Since the survey operations organised in 1855, the land-tax assessed on each holding is fixed at the discretion of revenue officers at each recurring settlement. The Madras Ryot has no fixity of rental, no security against enhancements, no adequate motive for improvements. The uncertainty of the land-tax hangs like the sword of Damocles on his head.

What is the Land Tax? The Court of Directors declared in 1856 that the right of the Government is not a rent which consists of all the surplus produce after paying the cost of cultivation and the profits of agricultural stocks, but a land revenue only.[2] Two years after this, the East India Company was abolished, and the first Secretary of State for India under the Crown, Sir Charles Wood, afterwards Lord Halifax, declared that he desired to take only a share, generally a half share, of the rent as Land Tax.[3]

This is a very high rate, but fixes a clear and intelligible limit. In practice, even this high limit is exceeded; and what is realised as Land Tax in Madras often sweeps away the whole of the economic rent. The maximum limit now fixed by the Government

[1] Letter of 18th February 1862.

[2] Despatch of 17th December 1856. [3] Despatch of 1864.

is one-third the field produce; and this is virtually the whole of the economic rent. For in small farms, yielding a produce of about £12 in the year, the cost of cultivation and the profits of agricultural stocks approximate to £7 or £8, and the claim of the Government to £4 as Land-Tax is virtually a claim, not to 50 per cent., but to 100 per cent., of the economic rent.

The evils of an uncertain State demand grew with the lapse of years; the Madras cultivators remained resourceless; the famine of 1877 found them helpless and swept away five millions of the population of that province. The Marquis of Ripon came to India as Viceroy three years after, and he at last grappled with the Madras Land Question.

Without conceding to the Madras cultivator that absolute fixity of the Land Tax which had been acknowledged as one of his rights by the Madras Government in 1856 and 1862, Lord Ripon laid down a rule that in districts which had once been surveyed and settled, the Land Tax would not be raised except on the equitable ground of a rise in prices.[1] It left the door open for the enhancement of the land revenue, while at the same time it gave the cultivators an assurance against such enhancement except on the reasonable ground of a rise in the prices of the field produce. It was the most reasonable compromise which could be effected after the right of an absolutely fixed rental had been ignored; and it gave some security to the agricultural population of Madras, without which agriculture cannot flourish in any part of the world.

The Marquis of Ripon left India in December 1884, and in January 1885, the Secretary of State for India cancelled the equitable rule he had established! The India Office thus proved itself as un-

[1] Despatch of 17th October 1882.

generous and harsh to the Indian cultivators as the old Court of Directors. And the Madras cultivator to-day (1901) has no effectual security against uncertain State demands and unjust enhancements, and has therefore no motive to save and no power to improve his own condition.

CHAPTER X

LORD WELLESLEY AND CONQUESTS IN NORTHERN INDIA (1795–1815)

THE Province of India now called the *North-Western Provinces and Oudh*, came under British rule at different dates. Benares and some adjoining districts were annexed by Warren Hastings on the death of the Nawab of Oudh in 1775 by a treaty with his successor. Allahabad and some other districts were ceded by the Nawab of Oudh to the British, under pressure from Lord Wellesley, in 1801. Agra and the basin of the Ganges and the Jumna were conquered by Lord Lake in the Mahratta war of 1803. And the remaining portion of Oudh was annexed by Lord Dalhousie in 1856.

Cornwallis and Shore were anxious to extend to Benares the same Permanent Zemindari Settlement which had been concluded in Bengal in 1793. Negotiations were conducted with the Raja of Benares from 1787 to 1794, and an agreement was concluded on the 27th October 1794. The Raja of Benares relinquished to the British the rights which he had hitherto exercised over the whole of his State, retaining his Zemindari rights over a small tract which had formed the patrimony of his family. On the conclusion of this agreement, Sir John Shore, then Governor-General of India, made land revenue settlements with village Zemindars in the relinquished tracts, and also restored many estates to old Zemindars who had lost them under the Raja's administration. The division of the crop between the Government and the cultivator, in proportions which varied slightly in different parts of the country, furnished the rule for fixing the land revenue; and a Permanent Settlement of the revenue was made in 1795 over the whole of the Benares country.[1] The Code of Regulations for Bengal, Behar, and Orissa were extended to Benares with little alteration, and the civil and criminal laws administered were the same.

Six years after this, the Nawab of Oudh ceded to the East India Company the district of Allahabad and other districts called by the general name of the "Ceded Districts." The long negotiations between the Nawab and Lord Wellesley relating to this event, the threats under which the cession was ultimately made in commutation of the subsidy, and the charge of high crimes and misdemeanours which was subsequently framed against Lord Wellesley for these transactions, are matters of political history which do not come within the scope of the present work.[2]

[1] Fifth Report, 1812, pp. 45–48.

[2] "The subsidy which, according to the treaty of Lord Teignmouth, was already paid by the Vizir [Nawab of Oudh] amounted to Rs.7,600,000; the annual expense of the additional force with which he was to be loaded was Rs.5,412,929; the whole would amount to Rs.13,012,929. The Nawab was required to make a cession of territory, in perpetual sovereignty to the English, the revenue of which even in its present unproductive state, and without any regard to the improvements of which it might be susceptible, should amount to such a sum, over and above the whole expense of collection. The revenue remaining to the Vizir after such a reduction would have been Rs.10,000,000. The territory, then, of which he was to be deprived, amounted to more than one-half, to not much less than two-thirds, of his whole dominions. . . .

"If, on the other hand, this measure should, unfortunately, not obtain his consent, he was desired to consider the territorial cession as a measure which force, if necessary, would be employed to accomplish."—Mill's *British India*, Book VI. chap. ix.

See also State Papers relating to Lord Wellesley's administration. By a singular good fortune I have in my possession the identical copy of the State Papers in four volumes, which belonged to Lord Wellesley himself, and which was sold with the rest of his books after his death. These volumes contain interlineations and occasional short notes in the Marquis's own handwriting. Very amusing are his remarks on the policy of his peaceful successors, Cornwallis and Barlow, who reversed some of his acts. "Most infamous," "an abrogation in itself iniquitous," are some of the notes made by the irate Marquis in reference to his successors' policy.

On the same day on which Lord Wellesley ratified the treaty by which the Company obtained the "Ceded Districts," he formed a Commission for the administration and settlement of those districts. Three civil servants were appointed to form a Board of Commissioners, and the Governor-General's brother, Henry Wellesley, was nominated Lieutenant-Governor of the new territory and President of the Board. Henry Wellesley made a settlement of the land revenue for three years with the Zemindars and farmers, and his first settlement report, dated 10th February 1803, discloses the same over-assessment which the Company's servants made in every newly-acquired territory in India.

"3. The settlement of the provinces had, however, been formed by the Collectors previously to my arrival at Bareilly, at a Jumma [assessment] fully equal to that at which it had been ceded by his Excellency the Nawab Vizir; and although I was still apprehensive that this settlement had been made upon an erroneous calculation of the existing assets of the country, and that the amount would be with difficulty realised, I determined not to annul the engagements which had been recently concluded by the Collectors, from an apprehension that any immediate interference on my part might tend to weaken their authority, which at that critical period, it appeared to me so necessary to support. . . .

"18. From the documents which I have been enabled to collect relative to the annual revenue of these provinces during the Moghal Government, it would appear that it amounted to nearly two and a half crores of rupees [two and a half millions sterling]. . . . Under the mild and equitable system of the British Government I have no hesitation in stating my expectation that the land revenue of these provinces, when fully cultivated, will amount to two crores and fifty lakhs of rupees [two and a half million sterling]. . . .

"24. Under the regulations recently introduced, the revenue arising from the Abkaree, or duty on the sale of spirituous liquors, will at least equal the amount for which credit is taken in the statement. . . .

"30. I now proceed to lay before your Lordship the arrangements which I have adopted for the purpose of placing the exclusive privilege of the purchase and sale of salt in the hands of the Company."[1]

In the statement appended to this report the following figures are given:

	Rupees.
Amount of the Nawab's land revenue assessment	13,523,474
Amount of the British assessment, first year	15,619,627
Amount of the British assessment, second year	16,162,786
Amount of the British assessment, third year	16,823,063

It will appear from these figures that the blunder which had been committed in Bengal and in Madras on the first acquisition of those provinces was repeated in Northern India. Large tracts of country, harassed by frequent wars and impoverished by severe exactions, had passed under the rule of a great and civilised power. It was a suitable occasion for giving the peaceful and industrious population some relief; it was an opportunity of lightening their burdens and improving their resources. But in the very first year of Henry Wellesley's administration, the Company's demand from the Ceded Districts was raised beyond the Nawab's demand by two million Rupees, or two hundred thousand pounds; and another million Rupees was added before the third year was out. And while the Nawab's demand was only nominal—collections being made according to the state of the crops—the Company's demand was realised with a rigidity which

[1] Paper 1 of Papers relating to East India Affairs, 1806, p. 34 *et seq.*

the people of India had never known before. One Collector, Mr. Dumbleton, complained that the settlement of 1802 "pressed beyond a reasonable demand," and that the British Government continued the heavy rates of the Nawab's Government "without the same elasticity in realising."

In other respects, every endeavour was made to bring the newly acquired territory under organised government. The Bengal Regulations were extended to it on the 24th May 1803, and the country was divided into seven districts. A civil servant, exercising the functions of Judge and Magistrate, was appointed to each district, and another civil servant performed the duties of Collector. A Court of Appeal and Circuit was established at Bareilly, and Tehsildars and landholders were empowered, as at Benares, to apprehend robbers and to preserve the peace within their jurisdiction.[1]

An important Regulation was also enacted,[2] recognising the triennial settlement of the land revenue already made, and notifying that, at the expiration of that term, another settlement would be made for three years, to be followed by a settlement for four years, at the expiration of which a Permanent Settlement would be concluded.

"In these terms," says the Select Committee of the House of Commons,[3] "the Supreme Government pledged itself to the landholders for the introduction of a Permanent Settlement" at the expiration of an aggregate period of ten years from the first settlement of Henry Wellesley.

In 1803 General Wellesley (another brother of the Governor-General, and afterwards Duke of Wellington) broke the Mahratta power in the south in the famous battle of Assaye; and Lord Lake crushed the same power in the north in the battle of Laswaree. The

[1] Regulation xxxv. of 1803.
[2] Regulation xxv. of 1803.
[3] Fifth Report, 1812, p. 51.

country between the Jumna and the Ganges was annexed, and this country was called the Conquered Provinces, as distinguished from the Ceded Districts obtained from the Nawab of Oudh two years before. Bandelkhand and Cuttack were also annexed in 1803.

The Conquered Provinces were first placed under the administration of Lord Lake; but in 1805 they were formed into five districts, under the administration of judicial and revenue officers, and placed under the control of the supreme authorities at Calcutta like the Ceded Districts. The Regulations recently introduced in the Ceded Districts were introduced in the Conquered Provinces, and the same pledge which had been given to the landholders of the former country was given in the latter; settlements of one, three, and four years were to be made in succession, and the last settlement was to be permanent, if agreed to by the landholders.[1] Two years after the pledge was repeated, but with the proviso that the conclusion of the Permanent Settlement would depend on the confirmation of the Court of Directors.[2]

Northern India had been ravaged by the Mahratta war of 1803, and the severe land assessments made by the servants of the Company gave the people no chance of improving their condition. The result was the widespread famine of 1804. The Government was then compelled to make large remissions of the land revenue; loans and advances were made to the landowners; and a bounty was offered on grain exported into Benares, Allahabad, Cawnpore, and Fatehgarh. A Special Commission was appointed in 1807 to superintend the settlement for four years, which was to become permanent according to the regulations already enacted.

We now enter upon the famous discussion which took place on the question of a Permanent Settlement in Northern India.

[1] Regulation ix. of 1805. [2] Regulation x. of 1807.

The Special Commissioners, R. W. Cox and Henry St. George Tucker, submitted their report admitting the benefits of a Permanent Settlement, but declaring themselves adverse to the immediate conclusion of such a settlement in the Ceded and Conquered Provinces.

"230. We are ourselves fully sensible of the many advantages which may be expected to result from a limitation of the public demand upon the land. We are aware that temporary settlements are harassing to the people, and that they afford opportunities for frauds and abuses. It has been questioned, indeed, whether a country can make any considerable advances in improvement while the public taxes are progressively increased, and the individual is not permitted to enjoy any benefit from the execution of greater industry; but with every previous disposition in favour of the principle of a Permanent Settlement, we submit to your Lordship in Council our deliberate and unqualified opinion that the measure, considered with relation to the Ceded and Conquered Provinces generally, is at this moment unseasonable, and that any premature attempt to introduce it must necessarily be attended with a material sacrifice of the public resources, and may, in particular cases, prove injurious to the parties themselves, whose prosperity it is the chief object of the measure to secure upon a durable foundation."[1]

This was the first note of alarm raised in Northern India against a Permanent Settlement, and the fear of a "material sacrifice of the public revenues" inspired this alarm. The arguments of the Special Commissioners, however, received a conclusive reply from H. Colebrooke.

"3. Government is pledged, by the proclamation of the 4th July 1802 and 11th July 1805, to con-

[1] Report dated 13th April 1808.

clude a Permanent Settlement with the landholders, at the expiration of the periods there specified, for such lands as may be in a sufficiently improved state of cultivation to warrant the measure, on fair and equitable terms. It was judged expedient, on full consideration of the subject, and with ample knowledge of the circumstances now alleged, to anticipate these periods; and accordingly, in June 1807, the Governor-General in Council notified to the Zemindars and other proprietors, by Regulation x., 1807, that the Jumma assessed for the last year of the ensuing settlement shall remain fixed for ever, if they be willing to engage, and the arrangement shall receive the sanction of the Court of Directors.

"4. The pledge which has thus been solemnly contracted cannot be forfeited without such a glaring violation of promise as would lose us deservedly the confidence of the people. . . .

"9. The argument on which, if I mistake not, the late Commissioners chiefly rely, is that the right of participating in future improvement ought not to be relinquished, because Government is in a manner the landholder and proprietor of a vast estate. . . .

"26. Upon the important occasions of the Permanent Settlement of Bengal and Behar, and of the territories on the coast of Coromandel, and after mature deliberation, a claim of participation in the future improvement of the waste lands was relinquished to a greater extent than the proportion at which they are computed by the late Board of Commissioners in the Ceded and Conquered Provinces.

"27. The happy result of the measure is now witnessed in Bengal. The reviving prosperity of the country, its increased wealth and rapid improvement, are unquestionably due to the Permanent Settlement, the principle of which was so wise that even the serious errors that were committed in filling up the outline of the plan could not ultimately disappoint its views. . . .

"32. I appeal to this experience in preference to any speculative argument. . . . It was expected that the improvement of estates by the culture of waste lands would enrich the landholder by the increase of his usual income, and enable him to meet the variations of seasons and temporary calamities of drought and inundation without needing remissions of revenue.

"33. These expectations have been realised. . . .

"38. It appears to be a very prevalent opinion that the British system of administration is not generally palatable to our Indian subjects. Admitting this opinion to be not unfounded, it follows that while they taste none but the unpalatable parts of the system, and while the only boon which would be acceptable to them is withheld, the landed proprietors, and with them the body of the people, must be more and more estranged from the Government, in proportion to the expectations which they formed, and the disappointment which they will have experienced. . .

"63. I shall conclude by declaring my concurrence in the Commissioners' recommendation, that steadiness, moderation, and justice should be the features borne by the administration of Government. But it is not by abandoning a measure deliberately resolved on, and beneficial to our subjects, that we shall prove our steadiness. It is not by grasping at the highest revenue, and wringing from our peasants the utmost rent, that we shall evince our moderation; nor is it by depriving the sons of our petty landholders of their birthright that we shall demonstrate our sense of justice."[1]

This Minute, together with a similar Minute from

[1] Colebrook's Minute of 1808.

Lumsden, another member of Council, was forwarded by Lord Minto, then Governor-General, to the Court of Directors. And Lord Minto himself was equally explicit in his opinion.

"That on a mature consideration of all the documents connected with the establishment of a Permanent Settlement in the provinces of Bengal, Behar, Orissa, and Benares, and in the territories dependent on the Presidency of Fort St. George, and of all the reports and minutes respecting the proposed Permanent Settlement in the Ceded and Conquered Provinces, he was entirely satisfied of the sound policy, or rather of the urgent necessity, of the measure." [1]

But the Directors had made up their minds. They had been once influenced by circumstances to sacrifice a prospective increase in their profits for the good of a nation. Lord Cornwallis was now dead, and the Directors were never guilty of such generosity again. "Grasping at the highest revenue and wringing from our peasants the utmost rent" was now their policy.

"No settlement," they replied, "shall be declared permanent in Cuttack or in any other of our Provinces till the whole proceedings preparatory to it have been submitted to us, and till your resolutions upon these proceedings have received our sanction and concurrence." Nine months after they again wrote that "the object of the present despatch is to caution you in the most pointed manner against pledging us to the extension of the Bengal fixed assessment to our newly acquired territories." [2]

The Governor-General was taken aback by these despatches. They directed not only the abandonment of a measure absolutely necessary for the good of the people of India, but also the violation of a solemn pledge

[1] Letter dated 15th September 1808.

[2] Despatches of 1st February 1811 and 27th November 1811.

twice made unconditionally to the people, and incorporated in the Regulations of 1803 and 1805. The Proclamation which formed a part of Section 29 of Regulation xxv. of 1803 (for the Ceded Provinces) contained this clause:

"At the end of these ten years, a Permanent Settlement will be concluded with the same persons (if willing to engage, and if no others who have a better claim shall come forward) for such lands as may be in a sufficiently improved state of cultivation to warrant the measure, on such terms as Government shall deem fair and equitable."

And the Proclamation embodied in Regulation ix. of 1805 (for the Conquered Provinces) repeated the pledge in these terms:

"At the end of ten years, expiring with the year 1222 Fusly, a Permanent Settlement will be concluded with the same persons (if willing to engage, and if no other persons having a better claim shall come forward) for such lands as may be in a sufficiently improved state of cultivation to warrant the measure, on such terms as Government shall deem fair and equitable."

These pledges were given unconditionally to the people of India by the responsible servants and agents of the Company, and were therefore binding on the Company. In 1807 the pledge was repeated a third time in Regulation x. of 1807 (for the Ceded and Conquered Provinces), and the condition was then inserted for the first time that the Permanent Settlement shall be made if "the arrangement shall receive the sanction of the Honourable the Court of Directors."

How could these pledges be violated by the mandate of the Directors issued in 1811? "Had the Honourable Court's dissent," wrote the Indian Government in 1812, "to the arrangements established by the Regulations of 1803 and 1805 been signified at an early period after the enaction of those Regulations, the inherent powers of control possessed by the Court might have been urged in support of such dissent, although those Regulations contained no reserve of the Court's approval; but now that the whole term of the contract has expired in the Ceded Provinces, and two-thirds of it in the Conquered Countries, the annulment of it, at this distant period, could not, we apprehend, as already intimated, be reconciled to the dictates either of policy or justice."[1]

And Lord Minto, in a Minute recorded by himself, endeavoured to construe the Directors' recent orders in a restricted sense, as he could not reconcile a literal construction of those orders "with the maintenance of the faith of Government so publicly and so solemnly pledged to the landlords."[2]

One more protest was submitted by Lord Minto against the Directors' orders before he left India in 1813. He pointed out that a Permanent Settlement involved no sacrifice of revenues; that a variable land-tax had been condemned even by Adam Smith, in his *Wealth of Nations*, as a discouragement to improvements in land; that a Permanent Settlement could be effected for the estates actually held by the landlords in Northern India without including the waste lands; and finally, if the object of good government was "to ameliorate generally the conditions of the natives, it is our firm conviction that no arrangement or measure will lend so speedily and effectually to the accomplishment of those important objects as the establishment of a Permanent Settlement."[3]

But the Directors of the Company were obdurate. Their professed desire for the good of the people of India would not move them to surrender their own profits. They had indeed fixed upon a plan of getting out of the pledges given in 1803 and 1805. They

[1] Letter dated 9th October 1812. [2] Minute dated 11th July 1812.
[3] Letter dated 17th July 1813.

suggested an evasion which would not be held valid by any Court of Justice, and which was unworthy of honest merchants, not to speak of the rulers of an empire.

"Continued possession and a punctual discharge of the dues of Government during the triennial leases formed only one part of the condition on which Government pledged itself to a Permanent Settlement with the landholders. There was another and still more important clause in the condition, viz. that the land should, in the interval, be brought to a sufficiently advanced stage of cultivation to warrant us in fixing perpetual limits to our demand upon it. The precise point of improvement at which such a measure might become expedient, or even justifiable, was not determined by the Regulation of 1803 and 1805, and would not, indeed, be determined by any prospective Regulation. The question was left completely open for the future exercise of the judgment of Government; nor is there anything in these Regulations by which its decision can, or ought to be, in the smallest degree fettered."[1]

If this argument had been used in good faith and honesty, it would have led to Permanent Settlements in some advanced estates at once, and delayed them in others. But it was used artfully to evade a pledge, and the pledge was evaded. No Permanent Settlements were made in any estates in 1813, or have been made since.

Lord Moira, afterwards Marquis of Hastings, succeeded Lord Minto as Governor-General of India. His administration is famous in history for the Nepal war, the Pindaree war, and the last Mahratta war, which led to the annexation of the Province of Bombay in 1817. In the midst of these distractions, Lord Hastings was unable for a time to devote his attention to the settlement of Northern India.

[1] Letter dated 16th March 1813.

CHAPTER XI

LORD HASTINGS AND THE MAHALWARI SETTLEMENT IN NORTHERN INDIA (1815–1822)

THE last Mahratta war was over, and the last of the Peshwas was captured in 1818; and Lord Hastings was forced to face the problem of a proper land administration in India, far more difficult to deal with than swarms of the Pindaries or armies of the Mahrattas. The task of conquests and annexations was easy enough, when disciplined troops faced undisciplined hordes in the field of battle. But the story of such conquests is not the history of India; the story of the administration, and of the condition of the people under the new rule, is the true history of the country.

The Board of Commissioners in the Conquered and Ceded Provinces (Northern India), consisting of Sir Edward Colebrooke and Mr. Trant, submitted their report on land settlements in the different districts—Moradabad, Bareilly, Shajehanpur, and Rohilkhand; and they once more pressed that the assessments made should be made permanent.

"We should not fulfil the duty of the station in which it has pleased the Government to place us if we were to abstain from offering it as our decided opinion that the greatest injury cannot but occur to the interests of the British Government in this quarter of its possessions by any longer withholding the benefits of a Permanent Settlement, which have been so long and so anxiously expected by the mass of the population of the Ceded and Conquered Provinces.

"We shall not enter upon any discussion of the advantages of the measure in a fiscal point of view, although we are fully satisfied of them, because we consider the faith of the Government to have been pledged by the promulgation of the two Regulations above quoted, which having been enacted, as we understood, after a full discussion of the question of the Permanent Settlement with the Honourable the Court of Directors, was to be considered as the absolute and final determination of the supreme authorities, both in this country and in Europe. . . .

"We at the same time take the liberty of again expressing our conviction, both individually and collectively, that no measure short of a general permanency to the settlements of the whole of these provinces will meet the expectations of the landholders, founded on what they consider a solemn promise of Government."[1]

In the following year, 1819, a minute was recorded by Mr. Dowdeswell on the same subject on the eve of his retirement from India after a long and distinguished service. And he spoke in no uncertain voice.

"The position, then, which I maintain is, that the faith of Government was irrevocably pledged to the great body of the people to extend to them the benefits of a Permanent Settlement, with the limited exceptions above stated, at the expiration of the term of ten years, reckoning from the period of the cession and conquest respectively. . . .

"It is painful to me to be compelled to state facts and opinions which, I am sensible, cannot prove agreeable to those for whose consideration they are chiefly intended; but the Honourable Court [of Directors] will, I am persuaded, do justice to the motives which actuate me. Had I thought myself free to choose, I

[1] Report dated 27th October 1818.

should most readily have declined the task in which I am at present engaged. It is only because I thought the exposition of my sentiments to be a duty of more than ordinary exigency that I have been led to place them on record. . . .

"It will answer every object which I have at heart if I can aid in showing that the measure would conduce to the best interests of the Government in promoting the agricultural improvement of the country, and more specially in cementing the attachment of the people to the British name and power, without any inordinate sacrifice of the public resources. The landholders, I doubt not, would be fully satisfied to improve their means of subsistence by gradually reclaiming such small portions of land as lie intermixed with those already reduced to a state of cultivation, or in other words, within the limits of a Pergana, Mouza, or other division of an estate for which the settlement might be formed; the rest, as shown in preceding paragraphs, would belong *de jure* to Government. . . .

"On the other hand, I neither deem it wise, just, or politic that Government should gradually so enhance the assessments as to draw from the land the maximum revenue which it can possibly pay. I believe that, generally speaking, the assessment has already been raised as high as is consistent with the well-being of the agricultural classes and the gradual improvement of the country. . . .

"I now quit the subject, in all probability for ever. It is equally a source of pride and satisfaction to me to reflect that I have contributed something towards the internal peace and good order of the country; that I have laboured according to the extent of my means for the improvement and the administration of civil and criminal justice; and that the public resources generally have not suffered from the share I have had in the management of them. Wide, therefore, as the range is, I should scarcely have had a wish ungratified could I have witnessed, previously to quitting the country, the establishment of a Permanent Settlement in the western provinces."[1]

A still more distinguished officer, Sir Edward Colebrooke, was now about to leave India after his forty-two years' useful and distinguished service in the country. And he too made one more endeavour, on the eve of his retirement, to secure to the people of the country some prospect of wealth and of future gain from the soil, against the ever increasing and impoverishing demands of the Court of Directors. With his Minute, recorded in 1820, he submitted a statement showing how the land revenue of the Ceded and Conquered Provinces had been continuously increased during twelve years, from 1807 to 1818; and he recommended the promised limitation of the land revenue demand which would leave "to the land-holders the fruits of their improved industry."[2]

The following figures are taken from Sir Edward Colebrooke's statement, accepting ten Rupees as equivalent to a pound sterling.

Conquered and Ceded Provinces, Northern India.

Year.	Land Revenue.	Gross Revenue.
	£	£
1807	2,008,955	2, 65,396
1808	2,042,347	2,304,004
1809	2,254,791	2,579,949
1810	2,392,852	2,782,643
1811	2,414,737	2,741,728
1812	2,274,709	2,646,858
1813	2,508,681	2,931,905
1814	2,502,223	2,815,579
1815	2,483,133	2,891,045
1816	2,665,667	3,130,853
1817	2,626,761	2,926,923
1818	2,892,789	3,262,366

[1] Minute dated 7th October 1819.
[2] Minute dated 17th March 1820.

In a later Minute, recorded in the same year, Sir Edward Colebrooke made his last recommendation for securing the prosperity of the people of India among whom he had lived so long.

"On the eve of finally quitting a country in which I have resided forty-two years, and a service in which, through the early partiality of the late Warren Hastings in selecting me for Persian Secretary to Government so long ago as the beginning of 1780, I have borne an efficient and responsible part from the age of eighteen, I should feel a true satisfaction if, by the last act of my official existence, I could flatter myself in having contributed to secure the blessings of a limited assessment to that portion of the British territories in which the last twelve years of an active life have been employed. . . . I cannot, however, forget that to the general character of the landholders of those provinces I am indebted for the success of my labours, and common gratitude, if even my conviction of the propriety of the measure were less strong, might dictate this return."

A noble sentiment this, but futile. The loyal and peaceful character of the Indian people has never induced the Government to abate its own pecuniary demands; it has often had the contrary effect of encouraging the Government to enhance its demands till the people became impoverished and resourceless, in spite of the peace and security secured by the British rule, and in spite of the thrift and industry of the people, and the richness and fertility of their land.

Armed with the Reports and Minutes of the Board of Commissioners, of Mr. Dowdeswell and Sir Edward Colebrooke, as well as of Messrs. Stuart, Adam, and Fendall, the Governor-General, Lord Hastings, made his final appeal to the Court of Directors for that measure of Permanent Settlement, which had been solemnly promised by the British Government, and which was needed for the prosperity of the people.

"It is, then, our unanimous opinion, that the system of a Permanent Settlement of the land revenue, either upon the principle of a fixed Jumma, or of an assessment determinable by a fixed and invariable rate, ought to be extended to the Ceded and Conquered Provinces."[1]

The Directors of a trading company, now owners of an empire, refused the proposals of Lord Hastings with a curtness which betrayed how little real regard they entertained for the happiness of the people when their own pecuniary interests were concerned.

"We must again pointedly apprise you that we are not prepared to assent to the opinion to which, you say, you have unanimously come, 'that the system of a Permanent Settlement of the land revenue, either upon the principle of a fixed Jumma, or of an assessment determinable by a fixed and invariable rate, ought to be extended to the Ceded and Conquered Provinces;' and we distinctly repeat the injunction contained in the eighty-sixth paragraph of our letter in this department, dated the 15th January 1819, against any Permanent Settlement of land revenue; and we desire that you will abstain not only from making any such settlement, but from taking any measures which may raise the expectation that a settlement in perpetuity will hereafter be formed."[2] The controversy was thus closed for forty years.

Holt Mackenzie, then Secretary to the Board, had in the meantime recorded his famous Minute of 1819,

[1] Revenue Letter to the Court of Directors, signed by the Governor-General, Lord Hastings, and members of his Council, Messrs. Stuart, Adam, and Fendall, dated 16th September 1820.

[2] Revenue Letter from the Court of Directors to the Governor-General in Council, dated 1st August 1821.

revealing the existence of Village Communities in Northern India, and recommending a settlement with these communities where they existed, after a systematic survey and inquiry.[1] The Minute contained a review of the different districts and suggested that the villages should now be surveyed, that a record of rights be prepared, and that Village Communities should be represented by head-men who should be called Lambardars, or persons having a "number" in the Collector's register of persons liable to pay land revenue to the State. It was also suggested that the rates of assessment should be equalised rather than enhanced; and that revenue payers should have their rights secured such as they were.

All ideas of a Permanent Settlement being abandoned in 1821, the minute of Holt Mackenzie was accepted as the basis of settlement. The idea was that settlements should be made with landlords where they existed, and with Village Communities where they held land in common tenancy. And it was specially desired that the land tax should be fixed at a moderate rate. This was particularly insisted upon in the Government Resolution of 1822.

"87. It appears, indeed, that the ancient Hindu laws assigned to the Sovereign a certain and moderate share of the produce. But if we judge of the practice of ancient times by that of more modern Hindu principalities, it may apparently be assumed that the actual sums levied from the cultivators were by no means always limited by the nominal rates. . . .

"88. So also in the Moghal system as described by Mr. Grant, who states the ordinary money rates to have been fixed by an average valuation of one-fourth of the produce. . . .

"93. On the whole, indeed, his Lordship in Council is disposed to conclude that although the

[1] Minute dated 1st July 1819.

native governments to which we succeeded allowed considerable weight to ancient customs, even in adjusting their pecuniary demands, and though in later days especially, they were too weak to enforce all that they might regard as their just dues, yet that (subject to the general obligation of consulting the case of the Ryots) the right of the ruling power to fix the rate of its demand was never questioned. . . .

"101. In the case of Government especial caution is necessary to guard against an excessive demand; for there must always be great danger lest, while we imagine that we take only a share of the *net* rent, we in fact encroach on the fair wages of labour and profits of stock. . . .

"129. When the rates of rent payable by the cultivators are settled, it will remain to determine the nature and extent of the advantages to be assigned to the intermediate managers and others [landlords], and the manner and proportion in which the *net* rent and profits arising out of the limitation of the Government demand is to be distributed. . . .

"373. His Lordship in Council has derived much satisfaction from the evidence afforded on other occasions, that the native revenue officers have a lively sense of the distinction of honorary rewards. That feeling it is most important to cherish, and it can never be the wish of Government to practise, in regard to any class of public functionaries, the fallacious economy which leaves to officers invested with extensive trust the alternative of poverty or dishonour.[1]

A week after the date of this Resolution was passed Regulation vii. of 1822, "declaring the principles according to which settlement of the land revenue in the Ceded and Conquered Provinces, including Cuttack, Pattaspore, and its dependencies, is to be hereafter made."

[1] Resolution of Government dated 1st August 1822.

The revision of the settlement was to be made village by village and estate by estate, and as an estate is called a Mahal in the Indian language, the settlement which was made in Northern India is known as the *Mahalwari Settlement.* The revenue demand was not to be raised in any estate unless it was clear that the landlords' profits exceeded one-fifth of that demand. In such cases "the assessment shall be so regulated as to leave the Zemindars and others aforesaid a net profit of twenty per cent. of the amount of the Jumma," or revenue demand. Thus in an estate with a rental of £1200, the State-demand was to be raised to £1000, so as to leave to the landlord £200, or one-fifth of the State-demand. The State-demand was thus to be over 83 per cent. of the rental of estates.

Revenue Collectors were empowered to grant leases to cultivators, specifying the rents payable by them. In cases in which estates were held not by landlords but by cultivators in common tenancy, the State-demand might be raised to 95 per cent. of the rents, *i.e.* to the entire rental "with a deduction of 5 per cent. on account of Malikana, or such other rate not being less than 5 per cent. as Government may determine." In such cases the Revenue Collector was empowered to make a fresh partition of the lands of the village, or of the proportion of the State-demand payable by each cultivator.

Revenue Collectors might be empowered to try suits between landlords and tenants, to determine the rents payable, to adjust accounts between them, and to decide all matters connected with lands, rents, leases, and engagements between landlords and tenants. An appeal was allowed from the decision of the Collector to the Board, and finally by a regular suit in Civil Courts.[1]

[1] Regulation vii. of 1822.

N

Such was the first comprehensive Land Act of Northern India, passed twenty years after Northern India was ceded to or conquered by the British; and a careful examination of its clauses discloses its defects. The Act prescribed no equitable standard of rents payable by cultivators except the judgment of the Revenue Collector. It prescribed no equitable margin of profits to landlords except a bare 17 per cent. of the rental. In curious contrast to frequent professions "to guard against an excessive demand," and to "take only a share of the net rent," it swept away virtually the whole of the rental of the country, leaving landlords and cultivators equally impoverished. It made any accumulation of wealth and any improvement in the material condition of the people impossible; and it fixed no limits to the State-demand in future and recurring settlements after the brief period of the first settlement was over.

The system broke down ultimately by reason of its own harshness. Some relief was at last given to the people of Northern India in 1833 by the best and greatest of the Company's Governor-Generals, Lord William Bentinck. To an account of the Land Settlement of 1833 we shall revert in a future chapter.

CHAPTER XII

ECONOMIC HISTORY OF SOUTHERN INDIA (1800)

In the preceding chapters we have dwelt on the history of Land Settlements in Bengal, Madras, and Northern India. We have seen that everywhere the local authorities pressed for a Permanent Settlement of the land revenues. In Bengal a Permanent Zemindari Settlement was made in 1793, and this was extended to Benares in 1895. In Madras a Permanent Zemindari Settlement was made in the Northern Circars and elsewhere between 1802 and 1805, and then there was a change in the policy of the Directors. Thomas Munro recommended a Permanent Ryotwari Settlement, and the Board of Revenue recommended a Permanent Village Settlement; a Ryotwari Settlement was made, but it was not declared permanent. In Northern India Lord Wellesley pledged the faith of the British Government in 1803 and 1805 to conclude a Permanent Zemindari Settlement, and Lord Minto and Lord Hastings pressed the Directors to redeem this pledge. The Directors broke the pledge and ordered a Mahalwari Settlement, not permanent.

Such is the history of Land Settlements in India during the second period of British rule in India. The first generation of British rulers—the generation of Clive and Warren Hastings—settled nothing; they were bewildered by the land question, and their harsh and ever-changing methods ended in oppression and failure. The second generation—that of Cornwallis and Wellesley and Lord Hastings—gave a *Permanent*

Zemindari Settlement to Bengal, Benares, and the Northern Circars; a *Ryotwari Settlement, not declared permanent,* to the newer acquisitions in Madras; and a *Mahalwari Settlement, not permanent,* to the Ceded and Conquered Provinces of Northern India.

We shall pause now in the course of our narrative to examine the economic condition of the people of India at the commencement of the nineteenth century. It is necessary to examine somewhat minutely how the people of India lived, and tilled their fields, and produced their manufactures, what incomes and wages were earned by men, what employment occupied the women. No study is more interesting and instructive in the history of nations than the study of the material condition of the people from age to age. And, fortunately, we have in the valuable works of Dr. Francis Buchanan—the first statistical inquirer employed by the British Government in India—some detailed information concerning the occupations and industries of the people of India.

On the 24th February 1800, Lord Wellesley, then Governor-General of India, directed Dr. Francis Buchanan, a medical officer in the employment of the East India Company, to make a journey through Southern India; with a view to make economic inquiries into the condition of the people and their agriculture and manufactures. Dr. Buchanan travelled from Madras territory into the Karnatic, Mysore, Coimbatur, Malabar, and Canara, and the diary of his journey and the results of his inquiries were published in London in 1807, in three quarto volumes. This work will be our guide in the present chapter, which deals with the condition of the people of Southern India in 1800. The later inquiries of Dr. Buchanan in Northern India will be dealt with in the next chapter.

THE JAIGIR OF MADRAS.

On the 23rd April 1800, Dr. Buchanan left Madras on his tour of statistical inquiry. There was little waste land in the immediate vicinity of Madras, and the soil produced a good crop of rice if the rainfall was sufficient. In some places the people irrigated their fields from old tanks and reservoirs, and these fields were covered with rice. Charitable people had built Choultries or inns on the wayside for the free accommodation of travellers.

Further on, the road westward passed through a country "at present naked," but showing some signs of improvement in the shape of plantations of cocoa-nut palms. At Condaturu the country assumed a different and pleasing aspect, and Dr. Buchanan saw one of those old Hindu irrigation works for which Southern India was always famous. It was a large reservoir formed by shutting up with an artificial bank an opening between two natural ridges of ground. The sheet of water was seven or eight miles in length and three in width, and was let out in numerous small canals to irrigate fields in the dry season. In the rains it was replenished from the Chir Nadi; there were sluices at different places twenty or thirty feet wide; and these sluices were fortified by stones, placed in a sloping direction, to let out the superfluous water. The reservoir could irrigate the lands of thirty-two villages during a drought of eighteen months. "In a country liable to famine from want of rain," wrote Dr. Buchanan, "a reservoir such as this is of inestimable value."

Further westward, between Condaturu and Sri-Parmaturu, the country was poor and overrun with low prickly bushes. There was little cultivation, and in most places a crop would not be worth the seed. Palms and wild dates grew, however, on the soil almost spontaneously, and the former produced drinks in the shape of Tari and Jagari.

At Sri-Parmaturu there was another old reservoir which irrigated the fields of the village containing over two thousand acres of rice lands. Beyond this spot the land was again bare and barren, and there was very little cultivation, until Dr. Buchanan came to the ancient Hindu capital of Kanchi, now called Conjeveram.

Conjeveram boasted of a large old reservoir which irrigated many fields covered with a thriving crop of rice. The Dewan of Nawab Mahomed Ali had also constructed a fine tank lined all round with cut granite, which descended to the bottom in steps. Choultries or inns were also built of granite on the sides of the tanks for the shelter of travellers, and the pillars were elaborately carved.

Conjeveram was a large town and regularly built, but was not populous. Many of the buildings were unoccupied, and the houses were only one storey high. They had mud walls and were roofed with tiles, and were built in the form of a square with a court in the centre. The streets were wide and clean and crossed each other at right angles, and on each side there was a row of cocoanut trees. Most of the Brahmans of the place were the followers either of Sankara-Acharya or of Ramanuja-Acharya. The former lived in the ninth century and was a rigid Vedantist, resolving all universe into the one Primal Soul. The latter lived in the eleventh century and was a more popular Vedantist, inculcating the faith of a Personal God. In modern times, the doctrines of Sankara are often identified with the cult of Siva, while those of Ramanuja blend themselves with the cult of Vishnu.

After leaving Conjeveram, Dr. Buchanan found the country once more a desert till he came to Damerlu, the last village in the Jaigir of Madras. A canal from the Palar river irrigated much valuable rice land between Damerlu and Oulur. At Oulur the soil was good but was fit only for dry grains, and bushes and trees grew in the midst of fields.

On the whole the Jaigir of Madras, which had been in the possession of the East India Company for half a century, was not in a flourishing condition. Frequent wars, a heavy land-tax, and the diversion of the revenues from possible local improvements to the purchase of the Company's Investments, left the country poor and the population sparse. At Condaturu the Collector, Mr. Place, had repaired the old reservoir during his administration, and had augmented the land-tax considerably. But long stretches of the country remained unirrigated, uncultivated, and sparsely populated—"a desert," as Dr. Buchanan calls it.

THE KARNATIC.

Lord Wellesley had not yet annexed the Karnatic when Dr. Buchanan travelled through the country, and it was therefore still nominally under the Nawab of Arcot, though virtually under the administration of the servants of the Company.

On his way to Arcot, Dr. Buchanan saw another splendid old Hindu reservoir, called the Kaveri-Pak. The reservoir "is about eight miles long and three broad, and fertilises a considerable extent of country. I never viewed a public work with more satisfaction, a work that supplies a great body of people with every comfort which their moral situation will permit them to enjoy."

The road from Kaveri-Pak to Arcot was bad, and scarcely fit for wheel-carriage. People travelled, however, on bullock carts, and Mahomedan women sometimes rode bullocks, wrapped in white veils. The city of Arcot was extensive, and produced coarse cotton fabrics. The houses were about as good as in the towns of the Madras Jaigir. The hills in the vicinity were barren, composed of granite rapidly decaying. The country between Arcot and the western hills contained some good land which served for gardens and dry grains, while others were altogether barren.

The road westward from Arcot to Vellore, and from Vellore to Paligonda, lay along the valley of the Palar river, and the country was fertile and verdant. The fort of Vellore was large and beautiful, and the town was also large and built in the Hindu fashion. The villages along the road were, however, poor and miserable, and some of them in ruins. The people of Paligonda procured water from the Palar river by digging canals in the sand six or seven feet deep. The water was then conveyed by other canals to irrigate the fields, and thus rendered the valley of Vellore the finest tract of country in the Karnatic.

BARAMAHAL.

Dr. Buchanan then ascended the Eastern Ghats and reached Venkatagiri in Baramahal on the 4th May. The country had been settled by Thomas Munro some years before, and reminded Dr. Buchanan of England by its swells and undulations. As far as he could judge, one-half of the country had been ploughed, while the remainder was copse land and served for pasture. Iron was smelted from ores and black sand, and common salt was found in many parts of the country. The soil was reddish ferruginous clay intermixed with quartz and granite, and walls of huts in towns and villages were built of this mud, and were smoothed and painted with alternate vertical broad stripes of white and red. In some places the flat roofs of the houses were also terraced with this mud.

Eastern Mysore.

Dr. Buchanan now entered into the territory of the Raja of Mysore, who had been placed on the throne by Lord Wellesley after the fall of Tipu Sultan in the preceding year. He found Waluru a large town with a weekly fair, and manufacturing coarse cotton cloths much of which was exported. Coarse blankets, known as Curnlies, were also largely manufactured in the neighbouring villages. The arable lands amounted to seven-tenths of the whole, and perhaps a twentieth part of them was irrigated. Rice grew on the banks of the Pennar river. Fields were manured by women who carried the manure in baskets, and were ploughed by buffaloes and oxen.

On the 10th May, Dr. Buchanan arrived at Bangalore, which had been constructed by Haidar Ali as a frontier fortress after the best fashion of Mahomedan military architecture, and had been destroyed by his son, Tipu Sultan, who found it useless against the valour of British troops. The gardens were extensive and divided into square plots, the cypress and vine grew luxuriantly in that climate, the apple and the peach produced fruits, and some pine and oak plants introduced from the Cape of Good Hope were thriving. The arable land in the vicinity of Bangalore did not exceed four-tenths of the country, and the small proportion of irrigated land, formerly under cultivation, was mostly waste, owing to the neglect of the reservoirs during the recent wars. Tipu Sultan had received the kingdom in a flourishing state from Haidar Ali, of whom all people spoke to Dr. Buchanan in terms of high praise. But the oppressions or wars of Tipu had caused much misery, and had driven four-tenths of the cultivators from their home and country.

On the 18th May, Dr. Buchanan presented his credentials at Seringapatam, then the capital of the

Mysore Raja. On the following day he had an interview with Purnea, the famous Hindu minister whose administration received the highest commendation from General Wellesley (afterwards Duke of Wellington), and from every other Englishman in India who came in contact with him. Purnea had enjoyed much authority even under Tipu Sultan, and might have saved him if he had listened to his counsels. After the fall of Tipu, he became the virtual ruler of Mysore under the new Raja.

Seringapatam, which had a population of perhaps 150,000 under Tipu Sultan, was now reduced to a miserable state by the wars, and had scarcely more than 32,000 people. The district on the north bank of the Kaveri was called Pattana Ashta-gram, while that to the south of the river was known as Mahasura Ashta-gram. The country rose gradually on both sides of the river, was naturally fertile, and was irrigated by a noble system of canals sending out branches to water the intermediate spaces. The water of the Kaveri river was forced into the sources of these canals by anicuts or dams, formed of large blocks of granite at a great expense. Dr. Buchanan does not tell us if these useful and noble works were constructed by Haidar Ali or by his Hindu predecessors; but during the wars of Tipu Sultan very great damage was done; temples, villages, and dams were broken down, and canals were choked. Under the administration of Purnea, however, agriculture and industries were reviving. "Everything wears an aspect of beginning restoration. The villages are rebuilding, the canals are clearing, and in place of antelopes and forest guards, we have the peaceful bullock returning to his useful labour."[1]

The manner of reaping and preserving rice in Mysore has been minutely described. Water was let

[1] Buchanan's *Journey from Madras*, &c. (London, 1807), vol. i. p. 83.

off from the rice fields a week before the reaping, and the rice was then cut down, about four inches from the ground, and stacked with the ears inwards. After another week it was spread on the threshing-floor and trodden out by bullocks, and then put up in heaps containing 60 Kandakas or 334 bushels. Each heap was marked with clay and covered with straw, and so left for twenty or thirty days till the division between the cultivator and the Government. The cultivators then stored their share in various different ways. Some kept it in narrow shafts, about 24 feet deep, in hard, stony soil, the floor, sides, and roof being lined with straw, and each pit containing 84 to 168 bushels. Others stored it in store-houses, strongly floored with planks. Others again stored it in cylinders made of clay, the mouth being covered by an inverted pot, and the rice being drawn out from a hole in the bottom when required. Lastly, some cultivators stored their rice in bags made of straw. Besides rice, Mung, sesamum, and sugar-cane were grown near Seringapatam. Ragi was extensively cultivated in dry fields, and supplied the lower classes of people with their common food; and Jowar and Bajra were the next most important dry corns.

Each farm near Seringapatam consisted generally of two or three ploughs of land. One plough was a poor stock, while the possessor of four or five was a great farmer. With five ploughs a man cultivated about 12½ acres of wet land and 25 acres of dry field. The farmer or cultivator was not turned out of his holding "so long as he pays his customary rent. Even in the reign of Tipu such an act would have been looked upon as an astonishing grievance." On the other hand, the Government which received the rent was "bound to keep the canals and tanks in repair." [1] The pay of farm labourers near Seringapatam was

[1] Buchanan's *Journey from Madras*, &c., vol i. p. 124.

6s. 8½d. a month, while away from the town it was 5s. 4d. a month. Women often worked in the fields and carried manure in baskets on their heads. They were generally well dressed, and elegantly formed; "I have never seen finer forms," says Dr. Buchanan, "than even the labouring women of that country frequently possess. Their necks and arms are, in particular, remarkably well shaped."[1]

On the 6th June, Dr. Buchanan left Seringapatam on his way back to Bangalore. At Mundium he found the rice land irrigated entirely from tanks and reservoirs. At Maduru he found a large reservoir, said to have been built by Vishnu Vardhana Raya seven hundred years before. It received a supply from the neighbouring river by means of a dam and a canal, and when in proper repair was capable of irrigating all the neighbouring fields, under the level of its bank, throughout the year. At Chinapattam, formerly the residence of a Polygar family known as Jasadeva Rayas, glass and ornamental rings, steel wires for musical instruments, pure white sugar, and various other commodities were manufactured. Ramagiri was the next important place on the way, but had grievously suffered by Lord Cornwallis's invasion of Mysore in 1792, and a large proportion of the inhabitants had perished of hunger. At Magadi the road passed through a wild and romantic country, consisting of low hills and valleys cultivated with dry grains. Valuable timber and bamboos grew near Savana-durga, which Lord Cornwallis had taken by assault, and had been deserted ever since. Iron was smelted in the neighbouring hills, and was repeatedly forged and purified for being wrought into instruments of husbandry, and steel was manufactured for weapons. Sandal-wood and much valuable timber was grown in the neighbourhood, and the lac insect was reared

[1] Buchanan's *Journey from Madras*, &c., vol i. p. 135

for that famous dye which used to be one of the best-known products of India from olden times. On the 21st June Dr. Buchanan reached Bangalore.

Bangalore had possessed a large trade and extensive manufactures under Haidar Ali. Tipu Sultan had foolishly forbidden all commerce, both with the Nizam's Dominions and with the Karnatic, and the trade of Bangalore had declined; but the place was again rising in importance after the restoration of the Hindu dynasty. Poona merchants brought shawls and saffron and musk from Kashmir and pearls from Surat; Burhanpur traders imported chintz and gold lace, cloth and thread; red cotton cloth, flowered with gold and silver, came from the Nizam's Dominions; and salt, tin, lead, copper, and European goods came from the Karnatic. The exports from Bangalore were chiefly betel-nut, sandal-wood, pepper, cardamoms, and tamarinds. A vast quantity of blankets and cotton-wool was also imported.

Goods were transported by cattle in loads. In one year, 1500 bullock-loads of cotton wool, 50 bullock-loads of cotton thread, 230 bullock-loads of raw silk, 7000 bullock-loads of salt, and 300 bullock-loads of foreign goods were imported; while 4000 bullock-loads of betel-nut and 400 bullock-loads of pepper were exported. Cotton weavers made cloths for home use, and silk weavers prepared a rich strong fabric. The silks were dyed red with lac, or orange colour with Capili-podi, or yellow with turmeric. Workmen who made cotton cloths with silk borders earned 8d. a day, and those who made silk cloth earned 6d. Weavers obtained advances from merchants, and sold their goods to merchants or to private customers, never carrying them to public markets. Various kinds of white muslins were manufactured, and had a considerable sale. Women of all castes, except Brahmans, bought cotton wool at weekly markets, spun them at home, and sold the thread to weavers. And thus people of all classes—men and women—found in spinning and weaving a profitable occupation.

Indigo was considerably used for dyeing; the tanning of leather was a paying industry; and castor oil, cocoanut oil, sesamum oil, and various other oils, were largely manufactured and sold.

In a village near Bangalore Dr. Buchanan was informed that merchants often advanced money to the cultivators to pay their rents, and were afterwards content to receive one-half of the crop for the advance and for interest. The system of division of crops in a Village Community, described by Dr. Buchanan, is interesting. A heap of grain, consisting on the average of twenty Kandakas or 2400 Seers (about 4800 lbs.), was thus divided—

	Seers.
Village priests	5
Village charity	5
Village astrologer	1
Village Brahman	1
Village barber	2
Village potter	2
Village blacksmith	2
Village washerman	2
Village measurer	4
Village beadle	7
Village chief	8
Village accountant	10
Village watchman	10
Village accountant	45
Village chief	45
Conductor of water	20
	169

Thus a payment of 5¼ per cent. of the produce of the fields secured to the villagers the professional services of the barber, the potter and the blacksmith, the priest and the astrologer. Of the remainder, the Deshmukh or Zemindar claimed 10 per cent.; and the balance was divided equally between the Government and the farmer. When Haidar Ali abolished the Deshmukhs, he claimed their share also for the Government.[1]

NORTHERN MYSORE.

Leaving Bangalore on the 3rd July, Dr. Buchanan made a long and circuitous tour through the northern portions of Mysore. In the country round Colar he found the lands watered entirely by means of the reservoirs, often excavated by private individuals, while the larger ones were excavated at the expense of the Government. The old Hindu rate of revenue, laid down in the ancient law-books, was one-sixth or one-eighth or one-twelfth the produce; and when rulers and chiefs in Southern India claimed so large a share as one-half the produce, they made cultivation possible by excavating and maintaining vast irrigation works at their own cost, and they took their share in kind, not in money.

Rice, sugar-cane, betel-leaf, and vegetables were grown on wet lands at Colar, and the quantity of rice grown was nearly equal to that of the dry crop Ragi. Poppy was also plentifully cultivated, both for making opium and on account of the seed which was used for sweet cakes. The quantity of wheat grown was about one-half of the rice. Farm servants got 29¼ bushels of grain and 13s. 5d. annually; the rate for day-labourers was about 3d. for men and 2d. for women.

Both Colar and Silagutta had suffered greatly under Tipu Sultan's arbitrary rule and frequent wars, but were reviving after his fall. Cotton cloths of various kinds were the most important manufactures. Travelling westwards, Dr. Buchanan came to the famous Nandi-Durga, in the vicinity of which the Northern Pennar, the Palar, and the Southern Pennar all take their rise. The country beyond the hills was desolate, one-third

1 Buchanan's *Journey from Madras*, &c., vol. i. p. 265 *et seq.*

of what had been formerly cultivated was waste, and villages were deserted since the invasion of Lord Cornwallis. The people said they had suffered from five great evils—the failure of rain, the three invading armies, and the defending army of Mysore!

On the 18th July, Dr. Buchanan came to the great Balapura, which had become an independent State under its Polygar Narayan Swami on the dissolution of the Vijainagar kingdom in the sixteenth century. The State, however, had subsequently fallen under the power of the Moghal and the Mahratta, the Nizam and Haidar Ali; and had finally passed under the administration of the restored Hindu dynasty. It imported chintz and muslin, and exported sugar.

Further to the west was Madhu-giri, which had also become the seat of an independent Polygar on the fall of the Vijainagar kingdom, but had since passed under the rule of Mysore. Haidar Ali had improved the fortifications of the hill, and turned it into a considerable mart with a hundred families of weavers. The place had declined under Tipu Sultan, and finally ruined by the wars of Mysore with the Mahrattas and with Lord Cornwallis. Rice and Ragi, sugar-cane and wheat, cotton, pulses, sesamum, and various kitchen vegetables were grown here when Dr. Buchanan visited the place. Dry soil, fit for Ragi, paid a rent of 1s. 1d. to 3s. 4d. the acre. If irrigated, it paid 9s. to 11s. an acre. The cultivator had a claim to his lands, and could reclaim them even after an absence of years. If, in the meantime, the temporary tenant had made improvements, the original cultivator was required to pay for them. A labouring man earned 4s. a month, and a woman 3s. 4d. There was frequent scarcity in this part of the country owing to failure of rain, but seldom any famine causing loss of life. "It is when war is joined to scarcity, and interrupts the transportation of grain, that famine produces all its horrors. These were never so severely felt here as during the invasion of Lord Cornwallis; when the country being attacked on all sides, and penetrated in every direction by hostile armies, or by defending ones little less destructive, one-half at least of the inhabitants perished of absolute want."[1]

On the 31st July Dr. Buchanan reached Sira, which was a large and prosperous town under the Moghals with 50,000 houses, and therefore a population of a quarter of a million. It then passed under the rule of Haidar Ali, and was ruined by the Mahratta invasions and the oppressions of Tipu Sultan. Rice and Ragi, wheat and sugar-cane, pulses and cotton, were the principal produce. Rent was paid sometimes in money and sometimes in a share of the crops. Betel-nut, pepper, sandal-wood, and spices were imported into Sira, while blankets, cloths, oil, butter, ginger, and cocoa-nuts were exported. A thin, coarse muslin and certain varieties of thick cloths were the principal manufactures.

Retracing his steps to Madhu-giri, Dr. Buchanan made some inquiries as to the famous cattle of the place, and found that every town and village in that hilly country had herds of breeding cattle. The Goalas or cowherds lived in small villages near the skirts of the woods, cultivated a little ground, and sold the produce of their dairy in the towns. Every family paid a small tax of four shillings a year to the Government, or rather to the Beni Chavedi or butter-officer, who paid an annual revenue to the Government. Iron was smelted and steel was manufactured at Madhu-giri and many neighbouring districts.

Travelling southwards, Dr. Buchanan found the fields well cultivated at Tavina-Karay, but saw much waste land at Tumkuru; and all the villages were fortified. Ragi was largely grown here, but there

[1] Buchanan's *Journey from Madras*, &c., vol. i. p. 390.

were also many rice fields. Gubi, further south, was a mart of some importance with 154 shops and a weekly fair. Coarse cotton cloth, both white and coloured, blankets, sackcloth, betel-nut, cocoa-nut, tamarind, grains, lac, iron, and steel from all the country round were sold at this mart.

Dora-Guda had iron mines, and Taniva-Karay was a place of importance with an outer and inner fort and an open suburb with 700 houses. It formerly belonged to a powerful family of Polygars, and one of them had built four temples and four great reservoirs for the irrigation of lands. The country round was once completely cultivated, but had been desolate since the invasion of the Mahrattas under Parasuram Bhao. Further south was Beluru, where there was a good deal of fine rice ground, as well as a fine reservoir. The whole of the country between Beluru in the north to Seringapatam in the south—a distance of forty miles as the crow flies—had been laid waste at the time of the invasion of Cornwallis in 1792; and the people had been forced by Tipu Sultan to leave the open country and retire to the woods, where they lived in huts and procured provisions as best they could. A large proportion of them had perished of hunger, and the country was only half populated even in 1800, when Dr. Buchanan visited it.

Not far from Beluru was the district of Naga-Mangala, where each Gauda or village-head partly rented his village and partly collected on the public account. The cultivators had a fixed property in the land, and so long as they paid rents according to the old valuation, they could not be turned out of possession. The rice ground paid its rent by a division of crops, and the dry field paid a money rent.

Mail-Kotay, about fifteen miles north of Seringapatam, was finely situated on a high hill, commanding a noble view of the valley of the Kaveri and the hills of

Mysore in the south, of the Ghats in the west, and of Savana-Durga and Siva-Ganga in the east. It was a famous place of Hindu worship with a temple of great dimensions surrounded by a colonnade; and the fine large tank was surrounded by many buildings for the accommodation of travellers. It is said that even Tipu Sultan was afraid of seizing the jewels of this temple; they were kept in the treasury at Seringapatam; and the British troops spared them when they captured that capital.

At Tonuru, to the south of Mail-Kotay, Dr. Buchanan saw the magnificent reservoir of Yadava-Nadi, ascribed to the famous religious reformer Ramanuja who lived in the eleventh century. "Two mountain torrents here had united their streams, and forced a way through a gap between two rocky hills. Ramanuja stopped up this gap by a mound, said to be 78 cubits high, 150 long, and at the base 250 cubits thick. The superfluous water is let off by a channel which has been cut with great labour through one of the hills, at such length as to enable it to water a great deal of the subjacent plain which is three or four miles in extent. When the reservoir is full it contains a sufficient quantity of water to supply the cultivators for two years."[1]

On the 1st September Dr. Buchanan returned to Seringapatam.

SOUTHERN MYSORE.

Leaving Seringapatam on the 5th September, Dr. Buchanan made a tour through the southern parts of Mysore. Near Pal-Hully, which had been entirely destroyed at the recent war, he saw the two canals from the Kaveri river which irrigated the district of Mahasura-Ashtagram. One of these canals contained a fine stream which never became entirely dry, and

[1] Buchanan's *Journey from Madras*, &c., vol. ii. pp. 82, 83.

which enabled the cultivators to have a crop of rice even in the dry season.

The Lakshman-Tirtha river, a tributary of the Kaveri, rises from the hills of Coorg. Six canals were constructed from this river to irrigate the country, and dams which forced the water into the canals were fine works and produced beautiful cascades. The whole land formerly irrigated by these canals was about 18,000 acres.

There were no hereditary Gaudas or village-chiefs in these parts, and the revenue was collected by renters, who could not take from the cultivators more than was fixed by the custom established by the old Mysore Rajas. Haidar Ali had appointed Harkaras, or superintendents of land revenue, who kept the renters in check, and listened to the complaints of the people. Tipu Sultan had abolished the Harkaras, with the effect that the people were oppressed and the Government defrauded.

Further west, the country had been depopulated first by the invasion of Baji Rao and his Mahrattas in 1761, and then by the invasion of Cornwallis in 1792. Priya-Pattan, called Periapatam in the English maps, was a place of great importance in olden days, and had belonged to a Polygar family called Nandi Raj. This family held the territory bounded by the Kaveri on the north and the Coorg frontier on the west, and yielding an annual revenue of £9361 to the Rajas of Coorg. It is said that a Polygar prince of this family defended himself gallantly against Mysore about 1640, and finding further resistance impossible, killed his women and children, and perished, sword in hand, in the midst of his enemies. Priya-Pattan continued after this to be the scene of frontier wars between Coorg and Mysore; suffered when Tipu Sultan conquered Coorg; and was utterly destroyed by Tipu's wars with the British.

"Tigers," says Dr. Buchanan, "have taken entire possession of its ruins, a horse that strayed in a few nights ago was destroyed, and even at midday it is considered as dangerous for a solitary person to enter. It was deemed imprudent for me, who was followed by a multitude, to enter into any of the temples, which serve the tigers as shelter from the heat of the day." [1]

The wet lands near Priya-Pattan were entirely irrigated from reservoirs, but in the southern parts of the district canals from the Lakshman-Tirtha river afforded water to the cultivators. The Hainu or wet rice, Karu or dry rice, sugar-cane, ragi, horse grain, pulses, sesamum and other crops were grown in this district. Farm labourers got from £1 to £1, 7s. a year besides one meal a day; and women labourers got 6s. a year besides two meals a day. Before the last Mysore war the poorest cultivator had two ploughs, and the richer ones had fifteen. A man who had two ploughs often possessed forty oxen and fifty cows, six or seven buffaloes, and one hundred sheep or goats. The produce of wet lands was equally divided between the Government and the cultivator after the village dues had been paid. There were extensive palm gardens before the war, and the pasture was good. Sandal-wood grew in the skirts of the forest.

South-east from Priya-Pattan, near Hanagodu, Dr. Buchanan saw one of the dams of the Lakshman-Tirtha river. "Advantage has been taken of a natural ledge of rocks which cross the channel, and stones have been thrown in to fill up the deficiencies. The whole now forms a fine dam, over which rushes a cascade about 100 yards long and 14 feet high, which in a verdant and finely wooded country looks remarkably well. This dam sends off

[1] Buchanan's *Journey from Madras*, &c., vol. ii. p. 96.

its canal to the eastward. . . . The ground irrigated will amount to 2678 acres."[1]

South-east from Hanagadu lay the old kingdom of Hegodu Deva, who was said to have cleared this country and peopled it about the beginning of the fifteenth century. Down to the time of Haidar Ali the town contained a thousand houses; there were only eighty when Dr. Buchanan visited it. The district was famous for its sandal-wood, while Mota-Beta, further to the east, was known for its rich iron ores.

On the 1st October Dr. Buchanan reached Taiuru on the Kampini river, a tributary of the Kaveri. In some villages of this district the Gaudas or village-chiefs were hereditary, and they were preferred, both by the Government and by the people, to the mere renters who also went by the same name. The hereditary Gaudas were better acquainted with the cultivators, were more cheerfully obeyed, and had greater credit with the money-lenders for the making up their rents at the fixed terms of payment. On failure of payment the crops were seized by the Government Accountant, whose duty it also was to sell the Government's share of the crops collected as rent. Both at Taiuru and at Narsingpur the country was beautiful, and every field was enclosed with quick-set hedges and well cultivated, the whole being high ground without rice lands.

Narsingpur was on the banks of the Kaveri river, and had two temples and about two hundred houses. There was rich black soil close to it where cotton was extensively grown. Wheat and Womun were raised in equal quantities, and Ragi was grown on the red soil fit for its cultivation.

[1] Buchanan's *Journey from Madras*, &c., vol. ii. p. 119.

COIMBATUR

Early in October, Dr. Buchanan left Mysore and entered into British territory on his way to Coimbatur. Colegala District was well cultivated, and contained forty or fifty large reservoirs for irrigation, repaired by the Mysore authorities eighty years before, and some of them repaired again by the Company's servants after the district had come to the possession of the Company. Passing through the grounds of the decayed reservoirs not yet repaired, Dr. Buchanan found the land entirely waste, so much did cultivation depend on irrigation works in this country. Major Macleod, the Collector, had set aside the authority of the Gaudas or village-chiefs, and had only employed them on fixed salaries to collect the land revenue from cultivators. The policy no doubt added to the land revenue, but weakened the ancient village-system of India.

The magnificent falls of Gangana-Chuki and the island of Sivana-Samudra struck Dr. Buchanan with wonder. The southern fall of Birra-Chuki was even more pleasing to his eye. He was told that the State of Sivana-Samudra had been founded by Ganga Raja about A.D. 1200, but he gives 1523 as a more probable date. The State fell, after the reign of three princes, under the combined attack of neighbouring powers.

The country near Colegala and Sategala lay immediately west, the mountains of the Eastern Ghats rising to a height of 2000 feet above the level of the upper country. The country was well cultivated as far as Pallia, but beyond that place more than half the lands were uncultivated, and the tanks were in ruins. Travelling farther eastwards, Dr. Buchanan entered the Ghats at Mathully, and threaded his way through the mountains until he reached Kaveripura on the Kaveri river, where a fort had been built by a frontier Polygar to protect the pass.

There was an old irrigation reservoir at Kaveripura which watered over five hundred acres of land; but it had burst fifty years before and had never been repaired. A considerable trade passed by Kaveripura between the upper and the lower country, and Dr. Buchanan met forty or fifty loaded cattle every day. Along the course of the Tumbula, a tributary of the Kaveri, there were five old reservoirs which had all burst fifty years before, and had never been repaired.

The village-heads, as stated above, had been set aside under the Company's rule, and the country under Major Macleod paid a land revenue of £10,293 to £16,545 a year, realised through paid Tahsildars, who combined in themselves the powers of revenue collector, civil magistrate, and police. Farm labourers got from cultivators a pay of 5s. to 6s. 8d. the year, and a house to live in, and 1⅔rds bushel of grain monthly; and their wives received daily wages if able to work. The implements of husbandry in the plains were more miserable and fewer in number than those used above the Ghats.

On the 19th October Dr. Buchanan arrived at Nala-Rayana on the Bhawani river, after travelling through a country three-fourths of which seemed to be waste. A dam on the Bhawani sent off a canal on each side of the river, and the lands watered by these canals gave one unfailing crop in the year. A little land watered by reservoirs gave two crops, but the supply of water was uncertain. Cultivators under the Company's rule were required to pay the full rent for the lands they cultivated, irrespective of the quantity of produce. This they felt as a hardship, and they desired to be placed on the old footing.

At Ana-Codavery, rice was grown on lands watered by canals taken from the Bhawani river. The dam on the river had been constructed by Nunjay Raja a hundred and twenty years before. In lands which were not irrigated, not over a sixth part of the ground was under cultivation. The soil was good, but the invasion of General Meadows had stopped cultivation; the inhabitants had retired to the hills and had perished in large numbers.

The Company's Commercial Resident at Salem had visited these parts some months before Dr. Buchanan's arrival, and had made advances to weavers for the Company's Investment. The cloth ordered was Shalambru, resembling the Bafta of Bengal, and was made 36 cubits long and 2¼ cubits broad.

Travelling southwards through much uncultivated country, Dr. Buchanan arrived at the important city of Coimbatur on the 28th October. The chief of the place was the twentieth in descent from the first founder of the town. The family originally paid tribute to the Rajas of Madura, and afterwards came under the rule of Mysore. The place had suffered much during the Mysore wars, but was recovering, and contained two thousand houses.

There was much rice ground in the neighbourhood, watered by reservoirs which were filled by canals from the Noyel river. Ragi and other crops were raised on dry lands; cotton and tobacco were grown in some places; betel-nut and cocoa-nut were cultivated by rich farmers; and iron was smelted at Topun Beta, five miles from Coimbatur. 459 looms worked in the district; the wives of all the low caste cultivators were great spinners; and the thread was dyed red or blue as required. The Commercial Resident at Salem had twice made advances to the Coimbatur weavers. The weavers formerly paid a duty of about 4s. on each loom annually, and this was replaced by a stamp duty under the Company's rule. The weavers thought this was harder, and requested the Collector to restore the former mode of assessment, without success.

Tripura, to the east of Coimbatur, was an open town with 300 houses and a weekly market. The rice land in the neighbourhood produced only one crop, and was irrigated partly from reservoirs and partly from canals brought from the Noyel river. Owing to want of repairs, more than one-third of the lands previously cultivated was out of cultivation. The poorest fields were set aside for pasture, and paid a small rent. Iron was smelted at China Mali, further east, and a duty of a thirtieth part of the smelted iron was paid as duty to Government in addition to a duty for cutting timber for fuel. China Mali had only 125 houses, and was suffering from small-pox. Lands in the district were irrigated from the Capely river, but no rice was grown.

Perenduru, north of China Mali, had 118 houses, and the district had 800 looms. Erodu on the Kaveri had had 3000 houses in the time of Haidar Ali, but had declined under Tipu Sultan. It was utterly destroyed during the invasion of General Meadows, but was reviving after the conclusion of peace. The canal passing by Erodu was a splendid work, said to have been constructed by one Kaling Raya four hundred years before, and still watered 3459 acres of land.

Further down the Kaveri river was the important town of Codomudi with an ancient temple and 118 houses. A canal taken from the Kaveri was conducted over the Noyel river to Pagolur village, and irrigated a large tract of land. The rent fixed in these parts by Tipu Sultan was four-tenths of the produce, but this was converted into a money rent, 3s. 5¾d. per acre, by the British Government in 1799, and the rent for 1800 had not yet been fixed.

Major Macleod, the Collector of the Northern Division of Coimbatur, informed Dr. Buchanan that by the custom of the country no tenant could be turned out of his holding as long as he paid his rent. The Major thought it was impracticable for the British Government to receive the land revenue in kind without leaving a door open to excessive embezzlements. When the Company obtained possession of the Salem country, the rice grounds, watered by the fine canals from the Kaveri, paid rent in kind. The Company's servants had changed this into money rent against the murmurs of the people, had extended cultivation and increased the land revenue. The Ryotwari system was preferred to the Zemindari system because it brought more revenue. "The regulations introduced by Colonel Read for collecting the revenue seem to me sufficient to secure the regular payment of more than can ever be procured from Zemindars; and I am persuaded that any deficiencies must arise either from a neglect of duty, or from dishonesty in the Collectors. I here allude to hereditary Zemindars merely as affecting the revenue and political state of the country, they must be considered as useful toward the improvement of agriculture."[1]

Caruru was a considerable town with 1000 houses on the Amaravati river, a tributary of the Kaveri. But the merchants were petty dealers, and the weavers were not numerous. Two canals from the Kaveri and several from the Amaravati irrigated this district. Sugar-cane, rice, and dry crops were grown.

On the 17th November Dr. Buchanan reached Daraporam (Dharma-pura), the headquarters of Mr. Hurdis, the Collector of the Southern Division of Coimbatur. The Collector was an active, intelligent and sympathetic young officer, mixed with the people, settled their caste disputes, and knew them well. "Mr. Hurdis thinks that the present rents are greatly too high; and, no doubt, the peasantry here, as well as in almost every part of India, are miserably poor. . . .

[1] Buchanan's *Journey from Madras*, &c., vol. ii. p. 296.

One great cause, indeed, of the poverty of the farmers, and consequent poverty of crops in many parts of India, is the custom of forcing land upon people who have no means of cultivating it. Thus all lands are apparently occupied, but it is in a manner that is worse than if one-half of them were entirely waste."[1] The reason for this has been explained elsewhere. The Company desired to obtain its revenue from the entire arable land, whether they could be properly cultivated or not. The rents were enormously high; betel-leaf lands were assessed at £3, 16s. 9d. an acre, rice lands at £1, 15s. 9½d. to £1, 5s. 2d. per acre.

Travelling further westwards, Dr. Buchanan reached Palachy on the 24th November. Roman coins in a pot had been dug up in this place, showing the trade of this ancient Pandya country with Rome at the time of Augustus and Tiberius. The worst grounds in this district were left for pasture and paid no rent, and the remainder belonging to each village was reckoned as arable, and had an average assessment fixed, ranging from 2s. 10¾d. to 7s. 3d. the acre. "The farmers complain that the land is forced on them, and that they are compelled to rent more than they have stock to enable them to cultivate. A man who rents seventeen Bullas of land (a Bulla = 4¼ to 6 acres) is able only to plough nine of them, whereas, if he had full stock, he would plough between eleven and twelve, leaving one-third part in fallow. The rents, however, have been lowered, in some villages one-fifth, in others one-third, in order to compensate the loss which the farmer suffers by this manner of renting lands, where there is not a sufficient stock to cultivate the whole. This sort of tenure seems to be a great evil."[2]

[1] Buchanan's *Journey from Madras*, &c., vol. ii. p. 309.
[2] *Ibid.*, vol. ii. pp. 319, 320.

MALABAR.

On the 29th November, Dr. Buchanan entered Malabar, which had been transferred from the Government of Bombay to the Government of Madras only a few months before. He entered the territory of the Tamura Raja, known as the Zamorin to European writers. High mountains on the south poured down cascades from great heights, and cornfields were mixed with lofty forests and plantations of fruit trees. But the dry land was neglected, and the quantity of rice land was not great. The town of Colangodu contained a thousand houses, many of them inhabited by weavers, who imported their cotton from Coimbatur. Palighat was the most beautiful country that Dr. Buchanan had seen, resembling the finest parts of Bengal, but the cultivation of high lands was neglected. The fort there had been built by Haidar Ali after his conquest of Malabar. There was no land tax under the Government of the old Rajas, but Haidar Ali had imposed one called Nagadi on the low and fertile lands, exempting the higher grounds. Tipu Sultan's oppression drove many of the proprietors into Travancore in the south.

The average produce of rice at the time of Dr. Buchanan's visit to Palighat was 7⅛ seeds, and the rental was 4¼ seeds, or over sixty per cent. of the produce. According to Mr. Smee's valuation, the Land Tax assessed on the landlords was at the enormous rate of 84 per cent. on their rental.[1] The annual rainfall was sufficient to bring one crop of rice into maturity, while reservoirs constructed and maintained at the expense of landlords secured a second. The cattle was of very small size, and insufficient for the requirements of the country. Iron was forged at Colangodu.

On the 6th December, Dr. Buchanan entered the

[1] Buchanan's *Journey from Madras*, &c., vol. ii. p. 369

territory of the Raja of Cochin, who paid an annual tribute to the East India Company, but retained full jurisdiction, civil and military, within his own realm. "His country is so far better administered than that more fully under the authority of the Company, that neither Moplas nor Nairs presume to make any disturbance."[1] At Cacadu the hills were mostly uncultivated, but the pasture was tolerable, the cattle in good condition, and the valleys were covered with corn, skirted by the houses of the inhabitants shaded by groves of fruit trees. Close by was a Christian village, and the Papa or priest informed Dr. Buchanan that Christianity had been introduced by St. Thomas who had visited Madras in the year A.D. 60.

The Moplas of Malabar had been rich traders about the middle of the eighteenth century, and possessed vessels which sailed to Surat, Mocha, and Madras. Dr. Buchanan found them quiet and industrious on the coast, but "fierce, bloodthirsty, and bigoted ruffians" in the interior. Their religious leader claimed descent from Fatima, the daughter of Mahomed.

Returning from Cochin to Malabar, Dr. Buchanan travelled northwards till he reached Vencata-Cotay on the 22nd December. The valleys were beautiful, the declivities of the hills were formed into terraces for cultivation, but the summits of the ridges were waste. The cultivators complained of the Land Tax; "every evil in Malabar is ascribed to that as its source."[2] Agriculture was much neglected between Tiruvana and Parupa-nada, and this was due to the want of people and the poverty of those who were in the country. The sea-coast near the latter place was, however, filled with highly productive cocoanut gardens. On Christmas day the doctor reached Calicut, the old capital of Malabar.

[1] Buchanan's *Journey from Madras*, &c., vol. ii. p. 388.
[2] *Ibid*, vol. ii. p. 468.

Mr. Torin, the commercial resident, was endeavouring to establish the manufacture of long-cloth at this place. The pieces were 72 cubits long, and the prices given to weavers were 18s. 6¾d. to 16s. 4½d. the piece. There were 344 weavers, brought from Travancore and Cochin, and they worked 237 looms, and produced 468 pieces of cloth monthly. Mr. Torin had also established a manufactory at Palighat, which was better and cheaper.

Dr. Buchanan made estimates of the produce, rental, and the Land Tax of this neighbourhood, with the following results:

For a Field of Poor Quality.

Land Tax	£0	12	9½
Charges of collection . . .	0	1	3¼
Seed	0	9	4½
Expense of cultivation . .	0	9	4½
Landlord	0	1	11
Interest of money advanced .	0	1	0¾
Cultivator	0	7	8
	£2	3	5½

Or approximately the gross Land Tax was 14s.; the expenses of cultivation came to 19s.; the owners of the land retained only 10s.

For a Field of the Best Quality.

Land Tax and collection charges .	£0	16	10
Seed	0	9	4½
Expense of cultivation . . .	0	9	4½
Interest	0	1	0¾
Landlord	0	8	6¼
Cultivator	1	5	6¾
	£3	10	8¾

Or approximately the Land Tax was 17s.; the expenses of cultivation came to 19s.; the owners of the land had £1, 14s.

On the 1st of January 1801, Dr. Buchanan reached Tamara-Chery. All the lands here had passed into the hands of Mopla mortgagees. Owing to the persecution of the Hindus by Tipu Sultan, and the warfare of the Moplas, one-fourth of the rice lands at Kurumbara was waste and overgrown with forest trees. Some great farmers had ten ploughs, twenty oxen, twenty male and female slaves, ten servants, and twenty-five milch cows, but the number of such farmers was small. Male slaves sold at the low price of 9s. 6½d. to 28s. 8d., and women slaves at half the price.

The Collector, Mr. Coward, who accompanied Dr. Buchanan through his district, was of opinion that one-fourth of the district was capable of irrigation and rice-cultivation, about one-half was high ground fit for dry grains or plantation, and the remainder was steep and rocky. "Mr. Coward thinks the Land Tax so high that it impedes agriculture."[1]

Leaving Mr. Coward on 5th January, Dr. Buchanan proceeded with Captain Osburne to Kutiporum, the residence of the Raja, who paid a tribute to the Company and had absolute authority in his territory. Here the Land Tax was 40 per cent., the landlord kept 27 per cent., and the cultivator 33 per cent. of the produce. Though accompanied by Captain Osburne, the worthy traveller did not receive kind greetings from the women of the country. "The Nairs being at enmity with Europeans have persuaded the women that we are a kind of hobgoblins who have long tails," and the women naturally ran away at their approach![2]

Tellicherry, Mahe, and Dharmapatam formed a circle under the management of Mr. Strachy, "a very promising young gentleman." The whole of the circle, Mr. Strachy thought, might be cultivated or planted

[1] Buchanan's *Journey from Madras*, &c., vol. ii. p. 502.
[2] *Ibid.*, vol. ii. p. 514.

with fruit trees, but much of it was waste. The tax on rice lands amounted to 25 per cent. of the rent. The commerce of the circle was of great importance, and the principal articles of commerce were pepper, sandal-wood, and cardamoms.

Mr. Hodgson, Collector of the Northern District of Malabar, received Dr. Buchanan at Cananore. A Mopla lady, who went under the title of Bibi or The Lady, was the descendant of those who had originally purchased Cananore from the Dutch, and entertained Dr. Buchanan at a grand dinner. The Biby paid 14,000 rupees to the Company as Land Tax, and owned Cananore and most of the Laccadive Islands. Succession, as among the Nairs, went by the female line.

Cherical was mountainous and very little cultivated, and the number of houses at Cananore and Cherical was 10,386. About the middle of January Dr. Buchanan left Malabar and went northwards to Canara.

CANARA.

Thomas Munro, the most distinguished and successful administrator of his time, had been sent after his settlement of Baramahal to settle Canara in 1798, as we have seen in a previous chapter. The Raja of Canara was then ill, but his sister's son or heir waited on Munro, and Munro had cautiously informed him that his claims to the State would be laid before the Company. In the meantime, it was placed under the management of Tahsildars or revenue collectors, the Raja was deprived of his powers, and was allowed a remission of the Land Tax on his private estate for his support. The Nairs complained of a want of good faith in the British officers in these arrangements.[1] Munro levied a Land Tax of 24,000 rupees against a nominal claim of 32,000 rupees under the government

[1] Buchanan's *Journey from Madras*, &c., vol. iii. p. 12.

of Tipu Sultan, but this reduced tax was all that the country could pay and consumed the whole rent of the lands. Trimula Rao, the Tahsildar, considered the tax heavier than at Arcot.

Dr. Buchanan stayed for a week at Mangalore, situated on a lake separated from the sea by a beach of sand. It had been a harbour at one time, but the depth of the opening had diminished, and vessels drawing more than ten feet could not enter at the time of Buchanan's visit. The fort of Mangalore had been destroyed by Tipu Sultan.

Imams or lands assigned for the support of temples had been reclaimed by Tipu, but some of them had been concealed. Thomas Munro and his successor Ravenshaw permitted things to remain as before, and the principal Hindu temple had an income of £193, 8s. 3d. the year. Munro's land assessment was felt as heavy, and gave rise to much complaint. "The proprietors allege that the tax amounts to more than the rent, and that they are obliged to borrow money, or to give part of the profit from the lands cultivated with their own stock, to enable them to satisfy the claims of Government. . . . The universal cry of poverty, however, that prevails in every part of India, and the care, owing to long oppression, with which everything is concealed, render it very difficult to know the real circumstances of the cultivator. We may safely, however, conclude from the violent contest for landed property of every kind in Canara that each occupant has still a considerable interest in the soil, besides the reward due to him for cultivating whatever his stock enables him to do. It is indeed sincerely to be wished that this property may long continue unmolested, as no country can thrive where the absolute property of the soil is vested in the State."[1] Dr. Buchanan did not know that the contest for land in

[1] Buchanan's *Journey from Madras*, &c., vol. iii. pp. 33–35.

India, even when the land is over-assessed, is due to the fact that land is virtually the sole means of subsistence for the nation; the cultivator must have his holding on any terms or starve.

Rice land was irrigated by canals from streams in the low valleys and from reservoirs in higher lands; while on very high lands the crop depended entirely on rains. Sugar-cane was cultivated mainly by the Christian population, and betel-nut and black pepper were grown in plantations. Salt was manufactured by the people as at Malabar, but the quantity produced was inadequate. Rice, betel-nut, and pepper were the principal articles of export; cotton and silk cloths, sugar and salt were imported.

Ten miles from Mangalore was Arcola, also called Firingy-Patta, because it was formerly inhabited by the Concan Christians. The whole country resembled Malabar, and the sides of the hills were formed into terraces for cultivation, but with less industry than at Malabar. Great damage had been done in the vicinity by Tipu Sultan and the Raja of Coorg in the recent wars. Dr. Buchanan found on the roadside many of the guns which Tipu had ordered to be transported from Mangalore to Seringapatam. A dam had been constructed across Bamala river, forming a large reservoir for cultivation.

On the 5th February Dr. Buchanan came to Einuru town, where he found eight Jain temples and a colossal Jain image, formed of one solid piece of granite and standing in the open air. The extent of lands held by the Jain temples at the time of Haidar Ali had been reduced by Tipu Sultan, restored by Thomas Munro, and again reduced by his successor Ravenshaw. The image of Gautama Raja (Buddha) at Carculla was one solid piece of granite, 38 feet high, and, according to the inscription, was made 369 years before Buchanan's visit, *i.e.* about 1432.

At Haryadika, further to the west, which Dr Buchanan reached on the 10th February, he made some inquiries into the incidence of the Land Tax, and found it was one-half of the rent. But "these people say that when the rice is cheap, the whole rent is not equal to the Land Tax."

On the following day he came within sight of the Arabian Sea once more at Udipu, where the name of Madhava-Acharya, the great Hindu scholar and reformer of the fourteenth century, was still revered, and his sect flourished. There were three temples and fourteen convents belonging to Sanyasins, who were religious teachers. Rice was grown from Udipu to the sea. "According to the valuation of five villages in this neigbourhood, I find that out of 2048 Pagodas, the gross value of their produce, the cultivators retain 1295 Pagodas. The share of the Government amounts in general to one quarter of the gross produce, and in these villages are 671 Pagodas, of which 37 are alienated in Inam or charity lands, as they are called. What remains to the landlord is 82 Pagodas."[1]

Travelling northwards, Dr. Buchanan reached Kundapura, and crossing the river, entered the Northern Division of Canara, then under the management of Mr. Read, "a young gentleman brought up in the same school with Mr. Ravenshaw." Further north were Beiduru with its temple dedicated to Siva and the larger town of Batuculla with 500 houses. Travelling further northwards, he found the plain between the sea and the low hills only half a mile to a mile and a half in breadth, and cultivated for rice. The temple of Murodeswara stood on a lofty fortified promontory. Not far from it was the Pigeon Island, frequented by wild pigeons, and also by boats for coral, with which the place abounded. On the

[1] Buchanan's *Journey from Madras*, &c., vol. iii. p. 103.

21st February Dr. Buchanan reached the great lake and town of Onore.

Onore was formerly a large town and a place of great commerce, and Haidar Ali had made a dock here for building ships of war. His foolish and despotic son demolished this great mart after he had recovered it by the treaty of Mangalore, and the town was desolate when Dr. Buchanan visited it. Boats came from Goa for trade, and merchants lived scattered near the banks of the lake, and purchased rice, pepper, cocoa-nuts, betel-nuts, and salt-fish for export. Most of the cultivated lands were private property, but the hills and forests belonged to the Government. Every man paid a Land Tax for the whole of his property, and cultivated it in whatever manner he pleased. Cultivators in moderate circumstances had four to six ploughs, but a great number of them had only one plough, and were poor. Cultivators obtained leases for four to ten years, and paid rents to proprietors, who paid the Land Tax to the Government.

"The proprietor ought to find security for the payment of the Land Tax. If he does not, a revenue officer is sent to superintend the harvest, to sell the produce, and to deduct the revenue from the proceeds. This is a miserable system, and one of true Hindustani invention, as the person sent to collect the harvest received an allowance from the farmer, and thus one of the idle tatterdemalions that formed part of the clamorous suite of some great man, had for a while the cravings of his appetite satisfied. If a man has given security, and fails in payment, on the third day after the term, the security is called upon and confined until the revenue is paid." [1]

An estate, which paid twenty Pagodas as Land Tax, sold for a hundred Pagodas, and could be mortgaged for fifty Pagodas. Sons divided their father's estate

[1] Buchanan's *Journey from Madras*, &c., vol. iii. p. 140.

equally among them, but the eldest managed the whole, and they all lived together. When a division took place among a number of cousins, the estate was commonly let and the rent divided. A good field produced 20 to 33 bushels of rice per acre, while poor soil produced 6 to 16 bushels. Sugar-cane, pepper, sandal-wood, cardamoms, betel-nut, and cocoa-nuts were articles of trade.

Gokarna, to the north of Onore, was a place of note, owing to the celebrated image of Siva, called Mahabaleswar, which was worshipped there. It is said that Ravana, King of Ceylon, was carrying this image from the northern mountains, and deposited it here to take rest, and could not lift it again. The town had 500 houses, one-half of which was occupied by Brahmans. There was a large tank with a convent near it, and an image of Sankara-Narayana was kept in a temple, "and it is a strong proof of the early prevalence of the doctrine . . . that Siva and Vishnu are different names for the same God."

Ancola produced an annual revenue of 29,000 Pagodas, while Onore yielded 51,000, and Kundapura 50,000. One-third of the good lands was waste. The Bazar in the town of Ancola had been frequently burnt by robbers, but was recovering under British rule. Thomas Munro's land assessment was nominally lighter than that of Tipu Sultan, but his collections were really higher. "Major Munro, according to the account of the revenue officers, considerably reduced the rate of the Land Tax, but owing to his care and strictness in the collections, the revenue which he raised was much greater than was ever before realised." [1] This is precisely what happened in most parts of India. The Company's servants sometimes maintained or raised, and sometimes reduced, the old revenue, but their collections were more rigorous than the people of India had ever known before.

[1] Buchanan's *Journey from Madras*, &c., vol. iii. p. 180.

The greater portion of three northern districts, Kundapura, Onore, and Ancola was rocky and barren, and unfit for cultivation. Mr. Read estimated the different kinds of land thus:

	Cultivated Land.	Capable of Cultivation.	Sterile.
Kundapura	0.32	0.08	0.60
Onore	0.26	0.12	0.62
Ancola	0.20	0.20	0.59

"The revenue, notwithstanding so much waste land, is said to have been greater during the first year of Major Munro's management than it was ever before known to have been. Mr. Read attributes this to an increase of rent on the lands actually under cultivation, but of this I have much doubt."[1]

It is unnecessary for us to trace the return journey of Dr. Buchanan through Mysore to Madras, which he reached on the 6th July 1801. The account of his journey through Southern India, from the eastern to the western sea, which we have condensed in this chapter, is one of the most valuable records we possess of the economic condition of the country under the old regime, and under the new rule of the East India Company. Everywhere the extension of the Company's rule meant the cessation of wars and disturbances, and the return of peace. With all these blessings which it conferred, the Company's administration committed the fatal blunder of over-assessing the soil; and the condition of the people under the Company's rule was therefore one of hopeless poverty—worse than in the native State of Mysore under the native minister Purnea.

[1] Buchanan's *Journey from Madras*, &c., vol. iii. p. 191.

CHAPTER XIII

ECONOMIC CONDITION OF NORTHERN INDIA
(1808–1815)

THE Court of Directors recognised the value of Dr. Francis Buchanan's economic inquiries in Southern India, and desired that similar inquiries should be made by the same eminent authority in Northern India. Dr. Buchanan was accordingly directed in 1807 to make a statistical survey of some of the districts of Bengal and Northern India. The inquiry was carefully conducted for seven years, at a cost of £30,000.

The valuable materials thus collected were forwarded by the Indian Government to England, but were left unused for a long time. Dr. Buchanan came in for a large property in Scotland, took the name of Hamilton on acquiring the estate, and died in retirement before his labours saw the light.

It was then that Montgomery Martin, historian of the British Colonies and a thoughtful and careful writer on Indian subjects, asked and obtained permission to examine the manuscripts left by Dr. Buchanan. A judicious selection from the information collected with so much labour was published in London, in three volumes, in 1838, and these volumes contain the best and most reliable account that we possess of the economic condition of Northern India in the first two decades of the nineteenth century. In pursuance of the scope and object of the present work we proceed to give a summary of the statistical portions of these volumes in the present chapter.

Patna City and Behar District.

(Area, 5358 square miles; population, 3,364,420.)

Rice was the most important crop throughout the district. Rice in husk sold on the average at the price of one rupee per 70 seers, or about 70 lbs. for the shilling. Wheat and barley were the next important crops, and were sometimes sown intermixed. Flour was taken as cakes (Roti), or parched and ground (Chhatu). Marua was raised entirely as a summer crop; maize and Janar were grown mostly on the banks of the Ganges.

Khesari, Bhut, pease, lentils, Arhar, Mung and succulent vegetables were also grown for food, and Til and other plants for oil. Potatoes had been introduced from Europe. Cotton was grown on 8000 acres of land, three-fourths of which yielded no other crop, and sugar-cane was raised on 7000 acres. Poppy was cultivated in garden lands near villages, and tobacco on 160 acres. The betel-leaf of Behar was considered superior to all others, and was exported to Calcutta, Benares, and Lucknow. The cultivation of indigo was on the decline, the landlords being averse to it, but Kusum or safflower was extensively grown.

The rents paid by cultivators to landlords were usually one-half the crop after deducting the expense of harvesting; but, on the other hand, the landlords paid all the expense of making and repairing canals and reservoirs required for irrigating lands.[1]

Large reservoirs, a mile and upwards in length, cost about 500 rupees (£50) in excavating, but the smaller ones, which were more numerous, cost from 25 to 100 rupees. Many canals were several miles in length, and often conveyed more water than remained in the channel of the river in the dry season. The greater portion of

[1] *History of Eastern India*, by Montgomery Martin (London, 1838), vol. i. pp. 282 and 294.

winter crops, vegetables, and sugar-cane was irrigated from wells. Of pasture, there were 27 square miles of inundated land, 384 miles of woods or scattered bushes, 640 miles of plantations, 205 miles of high lands, and 417 miles of broken corners, banks, and barren lands. Except in the cities of Patna and Gaya, the cultivators paid nothing for the ground occupied by their houses; "No person who rents a farm pays for his house." Artificers, traders, and labourers paid a ground rent, either in money or in work.[1]

It will thus appear that the cultivator's rent was half the produce after deducting the cost of harvesting, and this rent included the ground rent for his dwelling, the cost of irrigation, and free pasture. Nor was this half-produce rent very strictly levied. "The division is so troublesome that, instead of their respective shares, both master and tenant, when the crop is ripe, usually agree the one to take and the other to give a certain quantity of grain, or its value in money." "The arrears due by the tenantry to their landlords are quite trifling except in one estate, where the owner has been in the habit of giving much money in advance. . . . The custom of advances (Takavi) from the landlord to the tenant, to enable him to cultivate, is not very common, although it exists to some extent."[2] A general change, which was taking place at the time of Dr. Buchanan's inquiries, was the substitution of money rents for rents paid in kind.

A plough servant's annual wages ranged from 16 rupees to 22 rupees a year, or between three and four shillings the month. Day labourers employed with the hoe, or in transplanting rice, or in watering winter-crops, were paid three or four paisas (twopence) a day; and women employed to weed and transplant rice

[1] *History of Eastern India*, by Montgomery Martin (London, 1838), vol. i. p. 299.
[2] *Ibid.*, vol. i. pp. 303 and 305.

received the same allowance as men, and assisted in the harvest.

Spinning and weaving were the great national industry of India next after agriculture. All the spinners were women, and Dr. Buchanan estimates their number in this district at 330,426. "By far the greater part of these spin only a few hours in the afternoon, and upon the average estimate the whole value of the thread that each spins in a year is worth nearly 7 rupees, 2 anas, 8 pies, giving for the total annual value Rs.2,367,277, and by a similar calculation the raw material at the retail price will amount to Rs.1,286,272, leaving a profit of Rs.1,081,005 for the spinners, or Rs.3¼ (6s. 6d. the year) for each. . . . As the demand, therefore, for fine goods has for some years been constantly diminishing, the women have suffered very much."[1]

Cotton weavers were numerous. The total number of looms employed in the manufacture of Chadars or table-cloths was 750, and the value of the annual manufacture was Rs.540,000, leaving a profit of Rs.81,400, deducting the value of thread. This gave a profit of Rs.108 for each loom worked by three persons, or in other words an income of Rs.36 (72s.) a year for each person. But the greater part of the cotton weavers made coarse cloth for country use to the value of Rs.2,438,621 annually, which left a profit of Rs.667,242 after deduction of cost of thread. This gave a profit of Rs.28 (56s.) for each loom.

The system pursued by the East India Company is thus described: "Each man, on becoming bound (Asami) to the Company, received two rupees, and engaged not to work for any person until he had made as much as the Company required, and no other advance has ever been made by the Commercial Residents.

[1] *History of Eastern India*, by Montgomery Martin (London, 1838), vol. i. p. 350.

The agent orders each man to make a certain number of pieces of such or such goods, and he is paid for each on its delivery, according to the price stated in the tables."[1]

Weavers who made cloth wholly or in part of Tasar silk lived mostly at Phatuha, Gaya, and Nawada. The total annual value of the produce was Rs.421,710, leaving a profit ranging from 33 rupees to 90 rupees a year for each loom, requiring the services of a man and a woman.

Paper manufacture, leather work, perfumery, iron-work, gold and silver work, stone-cutting, pottery, bricklaying and lime manufacture, dyeing, blanket-weaving and the manufacture of gold and silver thread and cloth, were among the other important industries. Much of the internal trade of the district was carried on by Baldiya-Beparis, or traders possessing pack-bullocks. One ox and 5 rupees of capital enabled a Bepari to start his trade, he sold goods to the value of Rs.50 a month, making a profit of 6 to 12 per cent., and thus securing an income of 32 rupees (64s.) a year. Goods were conveyed from Patna to Calcutta by boats, and the freight was 12 to 15 rupees (24s. to 30s.) for carrying 100 maunds (8000 lbs.) of grain. Cartmen conveyed goods over shorter distances, and the hire for a bullock-cart for carrying 12 to 15 maunds (960 to 1200 lbs.) from Patna to Gaya (72 miles) was 3 rupees or 6s.

In going over this list of the principal trades and professions of India, a hundred years ago, one sees how greatly these sources of income have been narrowed within this period. Weaving and spinning are practically dead, as most of the thread and cloth used by the people are supplied by Lancashire. Paper manufacture has also declined; skins are now sent

[1] *History of Eastern India*, by Montgomery Martin (London, 1838), vol. i. p. 355.

to Europe for all the better kinds of leather work, the dyes of the country have been replaced by aniline dyes. The Beparis and their pack-bullocks have become things of the past, and the profits of the carrying trade are now earned, not by boatmen, but by railways owned by foreign capitalists. Agriculture has become virtually the sole means of subsistence for the people with the loss of their many trades and industries.

SHAHABAD DISTRICT.

(Area, 4087 square miles; population, 1,419,520.)

Rice was the greatest crop, but through the neglect of some landlords to repair the reservoirs on their estates, the cultivation of that grain had somewhat diminished. One-half of the district was under rice cultivation. With extended irrigation, Shahabad could be as productive as Patna and Behar, but the quality of the Shahabad rice was not as fine.

The lowest allowance given to the day labourer for mere reaping was nearly $3\frac{3}{4}$ per cent. of the gross produce, while the highest allowance was $8\frac{3}{4}$ per cent. On an average, 195 lbs. of grain were reaped by one man daily, for which, if he was a day labourer, he was allowed rather more than 6 per cent., and if a farm-servant, rather less than $7\frac{1}{2}$ per cent. The grain intended for seed was preserved in vessels made of clay; the most common granaries were composed of a kind of basket made, like the bee-hives usual in Scotland, of a straw-rope coiled spirally. These granaries contained 29,360 lbs. of rice. The large ones stood in the farm-yard, and were covered with a terrace of clay. The smaller ones were placed at the end of the hut.

"By far the greater part of the proprietors of

assessed estates in this District complain that the assessment [by the Company's Government] is too heavy, so as to leave them little or no profit, and in many cases to exceed the value of the lands, and as a proof quote that many estates having been put up to sale, no bidder has offered, and the arrears having been lost to Government, the lands have been let at a reduced price; and they also allege that the revenue is so high as leaving nothing to the owners, these have been unable to defray the expense of keeping the reservoirs in repair, and, of course, that the country is growing daily less able to pay the revenue."[1] Exclusive of the high table-land, the Government land revenue amounted to Rs.1,132,677 in Shahabad on an extent of 3151 square miles capable of being ploughed; while in Patna and Behar the land revenue was Rs.1,412,269 on an extent of 5051 square miles capable of being ploughed.

Spinning and weaving were the great national industries of Shahabad. 159,500 women were employed in spinning, and produced thread to the value of Rs.1,250,000 a year. Deducting the value of the cotton, each woman made only Rs.1½ or 3s. a year. This was little enough, but this little was added to the income of the families to which the women belonged.

Weavers worked in cotton only, as there were few silk weavers in Shahabad. 7025 houses of weavers working in cotton in the District had 7950 looms. Each loom made an annual income of Rs.20¾ or 41s. 6d. a year, and each loom required the labour of a man and his wife, as well as one boy or girl But as a family could not be supported for less than Rs.48 or £4, 16s. a year, Dr. Buchanan suspected that the income of each loom, given above, was understated.

[1] *History of Eastern India*, by Montgomery Martin (London, 1883), vol. i. p. 541.

Paper, perfumery, oils, salt, and spirituous liquors were manufactured in Shahabad. Rice was the great article both of import and export, barley was exported to Benares, and Arhar pulse to Murshedabad. Tobacco was imported from Chupra, sugar from Mirzapar, iron from Ramgarh, and zinc, copper, lead, and tin from Patna. Raw silk, cloth, salt, and fancy articles were exported to the Mahratta country of Ratanpur.

The weekly markets were fewer than in Behar, but most of the purchases and sales were made there. Bank notes had not entered into common currency, and "gold has almost totally disappeared, for the same reasons no doubt as in Behar." The milled copper coinage of the Company was current only in the city of Arra; in the interior rude masses of Gorukpur copper coins and Madhusahi and Sherguji Paisas were in use, and Cowri shells were current in exchange for copper coins.

Boats were fewer than in Behar; the fare for 100 maunds of goods (8000 lbs.) from Bindhuliya to Benares, a distance of 140 miles, was Rs.12 or 24s. Two great roads traversed the District, one the military road from Calcutta to Benares kept up by the public, and the other along the old bank of the Ganges kept up by a tax of 1 per cent. on the whole assessed land of the District. Both were impracticable in the rainy season.

The Raja of Bhojpur, Hardar Sing a Kayest, Abdul Nasur a Mahomedan landlord, Bibi Asmat a Mahomedan lady, Lala Rajrap and Lala Kananga, both Kayests, distinguished themselves among others by feeding all strangers and mendicants who came for help. This ancient rite of hospitality to the poor was known to the Hindoos as Sada-brata or ceaseless devotion to God.

BHAGALPUR DISTRICT.

(Area, 8225 square miles ; population, 2,019,900.)

Rice was the greatest crop, and 60 seers of the rough rice gave 37½ seers of clean husked rice. Wheat was the next large crop, and barley was sown a great deal mixed with the field pea. Maize was grown on the higher lands, and the next culmiferous crop Marua. Kheri, Kodo, Cheena, Janera and Bajra were also cultivated.

Kalai, Arhar, and Khesari were important leguminous plants. Til and numerous other plants yielding oil were extensively grown, and ginger, vegetables, greens, and spices were raised for consumption in the District.

Cotton was cultivated on 4000 acres, besides a considerable quantity raised by hill tribes on their native hills. Sugar-cane was chiefly grown near the banks of rivers where the fields could be irrigated by means of canals. The tobacco raised was not sufficient for the requirements of the District. One-half of the gross produce covered the cost of cultivation, and the rent paid to the landlords did not quite amount to one-half of the remainder.[1] Owing however to the system of advances being little known the people were not much involved in debt. The money rent was collected by instalments, rent in kind was taken when the crops were reaped. "Various deductions, before division, are made from the crop, specially the whole expense of harvest, and after these deductions the landlord in some places receives one-half, in others $\frac{22}{40}$; but then the landlord, as I have said, is at all the expense of the canals, and generally at all that of the reservoir for irrigation, and

[1] *History of Eastern India*, by Montgomery Martin (London, 1838), vol ii. p. 220.

the harvest, one of the heaviest deductions, is in favour of the tenant." [1]

Ploughmen in the northern tracts, who engaged themselves by the season, received an advance of Rs.5 to Rs.20, and laboured for their masters till this was worked off. In the southern tracts a curious division of the crops was made. The owner of the field first took double the quantity of the seed, and then two-thirds of the remainder; the labourer got the remaining third.

The hill tribes were less careful in cultivation, less industrious, and more addicted to drink, than the Hindu cultivators. Among these hill tribes the northern were more industrious and sober than the southern, though even among the former both men and women often get very drunk. The method of raising crops among the hill tribes was peculiar. Small holes, two or three fingers deep, were made in the interstices between the stones on the steepest declivities of hills, and in each hole were dropped ten or twelve seeds taken by chance from a promiscuous mixture, and the crops were reaped as they came month after month. Cotton was grown by the northern tribes, not by the southern.

All castes were permitted to spin. 160,000 women were supposed to spin, and each woman made an annual income of Rs.4½, or 9s., after deducting the cost of the cotton. This was added to the family income.

Few weavers worked in silk alone. A great many near the town of Bhagalpur made Tasar fabrics of silk and cotton intermixed; 3275 looms were so employed. The Company's Commercial Resident advanced Rs.10,000 annually for the fabrics known as Baftas and Namunas. The annual profit of each weaver employed in the

[1] *History of Eastern India*, by Montgomery Martin (London, 1838) vol. ii. p. 223.

mixed silk and cotton industry was supposed to be Rs.46, or 92s.—beside what his women made.

For the weaving of cotton cloths there were 7279 looms; each loom made an income of Rs.20, or 40s., in the year. By another calculation the profits of a man and wife engaged in this industry appeared to be Rs.32, or 64s., in the year. Cotton carpets, tapes, tent-ropes, chintz, and blankets were also made in this District.

Among the other important industries of the District may be mentioned bracelets of coarse glass, leather-tanning, iron-work, and carpentry, pottery, stone-cutting, gold and silver works, and pewter works. Indigo was produced by European planters, and the nitre produced was bought by the Company.

The people were less addicted to markets than in Bengal, and dealt more with shopkeepers and traders. Gold had almost entirely disappeared; the Calcutta Kuldar Rupees were by far the most common currency, and copper coins of different kinds were much used. "In the south-west part of the District coin is seldom seen, and most commercial transactions are carried on by exchange of commodities."[1]

There was not much river traffic in this district. The freight of 100 maunds (8000 lbs.) from Monghyr to Calcutta (300 miles) was 10 to 14 rupees, or 20 to 28 shillings. The greater part of the internal trade of the country was carried on by bullock-carts or pack-bullocks. There was only one important road through the District, that passing from Calcutta to Patna and Benares, but during the rains it became impassable even for loaded bullocks. The Baldiya-Beparis, or traders with pack-bullocks, were numerous. Travellers generally journeyed on foot, and found shelter at night in the shops of Mudis, or sweet-sellers, for one or

[1] *History of Eastern India*, by Montgomery Martin (London, 1898), vol. ii. p. 283.

two pice (a penny) the night, including cooking; while the articles required for food were separately paid for. Mahomedan travellers paid double for room and cooking, because they required special cooking by Bhatiyaras.

DISTRICT GORAKHPUR.

(Area, 7423 square miles; population, 1,385,495.)

Although in some parts little rice was grown, yet on the whole rice was a most considerable crop, and was reared where no artificial irrigation was required. Wheat was a most important crop, and in many divisions of the District exceeded the quantity of rice. Wheat and barley intermixed were in pretty common use. Some wheat was sown intermixed with oil seeds, and some barley was sown intermixed with pease.

Among leguminous crops, Arhar, Chanâ, Mas, Masur, Bhringi, and peas were common. Various farinaceous herbs were grown, and Tisi, Til, and Rai were cultivated for oils. Cotton was cultivated to a small extent; the date-palm and Mahua were grown for their saccharine juice, and sugar-cane was cultivated on 1600 acres. Tobacco and the betel-leaf was largely grown; poppy cultivation had been prohibited by the Company's Government.

Fields were watered from rivers, canals, tanks, and marshes by means of baskets swung by ropes, and ten men could irrigate three to five thousand square feet daily. Some fields were watered from wells by means of leathern bags raised by cattle. The greater part of the rent was paid in money, although in some places it was paid by a division of the crop. Where the latter system prevailed, the landlord received one-fourth of the crop after deducting ploughing, sowing, reaping, and other charges.[1]

[1] *History of Eastern India*, by Montgomery Martin (London, 1898), vol. ii. p. 537.

Gorakhpur was one of those Districts which had formerly flourished under Suja-ud-Dowla, Nawab of Oudh, which had suffered from exactions, rebellion, and depopulation, when the rents were assigned to Colonel Hanny under Asof-ud-Dowla, and which had been ceded to the Company in 1801 under the arrangement made by the Marquis of Wellesley. We have narrated these facts in preceding chapters, and have also shown that Lord Wellesley gave his pledge in 1803 and 1805 to conclude a Permanent Settlement in the Ceded and Conquered Provinces—a pledge which was never redeemed. It is interesting to read Dr. Buchanan's account of Gorakhpur, one of the Ceded Districts, and visited by him some ten years afrer the cession was made.

"It is indeed said, that during the government of Suja-ud-Dowla, the District was in a much better state than at present, and that the rents having been farmed to Colonel Hanny, that gentleman took such violent measures in the collection as to depopulate the country, and I certainly perceive many traces of cultivation where now there are wastes and woods. . . .

"When the country was ceded to the English, Major Rudledge, appointed to the management, acted with great vigour and prudence. He instantly, while the known power of our discipline gave him authority, dismantled every stronghold, and thus established the uncontrollable authority of the law, which gave a protection to the lower orders before unknown, and brought settlers from all quarters. His claims at first were very moderate, and the principal error committed was in making the settlement for too short a period. . . .

"On the whole I must say that the proprietors in this District appear to me to have been very hardly treated. Wherever the country is fully occupied, such as is the case on the right of the Ghagra, I would recommend a Perpetual Settlement on the footing of Bengal, Behar, and Benares."[1]

Here we have the old story told once again. Wherever the Company's dominions extended, disturbances were succeeded by peace, and the reign of law replaced disorder. But the land was subjected to a heavy and increasing assessment, and the hand of the tax-gatherer was felt heavier in Northern India for many decades than the occasional outrages of invaders and freebooters in previous times.

One hundred and seventy-five thousand six hundred women found employment in spinning cotton, and made an annual income of Rs.2½, or 5s. There were 5434 families of weavers, possessing 6114 looms, and each loom brought an annual income of Rs.23½, or 47s. Dr. Buchanan thought this was too low an estimate, and believed that each loom brought an income of Rs.36, or 72s., in the year. Chintz was made in Nawabganj, and blankets were woven for local consumption.

Carpenters worked in iron, or made doors, windows, carts, agricultural implements, palanquins, boxes, and sometimes boats. Between 200 and 400 boats were made every year. Braziers made vessels of bell-metal. Six men could turn out in three months articles to the value of Rs.240, which left them a profit of Rs.56. This meant a monthly earning of over Rs.3, or 6s. for each man. Many brass ornaments were also made. Sugar and salt were manufactured in the district.

Grain was largely imported from the kingdom still left to the Nawab of Oudh, and also from the level country possessed by Nepal. Sugar and tobacco were imported from Saran District and elsewhere; elephants and copper vessels came from Nepal, and brass and bell-metal articles from Patna. The carrying trade

[1] *History of Eastern India*, by Montgomery Martin (London, 1838), vol ii. pp. 547 and 549.

was done either by settled traders, or by traders with pack-bullocks, or by farmers owning bullock-carts. Kapariya merchants imported cloth, Banjara merchants brought salt and Nuniha merchants retailed it, Baniyas retailed grains, cotton merchants imported cottons, and Mahajans lent money to cultivators to pay their rents, and to landlords to pay their Land Tax to the Government.

There were weekly markets as at Shahabad, Lucknow, and Benares. Rupees were in common use, and the Calcutta Rupee was seldom seen. The local coinage of copper had been stopped, Nepal copper coins were in common use, and Cowri shells were also used as money.

A religious mendicant of Gorakhpur had built some very fine bridges for the good of his fellow-townsmen. There were four Sada-bratas, or houses of charity, at Gorakhpur, two at Bhewapur, one at Lalganj, and one at Magahar.

DINAJPUR DISTRICT.

(Area, 5374 square miles; population, 3,000,000.)

Rice was the most important crop of the District, and some lands produced two crops of rice, one reaped at the close of the summer and the other in winter. A third kind of rice called Boro was cultivated in small quantities and reaped in spring.

The higher lands which grew the summer rice received some manure, and grew winter crops such as mustard. The lower lands which grew the winter rice required no manuring, and produced only one crop. Women husked the rice by a wooden lever six feet long called Dhenki, and 40 seers of unhusked rice yielded a little over 28 seers of husked rice.

Wheat and barley were small crops in Dinajpur, and Marua was grown in poor lands. Among leguminous plants, Kalai, Khesari, and Masur were the most common, and field-pea was the most common pulse. Mustard, Rai, and linseed were grown for oils.

Nearly 37,000 acres were occupied by plantations —Mango, jack-fruit, tamarind, &c., and 83,000 acres were for vegetables for the kitchen. Jute was grown on 13,000 acres, cotton on 8000 acres, flax on 5000 acres, and sugar-cane on 8000 acres. Tobacco occupied 500 acres, and the betel-leaf 200 acres.

Indigo and safflower were grown for dyes, and the former was grown on 5000 acres. The practice which Dr. Buchanan found prevailing is the same which prevails to this day in some parts of Bengal. Each cultivator was required by the European planter to grow indigo in a portion of his holding.

Thirteen hundred acres of fine lands, all within a mile of the Mahananda river, and amidst noble groves of Mango, Banyan, and Pepul, grew mulberry plants for the silkworm. The Company's Commercial Resident made advances for a great part of the cocoons.

Irrigation of fields was in common use, though not so common as it ought to have been. The number of artificial lakes in the District was numerous, and most of them had springs, so that the supply of water was generally sufficient. Whenever rains failed, recourse was had to these lakes.

There were 480,000 ploughs in the District, which meant 960,000 plough bullocks and cows, besides 336,000 breeding cows. The pasture land consisted of 261 square miles of inundated lands which were overgrown with coarse grass in the dry season, 221 miles of woods and forests, about 300 miles of barren lands, and about 650 miles of lands occasionally cultivated, four-fifths of which was always untilled. No rent was demanded for the pasture of cattle, nor were they prevented from going on any field which was not producing some crop.[1]

Holdings of 55 acres were considered very large ones, those of 15 to 20 acres were comfortable and easy, while the poorer cultivators who, with their families, formed the bulk of the population, had holdings of 5 to 10 acres. The cost of cultivation was not more than one-half the produce, and the rent did not exceed one-fourth the produce, and was always paid in money.[2] In most parts of the District leases were granted in perpetuity to the cultivators, and in some places they "pretend to a right of perpetual possession at the usual rate of rent, if they have occupied a farm for ten years."

Cotton spinning, which was the principal manufacture, occupied the leisure hours "of all the women of higher rank, and of the greater part of the farmers' wives." Rs.3, or 6s., the year was the usual income each woman made by spinning in her afternoons. The total value of raw cotton bought by spinners in the District was Rs.250,000, the value of the yarn made was Rs.1,165,000, and the profit of the women was therefore Rs.915,000, or nearly £100,000.

The Maldai cloths, so called from their being manufactured at Malda, consisted of silk warp and cotton woof. Four thousand looms were employed on this work, and it was said that each loom made 20 rupees' worth of cloth in a month, which Dr. Buchanan considered too high an estimate. About 800 looms were employed for the larger pieces in the form of Elachis, and received advances from the Company's agents.

The manufacture of cloth made entirely of silk was confined to the vicinity of Malda and to some 500

[1] *History of Eastern India*, by Montgomery Martin (London, 1838), vol. ii. p. 889.

[2] *Ibid.*, vol. ii. pp. 907 and 908.

houses of weavers, and the total manufacture was valued at Rs.120,000, or £12,000.

The manufacture of pure cotton cloths was of more importance. The whole cotton cloth woven in the District was valued at Rs.1,674,000, or £167,400.

The lower caste Hindus—the Koch, the Poleya, and the Rajbansi—wove Pat or jute into fabrics for their own wear. Most families had looms, and most women worked in the afternoons.

The flowering cotton cloth with the needle gave a good deal of occupation to the Mahomedan women of Malda. The flowers were either Kosida having running patterns, or Chikon having detached flowers or spots. Some Mahomedan women also made silk strings for tying trousers or necklaces or bracelets.

Connected with the weaving industry was the important trade of dyeing. Indigo, lac, safflower, and turmeric, Moski, Horitoki, Moujista, and various flowers were the ingredients for dyeing. Building, pottery, mats, bracelets, leather-works, carpentry, bricklaying, copper, tin, and iron-works, sugar manufacture, and indigo manufacture, were among the other important industries. The last industry had already given rise to complaints against the European planters, and the reasons assigned for their unpopularity are classed by Dr. Buchanan under eight heads. Firstly, the planter considered the growers "as his slaves, beats and confines them whenever he is dissatisfied"; secondly, that the growers were "cheated both in the measure of their land and in the measure of the weed"; thirdly, that the whole produce of the field did not exceed the rent; fourthly, that the planters were "insolent and violent"; fifthly, that they interfered with the collection of rents; sixthly, that they belonged to the "governing caste"; seventhly, that they prevented the landlords' exactions; and eighthly, that they deterred cultivators from the work of cultivation.

Dr. Buchanan thought the complaints, though often exaggerated, were not unfounded, and held that "infinite advantage would arise from altogether refusing new licenses, and restricting Europeans, who are not responsible to the Company for their conduct, to a residence in the principal towns and seaports."[1] The action which the Company's Government took to prevent the growing evil will be narrated in the next chapter.

A great portion of the trade of the District had passed from the hands of native traders to that of the Company. There were no longer any Saudagars or great native merchants in the District. "One family, indeed, has acquired immense wealth in that line, and for nine generations the forefathers of Baidyanath Mandal carried on an extensive commerce with great reputation and propriety. The present head of the family has given up trade, has made large purchases of land, and is just as much despised as his forefathers were respected."[2]

Smaller merchants, called Mahajans, with capitals from Rs.2000 to Rs.25,000, residing in the District, exported rice, sugar, molasses, oil, and tobacco; and imported salt, cotton, metals, and spices. The whole number of fixed shops in the District did not amount to 2000, but open markets were numerous. Petty traders were called Paikars. Gold had become scarce, the Kuldar Rupee of Calcutta was the usual currency, and Cowri shells were largely used

In the rainy season boats reached most villages, but there was little carrying trade then. In the dry months goods were conveyed by pack-bullocks, there being "few or no roads" for the conveyance of goods. Boats conveyed a hundred maunds (8000 lbs.) to Calcutta for Rs.13, or 26s. Bullock-carts conveyed goods twelve miles for less than half a rupee.

[1] *History of Eastern India*, by Montgomery Martin (London, 1838), vol. ii. p. 996.

[2] *Ibid.*, vol. ii. p. 1001.

PURNIYA DISTRICT.

(Area, 6340 square miles; population, 2,904,380.)

The spring rice, the summer rice, and the winter rice were the principal crops of the District. Seventy seers of rice in husk produced 40 seers of clean rice when husked without boiling. When the operation was performed by boiling, 65 seers of unhusked rice gave 40 seers of clean. The Dhenki, or wooden lever, was everywhere used by women in this operation.

Wheat was more used than at Dinajpur, and barley was sown on the banks of rivers without previous cultivation and much used by the poor. Marua was also greatly used, specially on the west side of the Kosi. Maize, Janera, and different kinds of millets were also raised.

Among leguminous plants, Mas-kalai, Khesari, Arhar, Bhut, Kulti, and Mung were largely used. Mustard and Rai, Tisi and castor plant were grown for oils. Twenty-eight thousand acres were cultivated for vegetables.

Pat or jute was grown for its fibre; the cultivation of cotton was very limited. The cultivation of the sugar-cane was chiefly confined to the banks of the Kan Kayi river. Half the tobacco grown in the District was cultivated near the capital town, and the betel-leaf was an important article, although much less in use than in Dinajpur.

There were seventeen indigo factories under the management of Mr. Ellerton in the south-east part of the District, while there were some fifty other factories in other parts of the District. Safflower or Kusum was an article of somewhat greater importance than in the more eastern Districts. The cultivation of mulberry for silkworms was entirely confined to the south-east corner of the District.

The pasture of the District consisted of 234 square

miles of high fallow land, 4·82 miles of land not cultivated, and 186 miles of broken corners and roads. Besides this, there were some 389 miles of low lands covered with reeds and bushes. Finally in December and January, after the winter rice was reaped, the rice stubble was a great resource. Altogether the pasture lands would be inadequate for the cattle of the District but for the wilds of the Morang, belonging to the Nepal Government, where the owner of a herd of five or six hundred gave one male calf to the Gurkha officer as the pasture fee. "In some parts also of this District the Zemindars, although in other respects rigid Hindus, have had sense to take a rent for pasture."

The rents varied according to various circumstances, but "allowing one-half [of the produce] for the fair expense of cultivation, and one-half of the remainder for the net profit of the tenant, we may judge somewhat of the extent of the fair demands which the Zemindar might make, and which probably very far exceeds what they receive."[1]

In other words, Dr. Buchanan considered one-fourth of the produce would be fair rent; but the Zemindars of Purniya and elsewhere in Bengal were taking much less as *rent*, at the very time when the Company's Government was realising nearly half the produce from the cultivators of Madras as *land tax*.

No caste was considered disgraced by spinning, and a very large proportion of the women of the District did some spinning in their leisure hours. Dr. Buchanan found it very difficult to estimate their profits, but conjectured that the cotton used by them annually was worth Rs.300,000, and the thread spun valued at Rs.1,300,000, leaving a profit of Rs.1,000,000, or £100,000.

[1] *History of Eastern India*, by Montgomery Martin (London, 1838), vol. iii. p. 290.

Pure silk fabrics were woven by 200 looms, and the goods were worth Rs.48,600, out of raw silk worth Rs.34,200, leaving a profit of Rs.14,400. This would bring an annual income of Rs.72, or 144s. for each loom.

Weavers who made clothes of silk and cotton intermixed were nearly on the same footing as at Dinajpur.

Weavers of cotton were numerous, and were mostly employed in producing coarse goods for country use. Three thousand five hundred looms employed in finer work produced Rs.506,000 worth of goods, and brought a net profit of Rs.149,000, or about 86s. annually for each loom. Ten thousand looms employed on coarse goods produced cloths to the value of Rs.1,089,500, and brought a net profit of Rs.324,000, or about 65s. annually for each loom.

Weavers of cotton carpets (Satranjis) and tapes were confined to the capital. Coarse linen made of jute was largely produced, and a large proportion of the women in the eastern frontier used this for clothing. The blankets and woollen goods were coarse, but were of much use to the poor in the rains and winter.

Goldsmiths, carpenters, workers in the Bidri and other metals, blacksmiths, and dyers, were among the other industrious classes of Purniya. The manufacture of sugar was at a low ebb. Five hundred families made salt.

Cotton was imported from the west of India, and sugar from Dinajpur and Patna. There were seven houses of bankers at Purniya, and they granted bills of exchange for money paid to them, and also discounted bills of other houses. "If large exchanges of gold and silver are required, they can only be procured from these Kothi-walas (houses). Jagat Set's house will draw at once for Rs.100,000. The others will not exceed half that sum." The old unmilled rupees were as commonly in use as the milled (Kuldar) rupees of Calcutta. "In a country so exceedingly poor, a gold coinage is highly distressing to the lower classes, and in my humble opinion ought to be entirely discontinued. Even a rupee in this country is a large sum. . . . The gold has fortunately almost vanished, and perhaps should never be allowed to return, by being no longer held a legal proffer of payment. In most parts of the District the currency consists entirely of silver and Cowries. Towards the western parts a few of the copper coins called Paysa, worth about $\frac{1}{60}$ of a rupee, are current, but even these are too large for the small money of a country where two of them are equal to the comfortable daily board wages of a man-servant."[1]

The District was well provided with the means of using water carriage, and there were more boats than in Dinajpur. The hire for carrying 100 maunds (8000 lbs.) from the District to Calcutta was Rs.14, or 28s. A few roads had been made near the capital, and some indigo factories. Ponies were used for carrying loads, as well as oxen. Rich men provided accommodation and shelter to travellers, and the shops of Mudis or sweet-sellers were inns where they could find lodging and food.

SUMMARY.

The accounts given of the two remaining Districts, Rangpur and Assam, in Dr. Buchanan's volumes are incomplete, and do not contain details about agriculture and rents, industries and trade. It is unnecessary, therefore, to refer to those Districts in the present chapter.

[1] *History of Eastern India*, by Montgomery Martin (London, 1838), vol. ii. pp. 340–342.

The six Districts of which an account has been given above contained a much larger area than what is included in the Districts now known under those names. They formed an area of 36,000 square miles, and had a population of fourteen millions; and the account of these vast and populous Districts gives us a fair idea of the East India Company's entire possessions in Bengal and Northern India. The people were still miserably poor, but cultivation had revived since the time of Warren Hastings, and much waste land had been reclaimed since the Permanent Settlement of 1793.

The Zemindars, though willing enough to obtain as large a rental as they could, never exacted as much as the Company's servants did in Madras, and by this reason they afforded some protection to the people. In exceptional cases they claimed one-half the net produce, after deducting the cost of harvesting, but in return they considered themselves bound to maintain the irrigation works at their own cost. But generally in Bengal they received less than one-fourth the produce as their rents. And as the Government revenue had been permanently fixed, and the rents too were in many places fixed by custom, there was some motive for improvements and the reclaiming of waste lands as the years went by.

What threatened, however, the sources of the income of the people was the declining state of their industries and manufactures. The hardship was already felt in many places visited by Dr. Buchanan, and grew more severe later on. To an account of the industries of the people we now turn.

CHAPTER XIV

DECLINE OF INDUSTRIES (1793–1813)

It will appear from the facts stated in the last two chapters, that large portions of the Indian population were engaged in various industries down to the first decade of the nineteenth century. Weaving was still the national industry of the people; millions of women eked out the family income by their earnings from spinning; and dyeing, tanning, and working in metals also gave employment to millions.

It was not, however, the policy of the East India Company to foster Indian industries. It has been stated in a previous chapter that, as early as 1769, the Directors wished the manufacture of raw silk to be encouraged in Bengal, and that of silk fabrics discouraged. And they also directed that silk-winders should be made to work in the Company's factories, and prohibited from working outside "under severe penalties, by the authority of the Government."[1] This mandate had its desired effect. The manufacture of silk and cotton goods declined in India, and the people who had exported these goods to the markets of Europe and Asia in previous centuries began to import them in increasing quantities. The following figures[2] show the value of cotton goods alone sent out from England to ports east of the Cape of Good Hope, mainly to India, during twenty years.

1 General Letter dated 17th March 1769.

2 Return to an Order of the House of Commons, dated 4th May 1813.

Year ending 5th January.		Year ending 5th January.	
1794	£156	1804	£5,936
1795	717	1805	31,943
1796	112	1806	48,525
1797	2,501	1807	46,549
1798	4,436	1808	69,841
1799	7,317	1809	118,408
1800	19,575	1810	74,695
1801	21,200	1811	114,649
1802	16,191	1812	107,306
1803	27,876	1813	108,824

The Company's Charter was renewed in 1813. An inquiry was made, and witnesses were examined, previous to this renewal.

Very important witnesses, like Warren Hastings, Thomas Munro, and Sir John Malcolm were examined, and the House of Commons showed the utmost concern for the general welfare of the people of India. But in respect of Indian manufactures, they sought to discover how they could be replaced by British manufactures, and how British industries could be promoted at the expense of Indian industries.

India had suffered from repeated famines in the preceding half-century. A famine was desolating Bombay in the very year when the evidence was recorded. Industries and manufactures had declined in Bengal and in Madras. And yet we look in vain in this old volume of recorded evidence for any questions as to the means of reviving those sources of wealth which could insure the prosperity of a nation. We meet, on the contrary, with constant and never-ending inquiries how British goods could be forced on the people of India.

Warren Hastings was asked: "From your knowledge of the Indian character and habits, are you able to speak to the probability of a demand for European commodities by the population of India, for their own use?"

"The supplies of trade," replied Warren Hastings,

"are for the wants and luxuries of a people; the poor in India may be said to have no wants. Their wants are confined to their dwellings, to their food, and to a scanty portion of clothing, all of which they can have from the soil that they tread upon."[1]

Sir John Malcolm, who had lived a good deal among the people of India, and knew them as few Englishmen have known them since, bore high testimony to the many virtues of the nation. Speaking of Northern India, he said: "The Hindoo inhabitants are a race of men, generally speaking, not more distinguished by their lofty stature . . . than they are for some of the finest qualities of the mind; they are brave, generous, and humane, and their truth is as remarkable as their courage." And replying to the question as to whether they were likely to be consumers of British goods, he replied: "They are not likely to become consumers of European articles, because they do not possess the means to purchase them, even if, from their simple habits of life and attire, they required them."[2]

Graeme Mercer, who had served the East India Company as a doctor, and also in the revenue and political departments, described the people of India as "mild in their dispositions, polished in their general manners, in their domestic relations kind and affectionate, submissive to authority, and peculiarly attached to their religious tenets, and to the observance of the rites and ceremonies prescribed by those tenets." And in reference to the introduction of European goods in India he stated that Lord Wellesley had endeavoured to find markets for such goods by instituting fairs in Rohilkhand, exhibiting British woollens in those fairs, and by directing the British Resident

[1] Minutes of Evidence, &c., on the Affairs of the East India Company (1813), p. 3. The opinion of Warren Hastings about the general character of the people of India, expressed before the Lords' Committee, has been quoted in chapter iii. of this work.

[2] *Ibid.*, pp. 54 and 57.

to attend the great fair at Hardwar with the same object.[1]

But the most important witness examined by the Committee of the House of Commons on this memorable occasion was Thomas Munro; and the whole of his evidence was inspired by that sympathy with the people of India and that appreciation of their virtues which had distinguished that gifted Scotchman during his twenty-seven years' work in India, from 1780 to 1807.

Munro said that the average wages of agricultural labour in India was between 4s. and 6s. a month; that the cost of subsistence was between 18s. and 27s. a head per annum; that there was no probability of extending the sale of British woollen goods, because the people used coarse woollen of their own manufacture; and that they were excellent manufacturers, and were likely to imitate English goods. Asked if Hindu women were not slaves to their husbands, Munro replied, "They have as much influence in their families as, I imagine, the women have in this country" [England]. And asked if the civilisation of the Hindus could not be improved by the establishment of an open trade, he gave that memorable answer which has often been quoted and will bear repetition: "I do not understand what is meant by the civilisation of the Hindus; in the higher branches of science, in the knowledge of the theory and practice of good government, and in education which, by banishing prejudice and superstition, opens the mind to receive instruction of every kind from every quarter, they are much inferior to Europeans. But if a good system of agriculture, unrivalled manufacturing skill, a capacity to produce whatever can contribute to convenience or luxury; schools established in every village for teach-

[1] Minutes of Evidence, &c., on the Affairs of the East India Company (1813), pp. 88 and 89.

ing reading, writing, and arithmetic; the general practice of hospitality and charity amongst each other; and above all, a treatment of the female sex full of confidence, respect, and delicacy, are among the signs which denote a civilised people, then the Hindus are not inferior to the nations of Europe; and if civilisation is to become an article of trade between the two countries, I am convinced that this country [England] will gain by the import cargo."[1]

Munro had a high idea of the excellence of the Indian manufactures of his time. Among the causes which precluded the extended sale of British goods in India he mentioned "the religious and civil habits of the natives, and more than anything else, I am afraid, the excellence of their own manufactures." He had used an Indian shawl for seven years, and had found very little difference in it after that long use; while, with regard to imitation shawls produced in England, he said: "I have never seen an European shawl that I would use, even if it were given to me as a present."[2]

The evidence of one other witness deserves mention, that of John Stracey. He had served the East India Company in the Judicial Department, and as Under-Secretary to Government on the Bengal Establishment, and he deposed that the Indian labourer earned from 3s. 6d. to 7s. 6d. a month. How could such a nation use European goods? "I do not know that they use anything in their ordinary use from Europe, except it is some small woollens and broad cloths which they may have accidentally got at a cheap rate."[3]

Inquiries like these fairly disclosed the objects of the House of Commons Committee. It is not in human nature for any race of men to sacrifice their

[1] Minutes of Evidence, &c., on the Affairs of the East India Company (1813), pp. 124, 127, 131.
[2] *Ibid.*, pp. 123 and 172.
[3] *Ibid.*, p. 296.

own interests for those of another; and the British statesmen in the early years of the nineteenth century did all they could to promote British industries at the sacrifice of Indian industries. British manufactures were forced into India through the agency of the Company's Governor-General and Commercial Residents, while Indian manufactures were shut out from England by prohibitive tariffs. The evidence of John Ranking, a merchant, examined by the Commons Committee, will explain this.

"Can you state what is the *ad valorem* duty on piece-goods sold at the East India House?"

"The duty on the class called calicoes is £3, 6s. 8d. per cent. upon importation, and if they are used for home consumption there is a further duty of £68, 6s. 8d. per cent.

"There is another class called muslins, on which the duty on importation is 10 per cent., and if they are used for home consumption, of £27, 6s. 8d. per cent.

"There is a third class, coloured goods, which are prohibited being used in this country, upon which there is a duty upon importation of £3, 6s. 8d. per cent.; they are only for exportation.

"This session of Parliament there has been a new duty of 20 per cent. on the consolidated duties, which will make the duties on calicoes . . . used for home consumption, £78, 6s. 8d. per cent., upon the muslins for home consumption, £31, 6s. 8d."

There was no thought of concealing the real object of these prohibitive duties. The same witness, John Ranking said, further on, "I look upon it as a protecting duty to encourage our own manufactures."[1]

What was the result of these duties on Indian manufactures? Henry St. George Tucker, whose name has been mentioned in a previous chapter in connec-

[1] Minutes of Evidence, &c., on the Affairs of the East India Company (1813), pp. 463 and 467.

tion with land settlements in Northern India, retired to England ripe in Indian experience, and became a Director of the East India Company; and he did not conceal the scope and the effect of England's commercial policy towards India. Writing in 1823, *i.e.* only ten years after the date of the Parliamentary inquiry referred to above, he condemned that policy in the strongest manner.

"What is the commercial policy which we have adopted in this country with relation to India? The silk manufactures and its piece-goods made of silk and cotton intermixed have long since been excluded altogether from our markets; and of late, partly in consequence of the operation of a duty of 67 per cent., but chiefly from the effect of superior machinery, the cotton fabrics, which hitherto constituted the staple of India, have not only been displaced in this country, but we actually export our cotton manufactures to supply a part of the consumption of our Asiatic possessions. India is thus reduced from the state of a manufacturing to that of an agricultural country."[1]

Still more emphatic is the impartial verdict of H. H. Wilson, historian of India.

"It is also a melancholy instance of the wrong done to India by the country on which she has become dependent. It was stated in evidence [in 1813] that the cotton and silk goods of India up to the period could be sold for a profit in the British market at a price from 50 to 60 per cent. lower than those fabricated in England. It consequently became necessary to protect the latter by duties of 70 and 80 per cent. on their value or by positive prohibition. Had this not been the case, had not such prohibitory duties and decrees existed, the mills of Paisley and Manchester would have been stopped in their outset, and

[1] Memorials of the Indian Government, being a selection from the papers of Henry St. George Tucker (London, 1853), p. 494.

could scarcely have been again set in motion, even by the power of steam. They were created by the sacrifice of the Indian manufacture. Had India been independent, she would have retaliated, would have imposed prohibitive duties upon British goods, and would thus have preserved her own productive industry from annihilation. This act of self-defence was not permitted her; she was at the mercy of the stranger. British goods were forced upon her without paying any duty, and the foreign manufacturer employed the arm of political injustice to keep down and ultimately strangle a competitor with whom he could not have contended on equal terms."[1]

While such was the policy pursued in England to discourage Indian manufactures, the system pursued in India did not tend to improve them. The revenues of the country were spent on the Company's Investments, *i.e.* on the purchase of Indian goods for exportation and sale in Europe without any commercial return. How much of the country's revenues was applied in this manner will appear from the following list[2]:

Year.	Prime Cost of Investment, India.	Year.	Prime Cost of Investment, India.
1793-4	£1,220,106	1803-4	1,187, 07
1794-5	1,288,059	1804-5	1,088,700
1795-6	1,821,512	1805-6	1,335,460
1796-7	1,708,379	1806-7	986,310
1797-8	1,025,204	1807-8	887,119
1798-9	2,019,265	1808-9	1,013,740
1799-1800	1,665,689	1809-10	1,240,315
1800-1	2,013,975	1810-11	963,429
1801-2	1,425,168	1811-12	1,110,909
1802-3	1,133,526		
	Total of nineteen years		25,134,672
	Annual average		1,322,877

[1] Mill's *History of British India*, Wilson's continuation, Book I., chapter viii., note.

[2] Taken from statement in p. 487, of Minutes of Evidence, &c., on the Affairs of the East India Company, 1813.

The method pursued in supplying these Investments was this. On being informed of the amount required by the Directors, the Board of Trade in India forwarded a copy of the order to the several factories where the goods were produced. The Commercial Residents at the factories divided the order among the several subordinate factories, and required the weavers to attend on a specified day to receive advances. Each weaver was debited for the advance made to him, and credited for the deliveries he made. If the weavers objected to the rate, the Board of Trade decided the matter according to its own judgment.[1]

How this system was frequently abused appears from the evidence of many witnesses examined by the Commons Committee in 1813. Thomas Munro deposed that in the Baramahal the Company's servants assembled the principal weavers and placed a guard over them until they entered into engagements to supply the Company only.[2] When once a weaver accepted an advance he seldom got out of his liability. A peon was placed over him to quicken his deliveries if he delayed, and he was liable to be prosecuted in the courts of justice. The sending of a peon meant a fine of one anna (about 1½d.) a day on the weaver, and the peon was armed with a rattan, which was not unoften used to good purpose. Fine was sometimes imposed on the weavers, and their brass utensils were seized for its recovery.[3] The whole weaving population of villages were thus held in subjection to the Company's factories; and Mr. Cox deposed that 1500 weavers, not including their families and connections, were under his authority in the factory over which he presided.

[1] Minutes of Evidence, &c., on the Affairs of the East India Company (1813,) p. 532.

[2] *Ibid.*, p. 153.

[3] *Ibid.*, pp. 537–539.

The control under which the weaver population was held was not merely a matter of practice, but was legalised by Regulations. It was provided that a weaver who had received advances from the Company "shall on no account give to any other persons whatever, European or Native, either the labour or the produce engaged to the Company;" that on his failing to deliver the stipulated cloths, "the Commercial Resident shall be at liberty to place peons upon him in order to quicken his deliveries;" that on his selling his cloths to others the weaver "shall be liable to be prosecuted in the Dewani Adalat;" that "weavers possessed of more than one loom, and entertaining one or more workmen, shall be subject to a penalty of 35 per cent. on the stipulated price of every piece of cloth that they may fail to deliver according to the written agreement;" that landlords and tenants "are enjoined not to hinder the Commercial Residents or their officers from access to weavers;" and that they "are strictly prohibited from behaving with disrepect to the Commercial Residents" of the Company.[1]

Manufactures do not flourish when manufacturers are held under any sort of thraldom. But the worst result of this system was that, while the Company's servants assumed such power and authority over the manufacturers of India, other Europeans often assumed larger powers and used them with less restraint.

"The Englishman," said Warren Hastings, "is quite a different character in India; the name of an Englishman is both his protection and a sanction for offences which he would not dare to commit at home."

"There is one general consequence," said Lord Teignmouth, "which I should think likely to result from a general influx of Europeans into the interior of the country and their intercourse with the natives,

[1] Regulation xxxi. of 1793.

that, without elevating the character of the natives it would have a tendency to depreciate their estimate of the general European character."

"I find no difference in traders," said Thomas Munro, "whether their habits are quiet or not when they quit this country; they are very seldom quiet when they find themselves among an unresisting people over whom they can exercise their authority, for every trader going into India is considered as some person connected with the Government. I have heard that within these two or three years, I think in Bengal in 1810, private traders, indigo merchants, have put inhabitants of the country in the stocks, have assembled their followers and given battle to each other, and that many have been wounded."

"I have always observed," said Thomas Sydenham, "that Englishmen are more apt than those of any other nation to commit violences in foreign countries, and this I believe to be the case in India."[1]

So frequent were the acts of violence committed by European traders and indigo planters in the interior of the country in the early years of the nineteenth century, that the Government was compelled to issue circulars to magistrates on the subject. In a circular dated 13th July 1810 it was stated:

"The offences to which the following remarks refer, and which have been established, beyond all doubt or dispute, against individual indigo planters, may be reduced to the following heads:

"*First*, Acts of violence which, although they amount not in the legal sense of the word to murder, have occasioned the death of natives.

"*Second*, The illegal detention of the natives in confinement, specially in stocks, with a view to the recovery of balances alleged to be due from them, or for other causes.

[1] Minutes of Evidence, &c. (1813), pp. 2, 10, 138, 359.

"*Third*, Assembling in a tumultuary manner the people attached to their respective factories, and others, and engaging in violent affrays with other indigo planters.

"*Fourth*, Illicit infliction of punishment, by means of rattan or otherwise, on the cultivators or other natives."

And the circular directed magistrates to cause the destruction of the stocks, to report cases of flogging and inflicting corporal punishment on the cultivators, and to prevent European planters residing in the interior unless they conformed with the spirit of the Government orders. A further circular, issued on the 20th July 1810, directed magistrates to report cases in which indigo planters compelled the cultivators to receive advances, and adopted illicit means to compel them to cultivate indigo.[1]

The oppression of indigo planters in Bengal continued, however, for half a century, until the people of Bengal rose and resisted, and the cultivation of indigo by European planters terminated in most parts of Bengal after the Indigo disturbance of 1859.

Dina Bandhu Mitra, the greatest dramatist of Bengal, exposed the oppression of the planters in his memorable drama, entitled "The Mirror of Indigo." The Rev. James Long was fined and imprisoned by the High Court of Calcutta for translating this work into English. And the name of Ashley Eden, afterwards Lieutenant-Governor of Bengal, is gratefully remembered by the people for his endeavours to put a stop to this oppression.

A special law, which is called the "Slave Law" by the people of India, still exists for providing labourers for the cultivation of tea in Assam; ignorant men and women are bound down by penal clauses, upon their signing a contract, to work in tea gardens for a number

[1] Minutes of Evidence, &c. (1813), p. 567.

of years; and the utmost endeavours of the Chief Commissioner of Assam during the present year (1901) have failed to secure for these poor labourers an adequate pay during their enforced stay in the gardens. But we must return to our narrative of 1813.

The parliamentary inquiries of 1813 brought no relief to Indian manufacturers. The prohibitive duties were not reduced. The Company's Investments were not stopped. On the contrary, it was distinctly sanctioned by the Committee of the whole House.

"The whole or part of any surplus that may remain of the above described rents, revenues, and profits, after providing for the several appropriations, and defraying the several charges before mentioned, shall be applied to the provision of the Company's Investments in India, in remittances to China for the provision of Investments there, or towards the liquidation of debts in India, or such other purposes as the Court of Directors, with the approbation of the Board of Commissioners, shall from time to time direct."[1]

In the Parliamentary debates of 1813, says the historian, H. H. Wilson, "professions of a concern for the interests of India were, it is true, not unsparingly uttered, but it would be difficult to show that the majority of the party who engaged in the discussion were solely instigated by a disinterested regard for the welfare of the Indian subjects of the Crown. . . . The merchants and manufacturers of the United Kingdom avowedly looked only to their own profits."[2]

The real object of the Parliamentary inquiry of 1813 was to promote the interests of the manufacturers of England. Napoleon Bonaparte had excluded British manufactures from the Continental ports; the merchants and manufacturers of England were labouring

[1] Resolutions of the Committee of the whole House, 1813.
[2] Mill's *History of British India*, Wilson's Continuation, Book I. chap. viii.

under difficulties; the country was menaced with distress unless some new vent for the sale of its industrial products could be discovered. Under these circumstances the national demand against the monopoly of the East India Company increased in force, and the monopoly of the Company's trade with India was abolished when their Charter was renewed in 1813. British traders thus obtained, for the first time, a free outlet into the great field of India; it was not in human nature that they should concern themselves much with the welfare of Indian manufacturers.

CHAPTER XV

STATE OF INDUSTRIES (1813-1835)

It was thus that the monopoly of the East India Company in the Éastern trade was first abolished, when their Charter was renewed in 1813. Private trade, being once admitted, increased in volume, while the Company's trade declined. And when the time approached for renewing the Charter once more in 1833, the question arose whether the East India Company's trade should not be abolished altogether. Public opinion in England was strong in favour of the view that trade between England and India should be left altogether in the hands of private traders without the unfair competition of a Company with territorial possessions in India, and that the duties of traders were not consistent with the duties of the rulers of an empire. This last argument was urged with increasing vehemence by the traders of London and the other large commercial centres of England, who were jealous of the unfair advantages possessed by the Company in India, and who hoped to increase their own trade if the Company could be stopped from carrying on trade at all.

Accordingly the Company's trade was abolished altogether in 1833, and from that date they stood forth simply as administrators of India, drawing their dividends from the revenues of India.

A great deal of evidence on the trade and industries of India, and all branches of Indian administration, was recorded while the controversy was still going on in 1830, 1831, and 1832. Valuable evidence was given before the Lords' Committee in 1830. Still more valuable and copious evidence was conveyed in the Commons' Reports of 1830, of 1830–31, and of 1831. Fresh evidence was given before the Commons' Committee of 1832, and was published in six ponderous volumes, containing well-nigh six thousand folio pages.[1]

The portions of all this voluminous evidence which relate to trade and industries are somewhat one-sided. The Lords and Commons inquired into the state of the industries carried on by British capital, or which might give employment to British capital; the industries of the people of India, and the wages and profits of the artisans of India, did not interest them much. They inquired if the abolition of the Company's trade would increase the volume of British trade with India, and would benefit the private traders and manufacturers of England; the state of the internal trade of India, carried on by the people of that country, did not much attract their attention. To foster the indigenous trade and industries of the people of India was not the object of the inquiries made either in 1813 or in 1832, nor has this object been even seriously and steadily pursued during the seventy years which have elapsed since.

Nevertheless, we get a great deal of information from the evidence recorded, such as it is. And it will be our endeavour to condense this voluminous evidence in an intelligible form within the brief limits of this chapter.

COTTON.

Indian cotton was shorter stapled than the American, had more dirt, and there was more waste in the manufacture. It was generally used in making coarse

[1] The six volumes are: (1) Public, (2) Finance and Trade (3) Revenue, (4) Judicial, (5) Military, (6) Political.

goods, or mixed with wool in woollen fabrics. Surat cotton was considered the best, and the Dacca muslin, made in Bengal, was not equalled in England. A good quality of cotton was successfully grown in Tinnevelly from seed imported from the Isle of France. Long-stapled cotton was scarcely grown in India except near the sea, and was not required by the people for their own manufactures. All the cotton was spun by hand in India.[1]

The exportation of the Indian cotton had fallen off from the competition of the American market. The cotton of the East India Company's dominions was the worst that came to the British market. Between the cleaned Bombay cottons and the American upland cottons there was a difference in value of 10 to 15 per cent. The Surat cotton was generally applicable only to the coarser manufactures of England, and was also mixed in spinning the finer cottons. Attempts to improve the cotton in India had not succeeded; in some of the experiments the cotton deteriorated, in others the seeds did not come up well. Cotton was grown by the people of India, was brought to Bombay, and was purchased by Europeans. No lands producing cottons were in the hands of Europeans, and they had no share in the culture of it. The machine for cleaning cotton in India was a small hand-gin or wooden cylindrical machine, used from times immemorial. It cost 6d., was turned by hand, required no strength, and cleaned the cotton rudely. The East India Company's Investment of cotton was procured by their Commercial Residents principally from Tinnevelly. In 1823 the Investment was 8000 bales of 250 lbs., and was sent to China. Bengal was unfit for the cultivation of cotton by Europeans, but a fine variety was grown by the people near Dacca. The best Indian cotton was grown in Gujrat and Cutch. Indian cotton

[1] Evidence before the Lords' Committee, 1830. Digest.

was first imported into England in 1790, and American cotton in 1791. The total export of cotton from India in 1827 was 68 million lbs., valued at one million sterling. The total import of American cotton into England was 294 million lbs. A cotton mill had been started in Calcutta for spinning yarn.[1]

The Company exported cotton largely from Bengal and Bombay, and they did so from Madras till the factories were abolished. Cotton was conveyed from the interior to Calcutta in boats without sufficient protection from the weather, lying on board four or five months; it was then put into cotton screws, with a quantity of seeds screwed into it, and in a state of dampness and mouldiness it was shipped for England. It was impossible that the finest cotton could under such treatment arrive in England in a better state than Bengal cottons did.[2]

SILK.

The silkworm was principally confined to Bengal; it would not flourish in Northern India, and the soil of Bombay was not suited to the mulberry. The Company's Investment for England was provided by the agency of their Commercial Residents, who obtained it from the men who reared the cocoons, to whom advances were made. The Company had about twelve Residencies and extensive manufactories, but did not carry on the manufacture beyond reeling. In a few manufactories piece-goods were manufactured from "Putney silk." The manufacture of finer silks had much diminished, and English silks were imported to a considerable extent. Several European residents had factories, but not so large as the Company's, and the Company commanded the market. The defect of the

[1] Evidence in the Commons' Reports of 1830, 1830–31, and 1831. Digest.

[2] Evidence before the Commons' Committee, 1832. Digest.

Indian silk was its want of staple and want of cleanliness. The best Indian silk nearly sold as high as the best Italian silk, but the greater part of the Indian silk was inferior. The trade was in the hands of the Company, which could not exercise the strict superintendence required for production of fine quality. Very little Indian silk was sold for exportation; China silk would be preferred.[1]

There were three kinds of mulberry grown in India,—the white mulberry cultivated in Europe, the dark purple mulberry cultivated in China, and the Indian mulberry. There were two kinds of worm—the country worm, and the annual worm brought from Italy or China and producing a finer silk. The cultivation of the mulberry and the production of the cocoons were left to the people, the Company making advances to them, and settling the price after the delivery of the silk or the cocoons. The Company had eleven or twelve filatures in Bengal, the machinery being on the Italian principle and very simple. The Company's Residents were paid by a commission of 2½ per cent. on the quantity supplied, and were also allowed to purchase on their own account. They were not good judges of silk. The raw silk of Bengal had deteriorated in quality, but the quantity exported had increased owing to the opening of trade and a decrease in the duties. The shipments of raw silk to England between 1823 and 1828 had increased 35½ per cent., while the Company's Investments had increased only 17½ per cent.[2]

Mulberry and castor-oil plants were applied in Bengal for the feeding of silkworms. The mulberry trees were planted in rows about six or eight inches apart, and were three feet high. The extreme rapidity of the produce was what the people aimed at, which

[1] Evidence before the Lords' Committee, 1830. Digest.

[2] Evidence in the Commons' Reports, 1830, 1830–31, and 1831 Digest.

would give them an immediate return; but the return would be greater if the method pursued in the south of Europe were adopted, Leaves were first picked about four months after the trees were planted; afterwards there was a crop every eight or ten weeks; in the first year there were four crops, in the second six. One-third of an English acre would feed 1000 worms a day. The difference in the silk depended on the season in which it was spun: the best season was the November Bund, in which the cocoons were finished spinning early in December; the worst was the rainy season. The country worms hatched four times a year, the annual only once. The Company's Residents made advances through middlemen called Pykars, and received cocoons through them in their factories, where they were reeled by native workmen hired and paid by the factory. There were twelve Residencies; the Residents fixed the price after delivery, subject to the confirmation of the Board of Trade. The Residents were hardly such persons as a manufacturer would select to superintend his establishment. There was a steady rise in the produce of the raw silk from 1815 to 1830, and the Company increased its quantity. The Company also introduced into India the Italian method of winding. The trade was perfectly free, and persons had gone from England and built filatures, but had not succeeded; they could not compete with the Company. Italian silk was good, French silk was good, Bengal silk was also as much in demand as any other, but was not so strong as the silk of Italy, France, or Turkey. It was also coarser in quality than the Italian silk, because the people looked to the quantity rather than to the quality, and did not bestow the same care in reeling as in Italy or France. Hence the Bengal silk was more foul and uneven and "endy," having many breaks in it.[1]

[1] Evidence before the Commons' Committee, 1832. Digest.

The reader will perceive from the foregoing digest of evidence the change which had been effected during seventy years of the Company's rule in Bengal in the cotton and silk industries. Production by independent Indian manufacturers had been discouraged, sometimes by positive prohibition, later on by the influence of the Company's Residents. The weaving of fabrics had been largely discontinued. Men who had worked on their own capital, produced commodities in their own homes and villages, and obtained their own profits, were now dependent on the Company's Residents, who supplied them with raw cotton and raw silk, and received prices which the Residents settled. They had lost their industrial and economic independence with their political independence, and obtained wages and prices for what they were told to produce. Thousands of them looked up to the Company's factory for employment, having ceased to be independent producers for the world's markets. The factories demanded raw produce; the people of India provided the raw produce; forgot their ancient manufacturing skill; lost the profits of manufacture. The public in England marked the increase of trade between Europe and India—the increase in the import of raw produce and the export of manufactured articles—and argued increasing prosperity in India. The Lords and Commons inquired whether this increasing trade should be in the hands of the East India Company or in the hands of private traders. None cared to inquire if this increase in exchange meant the extinction of Indian industries and the loss of industrial profits to India. None desired to inquire if it was possible to revive the weaving industry of India for the economic welfare of the people.

FOOD GRAINS.

A great deal of misconception has always existed in England about the ignorance and the careless cultivation of the Indian cultivators; but those Englishmen who have taken the trouble to study agriculture have endeavoured to dispel this unjust and untrue idea. Dr. Wallick, who was Superintendent of the East India Company's Botanical Garden at Calcutta, gave his evidence on this subject on the 13th August 1832 before the Commons' Committee.

"The husbandry of Bengal has in a great measure been misunderstood by the Europeans out of India. The Bengal husbandry, although in many respects extremely simple and primeval in its mode and form, yet is not quite so low as people generally suppose it to be, and I have often found that very sudden innovations in them have never led to any good results. I have known, for instance, European iron ploughs introduced into Bengal with a view of superseding the extremely tedious and superficial turning of the ground by a common Bengal plough. But what has been the result? That the soil which is extremely superficial, as I took the liberty of mentioning before, which was intended to be torn up, has generally received the admixture of the under soil, which has deteriorated it very much."

Asked if the Indian husbandry was susceptible of any great improvement, Dr. Wallick replied: "Certainly, but not to so great an extent as is generally imagined; for instance, the rice cultivation. I should think, if we were to live for another thousand years, we should hardly see any improvement in that branch of cultivation."[1]

[1] Evidence before the Commons' Committee, 1832, vol. ii., Part I., p. 195. This is the opinion of all experts down to the present day. In 1889 Dr. Voelcker, Consulting Chemist to the Royal Agricultural Society of England, was deputed to India to make inquiries and suggest improvements, in respect of Indian agriculture. And he wrote: "On one point there can be no question, viz. that the ideas generally entertained in England, and often given expression to even in India, that Indian agriculture is, as a whole, primitive and backward, and that little has been done to try and remedy it, are altogether erroneous. . . . At his best the Indian Ryot, or cultivator, is quite as

The export of rice from Bengal in the husk increased to 1000 tons shortly before 1830, principally owing to the invention of machinery for freeing it from the husk after its arrival in England. Formerly it used to go husked, with a great deal of dirt and much broken in the grain. After the invention, it went in the husk, and was cleaned in England, and looked as fresh and bright as the American rice. If it could be cleaned in India as it was cleaned in Carolina it would be exported in larger quantities; for in the husk it paid double freight, as it occupied double the space.

INDIGO.

Somewhat contradictory evidence was given, as might be expected, as regards the condition of the cultivators under European indigo planters. Ramsay asserted that the condition of Ryots, who laboured for European planters, was worse than that of other Ryots; that European planters compelled them to sow a larger portion of their land with indigo than they would

good as, and in some respects the superior of, the average British farmer; whilst at his worst, it can only be said that this state is brought about largely by an absence of facilities for improvement which is probably unequalled in any other country, and that the Ryot will struggle on patiently and uncomplainingly in the face of difficulties in a way that no one else would.

"Nor need our British farmers be surprised at what I say, for it must be remembered that the natives of India were cultivators of wheat centuries before we in England were. It is not likely, therefore, that their *practice* should be capable of much improvement. What does, however, prevent them from growing larger crops is the limited facilities to which they have access, such as the supply of water and manure. But, to take the ordinary acts of husbandry, nowhere would one find better instances of keeping land scrupulously clean from weeds, of ingenuity in device of water-raising appliances, of knowledge of soils and their capabilities, as well as the exact time to sow and to reap, as one would in Indian agriculture, and this not at its best alone, but at its ordinary level. It is wonderful, too, how much is known of rotation, the system of mixed crops and of fallowing. Certain it is that I, at least, have never seen a more perfect picture of careful cultivation, combined with hard labour, perseverance, and fertility of resource, than I have seen in many of the halting-places in my tour."—*Report on the Improvement of Indian Agriculture.*

otherwise have done; that European planters interfered with the tiller's right to cultivate his land as he liked. Other witnesses contradicted him; but those who remember the state of things in Bengal down to 1860 are aware that the evils complained of by Ramsay prevailed in Bengal for a long period.

European planters made advances to cultivators who agreed to deliver so much weed at certain prices. If the planter was oppressive, "the Ryot had no other remedy against oppression than an appeal to the Courts where he has very little chance of having his appeal heard. Oppression is principally exercised in the lower parts of Bengal where a number of Europeans and half castes are settled."

Some Indian planters had considerable factories, but the indigo was not as good as that manufactured by Europeans. The manufacture of indigo by Indian planters was increasing. There were between five hundred and one thousand Europeans engaged as indigo manufacturers; they generally did not bring any capital from Europe, but borrowed it at Calcutta from Indians or from the Company's European servants or from Agency houses, and then started factories. There was no instance known of a man of capital going out to India to establish an indigo plantation.[1]

The importation of indigo from India commenced about 1790, and had so greatly increased in forty years as to supersede all other indigos. The cultivation was carried on from Dacca to Delhi, and the exportation was nine million lbs. The amount annually paid for rent and labour by British planters was £1,680,000; the commodity on its arrival at Calcutta was valued at £2,403,000, and realised in England £3,600,000. There were 300 or 400 factories in Bengal, chiefly in Jessor, Krishnaghar, and Tirhoot. The best soils were those subject to inundation from

[1] Evidence before the Lords' Committee, 1830. Digest.

the Ganges. Some indigo was grown in Madras and in Bombay. Generally speaking, planters borrowed their capital from great firms in Calcutta at an interest of 10 or 12 per cent. on a mortgage of their properties. The interest was high because there was considerable risk. Indian planters had begun to imitate the European process of manufacture. The manufacture and export were certainly not begun by Europeans, for indigo as a colour had been long known and used in the East, and manufactured and exported by the natives of India.[1]

The old Indian way of manufacturing indigo was imperfect; the East India Company advanced money to European planters for the production of the article, and began making large remittances to England in indigo in 1819. What caused the great and sudden prosperity of the indigo trade in Bengal was the destruction of St. Domingo, which had supplied nearly all the world with indigo previous to the French Revolution, and did not produce a single pound after the rebellion of the black population. The indigo factories were all destroyed during that rebellion.[2]

SUGAR.

Sugar was cultivated in various parts of the Deccan. It required irrigation. The Indian mode of manufacture was very simple, and their machinery imperfect; there was great room for improvement. The cultivation of sugar was perfectly free, like that of cotton and indigo. West Indian machinery was introduced, but did not extract so much from the cane as the simple Indian machinery, and the speculator was a loser. Two Europeans entered into speculations

[1] Evidence in the Commons' Reports of 1830, 1830–31, and 1831. Digest.

[2] Evidence before the Commons' Committee, 1832. Digest.

in Malabar, and both abandoned the project. An attempt was made to introduce the culture of sugar at Ganjam from 1796 to 1803, but the result was unsatisfactory.[1]

Europeans did not engage in the culture and manufacture of sugar in the same manner as they did in the manufacture of indigo; they simply purchased it in the Bazars or from cultivators to whom advances were made. The machinery used in India was inferior to that of the West Indies, and there were no large sugar plantations in India. The Indian sugar was inferior to the West Indian sugar. In Bengal the sugar-cane was as good as in the West Indies, and some superior sugar had been manufactured after undergoing a special process, but at a cost too high to make it profitable. Bengal sugar was subjected to a duty of 120 per cent. on the gross price, which was equivalent to a duty of 200 per cent. on the prime cost.[2]

The land fit for sugar was abundant in India, but the manufacture was ill-conducted. A more judicious selection of cane, and a more economical extraction and conversion of the juice into sugar, would increase the demand. The Company had a factory at Benares with agents to go about the country and buy sugar from the petty manufacturers; but orders had recently been issued to discontinue the import of sugar.[3]

TOBACCO.

Indian tobacco was not worth one-third of the American tobacco, owing to the want of skill in the grower and preparer. More attention should be paid to the selection of seed, the choice of soil, to weeding,

[1] Evidence before the Lords' Committee, 1830. Digest.

[2] Evidence given in the Common's Reports of 1830, 1830-31, and 1831. Digest.

[3] Evidence before the Commons' Committee, 1832. Digest.

reaping, preparing, and packing. India could not compete with America, but Indian tobacco might have an extensive demand if skill and capital were applied to it.[1]

Europeans did not engage in dealings in tobacco, and were not permitted to engage in the inland trade. Tobacco was extensively cultivated in the Northern districts of Bombay, and was of a very fine quality there. One bale imported into England sold higher than any American—it sold at 6d. when the latter was 5d.—but the average of an experimental exportation was found to be defective in the curing. The importations to England from Bengal and Bombay had been failures. The tobacco lands of Gujrat were the cleanest and best farmed, and tobacco was the most valuable product at Coimbatur in Madras."[2]

Tobacco had no Indian name, showing that it was not an indigenous produce of India, but it had been grown there from time immemorial. It was one of the smaller cultivations of India, and was only produced for domestic use. It was used in India mixed with molasses, spices, and fruits. On very rich land the produce was 160 lbs. the acre, but on average lands 80 lbs. would be considered a fair return in green leaf. Generally, Indian tobacco was bad, but very probably could be improved. The tobacco of the Northern Circars, converted into snuff at Masulipatam, was much prized in England. Some excellent Havanah tobacco was produced at Bhagalpur in Bengal.[3]

Dyes and Saltpetre, Coffee and Tea.

Lac-dye was imported to England in considerable quantities. Stick-lac was the gum, with the insect or

[1] Evidence before the Lords' Committee, 1830. Digest.
[2] Evidence in the Commons' Reports of 1830, 1830-31, and 1831. Digest.
[3] Evidence before the Commons' Committee, 1832. Digest.

its egg in it, from which the dye was made. The dyeing particles were separated and made the dye, while the gum made the shell-lac. Lac-dye was used in the dyeing of scarlet cloths, but was not adopted for the finest dyes. The lac was used as a varnish.

The cochineal insect was collected in the southern provinces of Madras, and was coarse and inferior compared to that of Mexico. The price of cochineal had fallen one-fourth since 1820, the fall being caused probably by the lac-dye. No cochineal was imported from Bengal.[1]

The import of saltpetre by the East India Company into England was 146,000 cwt. in 1814, but in 1832 it was only 37,300 cwt. Since the private traders began to import it, it fell to so low a price that it was bought as manure. In 1814 the price was 89s. 6d. per cwt., in 1832 it was only 37s. The import was profitable to the Company before 1814; since then it had become unprofitable.[2]

Coffee was extensively cultivated only since 1823. The Government then allowed coffee planters to engage in the cultivation, permitting them to hold lands for a long series of years, a concession not made to any other description of European planters. In Bengal, 4000 acres had been laid out in coffee. The Bangalore coffee was very good, though not so good as that of Mocha, and the cultivation was spreading. The attempt to cultivate coffee in Arcot failed, and cocoa plantations in Ganjam were failures. In Bengal the sun was too powerful for coffee. The cultivation of coffee did remarkably well at Coimbatur.[3]

The cultivation of tea had not yet been introduced

[1] Evidence in the Commons' Reports of 1830, 1830–31, and 1831. Digest.

[2] Evidence before the Commons' Committee, 1832. Digest.

[3] Evidence before the Lords' Committee, 1830; in the Commons' Reports of 1830, 1830–31, and 1831; and before the Commons' Committee, 1832. Digest.

in India, but Dr. Wallick, whose evidence in reference to rice cultivation has been quoted before, submitted a valuable paper on the possibility of introducing the cultivation of tea in the mountainous parts of Hindustan. Some extracts are given below.

"By far the most important cultivation of the plant is carried on in the provinces of the Chinese Empire, situated between the 27th and 30th parallels of north latitude, where the black teas are almost entirely produced; but it is also reared in vast quantities to the south, nearly as far as the seashore of Canton. . . .

"At Penang the late Mr. Brown, misled by the unconnected fact that the shrub stood well the climate of the island, conceived the project of cultivating it. . . . Upon the whole the plants grew remarkably well; but when the period arrived to reap the harvest of all the labour, time, and expense that had been incurred, the quality of the produce was found of a very inferior description. . . .

"In Java similar trials, made under very similar circumstances, have proved equally fruitless, and have, in consequence, been given up I am informed that no better success has attended some experiments which were made many years since by the Dutch Government in the southern parts of Ceylon.

"About twenty years ago the cultivation of the tea plant was commenced on a large scale at Rio Janeiro. . . . The produce proved to be so bad in its flavour that the plantation has of late been nearly relinquished.

"I have had an opportunity of examining a sample of tea produced in the Brazils. . . . The taste of the infusion was exceedingly bad. . . .

"There exist territories within the British dominions in the East Indies agreeing so perfectly with those of the tea provinces, that no doubt can be entertained of their being capable of producing tea equal to the best kinds ever obtained in China. . . . The provinces of Kumaon, Gurwal, and Sirmore contain situations corresponding entirely with what we know of those of China and Japan, in which the cultivation of the tea shrub is carried on to the greatest extent and perfection. . . .

"I have already had occasion to observe that a species of camellia grows wild in Nepal, and in publishing an account of it in 1818, I noticed that a tea shrub was thriving vigorously in a garden at Katmandu, 10 feet in height, and producing plentiful flowers and fruits during the last four months of the year. During my visit to that capital some years afterwards I saw the shrub, and I ascertained that the seeds of it had been brought from Pekin by the return of one of the triennial embassies which are sent to China by the Gurkha Government.

"If we take all these concurring circumstances into due consideration, we may surely entertain sanguine hopes that, under a well directed management, the tea plant may, at no distant period, be an object of extensive cultivation in the Honourable East India Company's dominions, and that we shall not long continue dependent on the will and caprice of a despotic nation for the supply of one of the greatest comforts and luxuries of civilised life."[1]

Dr. Wallick's letter is dated 3rd February 1832, and we may in fairness consider him one of the pioneers of the tea industry in India—next after the unknown Gurkha ambassadors who introduced it in Nepal.

Gold, Iron, and Copper.

Gold had been found in the Nilgiris and was collected of a pure kind, and in some quantity in

[1] Evidence before the Commons' Committee, 1832, Part II., Appendix 21.

the district of Wynaad, immediately below the mountains. Iron ore was abundant in most parts of India. At Ramnad it was sold at a higher price than British or Swedish iron, and was more pliable, but there was a great waste in working it. The native manufactured iron was inferior to the English owing to inferiority in the mode of manufacture. In the neighbourhood of Burdwan, in Bengal, there was some fine iron ore, but the better kind was found on the Madras coast. It could not be easily converted into steel, but when made, the steel was remarkably good. Mr. Heath had established an iron-foundry near Madras, and had established European machinery, and had the exclusive privilege of manufacture till the end of the Charter. The iron was very superior to any other Indian iron, or even to Swedish. Iron ore was found in great abundance on the frontier of Malabar, and was remarkably cheap at Coimbatur. The iron of Cutch was particularly fine; it was found principally on the surface, and was collected in baskets and burnt in charcoal. The finest steel in India was made in Cutch, and was fabricated into armour, sabres, &c. Copper had been found in the North-Western Provinces of India.[1]

Coal and Timber.

There were large coal mines in the Burdwan District of Bengal, worked in 1832 to the extent of 14,000 or 15,000 tons annually. The workings of the mines first began about 1814, but extensive operations began about 1825. The seam was 9 feet deep, and about 90 feet from the surface, and two or three thousand people were employed, receiving 6s. or 8s. a month. The coal was principally used for steam-

[1] Evidence in the Commons' Reports of 1830, 1830–31, and 1831 Digest.

engines, and was sent to Singapore for that purpose, and was also used for the burning of bricks. Coal had also been found in Bundelkhand, and was found in abundance in Cutch.[1]

Cutch coal had not been found good for steam-engines, and at Bombay English coal had been found cheaper. The Burdwan coal was the best in India, and none other was used in Calcutta. The price was 10 Annas (1s. 3d.) per bushel. It did not cake, but burnt to a white ash. It was not so good as English coal for the manufacture of iron. The best English coal was to the best Bengal coal in the proportion of 5 to 3 in regard to strength.

Indian forests contained every description of timber in the world, or a substitute for it. The principal kinds were Saigoon, Sal, Sisoo, Toon, Jarool, and Mango. Sal was used for ship and house-building, and for military purposes. Owing to bad and extravagant management there had been a falling-off in Sal, Sisoo, and Bamboo. There was an abundance of pine and oak. The timber of India might become an article of foreign trade.[2]

Opium and Salt.

In these articles the East India Company retained their monopoly as the India Government does to the present day, and they were an important source of revenue.

"The manufacture of opium and salt," said Holt Mackenzie, who was one of the principal witnesses examined by the Commons' Committee in 1832, "is conducted with a view to revenue, not trade. My opinion is that, of the suggested changes with regard to those articles, there is none that would not involve

[1] Evidence in the Commons' Reports of 1830, 1830–31, and 1831. Digest.

[2] Evidence before the Commons' Committee, 1832. Digest.

a large loss of revenue. In the salt department I do not think we could, by means of an excise, collect the same amount of net revenue as is yielded by the public sales. . . .

"From that source also [opium] they derive a very large revenue, the excess of the sale prices beyond the first cost constituting such a tax as I would think it hopeless to get by any other device; and though, commercially speaking, there are strong objections to the system, yet we must set against that the necessity of the revenue; and my belief is, that the same amount of revenue cannot be otherwise got."[1]

SUMMARY.

It will appear from the above summary that the evidence recorded between 1830 and 1832 by the Lords' and Commons' Committees contains the most valuable account that we possess of the industries of India at that time; as the records of Dr. Francis Buchanan contain the most valuable account of the state of industries between 1800 and 1815. Nevertheless the Parliamentary records are an incomplete account, as compared with Dr. Buchanan's. The Lords and Commons limited their inquiries to those industries in which British capital had been employed, or could be profitably employed. The humbler industries, which gave occupation to the people of India—like bricklaying and building, stone-cutting and carpentry, boat-building and furniture, brass, iron, and copper utensils, gold and silver work, dyeing and tanning, and the declining spinning and weaving industries of India—did not interest them much.

The evidence recorded discloses that in purely agricultural pursuits England had little to teach; but

[1] Evidence before the Commons' Committee, 1832, Part I., p. 26.

in cleaning and husking the food grains, in spinning and weaving, in the manufacture of indigo, tobacco, and sugar, in the growing of coffee and tea, in the forging of iron, in coal-mining and gold-mining, in all industries which were dependent on machinery, Europe had adopted more perfect methods than India in 1830. It is possible to conceive that a Government, working with an eye to the advancement of the national industries, might have introduced these superior methods among the industrious and skilful people of India, as they have been introduced among the people of Japan within our generation. But it was hardly possible that foreign merchants and rival manufacturers, working for their own profit, should have this object in view, and the endeavour was never made. A policy the reverse of this was pursued with the object of replacing the manufactures of India, as far as possible, by British manufactures. Writing five years after the date of the Parliamentary Inquiry of 1832, Montgomery Martin described and condemned the commercial policy of the time in the severest terms.

"Since this official report [Dr. Buchanan's economic inquiries in Northern India] was made to Government, have any effective steps been taken in England or in India to benefit the sufferers by our rapacity and selfishness? None! On the contrary, we have done everything possible to impoverish still further the miserable beings subject to the cruel selfishness of English commerce. The pages before the reader prove the number of people in the surveyed districts dependent for their chief support on their skill in weaving cotton, &c. Under the pretence of Free Trade, England has compelled the Hindus to receive the products of the steam-looms of Lancashire, Yorkshire, Glasgow, &c., at mere nominal duties; while the hand-wrought manufactures of Bengal and Behar, beautiful in fabric and durable in wear, have had heavy and almost prohibitive duties imposed on their importation to England."[1]

"In that part of India," the Commons' Committee asked the witness, Holt Mackenzie, "where the greatest number of British residents are found, has there been any increase among the natives in the indulgence of English tastes, fashions, and habits?"

"Judging from Calcutta," replied Holt Mackenzie, "there has been, I think, a marked tendency among the natives to indulge in English luxuries; they have well-furnished houses, many wear watches, they are fond of carriages, and are understood to drink wines."

A smile of grim satisfaction must have overspread the faces of the grave and reverend Commoners of England on obtaining this significant evidence of the spread of Western civilisation in India!

[1] *Eastern India*, by Montgomery Martin (London, 1838), vol. iii., Introduction.

CHAPTER XVI

EXTERNAL TRADE (1813-1835)

AN Act was passed in 1813 which directed a separation of the East India Company's Territorial Accounts from Commercial Accounts. It was directed that the Territorial Revenues should be applied (1) to Military Expenditure; (2) to Civil and Commercial Establishments; and (3) to the payment of Interest on the Indian Debt. And the Commercial Profits were to be applied (1) to the payment of Bills of Exchange and the current payment of other debts; (2) to the payment of Dividends; and (3) to the reduction of the Indian Debt or Home Bond debt.[1]

The Territorial Revenues of India during fifteen years from 1813 to 1828 were:—

Bengal	£196,121,983
Madras	82,042,967
Bombay	30,986,870
Oudh and Subordinate Settlements	1,931,480
Total	£311,083,300

This gives us an average annual Territorial revenue of over twenty millions sterling. The "Home Charges" spent in England out of this Indian Territorial Revenue came to an annual average of £1,693,472; and the total Territorial expenditure exceeded the total Territorial revenue, showing an annual average deficit of £1,227,343. Within this period of fifteen

[1] Act 53 Geo. III., 5, 155.

years the Territorial Debt had increased from thirty to forty-seven millions sterling; and the gradual and steady increase of the Company's Territorial Debt during thirty-seven years is shown in the following figures:[1]

April	1792	£9,142,720
"	1809	30,812,441
"	1814	30,919,620
"	1829	47,255,374

It will thus appear that large additions to the Debt were made during the warlike administrations of Lord Wellesley and Lord Hastings. The surplus Commercial Profit of the Company, after payment of Bills of Exchange and Dividends, was applicable to the reduction of the India Debt or the Home Bond Debt, as stated before. But this surplus Commercial profit, which exceeded a million sterling in 1814, 1817, and 1818, gradually declined with the extension of the Empire and the decline of the Company's trade, and was between £3000 and £42,000 only, between 1828 and 1830. After 1824, the Company ceased to export merchandise to India, and their only exports were military and political stores. The reason for discontinuing their export trade to India was the difficulty of obtaining any article of Indian produce or manufacture in return. Indian industries had declined, and the only articles which the Company continued to import into England from India were raw silk, some silk piece-goods, saltpetre, and indigo. The indigo was purchased at Calcutta, raw silk and saltpetre were prepared in their factories, and silk piece-goods were obtained by contracts with head-weavers. Even the import of Indian sugar into England had been discontinued. This steady decline

[1] Minutes of Evidence taken before the Commons' Committee, 1832. vol. ii. Report.

of the Company's commerce with India led to the final extinction of their trade when their Charter was renewed in 1833.

As the Company's Indian trade declined, it gradually passed into the hands of private merchants to whom it was first opened in 1813. During sixteen years after that date, the Company's trade averaged £1,882,718 annually, while private trade averaged £5,451,452 annually. The private trade was therefore three times as great as the Company's, and private traders thus proved themselves fitter to carry on the trade with India than the territorial masters of India. The process of the extinction of Indian manufactures went on, however, under the new arrangements; in 1813 Calcutta exported to London two millions sterling of cotton goods; in 1830 Calcutta imported two millions sterling of British cotton manufactures. The first import of British cotton twist into India was in 1823, in 1824 it was 121,000 lbs.; in 1828 it rose to 4,000,000 lbs. Woollen goods, copper, lead, iron, glass, and earthenware were also imported. British manufactures were imported into Calcutta on payment of a small duty of 2½ per cent., while the import of Indian manufactures into England was discouraged by heavy duties ranging up to 400 per cent. on their value.[1]

The duties which were imposed on the import of Indian manufactures into England between 1812 and 1832 on various articles of trade are shown in the following tables:[2]

---

[1] Evidence in the Commons' Report of 1830, 1830–31, and 1831. Digest.

[2] Evidence taken before the Commons' Committee, 1832, vol. ii., Appendix 5.

	1812.	1824.	1832.
	Per Cent. on Value.	Per Cent. on Value.	Per Cent. on Value.
Ornamental cane work . .	71	50	30
Muslins	27⅛	37½	10
Calicoes	71⅜	67½	10
Other cotton manufactures .	27⅛	50	20
Goat's wool shawls . .	71	67½	30
Lacquered ware . . .	71	62½	30
Mats	68⅛	50	20

	1812.	1824.	1832.
Raw silk . .	£2, 13s. 4d. on value *plus* 4s. per lb.	4s. per lb.	1d. per lb.
Silk manufactures	Prohibited	Prohibited	20 per cent. on value
Taffatees or other plain or figured silks . . .	Prohibited	Prohibited	30 per cent. on value
Manufactures of silk	Prohibited	Prohibited	20 per cent. on value
Sugar (cost price about £1 per cwt.). . .	£1, 13s. per cwt.	£3, 3s. per cwt.	£1, 12s. per cwt.
Spirits (Arrack) .	1s. 8d. per gallon *plus* 19s. 1½d. excise duty	2s. 1d. per gallon *plus* 17s. 0¾d. excise	15s. per gallon
Cotton wool .	16s. 11d. per 100 lbs.	6 per cent.	20 per cent.

Petitions were vainly presented to the House of Commons against these unjust and enormous duties on the import of Indian manufactures into England. One petition against the duties on sugar and spirits [1] was signed by some four hundred European and Indian merchants, among whose names we find *Ram Gopal Ghore*, which is probably a misprint of the name of the well-known Indian publicist Ram Gopal Ghose. An application to the British Government to reduce

[1] Evidence taken before the Commons' Committee, 1832, vol. ii., Appendix 6.

the duties on the cotton and silk fabrics of India. signed by a very numerous body of respectable Indians, was rejected; and some London merchants thereupon applied to the East India Company to allow a drawback of 2½ per cent. on these fabrics on their import into England.[1] The application was equally fruitless.

To what extent the unjust commercial policy of England discouraged and ruined the manufactures of India will appear from the following table of exports shipped from the port of Calcutta during thirty years. The figures represent the exports into the United Kingdom only:[2]

Year.	Cotton.	Cotton piece-goods.	Silk.	Silk piece-goods.	Lac and lac-dye.	Indigo.
	Bales.	Bales.	Bales.	Bales.	Maunds.	Chests.
1800	506	2,636	213	Figures not given.	Figures not given.	12,811
1801	222	6,341	238			9,928
1802	2,072	14,817	400			8,694
1803	2,420	13,649	1,232			12,986
1804	602	9,631	1,926			18,339
1805	2,453	2,325	1,327			13,486
1806	7,315	651	1,689			17,542
1807	3,717	1,686	482			19,452
1808	2,016	237	817			16,622
1809	40,781	104	1,124			8,852
1810	3,477	1,167	949			13,264
1811	160	955	2,623			14,335
1812	...	1,471	1,889			13,703
1813	11,705	557	638			23,672
1814	21,587	919	1,786			16,544
1815	17,228	3,842	2,796			26,221
1816	85,024	2,711	8,884			15,740
1817	50,176	1,904	2,260			15,583
1818	127,124	666	2,066			13,044
1819	30,683	536	6,998	468		16,670
1820	12,939	3,186	6,805	522		12,526
1821	5,415	2,130	6,977	704		12,635
1822	6,544	1,668	7,893	950		19,751
1823	11,713	1,354	6,357	742	14,190	15,878
1824	12,415	1,337	7,069	1,105	17,607	22,472
1825	15,800	1,878	8,061	1,558	13,491	26,837
1826	15,101	1,253	6,856	1,233	13,573	14,904
1827	4,735	541	7,719	971	13,756	30,761
1828	4,105	736	10,431	550	15,379	19,041
1829	...	433	7,000(?)	...	8,251	27,000(?)

[1] Evidence taken before the Commons' Committee, 1832, vol. ii., Appendix 7.

[2] *Ibid.*, Appendix 31.

These figures will show that while the manufacture of indigo by European planters increased, and the export of raw silk held its ground, that of silk piece-goods showed a decline. The export of cotton, too, was on the decline, but the most marked decrease was in that of cotton piece goods. In the first four years of the nineteenth century, in spite of all prohibitions and restrictive duties, six to fifteen thousand bales were annually shipped from Calcutta to the United Kingdom. The figure rapidly fell down to 1813. The opening of trade to private merchants in that year caused a sudden rise in 1815; but the increase was only temporary. After 1820 the manufacture and export of cotton piece-goods declined steadily, never to rise again. A similar decline took place in the export of Indian piece-goods to the other countries of the world, notably to America, Denmark, Spain, Portugal, Mauritius, and the markets of Asia. The export to America declined from 13,633 bales in 1801 to 258 bales in 1829; Denmark, which took 1457 bales in 1800, never took more than 150 bales after 1820; Portugal, which took 9714 bales in 1799, never took over a thousand bales after 1825; and the exports to the Arabian and Persian Gulfs, which rose to between four and seven thousand bales between 1810 and 1820, never exceeded two thousand after 1825.

On the other hand, as India lost her manufacturing industry, she began to import British and other foreign piece-goods, paying for it in food grains. The following figures are significant:[1]

[1] Evidence taken before the Commons' Committee, 1832, vol. ii., Appendix 33.

Some British and Foreign Goods imported through Madras into the Madras Province.

Year.	Chintz.	Long-cloth.	Muslin.	Piece-goods.	Satin.	Silk piece-goods.	Broad-cloth.	Shawls.	Woollen apparel.	Woollens.
	£	£	£	£	£	£	£	£	£	£
1824	No figures.	No figures.	No figures.	No figures.	No figures.	No figures.	No figures.	181	No figures.	No figures.
1825								920		
1826			342	903	312		835	1159		614
1827	510	470	941	536	637		2176	754	601	915
1828	219	380	789	958	593		915	1115	481	1310
1829	352	348	598	474	853	644	1417	409	581	844
1830	372	...	224	1121	577	136	1158	476	365	457

Some British and Foreign Goods imported through Calcutta into Bengal.

Year.	Broad-cloth pieces.	Cotton yarn, lbs.	Cotton twist, lbs.	Mule twist, lbs.	Piece-goods, value in £ sterling.	Liquors, value in £ sterling.
1813	3,381	Figures not given.	Figures not given.	Figures not given.	Figures not given.	52,253
1814	4,635					57,201
1815	3,908					59,462
1816	3,707					56,411
1817	2,355					53,157
1818	5,633					36,712
1819	9,244					20,988
1820	5,546					26,049
1821	7,590					30,382
1822	5,108					46,235
1823	7,346				64,449	30,129
1824	5,401				43,030	22,439
1825	13,981				158,076	14,223
1826	9,629				178,481	56,058
1827	5,430	82,738	432,878	339,234	296,177	80,595
1828	7,609	149,076	642,306	464,776	235,837	41,142
1829	11,838	98,154	398,930	918,646	197,290	31,311

In his evidence before the Commons' Committee in 1813, Thomas Munro had laughed at the idea of Paisley shawls replacing the excellent shawls of India. In 1824 he was Governor of Madras, and must have noticed with concern the introduction of European shawls, as well as of muslins and piece-goods, broad-cloths and woollens, to replace the manufactures of India. An equally sympathetic administrator, Sir John Malcolm, was the Governor of Bombay in 1830, and he, too, marked with consternation the ruin of Indian industries and the growing poverty of the Indian people.

"In the despatch of the Court [of Directors] it is observed that their attention has been directed in a special manner to this subject, and to look to India for the means of rendering great Britain independent of foreign countries for a considerable portion of raw material, upon which her most valuable manufactories depend. . . .

"I must add, that it is only by the introduction of produce like silk, by our improvement of the staple of cotton, and the success of our recent efforts to make and refine sugar, that we can restore heart to many of our districts, and maintain our territorial resources. . . .

"It is only by encouraging richer produce, such as that to which I have alluded, and other articles besides grain, reviving commerce, and inducing men of wealth and enterprise to remain or settle in the interior, that we can give heart to the country, and enable it to pay its revenue. There is no want either of talent or spirit among the native population subject to our rule and control to accomplish this object, but it requires to be drawn forth; and to effect this it is necessary to exert all the activity, energy, and enlarged policy of a Government which understands how to combine its own prosperity with that of the community subject to its authority." [1]

Even Sir John Malcolm did not see, or perhaps did not care to state, that the industrial prosperity of a subject population was impossible when the settled policy of the ruling nation was to convert India into a land of raw produce only, for the purpose "of rendering Great Britain independent of foreign countries for a considerable portion of raw material upon which her most valuable manufactories depend."

Public men and public writers in England never spoke or wrote of this policy pursued in India. The great political economists of the time, headed by Ricardo, had nothing to say on the subject. The leaders of the agitation against the Corn Laws, who rightly and successfully fought against the landlords of England for a measure which would bring cheap bread to the workman and labourer, said little and knew little of the policy which took the bread out

[1] Sir John Malcolm's General Minute of 30th November 1830, on his administration of the Bombay Government.

of the mouths of millions of weavers and artisans in India. Cobden and Bright, the most large-hearted, sympathetic, and enlightened Englishmen of their time, carried the agitation against the Corn Laws to the successful issue; and Sir Robert Peel, who repealed those Laws in 1846, trusted that his name would be remembered by Englishmen who would "recruit their exhausted strength with abundant and untaxed food, the sweeter because no longer leavened with a sense of injustice." But the bread of the Indian artisan and manufacturer is still leavened with a sense of injustice, and no statesman has yet seriously endeavoured to protect, foster, and revive their old and ruined industries.

Continental economists were able to take a more unbiassed view of the situation, and to speak more openly and freely. In a great work on Political Economy written in Germany in 1844, while the injustice of the Corn Laws was occupying the minds of English economists, a German economist pointed out the graver injustice which had been perpetrated in India.

"Had they sanctioned the free importation into England of Indian cotton and silk goods, the English cotton and silk manufactories must, of necessity, soon come to a stand. India had not only the advantage of cheaper labour and raw material, but also the experience, the skill, and the practice of centuries. The effect of these advantages could not fail to tell under a system of free competition.

"But England was unwilling to found settlements in Asia in order to become subservient to India in manufacturing industry. She strove for commercial supremacy, and felt that of two countries maintaining free trade between one another, that one would be supreme which sold manufactured goods, while that one would be subservient which could only sell agricultural produce. In the North American colonies, England had already acted on those principles in disallowing the manufacture in those colonies of even a single horse-shoe nail, and still more, that no horse-shoe nails made there should be imported into England. How could it be expected of her that she would give up her own market for manufactures, the basis of her future greatness, to a people so numerous, so thrifty, so experienced and perfect in the old systems of manufacture as the Hindus?

"Accordingly, England prohibited the import of the goods dealt in by her own factories, the Indian cotton and silk fabrics. The prohibition was complete and peremptory. Not so much as a thread of them would England permit to be used. She would have none of these beautiful and cheap fabrics, but preferred to consume her own inferior and more costly stuffs. She was, however, quite willing to supply the Continental nations with the far finer fabrics of India at lower prices, and willingly yielded to them all the benefit of that cheapness; she herself would have none of it.

"Was England a fool in so acting? Most assuredly, according to the theories of Adam Smith and J. B. Say, the Theory of Values. For according to them, England should have bought what she required where she could buy them cheapest and best; it was an act of folly to manufacture for herself goods at a greater cost than she could buy them at elsewhere, and at the same time give away that advantage to the Continent.

"The case is quite the contrary, according to our theory, which we term the Theory of the Powers of Production, and which the English Ministry, without having examined the foundation on which it rests, yet practically adopted when enforcing their maxim of importing produce and exporting fabrics.

"The English Ministers cared not for the acquisition of low-priced and perishable articles of manufacture, but for that of a more costly and enduring Manufacturing Power."[1]

The above extract will show that while British Political Economists professed the principles of free trade from the latter end of the eighteenth century, the British Nation declined to adopt them till they had crushed the Manufacturing Power of India, and reared their own Manufacturing Power. Then the British Nation turned free traders, and invited other nations to accept free trade principles. The other nations, including the British Colonies, know better; and are now rearing their Manufacturing Power by protection. But in India the Manufacturing Power of the people was stamped out by protection against her industries, and then free trade was forced on her so as to prevent a revival.

[1] *The National System of Political Economy*, by Friedrich List. Translated by Sampson S. Lloyd, M.P. (London, 1885), p. 42.

CHAPTER XVII

INTERNAL TRADE; CANALS AND RAILROADS (1813-1835)

THE internal trade of India still languished under the obnoxious transit duties which had been handed down from the preceding century. It will be remembered that the East India Company first obtained their footing in the country by an exemption of their export and import trade from those transit duties, to which the internal trade of the country was subjected. And it will also be remembered that when the servants of the Company claimed this exemption for their own private trade, Nawab Mir Kasim in a fit of noble generosity abolished all transit duties in Bengal, and that generosity cost him his throne. When at last the East India Company became the undisputed masters of Bengal in 1765, the time came for them to follow the example set by Mir Kasim, and to relieve the internal trade of India from those duties which repressed it. But the duties brought a revenue, however small, and the East India Company were slow to part with any portion of their revenues.

The transit duties became more oppressive under the British Rule than they had been under the Nawabs. For the Company's power was more far-reaching, absolute, and undisputed, and each low-paid officer, at each Chowki or toll-house, had the means of exercising greater oppression. The evil grew without cessation for sixty years, and as late as 1825, Holt Mackenzie, then Territorial Secretary, condemned it in the strongest terms.

"Some articles have to run the gauntlet through ten custom-houses, passing at each several subordinate Chowkis, before they reach the Presidency, and little or none of the great staple commodities of the country escape from being subjected to repeated detentions.

"Even supposing that there were no exactions and no delay, still the system would seriously hinder the commercial intercourse of the country, since no interchange of goods can take place between districts separated by a line of Chowkis, unless the difference of price shall cover not only the export of transportation and the other charges of merchandise, but also the duty of 5 or 7½ per cent. levied by Government. Thus also the natural inequalities of prices aggravated, and, contrary to every principle, justly applicable to a consumption tax, the burden falls on those places where the consumer would, independently of duty, have most to pay.

"But when to the Government demand are added those of the custom-house officers, it appears to be certain that much trade that would be carried on by persons of small capital must be absolutely prevented. The rich merchant can afford to pay the utmost demand likely to be made upon him, because a considerable douceur will not fall heavy on a large investment, and because his rank and wealth secures him from any outrageous extortion. But to the petty trader a moderate fee would consume the probable profit of his adventure, and he has little or no security for moderation. . . .

"Hitherto the attention of the authorities at home, and of the mercantile body generally in England, would appear to have been directed chiefly to the object of finding a market for the manufactures of the United Kingdom. They have consequently looked more to the import than to the export trade of India. The duties prescribed by Regulation ix. of 1810 have accordingly taken off a great number of articles sent from England hither; while of the exports, only indigo, cotton, wool, and hemp have been made free, and this more with a view, I apprehend, to English than to Indian objects. . . .

"The result of a pretty careful consideration of the articles which constitute the trade of Calcutta, and a consideration of the rate of duty which each could bear, have led to the conclusion that the country might be relieved from the mischief of our Inland Customs without any very considerable sacrifice, at least if the salt duties levied on our western frontier are, as would seem necessary for the protection of the Bengal monopoly, maintained. . . .

"Were Inland Duties abolished, without any change in the export and import duties, the immediate sacrifice of revenue would be about 33 lakhs (£330,000), and even though the duty on Western salts were maintained, there would still be a loss of 22 lakhs (£220,000). The whole of this, I fear, cannot be immediately replaced by the imposition of new duties on imports and exports by sea, but a considerable part may certainly be so, and inasmuch as the proposed arrangement will operate, as I hope, to extend trade, and will enable us to reduce establishments, the balance cannot be reckoned as a net loss." [1]

But Holt Mackenzie spoke to deaf ears. The East India Company would not willingly sacrifice even a revenue of £220,000, or any portion of it, for the prosperity of the internal trade of India. Professing the utmost anxiety for the material welfare of the people of India, they were unwilling to sacrifice a shilling to promote that welfare. If the abolition of the Inland Duties had depended on the East India Company, the duties would never have been abolished under their administration.

[1] Holt Mackenzie's Memorandum. Bengal Salt and Opium Consultations, 23rd June 1825.

Fortunately their hands were forced by their own servants. The greatest and best of the Company's Governor-Generals, Lord William Bentinck, went out to India in 1828, and that ruler employed Sir Charles Trevelyan to make an inquiry, and submit a report on Transit Duties. Trevelyan's famous report exposed mercilessly the evils of the system. It showed that the evils had grown under British Rule as compared with the state of things under the Nawabs of Bengal; that traders all over the country were subjected to delay and exactions; that manufactures were killed and internal trade paralysed by the extortions of Customs' Officers who were paid so low that it was possible for them to live only by extortion; that travellers were harassed and the honour of women passing through lines of customs' houses was not safe; and that this huge system of oppression was maintained in the country for the sake of an insignificant revenue.[1] Lord William Bentinck published Trevelyan's report, and thus sounded the death-knell to the Inland Duties.

Lord Ellenborough in England took up this report, and in his own forcible language pointed out to the East India Company in 1835 the evils of the system.

"While the cotton manufactures of England are imported into India on payment of a duty of 2½ per cent., the cotton manufactures of India are subjected to a duty on the raw material of 5 per cent., to a further duty on yarn of 7½ per cent., to an additional duty upon the manufactured article of 2½ per cent., and finally to another duty of 2½ per cent. if the cloth should be dyed after the Rowana [pass] has been taken out for it as white cloth. Thus altogether the cotton

[1] "Accustomed as I have been," wrote Macaulay, in referring to Trevelyan's Report, "to public affairs, I never read an abler state paper, and I do not believe that there is, I will not say in India, but in England, another man of twenty-seven who could have written it."—G. O. Trevelyan's *Life and Letters of Lord Macaulay*.

goods of India [consumed in India] pay $17\frac{1}{2}$ per cent. . . .

"The raw hide pays 5 per cent. On being manufactured into leather it pays 5 per cent. more; and when the leather is made into boots and shoes, a further duty is imposed of 5 per cent. Thus, in all, there is a duty of 15 per cent. [on Indian leather goods used in India]. . . .

"In what manner do we continue to treat our own sugar? On being imported into a town it pays 5 per cent. in customs, and 5 per cent. in town duty, and when manufactured it pays on exportation from the same town 5 per cent. more, in all 15 per cent. [on Indian sugar used in India].

"No less than 235 separate articles are subjected to Inland Duties. The tariff includes almost everything of personal or domestic use, and its operation, combined with the system of search, is of the most vexatious and offensive character, without materially benefiting the revenue. The power of search, if really exercised by every Custom-house officer, would put a stop to internal trade by the delay it would necessarily occasion. It is not exercised except for the purpose of extortion. . . .

"The effect upon the national morals is yet more serious than the effect upon national wealth. Every merchant, every manufacturer, and every traveller is, as it were, compelled, for the security of his property or the protection of his personal comfort, and not unfrequently for that of the feelings of the females of his family, to enter into unlawful collusion with the officers of Government. It is a system which demoralises our own people, and which appears to excite the aversion of all the foreign traders of Asia. . . .

"We may at once, by our own authority, give entire liberty to the internal communications of sixty millions of people. Industrious, possessing a fertile country, traversed in its whole extent by a navigable river, inaccessible to foreign war, and protected in their property by an impartial administration of the laws, the inhabitants of Bengal would thus obtain, by the enlightened policy of their Government, more extensive means of public prosperity than are enjoyed by any other nation in the world."[1]

But Lord Ellenborough too spoke to deaf ears. The Court of Directors replied that "the Indian Government is well aware of the opinion entertained by the home authorities of the injurious effects which attend the levying of this impost, and their desire to see it abolished whenever it can be considered safe to do so. The Court think it would be premature and inexpedient to go farther than this by giving peremptory instructions on such a subject to the Local Government."[2] In other words, the East India Company followed the practice, which unfortunately is not uncommon, of screening themselves and their disinclination to undertake reforms behind the imposing figure of the Local Government.

By an irony of fate that screen failed them for once. The publication of Trevelyan's report had stirred public opinion in India, and Mr. Rosse in the Upper Provinces took upon himself to abolish the Inland Customs Houses within his jurisdiction. And the successor of Lord William Bentinck followed this up by abolishing all the Customs Houses in Bengal on the 1st March 1836, and the town duties on the 1st May 1836. The Court of Directors, forced to approve of these measures, nevertheless expressed to the Governor-General their regret "that you were precipitated into its adoption without having been enabled

[1] Lord Ellenborough to the Chairman and Deputy-Chairman of the East India Company, dated 18th March 1835.

[2] Letter of the Court of Directors, dated 2nd April 1835.

to form any available plan for compensating the loss of revenue."[1]

We have now arrived at the date when Queen Victoria ascended the throne of the British Empire. But it is necessary to proceed with the narrative of the Inland Duties a few years further, in order to bring it to an end. Lord Auckland had arrived in India in 1836, and was the first Governor-General under the Queen. Unhappily, an act of astounding folly, ending in a grave calamity, marked the Indian administration at the very commencement of the new reign. Disregarding the policy of peace, retrenchment, and reform initiated by Lord William Bentinck, Lord Auckland launched himself into the first Afghan War of 1838. It ended in making enemies of a friendly and warlike race, in the disastrous retreat of 1842, in the destruction of 4000 troops and 12,000 followers, and in the sacrifice of Indian revenues in a war outside the frontiers of India.

Lord Ellenborough, who had pressed on the East India Company the abolition of the Inland Duties in 1835, went out as Governor-General to India in 1842. He abolished the Inland Duties in Sindh in 1843, in the territory of Jalun in 1844, and in the Province of Madras by Act VI. of 1844.

Nine years after, when the Charter of the East India Company came up again for renewal, Lord Ellenborough was one of the Select Committee of the House of Lords and Sir Charles Trevelyan was one of the witnesses. And referring to the abolition of the Inland Duties, Lord Ellenborough asked:

"Was it not owing to Lord William Bentinck sending you to make inquiries upon the subject, which was followed by your report, and by the Act of the Government abolishing those duties?"

Sir Charles replied: "If my report had remained

[1] Letter to the Governor-General in Council, dated 7th June 1837.

unpublished and had merely undergone the usual course of official discussion, years might have passed before the Transit and Town Duties would have been abolished. But instead of that the report was published, and everybody at once felt that the system was condemned."[1]

It is necessary to state, for the information of modern readers, that at the period of which we are speaking in this chapter India did not yet possess a uniform currency. The silver coin in Calcutta was the Sicca Rupee, the value of which was about 6⅜ per cent. above that of the Madras Rupee. The Gold Mohur was a legal tender for Rs.16, but as the value of gold had risen it sold for Rs.18, and ceased to be a current coin. Horsley Palmer, governor of the Bank of England, stated in his evidence in 1832: "Gold neither does nor will circulate to any extent as current coin in India, where silver forms the actual currency and is a legal tender. . . . I should be directly opposed to an opinion of the propriety of introducing gold into India as the current coin of the realm."[2]

Steam communication between England and India through the Red Sea had commenced, but was still enormously expensive. The *Hugh Lindsay* steamer reached Suez from Bombay in thirty-three days, a distance which is now performed in one-fourth the time.

The introduction of steam navigation in the rivers of Bengal and of an experimental voyage between Calcutta and Allahabad was also discussed. As early as 1828, H. T. Prinsep, then Secretary, submitted an interesting note on the subject. There was no river in the world, he said, except those of China, on which there was so large a navigation as on the Ganges. Thirty thousand boatmen found their livelihood on

[1] Second Report from the Lords' Committee, 1853, p. 161.
[2] Evidence before the Commons' Committee, 1832, vol. ii. p. 109.

that river as far back as 1780, and the number had since increased. Everybody "has been struck by the constant succession of boats moving up and down, the river never appearing for a moment altogether clear; and as this is nearly the same at all seasons and in all places, it leaves an impression of the extent to which this magnificent stream ministers to the wants of commerce and of the traveller such as defies the attempt at computation."[1] The present railway system of India ministers to the wants of commerce much more effectually; but it is constructed by foreign capital and pays interest to foreign shareholders; and millions of boatmen and boat-builders, cartmen and bullock owners, have lost their living.

The question of the applicability of canals, and railroads for conveyances drawn by animals, also came up for consideration. It was estimated that the cost of construction of a canal, and of a single railroad, would be the same, about £900 the mile; that the former would pay £190 and the latter £175 the mile.

"A canal would require works which are not required in irrigating channels, but not works of a very different nature. But a railroad for conveyances drawn by animals is one of the simplest works that can be executed, and would present much fewer obstacles than the various works now used in irrigation. The railroads would also be preferable to canals as requiring no water, which is so valuable in the Carnatic. . . . But the main question seems to be whether the same money and skill expended on works of irrigation, whether those now in use or new ones, would not, upon the whole, improve the country more than if expended in improving the means of internal communication. . . . It may be proper here to mention that all the above calculations and remarks respecting railroads refer only to those intended for animal power,

[1] H. T. Prinsep's Note, dated 31st July 1828.

for the use of locomotive engines alters the nature of the work materially and increases the expense prodigiously, because in the latter case neither such great inclinations nor such sharp turns can be allowed as in the former. Thus the Manchester and Liverpool railroad cost £25,000 per mile, while the average of double railways throughout England [for animal power] is about £5000 per mile. . . . It seems very advisable to send out a small quantity of rails and waggon wheels to be ready for any of the works that are constantly executing in the Tank Department. About a thousand yards of double rails, such as are used for temporary purposes in England, and wheels for forty railway waggons might be sent out for about £250."[1]

We have made the above extract because it is always interesting to trace the commencement of a controversy which has assumed vast proportions in recent years. The discussion about the comparative merits of canals and railways was carried on through succeeding decades, and, as might be expected, preference was given to railways which facilitated British trade with India, and not to canals which would have benefited Indian agriculture. So great was the influence of British traders on the Indian administration that the Indian Government guaranteed a rate of interest out of the Indian revenues to companies constructing railroads in India; and £225,000,000 were spent on railways, resulting not in a profit, but in a loss of £40,000,000 to the Indian taxpayer up to 1900. And so little were the interests of Indian agriculture appreciated that only £25,000,000 were spent on irrigation works up to 1900.

[1] Evidence before the Commons' Committee, 1832, vol. ii. Part ii Appendix xxiv.

CHAPTER XVIII

ADMINISTRATIVE FAILURES (1793-1815)

THE measures organised first by Warren Hastings, and then by Lord Cornwallis, for the civil and judicial administration of the Company's dominions in India have been briefly described in previous chapters. With much that was good and beneficial in those measures, they had some fatal defects which became more and more conspicuous with the lapse of time. In the first place, the judicial machinery set up was wholly inadequate for the requirements of a vast country, with a population which nearly amounted to a hundred millions in the tracts included in the Company's dominions at the time of the death of Cornwallis. And in the second place, a plan of administering justice, and giving protection to life and property to this great and civilised population, without accepting the help and co-operation of the people themselves, was doomed to failure.

European judges were imperfectly acquainted with the language of the people, and had a still more imperfect knowledge of their customs and manners. Their Indian ministerial officers were meanly paid and therefore corrupt, and justice was often sold to the highest bidders. Worse than this, the cases accumulated to such an extent, and their decision was delayed so long, that there was a virtual denial of justice to the people. Armies of witnesses were dragged from their homes and occupations to attend distant courts, until the people, Hindu and Mahomedan, considered it one of the severest of punishments to be cited as witnesses. Charges and fees were imposed in order to make justice more expensive and to discourage recourse to courts. Additional powers were given to judges, and the privilege of appeal was limited, in order to reduce the work. Every repressive measure was vainly adopted to remedy that evil which had but one true remedy,—to accept the co-operation of the people, and to entrust the task of judicial administration to the people themselves.

"It seems to have been forgotten that, for centuries prior to the introduction of European agency, law and justice had been administered solely by natives; yet society had been held together, and there had been times when, according to the testimony of travellers and historians, India had been populous and flourishing, the people thriving and happy."[1]

If such were the defects in the administration of civil justice in the early years of the nineteenth century, the defects in the administration of criminal justice were graver. Bengal was infested by gangs of robbers who were known by the name of Dacoits, and whom the Magistrates, helped by an ill-paid and corrupt police, were unable to check. Daring robberies were committed in large towns and centres of trade, and villages remained in a continuous state of terror, and often paid blackmail to renowned heads of robbers. From 1800 to 1810 the country was kept in a state of perpetual alarm; the deeds of Bengal Rob Roys were narrated in bazaars and market-places; the Magistrate and the Police were powerless; the people accepted their fate. "A monstrous and disorganised state of society existed under the eye of the Supreme British authorities, and almost at the

[1] Mill's *History of British India*, Wilson's continuation, Book I. chap. vii.

very seat of the Government to which the country might justly look for safety and protection. The mischief could not wait for a slow remedy; the people were perishing almost in our sight; every week's delay was a doom of slaughter and torture against the defenceless inhabitants of very populous countries."[1]

The measures which were adopted for remedying the evil were worse than the evil. Two European Superintendents of Police were appointed to act in concert with Magistrates for the suppression of crime. Special Magistrates were appointed and armed with special powers to put down robbery. They employed Goendas or spies to give information against suspected people, and thus the evils of an extensive system of espionage were added to the evils caused by crimes. Inhabitants of villages were indiscriminately apprehended on false information; they were kept in jail for months, and sometimes for years, before they were brought for trial; and they not unoften perished in prisons. Every large jail in Bengal was crowded with hundreds and thousands of innocent men; and the villagers dreaded the malice of the informer more than the wrath of the Magistrate.

In 1813 the Court of Directors circulated queries regarded the working of the judicial system in India to several of their distinguished servants, then in England. The majority of them still clung to the time-honoured tradition that the natives of India were unfit and unworthy of being entrusted with high duties—a tradition which had the merit of reserving all the high posts of India for their own sons and nephews, friends and relations. But the wisest and most thoughtful among the Company's servants saw the hollowness of the doctrine, and they boldly proclaimed—what was then a heresy—that India could not be governed except through the co-operation

[1] Lord Minto's Minute, dated 24th November 1810.

of the people themselves. Among the first who had the wisdom to see and the courage to declare this truth were Sir Henry Strachey of Bengal, Thomas Munro of Madras, and Colonel Walker of Bombay. It is necessary that some portions of their replies to the Court of Directors should be placed before the reader.

"The remedy I propose," wrote Sir Henry Strachey, "for the defects I have stated, is the establishment of more Courts, composed of natives, both Mahomedans and Hindus, to be guided entirely by our Regulations. Let the Native Judges be well paid, and they will do their duty well; of this I feel the strongest conviction. The expense would be little or nothing, as the fees might defray the whole, though it would be better to give the Native Judges liberal salaries. There should, at all events, in cases of undue exactions of rent, be no fees on documents, no stamps, no expense except the institution fee."

"If the powers of the Munsiffs [Native Civil Judges] were only extended to the decision of suits to the amount of Rs.200 [£20], the limit of the Registrar's authority at present, the institution fee alone would, I conceive, form an ample fund for the payment of the Native Judges and their Amla [clerks]. When I speak of a liberal salary for a Native Judge, I would be understood to mean somewhat less than one-tenth of the salary of the European Judge."

"It is my opinion that all the judicial functions of Bengal might gradually be thrown into the hands of the Natives, if such were the pleasure of the Company, and that the business would be as well conducted, under our Regulations, by the Natives as by Europeans, in some respects better, and at one-tenth of the expense."[1]

Speaking of European traders in India, Sir Henry

[1] *East India Papers* (London, 1820), vol. ii. p. 56.

wrote: "The trade of Bengal has been for the most part in the hands of Europeans for half a century and longer.

"It was not till the Courts, civil and criminal, had been some time established under their present form and in full operation, that oppression committed by European traders was put an end to. Labourers and manufacturers, in the employment of the Company and of private European traders, were imprisoned and beaten and harassed by peons.

"This I conceive to have been the ancient custom of the country, and not invented by Europeans; but the agents of the Company had most power, and were, of course, the worst tyrants.

"In the salt department a shameless system of cheating and severity was universally practised. Many thousands of men were compelled to work, and allowed a most scanty subsistence. Some hundreds were pressed every year into this service. They were, in some instances, bound hand and foot, and sent off to the most unhealthy parts of the Sundarbans, to manufacture salt for the Company's monopoly.

"All these practices remained till the Courts were established in 1793, and then it was soon discovered that they were wrong. They prevailed till that time; not that we had made laws to authorise them, but because the people seldom complained of them. Because, if they had been in the habit of complaining, the Collector could not have heard the hundredth part of the complaints, and because their practices were conformable to the custom of the country.

"Generally speaking, in the commercial transactions carried on by the Company and by Europeans out of the service, the Natives were treated ill, though signal acts of cruelty would occasionally be punished by the Collector.

"The decisions of the Civil Courts, and the sentences of the Magistrates in petty Foujdari [Criminal] cases, which last are speedy and expeditious, have produced, since 1793, a great change for the better." [1]

On the important question of Executive and Judicial duties, which were separated by Lord Cornwallis in 1793, Sir Henry Strachey's remarks are of special interest at the present time.

"It was not till the year 1793 that the powers of Collector and those of Judge and Magistrate were first separated and held by different persons in Bengal. The plan had been tried, I think, but partially, several years before, and given up; but till this period the administration of justice, whether committed to the Collector or not, appeared to be a secondary affair. It occupied less time than the other duties of the Collector, and the collection of the revenue was still considered, according to the ancient characteristic usage of the country, as the primary object, the chief function of the internal Government.

"It was not till this period [1793] that the Bengal Government, through the agency of its judicial servants, began seriously to attend to the welfare and protection of the numerous people subject to their dominion." [2]

Sir Henry Strachey had much to say of the oppression of the cultivators of Bengal under the Zemindari system, an oppression which has since been stopped by the Rent Acts of 1859, 1868, and 1885. And he also spoke in equally forcible words of the oppression of the cultivators of Madras under the Ryotwari system.

"Well may the Ryotwari Collectors talk of the incompatibility of their system with that of the judicial institutions of Bengal. Well might the Madras Government delay, from year to year, the introduction of the Bengal Regulations, lest the Collectors' influence should

[1] *East India Papers* (London, 1820), vol. ii. p. 58.

[2] *Ibid.*, p. 58. Judicial and Executive duties have unfortunately been reunited since.

be destroyed and the collection of the revenues impeded. . . .

"If the Ryotwari plan can be carried on successfully after the establishment of the judicial authorities, if rules can be framed under which the Ryotwar Collector shall act as Manager only of an estate, and the Judge shall have the usual power of redressing grievances, then I shall not condemn the plan; but I protest against the Ryotwar Collector having any judicial power whatever. As Manager of an estate only he ought to be considered; consequently we must be jealous of his power, lest he should pervert it to purposes of extortion. Every Manager of an estate has, in India, a natural inclination or tendency towards extortion. If any man, whose business it is to collect rent from the Ryots, shall persuade himself that, while so occupied, he is the fittest person in the world to defend these Ryots from the oppressions which he and his dependents commit, that his occupation supersedes the necessity of all control, that person, in my opinion, grossly errs."[1]

It is necessary to quote one more passage from Sir Henry's valuable letter, in which he emphatically asserts the fitness of the people of India for judicial duties of a high and responsible nature, without the superintendence of European officials.

"I think no superintendence of Europeans is necessary. I have already in my reply to Question 4th offered my opinion upon this subject. If the Natives are not qualified for these or any other offices, I conceive the fault to be ours, and not theirs. If we encourage them, if we allow them to aspire to high office, if we pay them well, if we raise them in their own estimation, they will soon be found fit for any official employment in India.

[1] *East India Papers* (London, 1820), pp. 64, 65. The Ryotwari Collector of Madras still continues [1901] to be the Magistrate of his District.

"I beg to repeat what I long ago said in substance upon this subject, that the Natives are depressed and humiliated, being confined by us to subordinate and servile offices. Although their education is most defective, and ignorance and credulity pervade all ranks, especially among the Hindus, they are nevertheless found to acquire easily the requisite qualifications for the duties which we are pleased to entrust to them. From temper, habit, and peculiar circumstances, they are in many respects fitter for the office of a Judge than ourselves.

"*But we place the European beyond the reach of temptation. To the Native, a man whose ancestors perhaps bore high command, we assign some ministerial office, with a poor stipend of twenty or thirty rupees* [£2 *or* £3] *a month. Then we pronounce that the Indians are corrupt, and no race of men but the Company's European servants are fit to govern them.*"[1]

We must here take leave of Sir Henry Strachey, though a great deal of what follows in the subsequent part of his letter is valuable. He quotes figures to point out the harshness of the measures adopted to suppress robberies in Bengal. Two hundred and nine prisoners were kept in confinement, some of them for five months, in the jail of the Twenty-four Perganas, on suspicion and without being even examined by the Magistrate. Sixty-two persons were arrested on suspicion after a robbery at Arwal; nine of them died in jail; not one was convicted on trial. Eighty-four persons were arrested on suspicion after a robbery at Dungain; only two of whom were found guilty by the Judge. One hundred and ninety-two persons were arrested on suspicion after a robbery at Madanpur; confessions were extorted from them or fabricated against them; forty-six of them were detained in irons

[1] *East India Papers* (London, 1820), vol. ii. p. 67. The italics are our own.

above a year; three of them died; the rest were proved innocent at trial and acquitted. In the District of Nadiya, 2071 persons were arrested on suspicion between November 1808 and May 1809. In six months forty-eight had died in jail, 278 were still under inquiry, and 1477 were not yet examined. "Such shocking cruelty," says Sir Henry, "such a monstrous perversion of justice, committed with our eyes open and with deliberation, the imprisonment of multitudes, the harassing, the subornation of perjury, the plunder, the death of innocent men in jail, these scenes I conceive to be most discreditable to those who permitted them. They ought not, under any circumstances, to have been endured. Dacoity itself, dreadful as it is, cannot be compared in its quantum of mischief to what was produced by this horrid system."[1]

We now turn to the opinions of Thomas Munro, which are equally significant.

"In a civilised, populous country like India, justice can be well dispensed only through the agency of the Natives themselves. . . . Most European Governments have deemed it advisable to purchase integrity in high public officers by honours and emoluments. If we want it in India, we must adopt the same means; *and if we pay the same price, we shall find it among the Natives of that country as readily, I am afraid, as among Europeans.* Under the sway of every Mahomedan conqueror, the Natives of India have been admitted to all the highest dignities of the State; it is only under the British Government that they have been excluded from this advantage, and held in a condition, even when employed in the public department, little superior to that of menial servants."[2]

In another Memorandum, Thomas Munro wrote of the ancient Hindu system of dispensing justice through

[1] *East India Papers* (London, 1820), vol. ii. p. 70.
[2] *Ibid.*, pp. 105, 110. The italics are ours.

Village Panchyets, with all their merits and all their defects.

"The strong attachment of the Natives to trial by Panchyet has, no doubt, in some degree arisen from the dread of the venality of their rulers; but it has probably been increased and confirmed by the conviction, resulting from experience, that no Judge, however upright or active, was so competent as such a body to dispense justly, correctly, and expeditiously."

Contrasting this old system with the system introduced under the British Rule, he made some thoughtful remarks.

"It is evident that our present system is not only most expensive and vexatious, but totally inefficient. There is, under the Bengal Government, about one hundred and thirty thousand suits in arrear. These suits will, on a moderate calculation, require a million of witnesses; and if we consider the expense, the distance, and the time they must be absent from their homes, it will not be easy to estimate the amount of injury which the country thereby sustains. But the evil, it has been asserted, is unavoidable, and springs from the litigious spirit of the people of India. Had this been their real character, it would have appeared when they paid nothing for trials. I have had ample opportunity of observing them in every situation, and I can affirm that they are not litigious. I have often been astonished at the facility with which suits among them were settled, and at the fairness with which the losing party acknowledged the claim against him. But when irritated by expense and by delay, it is not surprising that litigation should grow with the progress of the suit through its tedious stages. . . . Our system produces the litigation which we groundlessly impute to the character of the people."[1]

Lastly, we turn to the remarks of Colonel Walker

[1] *East India Papers* (London, 1820), vol. ii. pp. 116, 118.

of Bombay, who wrote with a commendable moderation and impartiality on the excellence as well as on the defects of the judicial system introduced in India under the British Rule.

"The excellence of the British judicial system has been often acknowledged and recorded with the fervour of national pride. The system has been dictated by the purest philanthropy, and is administered with the most honourable and scrupulous integrity. Justice is, in fact, administered with exactness to all ranks of subjects; and, allowing for the weakness of human nature, with strict and uniform impartiality. The disadvantages of the system may be principally ascribed to the great difference of manners, and the unfavourable situation of strangers in administering justice to a foreign people. This is a great disadvantage, which never can be effectually removed, but might be softened by admitting the Natives to a share in the administration. . . . The greatest defect of the present system, perhaps, is the employment of strangers to the total exclusion of the Natives of the country."[1]

To this subject Colonel Walker reverted again and again in his reply to the ninth question set by the Directors, in respect of the integrity and diligence of the natives of India.

"The most prominent feature in the civil government of the Company is the almost entire exclusion of native agency. The offices held by Natives are only those of the lowest description—such as could not be the object of ambition to any European; and the salary attached to these appointments is such as barely affords to themselves and families the means of subsistence. To Natives of rank and liberal education no temptation is held out which can induce them to engage in the service of the Company. Not only are the emoluments offered scanty, but the want of confidence reposed in

[1] *East India Papers* (London, 1820), vol. ii. pp. 183, 184.

them, the general light in which they are received, cannot fail to inspire them with insurmountable disgust. . . .

"The admission of the Natives to offices of honour and profit is the only mode by which they can be effectually conciliated. It is vain to expect that men will ever be satisfied with merely having their property secured, while all the paths of honourable ambition are shut against them. This mortifying exclusion stifles talents, humbles family pride, and depresses all but the weak and worthless. By the higher classes of society it is considered as a severe injustice; but these are the men of influence and consideration in the country, the men by whom the public opinion is formed. So long as this source of hostility remains, the British administration will always be regarded as imposing a yoke. . . .

"The Romans, whose business was conquest, and who extended their yoke over the greatest part of the civilised world, may be safely taken as guides in the art of holding nations in subjection; that wise people always left a great share of the administration of the countries they subdued in the hands of the natives."[1]

It is remarkable that a wide survey of historical antecedents suggested to Colonel Munro and to Colonel Walker the same conclusions. Colonel Munro pointed to the Mahomedan conquerors who ruled Northern India for five hundred years by admitting the Hindu natives of India "to all the highest dignities of state;" and Colonel Walker pointed to the Roman conquerors who held the Western world under their sway for a similar period by leaving "a great share of the administration of the countries they subdued in the hands of the natives." Those who are most keenly conscious of the blessings of England's Rule in India—and the educated people of India are the foremost among them

[1] *East India Papers* (London, 1820), vol. ii. pp. 185, 186.

—are, nevertheless, painfully aware how the virtual exclusion of Indians from the higher services and the control of the administration makes the British Rule needlessly unpopular and weakens the Empire.

And this exclusion is often justified by a misrepresentation of the Indian character which Colonel Walker guardedly refers to towards the end of his letter.

"There is no source of deception against which it would behove the Company to guard than the reports which they receive concerning the capacities of their native subjects. They are, of course, transmitted through the medium of Europeans holding employments in that country; *but they often undervalue the qualifications of the Natives from motives of prejudice or interest.* There are many, indeed, who would be superior to such motives, and few, perhaps, who would act upon them deliberately. But still the principle is secretly active, and will always have a powerful effect, though perhaps unfelt influence, on men's views and opinions." [1]

[1] *East India Papers* (London. 1820), vol. ii. p. 188. The italics are our own.

CHAPTER XIX

ADMINISTRATIVE REFORMS AND LORD W. BENTINCK (1815–1835)

THE opinions recorded by men like Sir Henry Strachey, Colonel Munro, and Colonel Walker, the famous Fifth Report submitted by the Select Committee of the House of Commons of 1812, and lastly, the evidence given by Munro and Malcolm before the House of Commons in 1813, had their effect on public opinion in England, and compelled the Court of Directors to take some measures to reform the judicial administration of India. They appointed a Special Commission to inquire into and reform the judicial system, and Colonel Munro was appointed President of the Commission.

Munro left England in June 1814, and arrived at Madras in September, after a quick voyage of eighteen weeks. Without any loss of time he entered into his work with his accustomed ardour, and on Christmas Eve of the same year he placed before the Government of Madras his suggestions under six heads. He proposed (1) that the Collector should be vested with the authority of Magistrate, and the management of the village police should be restored to the heads of villages; (2) that Village Panchyets should be reconstructed; (3) that Native District Judges or Commissioners should be appointed; (4) that Collectors should be empowered to enforce Pottah Regulations; (5) that the power of Zemindars to distrain should be restricted;

and (6) that cases of disputed boundaries should be decided by Collectors.[1]

It is impossible not to remark in these preliminary suggestions two predominating ideas which actuated Thomas Munro. In the first place, he insisted on placing all judicial work, as far as possible, in the hands of the people of India, appointed as Village Heads, District Judges, and Commissioners. In the second place, he desired to centralise all executive power—revenue, magisterial, and police—in the hands of a single official, the District Collector. His first idea has only been partially carried into execution, and the post of District Judge is, to the present time, virtually reserved for Europeans. His second idea, probably justified in an age of disorder and misrule, has unfortunately been acted upon down to the present time.

It is impossible within our limits to narrate the work of the Commission during the subsequent two years, and the vast amount of correspondence which ensued, and which fill nearly 500 folio pages of the East India Papers.[2] It is enough to state that the Commission at first prepared drafts of seven Regulations and submitted them to the Chief Civil and Criminal Courts of Madras for revision. A letter from the Court of Directors, dated 20th December 1815, was then received and forwarded to the Commission. Various alterations and additions to the original drafts were made in accordance with the suggestions of the Madras Government and of the Chief Courts. Finally a series of Fifteen Regulations were passed at different dates in 1816.

The immediate result of these Regulations was to largely extend the employment of the people of Madras

[1] Colonel Munro to the Madras Government, Letter dated 24th December 1814, para. 6.
[2] Vol. ii. (1820), pp. 291–769.

in responsible posts, and the transference of much of the judicial work to their hands. It was a reform which the most thoughtful of the Company's servants had advocated for years past, a reform which was needed in the interests of good administration. It fell to Thomas Munro to be the first to give effect to this needed reform.

"The most important and laborious part of that duty," wrote the Court of Directors to the Government of Madras, "fell on Colonel Munro, the first Commissioner, in whose commendation it would be superfluous for us to speak, were it not for the purpose of assuring you, for your information and that of the Civil Service in general, that we consider the services which he has rendered to the Company and to the natives, as Chief of the Commission, to be as deserving of our hearty acknowledgments as any act of his long and honourable public life."[1]

This encomium was well deserved, and has been endorsed by public opinion in India. Nevertheless, it is necessary to state that some of the objects aimed at by Munro in his Regulations have not been fulfilled. The endeavour to place the village police under village heads has been abandoned, and the Police now forms a separate force all over India. And the endeavour to reconstruct village Panchyets has also failed, for reasons which have been explained elsewhere. The time to construct Village Unions under wiser regulations has now come, and the Government in India will never be in touch with the mass of the people till this is effected.

On the other hand, the mistake made by Thomas Munro in combining the duties of the Collector, the Magistrate, and the Police, in the same hands has been perpetuated. The mistake was committed, not without a strong protest from the Madras Government

[1] Judicial Letter to Madras, dated 12th May 1819.

even in 1815 and 1816. Mr. Fullerton, a Member of the Madras Government, stated the cardinal objections to that combination of duties fully and clearly.

"The transfer of Magisterial duties to Collectors, also, I do certainly think must involve a departure that may go far to counteract the benefit of the judicial system, by arming the executive with too much power, and lessening that faith and confidence the people now begin to feel in the protection of the Judicial Department."[1]

The Madras Government was of the same opinion, and held that while the Collector might be vested with the superintendence of the Police, he should not be armed with magisterial powers. The question went up to the Court of Directors, and the Directors overruled the Madras Government, and directed the combination of revenue and magisterial duties in the same officers.

"The point on which a difference of sentiment has arisen between you and Colonel Munro regards that part of our despatch in which we enjoined the transfer of magisterial functions to the Collector, Colonel Munro thinking that we meant to include in the transfer not merely the superintendence and control of the police, but the whole duties of magistrate, and our Governor in Council, on the other hand, conceiving that we intended to confine the transfer to the superintendence and control of the police establishment.

"We have no hesitation in declaring our intention to have been that the transfer should take place in the sense and to the extent supposed by Colonel Munro."[2]

The Government of Madras submitted to this

[1] Minute, dated 1st January 1816.

[2] Judicial Letter from the Court of Directors to the Government of Madras, dated 20th December 1815, paras. 12 and 13.

decision with ill-grace. Robert Fullerton wrote again: "However much I must lament that the sentiments I had previously recorded should have proved at variance with the orders and opinions since received from superior authority, I cannot conscientiously recall them. Intermediate reflection, and the consideration of various public documents since received, have added strength to the belief that the whole and sole magisterial authority of the district, vested in the Collector, much of which must be delegated to Native Revenue officers, uncontrolled except by the occasional visits of the Judge of Circuit, will establish a degree of power in the Revenue Department, against the abuse of which no legal appeal can effectually be made."[1]

We now turn to the affairs of Bombay. No reference to Bombay has been made in preceding chapters, because the greater portion of the Province came under British Rule more than half a century after Bengal and Madras. British influence was firmly established in Bengal after the battle of Plassey in 1757, and in Madras after the battle of Wandewash in 1761, but the Mahrattas held their own in the west of India in spite of the wars of Warren Hastings and Lord Wellesley. The last of the Peshwas was seated on the throne of Poona by the help of British arms in 1802, and maintained a British subsidiary force within his dominions by the terms of his treaty with the British. This was the beginning of the end. He soon discovered the formidable power of his new allies, and chafed under the restraint he had placed on himself. At last he threw off the mask; he fought one battle and lost, and his dominions were annexed to British territory in 1817.

Mountstuart Elphinstone's name is as intimately

[1] Minute of 13th September 1816. Robert Fullerton might have been aware that the main concern of the Directors was their revenue, and the main purpose of their policy was to vest the utmost degree of power in the Revenue Department.

connected with the building up of British administration in Bombay as the name of Thomas Munro is connected with Madras. Elphinstone went out to India in 1796, a young lad of seventeen. Seven years after he had the good fortune of serving in the capacity of a private secretary under Arthur Wellesley, afterwards the famous Duke of Wellington. He rode by the Duke's side in the great battle of Assaye in 1803, and he first acquired his intimate knowledge of Mahratta affairs and administration as Resident at Nagpur from 1804 to 1808. A mission to Kabul enabled him to write a very readable work on the people and institutions of that unknown country, and on his return he was, in 1811, appointed Resident at Poona, where he was destined to play an important part in the revolution which followed within a few years. The revolution came, as stated before, in 1817; the rule of Baji Rao, the last Peshwa, was swept away; and the Deccan was annexed to the British Empire.

Elphinstone's unequalled experience in Mahratta affairs marked him out as the most capable man for settling the conquered territory. He was appointed Commissioner of the Deccan in January 1818, and the work performed by him in this capacity will be referred to in the following chapter. In 1819 he was appointed Governor of Bombay, and during the eight years that he held this high appointment, he laid the foundations of British administration in Western India.

His fame as a liberal administrator rests mainly on his work in three directions. His first endeavour was to codify the law. His second great object was to confer on the people of India as large a share in the work of administration as was then possible. His third and last purpose was to spread a sound education among the people, so as to enable them to take a higher and more responsible share in the future in the management of their own concerns.

The first task was well and satisfactorily done. "The whole of the Bombay Regulations were formed into a code, regularly arranged according to their subject-matter. This code consists of twenty-seven Regulations, subdivided into chapters and sections. It refers to the same subjects as the Bengal Regulations, but differs from them in the circumstance that it contains a body of substantial criminal law."[1] Beyond this, Elphinstone endeavoured to prepare a digest of the laws, customs, and usages of the people themselves. "What we call Hindu law," he wrote, "applies to Brahmans only; each caste has separate laws and customs;" and Elphinstone's idea was to compile a complete digest of these varying customs of all castes and tribes. Such an idea was worthy of him, but was impossible of execution, and the work remained unaccomplished.

How intimate the best administrators in India have always been with the highest thought and culture of England will appear from the fact that while Elphinstone was seeking to compile a digest of Hindu usages and laws, he was studiously applying himself to the works of Jeremy Bentham. He wrote of him to Strachey:

"I was greatly delighted with your account of Jeremy Bentham. I had a great curiosity about him, which was fully gratified. He is certainly a man of first-rate talents, but also of first-rate eccentricity, which, both in his doctrines and his personal habits, probably arises from his little intercourse with the world. I was extremely flattered by his present of books, and knew no author from whom I should so highly have valued such a distinction. When I last

[1] Sir James Stephen. Proceedings of the National Association for the Promotion of Social Science for 1872–73.

wrote to you at length, I was thinking of employing the Bengal counsellors whom I expected to get at Poona to form a code from the Hindoo law as administered under the Brahmans and the customs of the Mahratta country, corrected in some cases by our own; but I got no counsellors, and the more I contemplated the undertaking the more formidable it seemed."[1]

Historians of India have not always made it sufficiently clear that British administration in India during the last 150 years has been always shaped by European influences. The wars of Frederick the Great fostered those wars between the English and the French in the eighteenth century which ended in the effacement of the latter in India; and the Napoleonic wars inspired the ambitious conquests of Lord Wellesley and Lord Hastings. The endeavour after judicial, civil, and domestic reforms which followed, and which culminated in England in the Reform Act of 1832, led to similar reforms in India, and admitted the people into a larger share of administrative work in Madras, Bombay, and Bengal. And during the seventy years which have elapsed since, every period of peace and reforms in England has been marked by some tangible reforms in India; and every wave of the war feeling in England has inspired ambitious projects and often foolish wars in India. The want of any popular representation in India makes that country dependent on England in more senses than one; and the people of India have often had to endure unwise and retrograde administration, and to pay for unwise and foolish wars, during periods of England's temporary madness!

At the period of which we are speaking in this chapter the English influences were of the healthiest kind, and induced Munro, Elphinstone, and Bentinck not only to reform the laws of India, but to regard

[1] Letter of September 3, 1820. *Life of the Hon. Mountstuart Elphinstone*, by Sir J. E. Colebrooke (1884), vol. ii. p. 115.

favourably the claims of the people to a legitimate share in the administration. Elphinstone was as thorough in this opinion as Munro, and gave expression to it in all his correspondence and minutes in which the question came up for consideration. The following extract from a letter to Sir Thomas Munro, dated 1822, will serve as an example:

"I hear you have instituted something like a Native Board at Madras, and I should be much obliged if you would inform me of the nature of the plan. It seems to be one great advantage of the arrangement that it opens a door to the employment of natives in high and efficient situations. I should be happy to know if you think the plan can be extended to the judicial or any other line. Besides the necessity for having good native advisers in governing natives, it is necessary that we should pave the way for the introduction of the natives to some share in the government of their own country. It may be half a century before we are obliged to do so; but the system of government and of education which we have already established must some time or other work such a change in the people of this country that it will be impossible to confine them to subordinate employment; and if we have not previously opened vents for their ambition and ability, we may expect an explosion which will overturn our Government."[1]

Four years later, in a letter to Henry Ellis, Elphinstone expressed his matured opinion on the subject still more emphatically.

"It has always been a favourite notion of mine that our object ought to be to place ourselves in the same relation to the natives as the Tartars are in to the Chinese: retaining the government and military power, but gradually relinquishing all share in the

[1] *Life of the Hon. Mountstuart Elphinstone*, by Sir J. E. Colebrooke (1884), vol. ii. p. 142. Letter dated 27th October 1822.

civil administration, except that degree of control which is necessary to give the whole an impulse and direction. This operation must be so gradual that it need not even alarm the Directors, as you suppose, for their civil patronage; but it ought to be kept in mind, and all our measures ought to tend to that object."[1]

Elphinstone always upheld and preached this idea to the end of his life. Over twenty years after his retirement from India, when he was living a retired life among his books in his quiet country house at Surrey—esteemed by all as the highest authority on Indian affairs, and pressed more than once to go out to India as Governor-General—he still entertained and expressed the same opinion in his correspondence.

"We . . . must apply ourselves to bring the natives into a state that will admit of their governing themselves in a manner that may be beneficial to our interest as well as their own and that of the rest of the world, and to take the glory of the achievement and the sense of having done our duty for the chief reward of our exertions."[2]

It remains to add that Elphinstone did all he could to give effect to this policy during his administration; and the example set in Madras by Sir Thomas Munro enabled him to place a large share of the judicial work of Bombay in the hands of Indian Civil Judges of different grades.

The third and last great object of Elphinstone's administration was the promotion of education among the people. Bombay was then probably the most

[1] *Life of the Hon. Mountstuart Elphinstone*, by Sir J. E. Colebrooke (1884), vol. ii. p. 186. Letter dated 30th October 1826. The Directors and their civil patronage have ceased to exist, but the desire to find a career for English boys in India has still kept the door to the higher services virtually closed to the sons of the soil.

[2] Cameron's Address to Parliament on the Duties of Great Britain to India (1853). Quoted in J. S. Cotton's *Mountstuart Elphinstone and the Making of South-Western India* (1896), p. 190.

backward of all the Presidencies in point of education. The chaplains of the East India Company supervised a few charity schools, and missionary effort was almost confined to a small body of American missionaries who came to Bombay in 1814.

Elphinstone presided at a public meeting in 1820, and a Society for the promotion of the Education of the Poor was formed. He obtained a grant of £5000 for this Society for printing works and purchasing prizes, and all education in the vernacular languages was conducted during the next sixteen years through the agency of this Society, Elaborate inquiries were also conducted into the system of primary instruction, and the result of these inquiries, published in 1832, disclosed a total of 1705 schools with 35,143 scholars in the Bombay Province, with its populatian of nearly five millions.[1]

In his endeavour to spread higher education, Elphinstone met with opposition from his own Council, and also from the Court of Directors. Elphinstone desired to found a College at Bombay for young civilians with a special department for the training of native officials; the latter part of the scheme was opposed by his Council; and the whole project failed to obtain the sanction of the Directors.

For the spread of general education Elphinstone proposed (1) to improve and increase the native schools; (2) to supply them with school-books; (3) to encourage the lower classes to obtain education; (4) to establish new schools for the teaching of European sciences; (5) to prepare books of moral and physical science in the vernaculars; (6) to establish new schools for teaching English; (7) to hold forth encouragement to the people. To conciliate the Directors, Elphinstone pointed out that the cost

[1] J. S. Cotton's *Mountstuart Elphinstone and the Making of South-Western India*, 1896, p. 193.

of the schools to the Company would be small, and would be largely borne by villages. Nevertheless no sanction to his scheme was received before he left India. The first English school was opened in Bombay in 1828, the year after Elphinstone's departure; an English department was attached to the Sanscrit college at Poona in the same year; and the great Elphinstone Institution of Bombay was not opened till 1834.

We conclude this brief account of Elphinstone's educational work in India by making one or two extracts from his Minutes of 1824.

"It has been urged against our Indian Government that we have subverted the States of the East, and shut up all the sources from which the magnificence of the country was derived, and that we have not ourselves constructed a single work, either of utility or of splendour. It may be alleged with more justice that we have dried up the fountains of native talent, and that from the nature of our conquest, not only all encouragement to the advancement of knowledge is withdrawn, but even the actual learning of the nation is likely to be lost and the productions of former genius to be forgotten. Something should surely be done to remove this reproach." [1]

And he wrote in the same year:

"If care were taken to qualify the natives for the public service, and afterwards to encourage their employment, the picture would be soon reversed. At no very distant day we might see natives engaged in superintending a portion of a District as the European Assistants are doing now. In a more advanced stage, they might sometimes be Registrars and Sub-Collectors, or even Collectors and Judges;

[1] Forrest's *Selections from the Minutes and other Official Writings of the Hon. Mountstuart Elphinstone* (1884), p. 102.

and it may not be too visionary to suppose a period at which they might bear to the English nearly the relation which the Chinese do to the Tartars, the Europeans retaining the government and the military power, while the natives filled a large portion of the civil stations, and many of the subordinate employments in the army." [1]

The two greatest administrators of their time were removed from India in the same year. Sir Thomas Munro died in July 1827, and Mountstuart Elphinstone left India four months after. In the same year Lord William Bentinck was appointed Governor-General of India, and it fell to him to complete the work which Munro and Elphinstone had so happily begun.

No administrator went out to India under stronger influences of that healthy public opinion which was forming itself in Europe after the Napoleonic Wars. He had been Governor of Madras early in the nineteenth century, had been removed from the post on the occurrence of a mutiny, and had then plunged into European politics. He was in Sicily and in Italy, planning with the Duke of Orleans (afterwards Louis Philippe, King of France) for the emancipation of Italy; and after the capture of Genoa in 1814, he restored to the Genoese their old constitution, and called on the Italians to struggle and be a free nation. The victorious Allies, however, wanted to keep up the old order of things, and the Congress of Vienna forced Italy under the hated rule of Austria. Thirteen years after this, when France was on the eve of the revolution of 1830, when England was already agitating for a Reform Act, Lord William Bentinck arrived in India as Governor-General in 1828.

The administrative and educational reforms effected by Lord William Bentinck were on the lines laid down by Munro and Elphinstone. A larger share of judicial

[1] Quoted in J. S. Cotton's work, cited before.

work was given to qualified Indian officials, and a higher grade of Indian judges was created under the name of Sudder-Ameens. Some executive and revenue work was also entrusted to them, and a higher grade was created for them under the name of Deputy-Collectors. During a period of over seventy years, the educated people of India have proved their ability, integrity, and fitness for the most difficult and responsible administrative work.

The Land Settlements of 1822 in Northern India, under which the State claimed more than three-fourths of the rental as the Land-Tax, had proved oppressive in the extreme. Lord William Bentinck changed the system, and reduced the State demand to two-thirds of the rental. A new settlement commenced in 1833, and effected by R. M. Bird, gave much relief to the people, while it actually increased the revenue from the soil. We shall speak of this new settlement in a subsequent chapter.

Raja Ram Mohan Roy, the most advanced among the educated Hindus, gave the Governor-General his support in abolishing that cruel custom of permitting Hindu widows to burn themselves on the funeral pyre of their deceased husbands, known under the name of Sati. And Sleeman's name stands prominent in connection with the suppression of the class of criminals known as Thugs or wayside murderers, who infested various parts of India.

The Company's Charter was renewed in 1833, and the Company's trade was abolished. They stood forth henceforward as administrators of India, not as traders; and they found in Lord William Bentinck the most efficient helper in the cause of good administration. The post of a Legal Member of the Governor-General's Council was created, and the illustrious Macaulay went out to India as the first Legal Member.

Never had any Governor-General more enthusiastic

colleagues. Trevelyan, as has been stated in the preceding chapter, took the first decisive step in abolishing the Inland Duties which had so long impeded trade in India. Macaulay helped in all legal work, and made the first draft of that celebrated Penal Code of India which is still one of the finest penal laws in the world. And Metcalfe followed out Lord William's policy after his retirement, and granted liberty to the Press of India during his short administration.

True reforms always lead to retrenchment, and Lord William Bentinck changed the chronic deficit in the Indian budget into a surplus. The total deficit during fifteen years, from 1814 to 1828, was nearly twenty millions sterling, while the deficit during the last six years of this period amounted to nearly three millions a year. Lord William Bentinck's administration changed this into a surplus of two millions.

No true reformer in Indian administration has escaped obloquy and censure. The extension of the civil powers of the Indian officials gave offence to the Europeans in India; and the Act which withdrew from them their privilege of bringing civil appeals before the Supreme Court at Calcutta was called the Black Act, and brought upon Macaulay and Lord William Bentinck a torrent of abuse.[1] The historian Thornton was himself carried away by this race prejudice, and wrote of Bentinck that he "added the treachery of the Italian to the caution of the Dutchman." Such is the fate which has overtaken, not once or twice, those British administrators who have laboured to work in the interests of the unrepresented people. Canning and Ripon are more recent instances.

[1] Macaulay refers to this European agitation in these words: "That Public Opinion means the opinion of five hundred persons who have no interest, feeling, or taste in common with the fifty millions among whom they live; that the Love of Liberty means the strong objection which the five hundred feel to every measure which can prevent them from acting as they choose towards the fifty millions."—Trevelyan's *Life and Letters of Lord Macaulay*.

English education had made more progress in Calcutta than in Bombay. David Hare, a watchmaker of Calcutta, started an English school, and his name is remembered in Bengal to this day as the Father of English education. Subsequently, in 1817, the Marquis of Hastings founded the Hindu College of Calcutta. The question soon arose whether education should be imparted in India through the English language, or through the Sanscrit and Arabic and the vernacular languages of India. Oriental scholars, with a generous appreciation of all that was great and noble in the Oriental classics, urged that education should be imparted to the people through their own language. But more practical men, like Macaulay and Trevelyan, thought that no true education in modern knowledge and sciences could be imparted except through the medium of a modern language. Macaulay's masterly Minute, which has become a historical document, virtually decided the controversy. With a very imperfect appreciation of Sanscrit literature, he nevertheless came to a conclusion which was correct—that modern education could only be imparted through a modern language.

"Suppose that the Pasha of Egypt, a country once superior in knowledge to the nations of Europe, but now sunk far below them, were to appropriate a sum for the purpose of reviving and promoting literature, and encouraging learned natives of Egypt, would anybody infer that he meant the youth of his Pashalic to give years to the study of hieroglyphics, to search into all the doctrines disguised under the fables of Osiris, and to ascertain with all possible accuracy the ritual with which cats and onions were anciently adored? Would he be justly charged with inconsistency if, instead of employing his young subjects in deciphering obelisks, he were to order them to be instructed in the English and French languages, and in all the sciences to which those languages are the chief keys? . . .

"We have to educate a people who cannot at present be educated by means of their mother tongue. We must teach them some foreign tongue. The claims of our own language it is hardly necessary to recapitulate. It stands pre-eminent even among the languages of the West. . . . Nor is this all. In India, English is the language spoken by the ruling class. It is spoken by the higher class of natives at the seats of Government. It is likely to become the language of commerce throughout the seas of the East. It is the language of two great European communities which are rising, the one in the south of Africa, the other in Australasia, communities which are every day becoming more important and more closely connected with our Indian Empire. Whether we look at the intrinsic value of our literature or at the particular situation of this country, we shall see the strongest reason to think that, of all foreign tongues, the English tongue is that which would be most useful to our native subjects."[1]

The Orientalists were routed by the irresistible logic and the matchless power of Macaulay's Minute. It was decided that education should be imparted to the people of India through the medium of the English language. Nineteen years after, this decision was supplemented by the famous Education Despatch of 1854, which provided that primary education should be imparted in Indian schools through the Indian vernaculars, and should lead up to higher education in English. This is the educational policy of India to the present day.

On the 20th March 1835, Lord William Bentinck left India after a benevolent and successful rule of seven years. In the graphic words of Macaulay, inscribed on the pedestal of Bentinck's statue in

[1] Macaulay's Minute, dated 2nd February 1835.

Calcutta, he "never forgot that the end of government is the happiness of the governed."

After his retirement from India, Lord William Bentinck was elected Member of Parliament in the Liberal interest for the city of Glasgow in 1837; but he spent a good deal of his time in France, where his friend Louis Philippe was then king, and he died in Paris in June 1839. The calumnies and censure with which privileged classes had assailed him in India passed away; and fourteen years after his death, Sir Charles Trevelyan, who had been his colleague in India, spoke of Bentinck's administration in his evidence before the Lords' Committee in words which have received universal assent from the people of India.

"I must bear my testimony to Lord William Bentinck, that although the honour of having established our dominion in India belongs to others, to Lord William Bentinck belongs the great praise of having placed our dominion in India on its proper foundation in the recognition of the great principle that India is to be governed for the benefit of the Indians, and that the advantages which we derive from it should only be such as are incidental and inferential from that course of proceeding."[1]

There is no doubt that men like Munro, Elphinstone, and Bentinck, Trevelyan, Metcalfe, and Macaulay, set this high ideal before them in their administration of India; and if it had been possible for one nation to work in the interests of another, India to-day would have been governed "for the benefit of the Indians." But it is not in human nature for one race to work for another; and it were idle to ignore the fact that all Indian interests, commercial, industrial, economic, and financial, have been subordinated to the interests of

[1] Trevelyan's Evidence. Second Report from the Select Committee of the House of Lords, 1853, p. 159.

England down to the present time. Mankind has yet discovered no method of ruling a subject nation for the benefit of that nation except by conceding to them some hand in the administration of their own concerns, some degree of representation and self-government. And until this policy is adopted in India, the words that "India is to be governed for the benefit of the Indians" will remain an idle maxim, if not a cruel satire.

CHAPTER XX

ELPHINSTONE IN BOMBAY (1817–1827)

THE dominions of Baji Rao, the last of the Mahratta Peshwas, were annexed in 1817, and he himself was captured, after a long pursuit, in the following year. He retired on a pension, and his extensive territory now forms the most important portion of the Province of Bombay.

The duty of settling this wide tract of country fell on one of the ablest and best servants of the Company. Mountstuart Elphinstone, son of the eleventh Lord Elphinstone, had come out to India in 1796, as has been stated in the last chapter, and after varied experience had been appointed to Poona in 1811. In 1818 he was appointed Commissioner of the territories annexed from Baji Rao.

No better selection could have been made. Junior to Thomas Munro by nearly twenty years, Elphinstone had the same capacity for revenue work, the same sympathy with the people, the same literary instincts, the same broad and statesmanlike desire to promote the prosperity of the Indian Empire. The first half of the nineteenth century produced a number of great administrators in India, distinguished no less by their sympathy with the people than by their capacity for organisation and work. But it is perhaps no injustice to the other meritorious servants of the East India Company of this period to acknowledge that Munro of Madras and Elphinstone of Bombay stand a head and shoulders above the rest. It is a melancholy reflection which forces itself on all thoughtful observers that this class of sympathetic administrators became rarer in the latter half of the nineteenth century; and that a desire to repress the political advance of the people, rather than to promote their progress and self-government, has often influenced later administration.

Elphinstone's "Report on the Territories Conquered from the Peshwa," submitted to the Governor-General in October 1819, is a masterly account of the country and of the measures adopted for its settlement. It is a voluminous paper, and covers nearly seventy folio pages of the fourth volume of "East India Papers," and all that we can do here is to make a few extracts.

VILLAGE COMMUNITIES.

"In whatever point of view we examine the Native Government in the Deccan, the first and most important feature is, the division into villages or townships. These Communities contain in miniature all the materials of a State within themselves, and are almost sufficient to protect their members, if all other governments are withdrawn. Though probably not compatible with a very good form of government, they are an excellent remedy for the imperfections of a bad one; they prevent the bad effects of its negligence and weakness, and even present some barrier against its tyranny and rapacity.

"Each village has a portion of ground attached to it, which is committed to the management of the inhabitants. The boundaries are carefully marked and jealously guarded. They are divided into fields, the limits of which are exactly known; each field has a name and is kept distinct, even when the cultivation of it has long been abandoned. The villagers are almost entirely cultivators of the ground, with the addition of the few traders and artisans that are required to supply their wants. The head of each village is the Patil, who has under him an assistant, called a Chaugulla, and a clerk called a Kulkarni. There are, besides, twelve village officers, well known by the name of the Bara Baloti. These are the astrologer, the priest, the carpenter, barber, &c., but the only ones who are concerned in the administration of the government are the Sonar or Potdar, who is silversmith and assayer of money, and the Mhar, who, in addition to various other important duties, acts as watchman to the village. Each of these classes consists of one or more individuals, according as their original families have branched out. The Mhars are seldom fewer than four or five, and there are besides, where those tribes are numerous, very frequently several Phils or Ramoshis, employed also as watchmen, but performing none of the other duties of the Mhar.

"The Patils are the most important functionaries in the villages, and perhaps the most important class in the country. They hold office by a grant from the Government (generally from that of the Moguls), are entitled by virtue of it to land and fees, and have various little privileges and distinctions, of which they are as tenacious as of their land. Their office and emoluments are hereditary, and saleable with the consent of the Government, but are seldom sold, except in cases of extreme necessity, though a partner is sometimes admitted, with a careful reservation of the superiority of the old possessor. The Patil is head of the police and of the administration of justice in his village, but he need only be mentioned here as an officer of revenue. In that capacity he performs on a small scale what a Mamlatdar or a Collector does on a large; he allots the land to such cultivators as have no landed property of their own, and fixes the rent which each has to pay; he collects the revenue for Government from all the Rayats; conducts all its arrangements with them, and exerts himself to promote the cultivation and the prosperity of the village. Though originally the agent of the Government, he is now regarded as equally the representative of the Rayats, and is not less useful in executing the orders of the Government than in asserting the rights, or at least in making known the wrongs, of the people."

Mirasdars or Peasant Proprietors.

"A large portion of the Rayats are the proprietors of their estates, subject to the payment of a fixed Land-Tax to Government; that their property is hereditary and saleable, and they are never dispossessed while they pay their tax, and even then they have for a long period (at least thirty years) the right of reclaiming their estate on paying the dues of Government. Their Land-Tax is fixed, but the late Mahratta Government loaded it with other impositions, which reduced that advantage to a mere name; yet so far, however, was this from destroying the value of their estates, that although the Government took advantage of their attachment to make them pay considerably more than an Upri, and though all the Mirasdars were, in ordinary cases, obliged to make up for failures in the payment of each of their body, yet their lands were saleable, and generally at ten years' purchase. . . .

"An opinion prevails throughout the Mahratta country, that under the old Hindu Government all the land was held by Mirasis, and that the Upris were introduced as the old proprietors sank under the tyranny of the Mohammedans. This opinion is supported by the fact that the greater part of the fields now cultivated by Upris are recorded in the village books as belonging to absent proprietors; and affords, when combined with circumstances observed in other parts of the peninsula, and with the light Land-Tax authorised by Manu, a strong presumption that the revenue system under the Hindus (if they had a uniform system) was founded on private property in the soil."

Changes under the British Rule.

"The outline of the revenue system adopted since our acquisition of the country is contained in my letter dated July 10th, conveying instructions to the Collectors, and in that dated July 14th, enclosing instructions for Mamlatdars. The leading principles are to abolish farming, but otherwise to maintain the native system; to levy the revenue according to the actual cultivation, to make the assessment light, to impose no new taxes, and to do none away unless obviously unjust; and, above all, to make no innovations. Many innovations were, however, the result of the introduction of foreign rulers and foreign maxims of government; but in the revenue department most of them were beneficial. The country, which had been under many Mamlatdars, with very unequal extent of territory and power, was placed under five principal officers (I include Satara), with much superior weight and respectability. The chief authority now resided in the District, and devoted his whole time to its affairs, and all subordinate agents were obliged to follow his example. The straggling revenue divisions of the Mahrattas were formed into compact districts, each yielding from Rs.50 to Rs.70,000 a year, and placed under a Mamlatdar."

Evils of a Foreign Government.

"Many of the evils from which this country has hitherto been exempt are inseparable from the introduction of a foreign Government; but perhaps the greater may be avoided by proper precautions. Many of the upper classes must sink into comparative poverty, and many of those who were employed in the court and army must absolutely lose their bread. Both of these misfortunes happened to a certain extent in the commencement of Baji Rao's reign; but as the frame of Government was entire, the bad effect of these partial evils was surmounted. Whether we can equally maintain the frame of Government is a question that is yet to be examined. The present system of police, as far as relates to the villages, may be easily kept up; but I doubt whether it is enough that the village establishment be maintained and the whole put under a Mamlatdar. The Patil's respectability and influence in his village must be kept up, by allowing him some latitude both in the expenditure of the village expenses, and in restraining petty disorders in his village. So far from wishing that it were possible for the European Officers to hear all complaints on such subjects, I think it fortunate that they have not time to investigate them, and think it desirable that the Mamlatdars also should leave them to the Patils, and thus preserve a power on the aid of which we must, in all branches of the Government, greatly depend. Zealous co-operation of the Patils is as essential to the Collector of the revenue, and to the administration of civil justice, as to the police; and it ought, therefore, by all means to be secured. Too much care cannot be taken to prevent their duty becoming irksome and their influence impaired by bringing their conduct too often under the correction of their superiors. I would lend a ready ear to all complaints against them for oppression, but I would not disturb them for inattention to forms; and I would leave them at liberty to settle petty complaints their own way, provided no serious punishment were inflicted on either party."

EDUCATION.

"Books are scarce, and the common ones probably ill chosen, but there exist in the Hindu languages many tales and fables that would be generally read, and that would circulate sound morals. There must be religious books tending more directly to the same end. If many of these were printed and distributed cheaply or gratuitously, the effect would, without doubt, be great and beneficial. It would, however, be indispensable that they should be purely Hindu. We might silently omit all precepts of questionable morality, but the slightest infusion of religious controversy would secure the failure of the design.

"It would be better to call the prejudices of the Hindus to our aid in reforming them, and to control their vices by the ties of religion, which are stronger than those of law. By maintaining and purifying their present tenets, at the same time that we enlighten their understandings, we shall bring them nearer to that standard of perfection at which all concur in desiring that they should arrive; while any attack on their faith, if successful, might be expected in theory, as is found in practice, to shake their reverence for all religion, and to set them free from those useful restraints which even a superstitious doctrine imposes on the passions."

VILLAGE PANCHYETS.

"But with all these defects, the Mahratta country flourished, and the people seem to have been exempt from some of the evils which exist under our more perfect Government. There must, therefore, have been some advantages in the system to counterbalance its obvious defects, and most of them appear to me to have originated in one fact, that the Government, although it did little to obtain justice for the people, left them the means of procuring it for themselves. The advantage of this was particularly felt among the lower orders, who are most out of reach of their rulers, and most apt to be neglected under all Governments. By means of the Panchayat, they were enabled to effect a tolerable dispensation of justice among themselves; and it happens that most of the objections above stated to that institution do not apply in their case. . . .

"I propose, therefore, that the native system should still be preserved, and means taken to remove its abuses and revive its energy. Such a course will be more welcome to the natives than any entire change, and if it should fail entirely, it is never too late to introduce the Adalat. . . .

"Our principal instrument must continue to be the Panchayat, and that must continue to be exempt from all new forms, interference, and regulation on our part."[1]

It will appear from the preceding extracts that the great aim of Elphinstone was to conserve what was good in the old institutions of the Mahrattas. It were well for the country if Elphinstone's successors were as cautious in introducing innovations. But under the administration of succeeding generations of rulers, Village Communities have disappeared, and the right of peasant proprietors to hold their lands at fixed rates has been crushed under increasing revenue demands.

Elphinstone's great ability marked him out as the most suitable head of the Government, and he was appointed Governor of Bombay in 1819, a year before Sir Thomas Munro was appointed Governor of Madras. It is necessary now to describe briefly his endeavours to arrive at a proper land settlement in Bombay within the eight years of his administration.

[1] Report on the Territories conquered from the Peshwa, dated 25th October 1819.

Broach.

In 1821 the Governor recorded a Minute on the land revenue arrangements at Broach, and did not contemplate with pleasure the increase in the Land-Tax which had already commenced under the British Rule.

"The assessment is made entirely by villages, without any inquiry into the circumstances of individuals. One of the hereditary revenue officers is sent to inspect the crops of each harvest. He makes a statement of the quantity of land cultivated with each sort of produce by each Ryot, and calculates the quantity of each sort that will be produced in each field. The sum of these gives the whole amount of each sort of grain produced in the village. . . . The general principle is to take half of the money produced by the sale of the crops, and leave the rest to the Ryot. . . .

"It is always difficult to guess whether the assessment is light or heavy. On the plan here adopted it is utterly impossible. An increase of four lakhs and a half [£45,000] has taken place this year: a circumstance which I cannot contemplate with pleasure."[1]

Ahmedabad.

On the same date Elphinstone recorded another Minute on the land revenue operations in Ahmedabad and Kaira, and his remarks betray the same caution and hesitation.

"In the Ahmedabad Zilla, the number of villages that have been let to the highest bidder, the consequent detection of all sources of revenue, and in some cases the raising of the Bigoties by Panchyats granted

[1] Minute dated 15th August 1821.

at the suggestion of the farmer, have a tendency to strain the revenue to the highest pitch."[1]

SURAT.

In May 1821 Elphinstone recorded a Minute on Surat, in which he once more deplored the heaviness of the land assessment.

"If I were to decide on the present condition of the people in this Collectorship, I should pronounce it to be very much depressed. The Ryots seem to be ill-clothed and ill-lodged, and although some parts of the District are highly productive, I should think that in others the cultivation was very imperfect. . . . These evils are by no means to be ascribed to the present system. On the contrary, I am persuaded that the measures now in progress will go far to relieve us from the system which we inherited from our predecessors. The great obstacle will be the extreme heaviness and perhaps the inequality of the assessment."[2]

THE CONCAN.

The state of things in the Northern Concan was unsettled. The Collector recommended "that the demand of the Government be fixed at one-third of the gross produce, and at a reduced ratio on the inferior kinds of soil, to be divided into three, or at the utmost into four classes of land; that no rent be paid in kind, which is a system expensive to Government and offers opportunities of peculation to the inferior native officers; that the commuted money-payment be fixed for six years; that the rate of assessment be not fixed in perpetuity, but that a settlement be made for twelve years."[3]

[1] Minute dated 15th August 1821.
[2] Minute dated 6th May 1821.
[3] Revenue Letter from Bombay to the Court of Directors, dated 19th April 1822.

A separate letter was recorded in the same year in reference to Southern Concan, which gives us some information with regard to the Khotes and the rights of cultivators generally.

"The villages are either termed Kulargee or Khotegee. In the former, each cultivator is understood to stand assessed at a certain fixed rental on the public records, beyond which nothing can be properly levied from him; whilst in the Khotegee villages, though a Khote or head of the village can only levy a particular sum from one particular class of Ryots, yet with others, either occupying new lands or renting the Khote's own, he may make what bargain he pleases. And this naturally leads to an explanation of the only two descriptions of tenures prevalent in this Zilla, viz., the first Dharekari, and the second Ardheli.

"The former of these seems very nearly to correspond with the Mirasi of the Deccan, for he cannot be dispossessed as long as he makes good his payments according to the custom of the country; and if he cannot actually sell, he may unquestionably mortgage his property, though it is generally believed he may even dispose of it. . . .

"The Ardheli Ryot is on the footing with the Upri elsewhere. He is the tenant of the Khote, or of some other holder of land, as the case may be. He cannot either sell or mortgage what he occupies, because it, of right, belongs to another, and he only holds it by sufferance. He may be dispossessed either by the owner choosing to take the land into his own hands, or to assign it to some one else, though this latter course would be considered a hardship if the Ryot regularly fulfilled his engagements. These engagements are, however, mostly annual, and it is therefore obvious the owner of the land might easily effect an ejectment by raising his demands till the land would not be worth the cultivation. The Ardheli Ryot who may cultivate rice-land generally pays his landlord half the produce in kind. . . .

"From the foregoing description, your Honourable Court will perceive that the Khotes very much resemble the smaller class of zemindars in Bengal."[1]

The Deccan.

We have so far referred to the reports of experimental Settlements in the Western Coast, from Broach to the Concan. We turn now once more to the Deccan. Mr. Chaplin had succeeded Elphinstone as Commissioner of the Deccan, and his lucid reports of November 1821 and August 1822 cover, with their enclosures, over five hundred folio pages of the East India Papers.

The population of the newly acquired territory, including Poona, Ahmadnagar, Khandesh, Dharwar, Satara, and the Southern Jaigirs, was estimated at nearly four millions. An endeavour was made, in the early land settlement, to combine the Ryotwari system, which had been introduced in Madras by Sir Thomas Munro, with the village system, which had been so strongly advocated by the Madras Board of Revenue. The settlement made was professedly the Ryotwari, and was so essentially; but the individual distribution was left with a good deal of latitude to the village officers. The new system did not at first essentially differ from that which had been followed under the Mahratta Rule at the time of their renowned minister, Nana Farnavis, except that the Mamlatdars or district officers had less power in increasing or decreasing the revenue. The payments of the Ryots were fixed by the Company's servants with reference to their cultivation and the receipts of former times, and the levy of the State demand was more rigorous than before. In 1817 the

[1] Revenue Letter from Bengal to the Court of Directors, dated 23rd February 1822.

revenue of the newly acquired territory was £800,000; in 1818 it was raised to £1,150,000, and in a few more years to £1,500,000. The village officials were allowed less and less power of interference; the Company's servants liked to come in closer contact with each individual cultivator; and the Village Communities virtually disappeared in a few years in Bombay, as they had disappeared in Madras.

KHANDESH.

The district of Khandesh was under the administration of Captain Briggs, who distinguished himself in later years by his great work on the Land-Tax of India, and his translation of Ferishta's History of India, and who with Elphinstone and Malcolm, Grant Duff, Todd, and Horace Hayman Wilson, stands foremost among the Anglo-Indian writers and historians of the first half of the nineteenth century. He found in Khandesh "the dilapidated remains of more than one hundred substantially built dams for diverting the water into channels for irrigation, many of them constructed at prodigious expense," which attested "the liberal and enlightened policy of the early Mahomedan monarchs." But Khandesh in his time was desolated and impoverished. Frequent wars, the incursion of the Bheels, and the havoc caused by tigers, which in three months had destroyed 500 men, and 20,000 head of cattle, added to the miseries of the district. And Captain Briggs experienced "the difficulty of drawing the line between a moderate and a high assessment in the absence of all authentic records of the resources."

POONA.

The District of Poona was under the administration of Captain Robertson, and his answers to queries put to him by the Commissioners throw a flood of light on the institutions and the condition of the cultivators of the Deccan. The Mirasi tenant in the Deccan was virtually a peasant proprietor, subject to the payment of a Land-Tax to the Government. "He is in no way inferior," wrote Captain Robertson, "in point of tenure on its original basis, as described in the quotation, to the holder of the most undisputed freehold estate in England. The ancestors of many of the present occupants of the lands of the Deccan were probably holders of land antecedent to the Musalman conquest of their country, on the condition of paying a *reddendum* equal to a sixth part of the produce of the land they held." "If I were to make any such distinction respecting the payment made by the Thalkaris [Mirasi tenants] of the Deccan, I should term it a tax and not a rent." [1] Modern administrators who speak of the cultivators' rights to the soil in Southern India, and the Zemindars' rights to the soil in Northern India, as the creation of British legislation, will find from the voluminous reports of early British administrators that private property in the soil, heritable and transferable, was stronger in India before the British conquest than under modern revenue settlements. The soil belonged to the nation and not to the State, and the State was never entitled to anything except a Tax—*a fixed Tax*—from the Mirasdars.

Captain Robertson's remarks on the common possession of villages by families of cultivators are equally instructive.

"Every original paper relating to Thalkaris [Mirasi tenants] and their occupation of land, every return I have obtained from the districts concerning them and the ancient distribution of land, proves beyond

[1] Paragraphs 19, 20, and 22 of Robertson's Report, dated 10th October 1821.

a shadow of doubt that at a former time the whole of the arable land of each village was apportioned out among a certain number of families. . . . Their descendants collectively are termed a Jutha; they are inferred to possess the whole of the original estate among them; they are responsible as a body corporate for the payment of whatever is due to Government and others for the whole estate. . . . One Jutha appears to have been selected, either by Government or the other Juthas, to perform, through the representation of its elder branch, the duty of collecting from all other Juthas, and to be responsible for the claims of Government on them all; thus collectively rendered under one head a body corporate, for the discharge of certain obligations and for the enjoyment of certain privileges. The members of the Jutha thus selected have the distinguishing appellation of Patils, and probably always had that or some other distinguishing name, and a person of the elder branch of it actually *in officio* as its head is styled Mukaddam. . . . He was and is still a Magistrate, by the will of the community as well as by the appointment of Government; he enforces the observance of what in England would be termed the bye-laws of the Corporation; he formerly raised by contribution a sum of money for the expenses of the Corporation as such, and for the support of his own dignity as its head; he suggested improvements for the benefit of the association, and marshalled the members to aid him in maintaining the public peace; he dispensed, and still dispenses, civil justice as a patriarch to those who choose to submit to his decision as referee or arbitrator; or he presides over the proceedings of others whom either he himself or the parties might nominate as arbitrators on their disputes." [1]

For the rest, Captain Robertson proved the heritable

[1] Paragraphs 26, 27, 30, and 32 of Robertson's Report.

and transferable nature of the Mirasi tenure by many documents, and added that "the Mirasi tenure may be said to have existed in all villages in this Collectorship. There are not many in which it does not now exist."[1] This was written in 1821, and gives us some idea of the status and rights of Bombay cultivators under Mahratta rule.

AHMADNAGAR.

Captain Pottinger administered the District of Ahmadnagar, and reported that "those Ryots who are Mirasdars can dispose of or mortgage their lands when they like." "The Mirasi tenure has existed in this part of India (in common, I believe, with all others) from time immemorial; and when I have asked about the period of its establishment, I have been told I might as well inquire when the soil was made. I observe that Mr. Ellis, in his numerous replies on Mirasi, states in a note, 'the fact is, that the thing (Mirasi) existed in India when the lawgivers of the land wrote;' and his authority is, in my humble judgment, quite definitive."[2]

DHARWAR.

The District of Dharwar was under the administration of Mr. St. John Thackeray. He was an experienced revenue officer, mixed much with the cultivators, and gave some characteristic replies to the queries sent to him. "With respect to the personal exertions of revenue officers," he wrote, "in promoting agriculture, I have generally found them more inclined to bully than to encourage the Ryots; and their object is rather to display their zeal by showing an increase of cultivation on paper, than to augment the resources

[1] Robertson's Report, para. 132.
[2] Pottinger's Report, dated 31st July 1822, Answer to Query 37.

of the country. . . . The Ryot cultivates for his profit and when this is adequate, he needs no spur."[1]

THE DECCAN.

Enclosing these and other District Reports, the Commissioner Chaplin submitted his own exhaustive Report on the revenue settlements of the Deccan. He referred to the previous settlement of Malik Ambar, which was as famous in the Deccan as the settlement of Todar Mall was in Northern India. Malik Ambar's settlement was in the nature of a fixed money demand for each village, and his policy was greatly to encourage the ancient Mirasi tenure, by which the arable land of the country "acquired most of the substantial qualities of private property."

Passing on to the subject of the assessment of the soil under the newly established British Rule, Chaplin assumed that a cultivator of middling circumstances held ten acres of dry land and probably one-third acre of garden land, and had two ploughs and four bullocks, and made an income of £12 in the year. His expenditure is thus estimated:[2]

Land-Tax	£4	4	0
Proportionate annual cost of bullocks, assuming each pair to be serviceable for eight years	1	5	0
Cost of ploughs and occasionally hired labour	0	16	0
Seed for dry lands and garden . .	0	19	0
Fees of officers and village dues . .	0	12	0
Grain for the cultivator and his family's daily food	2	4	0
Clothes for cultivator and family . .	1	10	0
Sundry necessary expenses . . .	0	12	0
	£12	2	0

[1] Mr. Thackeray's Report, para. 51.

[2] Mr. Chaplin's Report, dated 20th August 1822, para. 105. There is an error in the totalling of the figures in the original report.

It will be seen that a State demand of £4, 4s. out of an estimated income of £12 is less than 45 or 50 per cent. of the gross produce which the Government originally demanded both in Madras and Bombay from the peasantry, But even this tax of £4, 4s. out of £12 left the cultivator no savings and no resources. It is quite clear that the Ryotwari system found favour with the Directors of the Company for this very reason, viz., that there were no intermediate landlords or Village Communities to intercept a part of the profits. The Company had as good a grip over the cultivators as a slave-owner has over his slaves, and could take away all that was not needed to keep them alive. "It cannot be concealed or denied, I think," said one Director, "that the object of this [Ryotwari] system is to obtain for Government the utmost that the land will yield in the shape of rent."[1]

With regard to the Mirasi tenure, Chaplin wrote that it "is very general throughout the whole of that part of the conquered territory which extends from the Krishna to the range of Ghats that divide Gungterre from Khandesh." That "a Ryot having once acquired the hereditary right of occupancy is, together with his heirs, entitled to hold it by sale, gift, or mortgage, and according to the usage of the Deccan, without previously obtaining the permission of the Government." That a Mirasdar "has a voice in all the village councils, has a right of pasture on the village commons, can build a house or dispose of it by sale." That in Poona the proportion of Mirasdars to Upris or tenants at will "may be about three to one." That to the north, beyond the Godavari, "the existence of the Miras right becomes less general, and

Chaplin also thinks the dairy produce brought 14s. annually to the cultivator.

[1] Henry St. John Tucker: *Memorials of Indian Government* (London, 1853), p. 113.

the difference between it and the Upri tenure more faint and indistinct." That in the Southern Mahratta country, "Miras does not exist at all," but "permanent occupancy is, however, recognised." That "the privileges of Miras in Sâtara are the same as in other parts of the Deccan."[1]

"The Collector [of Poona] is very properly an advocate," Chaplin wrote, "for preserving the rights of Mirasdars, a line of policy which he strenuously recommends in several places; but as nobody, I trust, has ever thought of invading their rights, the discussion of the question at any length would be superfluous."[2] Mr. Chaplin did not anticipate that later British administration would virtually cnnfiscate the ancient Mirasi rights of the Deccan cultivators.

Chaplin's long report ended with an exhortation to English officials to observe forms of civil intercourse with the people of India.

"It ought to be recollected that since the change of Government has inevitably deprived them of so much consequence, it is the more incumbent on us to continue to them the forms of civil intercourse which are yet in our power; and that although we may be apt to consider them as far beneath us, yet that they held a respectable rank under their native prince, which, as we now occupy his place, we ought to preserve to them as far as lies in our power.

"Young men on their first arrival in India, and their first appointment to office, are so prone to form opinions entirely at variance with those which I have just expressed, and to act on notions so diametrically opposite, that I have deemed it proper to inculcate these principles to the assistants who have been appointed to the Deccan; and I lately circulated for their guidance the judicious instructions of Sir John

[1] Mr. Chaplin's Report, paragraphs 107, 114, 125, 131, 133, 135, 136.
[2] Ibid., para. 143.

Malcolm on this subject. It would, I think, be attended with good effect if a code of this kind were given as a sort of manual for every one newly arrived from England. The motto of it might be in the words of Shakespeare:

'O but man, proud man,
Drest in a little brief authority,
Most ignorant of what he's most assured,
His glassy essence
Plays such fantastic tricks before high Heaven
As make the angels weep.'"[1]

On receipt of this valuable and exhaustive report with its many enclosures, the Governor of Bombay, Mountstuart Elphinstone, directed a gradual survey and assessment of the whole of the conquered territories. He also insisted on the preservation of the Patil's authority in each village; recommended that the assessment should be light and equally distributed; and urged on the Commissioner the importance of preserving the rights of the cultivators under every species of tenure in use. The Court of Directors also expressed their satisfaction with the proposal of a general survey.[2]

The Commissioner of the Deccan submitted one set of survey rules in September 1824, and a modified set of rules in February 1825. Sir Thomas Munro had reduced the Land-Tax in Madras to about one-third of the field produce; and Chaplin adopted the same standard for the Deccan in paragraph 7 of his Circular issued with the revised Survey Rules. This severe State demand has been the ruin of agricultural prosperity in Southern India. In Madras the rule is still maintained as the maximum of the Government demand; in Bombay, while all endeavour to fix any specific share of the produce has been abandoned, the

[1] Mr. Chaplin's Report, paragraphs 392, 393.

[2] Revenue Letter from Bombay to the Directors, dated 5th November 1823; and Revenue Letter from the Directors to Bombay, dated 4th May 1825.

actual Land-Tax levied often approximates to or exceeds one-third of the field produce. Thus Henry St. John Tucker's shrewd remark, quoted above, as to the cause of the extension of the Ryotwari system, is justified by facts.

The proposal of a general survey still hung fire. Mountstuart Elphinstone endeavoured to keep the village system untouched in the Deccan. His idea, as stated before, was to combine the principle of the Ryotwari system with the principle of the village system. His object was to settle, after a Survey, what each cultivator should pay to the State, and then to realise this from each village through its Patil. "The Survey will fix the rights and the payment of each Ryot, after which the village may be farmed for a certain number of years to the Patil."[1]

It must be admitted there was an initial weakness in this proposal. If the village Patil and the village Council were to be deprived by the proposed Survey of all their power of distributing the collective village assessment among the cultivators forming the village, what was the good of keeping up the Patil and his Council at all? If the functions which they had discharged in past centuries of assessing the Ryots of the village in order to make up the collective State demand was to be taken away from them, where was the necessity of maintaining them only as farmers of revenue?

The question had been fought out in Madras on first principles. The Madras Board of Revenue were out and out "Collectivists," and desired to maintain the village institutions and their authority unimpaired. Thomas Munro was an out and out "Individualist," and insisted on direct relations between the State and each individual cultivator, without any interference from the village authorities so far as the Land-Tax

[1] Revenue Letter from Bombay to the Court of Directors, dated 5th November 1823, para. 452.

was concerned. Thomas Munro had his way, and the Village Communities of Madras at once lost their vitality, in spite of Munro's own endeavours to keep them up by bestowing upon them other powers.

These experiments and results carried their own lesson. Village Communities could only be maintained in India, as they had been maintained for centuries, by leaving the work of internal assessment to the Village Councils and Panchyets. A few rules might have been framed against excessive assessment in view of the produce of lands, and subject to these rules the village elders might have been permitted to continue their work of separate assessments and realisations, and their collective payment to the State. Such an arrangement would have had the obvious advantage of a continuity of the ancient system of India, as well as of leaving an organised popular body in every Indian village. But such an arrangement was against the very spirit of the Company's rule. The Company's policy was to deal individually with every taxpayer in the land, and to levy as much tax as he could pay. Elphinstone himself was so far carried away by this spirit as to approve of a Survey which would fix the liability of each individual cultivator. And after this, when he still desired to deal with villages collectively through the headman, his plan was open to the obvious criticism that the headman's occupation was gone!

Elphinstone left India in 1827, and in the same year the Court of Directors found out the weak point in Elphinstone's plan, and took advantage of it.

"If the survey should really fix the rights and payments of each Ryot, and if the Ryot has immediate access to redress on account of any infringement of his rights, the Patil may be usefully employed in the manner adverted to in a preceding paragraph of this despatch. The experience which you have had of the evils produced by the system of revenue-farming during the administration of the late Peshwa ought to make you extremely cautious in confiding powers to individuals which their previous habits and practice must render them liable to abuse. Nor can we place any confidence in the security which a moderate assessment, payable by the village contractor to Government, would afford against exaction."[1]

This was the beginning of the end of the Village System.

[1] Revenue Letter from the Court of Directors to Bombay, dated 23rd May 1827, para. 87.

CHAPTER XXI

WINGATE AND THE RYOTWARI SETTLEMENT IN BOMBAY (1827–1835)

We have brought our narration to the year of the departure of Mountstuart Elphinstone from India. The land assessment in every Province of India was felt at that time to be excessive, not only by the people, but also by the Company's servants and revenue officers. In Madras, the revenue officers had told Dr. Francis Buchanan, as we have seen in Chapter XII., that the heavy Land-Tax impeded agriculture and the prosperity of the people, and Sir Thomas Munro gradually reduced the rate from one-half to one-third the gross produce, which last was still an excessive tax. In Northern India, Sir Edward Colebrooke and successive Governor-Generals had implored the Court of Directors, in vain, to redeem the pledge given by the British Government, and to permanently settle the Land-Tax, so as to make it possible for the people to accumulate wealth and improve their own condition. And in Bombay, Elphinstone had viewed with concern the rapid growth of revenue in several Districts, and Chaplin's decision to fix it at one-third the gross produce was calculated to give little relief. Throughout the continent of India, except where the Land-Tax had been permanently fixed, the people groaned under the assessments of the new rulers of the country. The Directors were deaf to representations, and the servants of the Company, who felt the injustice done to the people, expressed their opinions with bated breath, and were powerless to afford relief.

One of the most distinguished Englishmen then in India was Bishop Heber. He made a tour through India in 1824, 1825, and 1826, and during this extensive tour he inquired with great care into the condition of the people in the different provinces through which he travelled. What created the saddest impression on him was the poverty of the people, and the heavy Land-Tax which was levied by the East India Company in their dominions. He did not mention this explicitly in his Journal, which was recorded with an eye to publication, but in his private letters he opened his mind and stated his opinions more freely. His letter to the Right Honourable Charles Williams Wynn, dated Karnatic, March 1826, will serve as an example.

"Neither Native nor European agriculturist, I think can thrive at the present rate of taxation. Half the gross produce of the soil is demanded by Government, and this, which is nearly the average rate wherever there is not a Permanent Settlement, is sadly too much to leave an adequate provision for the present, even with the usual frugal habits of the Indians, and the very inartificial and cheap manner in which they cultivate the land. Still more is it an effective bar to anything like improvement; it keeps the people, even in favourable years, in a state of abject penury; and when the crop fails in even a slight degree, it involves a necessity on the part of the Government of enormous outlays in the way of remission and distribution, which, after all, do not prevent men, women, and children dying in the streets in droves, and the roads being strewed with carcasses. In Bengal, where, independent of its exuberant fertility, there is a Permanent Assessment, famine is unknown. In Hindustan [Northern India], on the other hand, I found a general feeling among the King's officers, and I myself was led from some circumstances to agree with them, that *the peasantry in the Company's Provinces are, on the whole, worse off, poorer, and more dispirited, than the subjects of the Native Princes;* and here in Madras, where the soil is, generally speaking, poor, the difference is said to be still more marked. The fact is, no Native Prince demands the rent which we do, and making every allowance for the superior regularity of our system, &c., *I met with very few men who will not, in confidence, own their belief that the people are overtaxed, and that the country is in a gradual state of impoverishment.* The Collectors do not like to make this avowal officially. Indeed, now and then, a very able Collector succeeds in lowering the rate to the people, while by diligence he increases it to the State. But, in general, all gloomy pictures are avoided by them as reflecting on themselves, and drawing on them censure from the Secretaries at Madras or Calcutta, while these, in their turn, plead the earnestness with which the Directors at home press for more money.

"I am convinced that it is only necessary to draw less money from the peasants, and to spend more of what is drawn within the country, to open some door to Indian industry in Europe, and to admit the natives to some greater share in the magistracy of their own people, to make the Empire as durable as it would be happy."[1]

It will appear from the above account, that while there were few officials in India who did not know the

[1] Bishop Heber's *Memoirs and Correspondence*, by his Widow, London, 1830, vol. ii. p. 413. The italics are our own. There has been some reduction in the Land-Tax in Bombay and Madras since Bishop Heber's time; but it is still excessive, and, what is worse, uncertain; and it still "keeps the people, even in favourable years, in a state of abject penury." "To draw less money from the peasants, and to spend more of what is drawn within the country," are the remedies against poverty and famines in India, more needed to-day than they were seventy-five years ago.

people to be overtaxed, they were unwilling to make the avowal openly. It is, however, to the honour of the Service that, when questioned on the subject openly in England, some of them stated their opinions in the most emphatic manner. Robert Richards was one of them; and some of his replies given to the Committee of the House of Commons deserve to be quoted.

"Where the revenue is collected, as it is in India, on the principle of the Government being entitled to one half of the gross produce of the soil, and vast numbers of officers, whose acts it is impossible to control, are also employed in the realisation of this revenue, it is a moral impossibility for any people whatever to live or prosper so as to admit of a very extensive commercial intercourse being carried on with them. . . .

"It may be done [*i.e.* manufacture of articles for foreign exportation] in lands not subject to the aforementioned exorbitant tax. It may also be the case in Bengal, where the Permanent Settlement has been enforced for many years, and where its original ruinous pressure is no longer so severely felt; but it would be quite impossible in lands, for example, subject to the Ryotwari Tax, or from lands where from 45 per cent. to 50 per cent. of the gross produce is actually levied as revenue. . . .

"I am personally acquainted with instances where the revenue assessed upon certain lands has actually exceeded the gross produce. I have also known other lands in India where a revenue has been assessed as being specifically derivable from rice lands, plantations of fruit trees, pepper, vines, and other articles, and each portion particularly described; but on comparing the assessment with the lands in question, those very lands have been found to have been nothing but jungle within the memory of man."[1]

The general feeling of the officers engaged in land

[1] Answers to Queries 2825, 2828, and 2829.

assessments in India at last found expression in a great and memorable work. To Lieutenant-Colonel Briggs belongs the credit of expounding for the first time the true nature of the Land-Tax in India, after an exhaustive inquiry into the laws and usages of ancient and modern times. The East India Company had so far regarded India as their estate, and had sought to derive from it the utmost possible land revenue, in disregard of ancient rights and customs. Against this practice John Briggs took his stand. In his great and epoch-making work on the subject,[1] he explained to Englishmen of his time, and of all succeeding time, that land in India had never been the property of the State; that the soil was private property in India, as among all other civilised nations; and that the State was only entitled to impose a tax on this form of private property, as on other private properties.

It is not possible, within our limits, to give an analysis of this great work of nearly five hundred pages; but it is necessary to place before the reader a few of the conclusions arrived at, which have their value at the present time as they had seventy years ago. John Briggs pointed out that among ancient nations—the Greeks, the Romans, the Persians, and the Chinese—the right of the State consisted in levying a tax of one-tenth of the produce. Among the ancient Hindus the right of the King or the State was to levy of grain one-eighth part, a sixth, or a twelfth, according to the difference of the soil and the labour necessary to cultivate it."[2] And Briggs showed, after an exhaustive inquiry into the practice of succeeding ages,—

"That the occupant of the land alone was its sole proprietor; that the demand on him for contributing to the support of the State was a sort of income-tax, viz., a limited portion of the produce of his estate; and

[1] *The Present Land-Tax in India*, by John Briggs, London, 1830.

[2] Quoted from Manu's *Institutes*, in p. 31 of Briggs' work.

that this portion was fixed in time of peace, but liable to increase in time of war; and that, under all circumstances, it left a certain surplus profit to the owner, equivalent to a rent. Moreover, I hope I have established that the Sovereign never claimed to be the proprietor of the soil, but of the Land-Tax."[1]

The disregard of this cardinal principle by the East India Company, and their endeavours to sweep away the entire profits from the land, leaving to cultivators barely enough to support their lives, were regarded by John Briggs as the main causes of the poverty of India under British rule.

"The flourishing condition of the country under the Moghal Emperors is recorded by all European travellers who have visited the East within the last three centuries; and the wealth, the population, and the national prosperity of India, far surpassing what they had seen in Europe, filled them with astonishment. That the condition of the people and the country under our Government presents no such spectacle, is every day proclaimed by ourselves, and we may therefore assume it to be true. . . .

"If I have proved that we have departed from the practice of our predecessors, that we have established a system far exceeding theirs in rigour, even in the worst of their regular governments, then indeed there is some reason to call for a reform, and to hope at least for investigation. . . .

"I conscientiously believe that under no Government whatever, Hindu or Mahomedan, professing to be actuated by law, was any system so subversive of the prosperity of the people at large as that which has marked our administration. . . .

"Although we have everywhere confessed that the heavy pressure of taxation was the most cruel injury they sustained, we have in no instance alleviated that

[1] *Ibid.*, p. 108.

pressure. So far from it, we have applied a false measure for fixing the impost, that of money instead of produce; we have pretended to abolish minor taxes on other classes, but have laid the amount on the landholder; and by minute scrutiny into every individual's concerns, have, under the plea of justice to ourselves, in many instances deprived the cultivators of the means they enjoyed of paying the heavy taxes from which they sought relief under us, till by rigid exactions we have increased our own revenue and reduced the people to the condition of mere labourers. This is the professed maxim of our rule, the certain and inevitable result of taking the whole surplus profit of land. . . .

"Having assumed that the Government is the sole landlord, it [the present Government] considers the land to be the most profitable source of all revenue; it employs a host of public servants to superintend the cultivator; and it professes to take all the profit. A Land-Tax like that which now exists in India, professing to absorb the whole of the landlord's rent, was never known under any Government in Europe or Asia."[1]

A great and thoughtful work like this would have created a revolution in any other country in the world. In India it did not produce the slightest change in the procedure of the Bombay revenue officials. The Survey Settlements, recommended by Elphinstone, had already been commenced by Pringle of the Bombay Civil Service in 1824–28; and the Settlements were conducted on untrue and exaggerated estimates of the produce of the soil, and therefore led to disastrous results.

"His [Pringle's] assessment was based on a measurement of fields, and an estimate of the yield of various

[1] *The Present Land Tax in India*, by John Briggs, pp. 393, 410, 414, 416.

soils, as well as of the cost of cultivation; the principle adopted being to fix the Government demand at 55 per cent. of the net produce. . . . The preliminary work of measurement was grossly faulty, and the estimates of produce which formed such an important element in the determination of the assessment, and which had been prepared in the most elaborate manner, were so erroneous as to be worse than useless. But meanwhile the Settlement had been introduced, and with the result of aggravating the evils it had been designed to remove. From the outset it was found impossible to collect anything approaching to the full revenue. In some districts not one half could be realised. Things now went rapidly from bad to worse. Every year brought its addition to the accumulated arrears of revenue, and the necessity for remission or modification of rates. . . . Every effort, lawful and unlawful, was made to get the utmost out of the wretched peasantry, who were subjected to torture, in some instances, cruel and revolting beyond all description, if they would not or could not yield what was demanded. Numbers abandoned their homes, and fled into the neighbouring Native States. Large tracts of land were thrown out of cultivation, and in some Districts no more than a third of the cultivable area remained in occupation."[1]

The system was eventually abandoned. A re-survey was commenced in 1835 by Goldsmid of the Bombay Civil Service and Lieutenant Wingate, afterwards Sir George Wingate.

"Abandoning all attempts to arrive at a theoretical ideal of assessment by endeavouring to discover the yield of soils and assigning a certain proportion of them as the Government demand, the Survey officers adopted the simple expedient of ascertaining the average character and depth of soil in each field, and classing it accordingly; no more than nine gradations

[1] Bombay Administration Report of 1872–73, p. 41.

of valuation being employed for the purpose. In fixing the rates of assessment they were guided by purely practical considerations as to the capability of the land and the general circumstances of the District."[1]

In spite of the official approval of this latter system, the reader will perceive that the new method was wrong in principle. The principle of fixing the assessment on the basis of the average produce of the fields was the ancient and correct principle; though Pringle failed because he worked it badly. The new method of fixing the assessment by "ascertaining the average character and depth of soil" was absurd on the face of it; though Wingate succeeded because he worked it with that moderation and leniency which was a part of his nature. A geological examination of the soil is not a safe basis for an estimate of its produce; and the continuous increase in the land revenue in later settlements, made on this unreliable basis, has led to impoverishment and widespread distress in the Province.

The Survey, which commenced in 1835, is the commencement of the present land revenue system of Bombay; and the first Regular Settlement in that Province was commenced in the following year, on the eve of the accession of Queen Victoria. It is necessary to examine this Settlement somewhat minutely, because it is virtually the system which is followed in Bombay down to the present time.

The Settlement operations were carried on for many years, and were gradually extended to the whole of the Province. As experience widened, it was thought necessary to gather up the results and to formulate rules for future guidance. This was done in 1847 by what is known as the JOINT REPORT, signed by H. E. Goldsmid, Captain Wingate, and Captain Davidson.[2]

[1] Bombay Administration Report of 1872–73, p. 42.
[2] Joint Report, dated 2nd August 1847.

The principles of the Settlement, as explained in the Joint Report, were, *Firstly*, that it was based on the assessment of each field separately, and not of holdings or villages collectively; *Secondly*, that it granted long leases for thirty years instead of the short leases which had preceded; and *Thirdly*, that it abandoned the basis of produce-estimates, and substituted the estimated value of lands as the basis of assessment. A few extracts from the Joint Report will make this clear.

"The cultivator's title to the occupation of the fields is indestructible while he continues to discharge the assessment laid upon them, though his engagement for each be annually renewed; and by placing the assessment upon each field, instead of on his whole holding, he is enabled, when circumstances make the course desirable, to relinquish any of the former or take up others which may be unoccupied, so as to accommodate the extent of his liabilities to his means to meet them. The fixed field assessment for the term of thirty years, introduced by our surveys, thus secures to the cultivator the full advantages of a thirty years' lease without burdening him with any condition beyond that of discharging the assessment for the single year to which his engagement extends."

"We have retained the practice of referring every variety of soil to one of nine classes which experience has proved to afford a sufficiently minute classification for all practical purposes. But in preference to trusting entirely to the judgment of the Classer for determining to what class any particular soil should be referred, we have formed a set of rules for the purpose of determining the soils which should fall into any class. The fertility of a soil in this country, or at least in all parts of it to which our operations have yet extended, being chiefly dependent on its power of imbibing and retaining moisture, and as this quality is mainly affected by depth, we have chosen the latter peculiarity as the principal regulating influence in the formation of our estimates."

"If all soils of the same depth were of uniform fertility the depth alone would suffice to determine their class, but this is not the case. . . . We deem it sufficient for the purpose of valuation to range them [the soils of different degrees of fertility] under three orders, which again are distributed among the nine classes of our scale on a consideration of their depth, as will be readily understood from the following table:

Class.	Relative value of class in annas or 16ths of a rupee.	Soils of the First Order. Of a fine uniform texture, varying in colour from deep black to dark brown.	Soils of the Second Order. Of uniform but coarser texture than the preceding and lighter also in colour, which is generally red.	Soils of the Third Order. Of coarse gravelly or loose friable texture, and colour varying from light brown to grey.
		Depth in cubits (1 cubit = 1½ ft.).	Depth in cubits (1 cubit = 1½ ft.).	Depth in cubits (1 cubit = 1½ ft.).
1	16	1¾	...	...
2	14	1½	1¾	...
3	12	1¼	1½	...
4	10	1	1¼	...
5	8	¾	1	...
6	6	½	¾	1
7	4½	¼	½	¾
8	3	...	¼	½
9	2	...	...	¼

"The first column of this table contains the nine classes of our scale; the second, the relative values of these, estimating the highest at sixteen annas or one rupee, which is the mode of valuation most familiar to natives."

"Detailed figured statements should be furnished, exhibiting the source and amount of every item of revenue hitherto derived from land of every description."

"The information thus collected and exhibited with that obtained by local inquiries into the past history of the District will generally enable us to trace the causes which have affected its past condition; and a knowledge of these, aided by a comparison of the capabilities of the District with those of others in its neighbourhood, will lead to a satisfactory conclusion regarding the assessment to be imposed."

"But instead of a particular sum at which a District should be assessed, it amounts to the same thing, and is more convenient to determine the rates to be imposed on the several descriptions of soil and culture contained within its limits, so as to produce the amount in question. And to do this it is only requisite to fix the maximum rates for the different descriptions of cultivation, when of course all the inferior rates will be at once deducible from the relative values of our classification scales."[1]

The above extracts give us the substance of the famous Joint Report, the basis of the Bombay Land Revenue system. It recognised the transferable and heritable right of the cultivator to his field, but it finally swept away the equally ancient right to a fixed Land-Tax which the Mirasi cultivator had enjoyed under the Mahratta rule. It made an elaborate scale for the distribution of the District revenue demand among a million of fields contained in the District, but it prescribed no limit to that demand. It substituted for the equitable basis of the field produce an impracticable geological basis for the purposes of assessment. And it let loose swarms of Classers, on a pay of ten or twelve shillings a month, to determine the depth and nature of the soil in each field in order to fix its

[1] Joint Report, paras. 9, 41, 42, 43, 75, 76, and 77.

relative value! The total District demand was to be distributed among the fields according to their relative values thus determined, but the District demand itself was to be vaguely determined from "the past history of the District" and the past condition of the people. Thus on the one point on which the people looked up to the Government for some assurance after thirty years of British rule in the Province, they received none; the East India Company and their servants would prescribe no limits to their own demand; they retained the power to shape the demand, to vary it, to increase it, at each recurring settlement, according to the condition of the people. No system could be devised by human ingenuity better calculated to keep an agricultural nation permanently poor and resourceless than the system which left to the revenue officials the absolute and unrestricted power to increase the revenue demand at each recurring settlement. The cultivator had no voice in the settlement of the Land-Tax; he was not consulted in fixing that tax; he was called upon, after the demand was settled, to pay it or to quit his ancestral land and starve.

That we are not exaggerating the evils of the new system will appear from the testimony of those who took a part in the making of the Settlement. The Company's charter came up for renewal in 1853, and, as usual, there was a Parliamentary inquiry into all branches of the Company's Indian administration before the charter was renewed. Select Committees of the Houses of Lords and Commons recorded evidence in 1852 and framed their Reports. They recorded further evidence in 1853, and the Lords submitted three Reports and the Commons six. From this voluminous mass of evidence we will select that of a young officer, Goldfinch, who had himself done Settlement work in Bombay, and described it on the 20th June 1853.

"6714. After the survey was finished, when you found a field, say No. 11, of five Bighas [about two acres] of land, in the possession of some particular person, did the Collector assess the revenue upon it arbitrarily, or did he ask the occupant or proprietor whether he was willing to pay the amount?

"The assessment was fixed by the Superintendent of Survey, without any reference to the cultivator; and when those new rates were introduced, the holder of each field was summoned to the Collector and informed of the rate at which his land would be assessed in future; and if he chose to retain it on those terms, he did; if he did not choose, he threw it up."

"6720. Does the assessment bear the same proportion to the nett produce of all the villages in that District, or does it vary?

"I cannot answer that question; I can only give a guess as to what proportion the assessment bears to the nett produce of the land."

"6722. Is there one officer superintending the survey for the whole District?

"Yes.

"6723. Therefore the principle of assessment is uniform throughout the Presidency?

"Certainly.

"6724. What service does the Superintendent of Survey belong to?

"He belongs to the Engineers—Captain Wingate."[1]

To Goldfinch it appeared that to fix the Land-Tax "without any reference to the cultivator," and then to ask him to accept the assessment or to throw up his land, was a fair and equitable procedure. It did not strike him that the land belonged to the cultivator,

[1] Fourth Report from the Commons' Select Committee, 1853, p. 141.

and had been held by his ancestors at a fixed Land-Tax; and that the option of throwing up the land meant a confiscation of his hereditary property. A fuller account of the results of this settlement will be given in another work,—*India in the Victorian Age.*

It is fair to Captain Wingate to state that he worked this bad system with moderation and leniency. And it is fair to the East India Company to state that they saw the iniquity of the system, and endeavoured to prescribe some general limits to the assessment. Three years after the renewal of the charter they recorded their famous Despatch of the 17th December 1856, in which they laid down that the "right of the Government is not a *rent* which consists of all the surplus produce after paying the cost of cultivation and the profits of agricultural stocks, but a *land revenue* only." And after the abolition of the East India Company, Sir Charles Wood (afterwards Lord Halifax), then Secretary of State for India, recorded in his equally famous Despatch of 1864 that he desired only to take a share, and only a *half share of the rent* as Land-Tax.

But these were pious wishes which could not be carried into effect when, under the Bombay system, the produce of the field and its economic rent were never ascertained, and the Land-Tax in each District was fixed by an examination into what the people had paid in the past, and what they could pay in the future. Under such a system, where the cultivators were not consulted, and could appeal to no Land Courts, the revenue demand was increased at each recurring Settlement, and the peasantry remained resourceless and poor.

Lord Canning, who was Viceroy of India from 1858 to 1862, proposed to permanently settle the land revenue of Bombay as of other Provinces of India; but the proposal was rejected by the India

Office in London in 1883. The Marquis of Ripon, who was Viceroy of India from 1880 to 1884, proposed that the increase of land revenue should be limited to the reasonable ground of an increase in prices; but that proposal too was rejected by the India Office in 1885.

All equitable and intelligible limits to the Land-Tax, proposed from time to time, have thus been ignored or rejected; and the present system is as well calculated to keep the Bombay cultivator permanently resourceless as any system that the wit of man could devise. The cultivator has accordingly sunk more and more under the thraldom of the money-lender; and the nineteenth century closed in Bombay with the worst and most widespread famine that has ever afflicted India.

CHAPTER XXII

BIRD AND THE NEW SETTLEMENT IN NORTHERN INDIA (1822–1835)

THE Settlement of Northern India, commenced in 1822, and described in Chapter XI. of this work, was a failure. Inquiries needed for the preparation of a Record of Rights made no progress. Minute investigations relating to the produce of fields proved vexatious and futile. The Government demand of over 80 per cent. of the rent was severe and impracticable. The system broke down through its own harshness. A reform was needed, and a true reformer appeared on the scene.

Lord William Bentinck had come to India as Governor-General in 1828, and the East India Company never sent out a truer friend of the people. He made a tour in Northern India, and he described what he saw in a letter to the Court of Directors.

"2. Your Honourable Court is already aware that my visit to the Western Provinces was in a great measure prompted by my anxiety to satisfy myself by personal observation of the progress which was making in the work of Settlements under the operation of the provisions of Regulation VII. of 1822, and to ascertain whether it might not be practicable to expedite the progress, or to adopt other measures equally adapted to secure the objects contemplated by your Honourable Court to promote the prosperity of the country."

"4. Among the officers whom I consulted, I found

no deficiency of zeal, and no want of intelligence; but it is nevertheless my duty to assure your Honourable Court that, to whatever cause the failure may be attributable, little or nothing has been effected towards a Settlement of these Provinces.

"8. It is with sincere gratification that I perused the remarks contained in the 58th paragraph of your Honourable Court's despatch dated the 9th February last, which evince your sense of the necessity of long leases, and which detail your views, so nearly corresponding with my own, as to the mode by which the process of settlement may be expedited, and the rights of the subordinate tenantry protected."[1]

In a letter addressed to the Board of Revenue in the same year, Lord William Bentinck pointed out the main causes of the failure of the scheme of 1822. He condemned the exorbitant Government demand of over 80 per cent. of the rental, and he had the courage to suggest that this should be reduced.

The Regulation prescribes, he wrote, "that where an increase may be demanded, the assessment shall be so regulated as to leave the Zemindars and others a nett profit of 20 per cent. on the amount of the Jumma [Government demand] payable by or through them respectively, while his Lordship understands it to be a prevalent notion among revenue officers whose opinions are entitled to respect, that the allowance in favour of the Zemindars should in no instance fall short of 30 or 35 per cent. of the Government Jumma; and after all may not this be considered as the capital by which improvement is to be accomplished?

"This however is exclusive of charges of collection, and is calculated upon the nett rental. The deductions to be made in favour of the Zemindar or other

[1] Letter from the Governor-General to the Court of Directors, dated 15th September 1831.

proprietor from the gross rental on every account is that which his Lordship is desirous of having fixed; and whatever may be the proper rate, his Lordship desires me to suggest for your consideration whether it would not be more practicable to consolidate the whole of the deducted allowances to be made in favour of Zemindars from the gross rental, and to fix it so that it shall operate uniformly and universally, instead of being assigned, as appears to have been hitherto the custom, at the discretion of individual officers." [1]

It will appear from these extracts that as early as 1831 Lord William Bentinck had grasped the cardinal principles of the New Settlement which was to follow, viz., *long leases*, which would give landlords and tenants a motive for improvement, and a *moderate Government demand*, which would leave with them some portion of the profits from the soil.

Another matter which also received the attention of the Governor-General was the preservation of the Village Communities of Northern India. This was forcibly laid down by Sir Charles Metcalfe, then a member of the Governor-General's Council, and afterwards Acting Governor-General of India, in his famous Minute of 1830, which has often been quoted.

"The Village Communities are little Republics, having nearly everything that they want within themselves, and almost independent of any foreign relations. They seem to last where nothing else lasts. Dynasty after dynasty tumbles down; revolution succeeds to revolution; Hindu, Pathan, Moghal, Mahratta, Sikh, English, are masters in turn; but the Village Communities remain the same. In times of trouble they arm and fortify themselves; a hostile army passes

[1] Letter to the Board of Revenue, dated 7th April 1831, paragraphs 106 and 107.

through the country; the Village Community collect their cattle within their walls, and let the enemy pass unprovoked. If plunder and devastation be directed against themselves and the force employed be irresistible, they flee to friendly villages at a distance, but when the storm has passed over they return and resume their occupations. If a country remain for a series of years the scene of continued pillage and massacre, so that the villages cannot be inhabited, the scattered villagers nevertheless return whenever the power of peaceable possession revives. A generation may pass away, but the succeeding generation will return. The sons will take the places of their fathers, the same site for the village, the same position for the houses, the same lands, will be re-occupied by the descendants of those who were driven out when the village was depopulated; and it is not a trifling matter that will drive them out, for they will often maintain their post through times of disturbance and convulsion, and acquire strength sufficient to resist pillage and oppression with success.

"The union of the Village Communities, each one forming a separate little State in itself, has, I conceive, contributed more than any other cause to the preservation of the people of India through all revolutions and changes which they have suffered, and it is in a high degree conducive to their happiness and to the enjoyment of a great portion of freedom and independence. I wish, therefore, that the Village Constitutions may never be disturbed, and I dread everything that has a tendency to break them up. I am fearful that a Revenue Settlement with each individual cultivator, as is the practice in the Ryotwari Settlement, instead of one with the Village Community through their representatives, the headmen, might have such a tendency. For this reason, and for this only, I do not desire to see the Ryotwari Settlement generally introduced into the Western Provinces." [1]

Sir Charles Metcalfe was correct in ascribing the disappearance of Village Communities in Madras and in Bombay to the introduction of the Ryotwari Settlement. When a settlement is made with each individual cultivator, the *raison d'être* of Village Communities ceases. The endeavours of Munro and Elphinstone to keep the Communities alive, after depriving them of their chief function, failed. In Northern India too, the Village Communities have virtually disappeared within the last seventy years through similar causes. The British Government, in obedience to Western ideas, endeavoured to fix the responsibility of the Land-Tax on particular men—zemindars or headmen—until they became the responsible revenue payers and landlords, and the Communities declined. And in trying also to centralise all judicial and executive powers in the hands of its own officers in the spirit of Western institutions, the Government withdrew or weakened the ancient powers of the Communities, until they fell like trees whose roots had been severed. With the most sincere desire to preserve this ancient form of self-government—a desire earnestly and eloquently felt and expressed by Munro, Elphinstone, and Metcalfe—they nevertheless failed in their object because they withdrew the powers of Self-Government from the little republics, because they centred all powers in their own civil courts and executive officers, because they reposed no real trust in the old institutions of the people. One of the saddest results of British rule in India is the effacement of that system of village Self-Government which was developed earliest and preserved longest in India among all the countries of the earth.

[1] Sir Charles T. Metcalfe's Minute, dated 7th November 1830.

Lord William Bentinck had now completed his scheme in consultation with his Councillors, his Board of Revenue, and the Court of Directors; and he convened a conference of officers at Allahabad in 1833, over which he presided in person. The result was the passing of Regulation IX. of 1833, which is the true basis of Land Settlements in Northern India. By this Regulation the majority of judicial cases were transferred from the Courts of Settlement Officers, estimates of produce and of rents were simplified, and the system of average rents for different classes of soil was introduced. The general use of the field map and the field register was prescribed for the first time. The Government demand was reduced to two-thirds of the gross rental; and the settlements which took sixteen years to complete, from 1833 to 1849, were made for a period of thirty years.

The direction of this vast operation fell on a man who was worthy of the work. This man was Robert Merttins Bird, the Father of Land Settlements in Northern India. He was originally a judicial officer, and the training he had received in the discharge of his judicial work rendered him better qualified as a great revenue administrator.

"The greater part of the measures," he wrote in 1842, "which have now been carried through, had been many years before planned and elaborated by me, as measures of a purely judicial character, when I was holding a judicial office, and had no prospect of ever being employed in the Revenue Department. . . .

"A judicial officer has no official facilities for bringing plans of general usefulness into practical operation. I embraced therefore with avidity the offer of the appointment of Revenue Commissioner to conduct the settlements of the Goruckpur Division, as affording the ready means of carrying out my purposes and testing both the soundness and the practicability of my views by actual experiment. . . .

"I saw no reasen to doubt the assessment of a fair and moderate revenue on the land might be so combined with the ascertainment of private rights and the cultivation of the Village Communities, that such records might be framed, such principles fixed, and such sanatory processes put in action, as would correct the evils which had eaten like a canker into the very vitals of landed property and agricultural prosperity.

"On these principles I commenced operations at Goruckpur. The late Lord William Bentinck, having visited that district in the following year, communicated fully with me on my plans, and by his command I maintained a constant correspondence with him on the subject; the result was his calling me in the year 1832 to the office in which the superintendence of the settlements of the North-Western Provinces had devolved principally on me. . . .

"On the whole, there is, I think, just reason to consider that a moderate, fair, and equal demand on the land, such as can and ought to be collected without interfering with the accumulation of property, and the march of agricultural prosperity, has, generally speaking, been fixed."[1]

It is not necessary in the present work to go through the history of the settlements in the different divisions and districts in Northern India; but the results of the assessments may be seen from the following figures taken from a statement appended to Bird's Report.[2]

[1] T. M. Bird's Report on the Settlement of the North-Western Provinces, dated 21st January 1842.

[2] The statement excludes tracts permanently settled. One mistake in calculation about Hariana District has been corrected. Fractions of acres and pies have been omitted.

Name of Division and District.	Total Area in Acres.	Cultivated Area in Acres.	Rate of Government Revenue per Acre of the Land in Cultivation.		
			Rupees.	Annas	Pies.
Delhi Division—					
District Hariana . . .	1,657,975	696,147	0	14	4
,, Delhi	364,534	174,605	2	1	3
,, Rohtuck . . .	844,666	474,465	1	5	2
,, Gurgaon . . .	1,160,437	647,353	1	9	0
Meerut Division—					
District Saharanpur . .	1,018,705	606,847	1	10	6
,, Muzaffarnagar .	691,706	392,377	1	11	2
,, Meerut . . .	1,776,430	1,034,016	2	1	9
,, Bulandshahar .	1,025,096	592,630	1	9	8
,, Alighar . . .	1,119,238	900,562	1	4	0
Rohilkhand Division—					
District Bijnaur . . .	1,027,533	459,409	2	2	10
,, Moradabad . .	Not stated	Not stated	Not stated.		
,, Budaon . . .	1,450,418	752,103	1	7	6
,, Pilibeet . . .	Not stated	Not stated	2	0	1
,, Bareli	1,116,174	639,579	1	15	7
,, Shajehanpur .	1,309,211	651,549	1	9	0
Agra Division—					
District Muttra. . . .	Not stated	Not stated	Not stated.		
,, Agra	935,815	646,818	2	2	5
,, Farakkabad . .	1,247,288	614,253	2	6	0
,, Mynpuri . . .	1,280,927	613,422	2	4	0
,, Etawa	1,071,756	477,901	2	11	10
Allahabad Division—					
District Cawnpur . . .	1,497,795	782,276	2	1	3
,, Fattehpur . .	990,584	506,905	2	12	9
,, Allahabad . .	1,790,244	997,508	2	2	6
Benares Division—					
District Goruckpur . .	4,115,214	1,927,234	1	1	3
,, Azimgarh . .	1,652,293	773,616	1	15	4

These were the general results of Robert Bird's work up to the date of his leaving India. Ten years after, when he was examined as a witness before the Select Committee of the House of Commons, he explained clearly and lucidly the procedure he had followed in India.

"I first of all proceeded to make a survey of all the land. . . . The next process was to make a map, including every field, exactly in the same manner as the English tithe commutation maps. . . . Then the next thing was the professional survey of the boundary made by an educated officer, that shows the cultivated and the uncultivated land, and the real shape of the village as taken by a regular survey. . . . We then proceeded to investigate the assessment of the Government Land-Tax upon that tract. . . . As soon as that was ascertained, we fixed the amount of the Government tax we should require upon the whole of that tract, and then we proceeded to set down the amount that we should require upon each village. . . . The people then came forward and met the Collector. They generally met, as is our way of doing business in India, under the shade of a tree or in an open field. . . . In many instances objections were made: they said, 'This is too high; my village will not pay this; it is a poor village.' They were then told that we intended to have that amount of revenue from the whole tract, and that, therefore, if there was any objection regarding that village, they must point out who could pay more; and this set them to discuss the matter among themselves. . . The assessment upon the whole tract was not strictly maintained; it was not our object to do so; we were ready to reduce it if we found cause to do so; but the object of demanding this first in a lump was to induce them to look into their own concerns, and to come to such an adjustment as they should find to be satisfactory."

This procedure, as described by Robert Bird himself, was by no means perfect: but it was far better than that of Bombay, where, according to Goldfinch, each cultivator was called upon to take his field on the revenue fixed by Government, or to throw it up.

Asked what was the proportion of the Government revenue assessed by him on the produce of the soil, Robert Bird replied: "My general impression is that *it was not above a tenth of the produce.*" And he added that "in Madras and other places it is a matter notorious now that the error is that *the revenue was fixed too high at the beginning, and impoverishes the people.*" [1]

A fuller account of Robert Bird's Settlement will be given in another work,—*India in the Victorian Age.* In the present chapter we will only add a few words to complete the land revenue history of Northern India.

When Robert Merttins Bird left India, the work he had commenced, and almost completed, passed under the control and supervision of a worthy successor. James Thomason was the Lieutenant-Governor of the North-Western Provinces from 1843 to 1853, and a more kind-hearted and benevolent Englishman never went out to India. His "Directions for Settlement Officers," drawn up in 1844, was the first complete Code of Land Settlement compiled in India. These, with the "Directions for Collectors," were published five years after under the name of "Directions for Revenue Officers," and continued for many years to be the standard of official reference. The underlying principles of the Land System of Northern India are enunciated in a Preface to these Directions.

"*First,* All the inhabited part of the country is divided into portions with fixed boundaries called Mahals or estates; on each Mahal a sum is assessed for the term of twenty or thirty years, calculated so as to leave a fair surplus profit over and above the

[1] Fourth Report from the Select Committee, 1853. The italics are our own. A tenth of the produce is consistent with the ancient Hindu law of Manu and the Mahommedan law of the Hedaya, and ought to be the maximum limit of the Government Revenue where it is not permanently settled. In Madras and Bombay the Government revenue is still too high and impoverishes the people. The percentage of the revenue on the gross produce is between 12 and 31 in Madras, according to the Board of Revenue's Statement submitted to the Famine Commission of 1880 (Appendix III. p. 394), and the percentage is 20 in some parts of Bombay, according to the Famine Commission's Report of 1901.

nett produce of the land, and for the punctual payment of that sum the land is held to be perpetually hypothecated to the Government.

"*Secondly,* It is determined who are the person or persons entitled to receive this surplus profit. The right thus determined is declared to be heritable and transferable, and the persons entitled to it are considered the proprietors of the land, from whom the engagements for the annual payment of the sum assessed by the Government on the Mahal are taken.

"*Thirdly,* All the proprietors of a Mahal are, severally and jointly, responsible in their persons and property for the payment of the sum assessed by the Government on the Mahal."[1]

Thomason laboured for ten years to complete the great work initiated in Northern India by Lord William Bentinck. And if Bentinck had able and distinguished colleagues in Metcalfe, Trevelyan, and Macaulay, Thomason too trained up under him a school of no less distinguished administrators, such as John Lawrence, Robert Montgomery, and William Muir. They were inspired by that practical desire to work in the interests of the people which animated Lord William Bentinck; a desire which unfortunately became less conspicuous in the last decades of the century. Thomason's good work of ten years was recognised in England; and on the 27th September 1853 an order was signed by Her Majesty's command appointing the wise and able administrator of Northern India to the higher post of Governor of Madras. The reward came too late: on that very day, the 27th September 1853, James Thomason died in the country in which he had passed the best part of his life in the service of its people.

Two years after, Bentinck's wise policy of reducing

[1] Selection of Papers relating to Revenue Survey and Assessment in the North-Western Provinces, 1853, pp. 4, 5.

the Government demand was more than vindicated. He had reduced that demand to two-thirds of the rental, but in practice, even this was found to be harsh and unworkable. Under the administration of Lord Dalhousie it was decided by the famous Saharanpur Rules of 1855 that the Government demand should be limited to one-half the rental.

"The assets of an estate can seldom be minutely ascertained, but more certain information as to the average nett assets can be obtained now than was formerly the case. This may lead to over-assessment, for there is little doubt that two-thirds, or 66 per cent., is a larger proportion of the real average assets than can ordinarily be paid by proprietors or communities in a long course of years. For this reason the Government have determined so far to modify the rules laid down in paragraph 52 of the Directions to Settlement Officers as to limit the demand of the State to 50 per cent. of the average nett assets. By this it is not meant that the Jumma [Government revenue] of each estate is to be fixed at one-half of the nett average assets, but in taking these assets, with other data, into consideration, the Collector will bear in mind that about one-half, and not two-thirds as heretofore, of the ascertained nett assets should be the Government demand. The Collectors should observe the cautions given in paragraphs 47 to 51 of the treatise quoted, and not waste time in minute and probably fruitless attempts to ascertain exactly the average nett assets of the estates under settlement."[1]

[1] Rule XXXVI. of the Saharanpur Rules of 1855. It will help the reader's memory to note that the great land reforms in Northern India were effected, curiously, once in every eleven years. The first great Land Act was Regulation VII. of 1822. Regulation IX. of 1833 reduced the Government demand to two-thirds the rental, and saw the commencement of the New Settlement by R. M. Bird. In 1844 Thomason's Directions to Settlement Officers were promulgated. In 1855 the Saharanpur Rules were passed, reducing the Government demand to half the rental.

Thus after the persistent blunders of half a century, the Government at last decided to limit its demand to one-half the rent. This is now the recognised principle all over India, where the revenue has not been permanently fixed. In Madras and Bombay the Land-Tax is fixed at one-half the economic rent by Sir Charles Wood's despatch of 1864; in Northern India it has been fixed at one-half the rental by the Saharanpur Rules of 1855. It would be a distinct gain to the cause of good government in India if this principle were strictly and honestly adhered to.

But it is the unavoidable result of a system of administration in which Revenue Collectors dictate the revenue policy, and the people have no voice whatever, that the clearest and most unmistakable rules are strained, misinterpreted, and evaded. How this was done in Madras and Bombay has been described elsewhere. How this was done in Northern India, it is painful to note. Lord Canning's recommendation for a Permanent Settlement of the land revenue all over India, made in 1862, and supported by Lord Lawrence, Sir Charles Wood, and Sir Stafford Northcote, was rejected in 1883. Eeven the Saharanpur Rules, which were still binding on revenue collectors, were virtually evaded in practice. The purport of the Saharanpur Rules is unmistakable. The rule quoted above limits the Government demand to one-half of "the average nett assets," "the real average assets." But in later settlements the Government interpreted this to mean one-half of "the prospective and potential" rental of estates. If an estate had a rental of £1200 a year, the claim of the Government was to a revenue of £650, or might be £700, on the ground that the rental *might rise hereafter* to £1300 or £1400. More than this, while the Land-Tax is still theoretically one-half the rental, a number of new taxes for education, post-office, &c., have been introduced and assessed on the rent, adding to the share of the Government on the produce of the soil. Is this not paltering with the people of India in a double sense, keeping the word of promise to their ear, and breaking it to their hope?

CHAPTER XXIII

FINANCE AND THE ECONOMIC DRAIN (1793–1837)

THE East India Company's Charter was renewed in 1833 for twenty years, dating from April 1834. The financial arrangements which were effected by this Act deserve our attention in the present chapter.

It was provided that the East India Company should henceforth "discontinue and abstain from all commercial business," and stand forth only as Administrators and Rulers of India. It was enacted that all the territorial and other debts of the Company "shall be charged and chargeable upon the revenues of the said territories" of India. It was declared that out of the revenues of India there should be paid to the Company "a yearly dividend after the rate of £10, 10s. per annum on their capital stock." It was further provided that the Company's dividend should be subject to be redeemed by Parliament after 1874 on payment to the Company of £200 sterling for every £100 of the capital stock." And lastly, it was enacted that if the Company ceased to exist after 1854, or was deprived of the possession and government of India by the authority of Parliament, they would be entitled to demand the redemption of the said dividend within one year, "and provision shall be made for redeeming the said dividend, after the rate aforesaid, within three years after such demand."

Comments on these arrangements are superfluous. The British nation had spent millions of their own money in acquiring dominions in other parts of the world; but in India an empire had been acquired, wars had been waged, and the administration had been carried on, at the cost of the Indian people; the British nation had not contributed a shilling. The trading Company which had acquired this empire had also drawn their dividends and made their profits out of the revenues of the empire for two generations. When they ceased to be traders in 1834, it was provided that the dividends on their stock should continue to be paid out of the taxes imposed on the Indian people. And when, finally, the Company ceased to exist in 1858, their stock was paid off by loans which were made into an Indian Debt. The empire was thus transferred from the Company to the Crown, but the Indian people paid the purchase-money. And the Indian people are thus virtually paying dividends to this day, on the stock of an extinct Company, in the shape of interest on Debt!

It is necessary here to place before the reader the Indian revenue and expenditure of the Company year by year from 1792 to the year of the Queen's accession.[1]

	Land Revenue.	Gross Revenue.	Gross Expenditure.
	£	£	£
1792–93.			
Bengal	3,091,616	5,512,761	3,873,859
Madras	742,760	2,476,312	2,222,878
Bombay	79,025	236,555	844,096
Total	3,913,401	8,225,628	6,940,833
1793–94.			
Bengal	3,177,028	5,871,945	3,714,160
Madras	789,050	2,110,089	1,972,224
Bombay	82,050	294,736	906,745
Total	4,048,128	8,276,770	6,593,129

[1] Returns of the Gross Revenue, &c., in India since 1792. Ordered by the House of Commons to be printed, 22nd June 1855.

	Land Revenue.	Gross Revenue.	Gross Expenditure.
1794-95.	£	£	£
Bengal	3,235,259	5,937,931	3,863,566
Madras	891,640	1,775,782	1,880,332
Bombay	70,238	312,480	823,910
Total	4,197,137	8,026,193	6,567,808
1795-96.			
Bengal	3,130,697	5,694,194	3,986,744
Madras	929,200	1,894,304	2,119,196
Bombay	64,085	277,596	783,057
Total	4,123,982	7,866,094	6,888,997
1796-97.			
Bengal	3,118,556	5,703,906	4,126,644
Madras	900,534	1,996,328	2,449,000
Bombay	39,724	315,937	932,394
Total	4,058,814	8,016,171	7,508,038
1797-98.			
Bengal	3,097,443	5,782,741	4,351,926
Madras	732,983	1,938,950	2,665,232
Bombay	38,872	338,189	998,169
Total	3,869,298	8,059,880	8,015,327
1798-99.			
Bengal	3,072,743	6,153,615	4,416,954
Madras	856,666	2,123,831	3,442,094
Bombay	37,007	374,587	1,280,315
Total	3,966,416	8,652,033	9,139,363
1799-1800.			
Bengal	3,213,230	6,498,473	5,058,661
Madras	883,539	2,822,536	3,319,547
Bombay	31,364	415,663	1,577,182
Total	4,128,133	9,736,672	9,955,390
1800-1.			
Bengal	3,218,766	6,658,334	5,420,966
Madras	957,799	3,540,268	4,614,387
Bombay	45,130	286,457	1,432,832
Total	4,221,695	10,485,059	11,468,185
1801-2.			
Bengal	3,296,303	7,127,988	5,647,415
Madras	1,095,972	4,729,609	5,347,805
Bombay	54,571	305,992	1,414,825
Total	4,446,846	12,163,589	12,410,045

	Land Revenue.	Gross Revenue.	Gross Expenditure.
1802–3.	£	£	£
Bengal	3,295,761	8,380,087	5,798,858
Madras	933,108	4,724,904	5,117,769
Bombay	68,015	359,546	1,410,253
Total	4,296,884	13,464,537	12,326,880
1803–4.			
Bengal	3,252,621	8,060,993	6,193,638
Madras	921,646	4,651,744	6,306,284
Bombay	305,861	558,648	1,895,483
Total	4,480,128	13,271,385	14,395,405
1804–5.			
Bengal	3,225,436	9,336,707	7,464,291
Madras	993,849	4,897,140	6,312,613
Bombay	384,740	715,548	2,338,279
Total	4,604,025	14,949,395	16,115,183
1805–6.			
Bengal	3,311,673	9,542,430	8,931,958
Madras	1,097,416	5,014,493	5,728,164
Bombay	471,344	846,486	2,761,296
Total	4,880,433	15,403,409	17,421,418
1806–7.			
Bengal	3,296,684	9,160,149	9,291,826
Madras	963,440	4,602,721	5,742,829
Bombay	388,536	772,869	2,474,209
Total	4,648,660	14,535,739	17,508,864
1807–8.			
Bengal	3,729,098	9,971,695	7,760,920
Madras	1,039,671	4,927,519	5,717,228
Bombay	417,186	770,691	2,372,142
Total	5,185,955	15,669,905	15,850,290
1808–9.			
Bengal	3,851,128	9,816,458	7,898,924
Madras	1,057,628	4,968,321	5,431,151
Bombay	427,033	740,276	2,062,814
Total	5,335,789	15,525,055	15,392,889
1809–10.			
Bengal	3,706,200	9,590,880	7,815,675
Madras	1,184,253	5,373,191	5,637,365
Bombay	396,482	691,914	2,081,671
Total	5,286,935	15,655,985	15,534,711

	Land Revenue.	Gross Revenue.	Gross Expenditure.
1810–11.	£	£	£
Bengal	3,295,382	10,682,249	7,241,839
Madras	1,071,666	5,238,576	5,110,977
Bombay	437,108	758,372	1,557,165
Total	4,804,156	16,679,197	13,909,981
1811–12.			
Bengal	3,296,905	10,706,172	7,058,871
Madras	1,048,844	5,156,717	4,619,610
Bombay	433,785	742,726	1,542,485
Total	4,779,534	16,605,615	13,220,966
1812–13.			
Bengal	3,310,874	10,390,257	7,222,936
Madras	1,159,778	5,258,244	4,799,630
Bombay	420,323	687,789	1,493,262
Total	4,890,975	16,336,290	13,515,828
1813–14.			
Bengal	3,310,617	11,172,471	7,135,172
Madras	892,793	5,297,088	4,893,224
Bombay	400,802	759,152	1,589,329
Total	4,604,212	17,228,711	13,617,725
1814–15.			
Bengal	7 370,741	11,155,912	9,145,560
Madras	3,889,555	5,322,164	5,134,246
Bombay	488,998	819,204	1,675,200
Total	11,749,294	17,297,280	15,955,006
1815–16.			
Bengal	7,566,439	11,312,896	9,833,062
Madras	3,609,668	5,106,107	5,289,476
Bombay	467,777	818,816	1,937,430
Total	11,643,884	17,237,819	17,059,968
1816–17.			
Bengal	7,875,647	11,856,953	10,200,303
Madras	3,826,107	5,360,220	5,201,399
Bombay	498,102	860,405	1,902,460
Total	12,199,856	18,077,578	17,304,162
1817–18.			
Bengal	7,639,154	11,692,068	10,685,154
Madras	3,856,433	5,381,307	5,475,254
Bombay	868,047	1,302,445	1,885,786
Total	12,363,634	18,375,820	18,046,194

	Land Revenue.	Gross Revenue.	Gross Expenditure.
	£	£	£
1818-19.			
Bengal	8,548,138	12,437,385	11,925,349
Madras	3,799,410	5,361,432	5,979,045
Bombay	1,143,041	1,660,200	2,492,193
Total	13,490,589	19,459,017	20,396,587
1819-20.			
Bengal	8,163,919	12,245,526	11,598,419
Madras	3,791,931	5,407,004	5,694,844
Bombay	1,078,164	1,577,932	2,395,844
Total	13,034,014	19,230,462	19,689,107
1820-21.			
Bengal	8,139,415	13,547,423	11,287,397
Madras	3,738,460	5,403,506	5,572,489
Bombay	1,818,314	2,401,312	3,197,366
Total	13,696,189	21,352,241	20,057,252
1821-22.			
Bengal	8,258,903	13,390,339	10,841,003
Madras	3,708,404	5,557,029	5,405,592
Bombay	1,761,910	2,855,740	3,609,894
Total	13,729,217	21,803,108	19,856,489
1822-23.			
Bengal	8,261,843	14,312,044	10,746,301
Madras	3,769,369	5,585,210	5,072,992
Bombay	1,551,592	3,274,447	4,264,448
Total	13,582,804	23,171,701	20,083,741
1823-24.			
Bengal	8,211,251	12,992,069	11,397,024
Madras	3,741,100	5,498,765	6,228,823
Bombay	1,607,088	2,789,550	3,228,150
Total	13,559,439	21,280,384	20,853,997
1824-25.			
Bengal	8,081,462	13,524,223	13,509,910
Madras	3,765,212	5,440,743	5,714,848
Bombay	1,208,735	1,785,217	3,279,398
Total	13,055,409	20,750,183	22,504,156
1825-26.			
Bengal	8,133,625	13,151,080	14,456,164
Madras	3,978,682	5,714,915	5,704,829
Bombay	1,627,237	2,262,393	4,007,020
Total	13,739,544	21,128,388	24,168,013

	Land Revenue.	Gross Revenue.	Gross Expenditure.
	£	£	£
1826-27.			
Bengal	8,355,800	14,812,833	13,904,322
Madras	3,669,312	5,981,681	5,432,562
Bombay	1,873,427	2,588,983	3,975,411
Total	13,898,539	22,383,497	23,312,295
1827-28.			
Bengal	8,331,604	14,973,110	14,012,763
Madras	3,605,226	5,347,828	6,007,597
Bombay	1,817,873	2,542,325	4,033,477
Total	13,754,703	22,863,263	24,053,837
1828-29.			
Bengal	8,200,779	14,833,840	12,563,550
Madras	3,649,012	5,575,049	5,502,224
Bombay	1,722,335	2,331,802	3,652,786
Total	13,572,126	22,740,691	21,718,560
1829-30.			
Bengal	8,197,563	13,858,178	11,710,870
Madras	3,522,100	5,415,587	5,256,647
Bombay	1,585,432	2,421,443	3,600,841
Total	13,305,095	21,695,208	20,568,358
1830-31.			
Bengal	8,228,161	14,119,914	11,532,398
Madras	3,460,329	5,358,260	5,107,020
Bombay	1,650,061	2,541,136	3,594,472
Total	13,338,551	22,019,310	20,233,890
1831-32.			
Bengal	6,942,324	11,748,757	13,464,520
Madras	3,252,117	4,472,137	2,167,574
Bombay	1,395,891	2,096,343	1,416,079
Total	11,590,332	18,317,237	17,048,173
1832-33.			
Bengal	7,099,249	12,244,523	10,539,527
Madras	2,940,703	4,108,061	4,312,452
Bombay	1,441,986	2,125,340	2,662,741
Total	11,481,938	18,477,924	17,514,720
1833-34.			
Bengal	6,637,961	11,616,954	9,881,927
Madras	3,176,708	4,358,207	4,382,368
Bombay	1,629,580	2,292,207	2,660,037
Total	11,444,249	18,267,368	16,924,332

	Land Revenue.	Gross Revenue.	Gross Expenditure.
1834-35.	£	£	£
Bengal	3,234,336	15,290,414	8,470,472
N.W. Provinces	4,018,344	4,899,274	1,494,027
Madras	3,256,855	4,480,025	4,128,753
Bombay	1,544,183	2,186,934	2,591,244
Total	12,053,718	26,856,647	16,684,496
1835-36.			
Bengal	3,304,294	8,286,287	7,942,501
N.W. Provinces	4,217,981	4,838,133	1,640,478
Madras	3,297,602	4,599,261	3,839,758
Bombay	1,719,895	2,424,444	2,572,067
Total	12,539,772	20,148,125	15,994,804
1836-37.			
Bengal (includes Excise)	3,575,059	8,618,470	8,455,287
N.W. Provinces	4,478,417	5,056,489	1,735,419
Madras	3,161,490	4,618,309	4,172,784
Bombay	1,842,759	2,705,862	2,999,878
Total	13,057,725	20,999,130	17,363,368
1837-38.			
Bengal (includes Excise)	3,615,975	9,081,014	8,536,423
N.W. Provinces	3,765,973	4,369,351	1,807,209
Madras	3,431,270	4,819,890	4,295,036
Bombay	1,858,525	2,588,565	2,914,857
Total	12,671,743	20,858,820	17,553,525

These long columns of dry figures have a meaning and a significance, if we read in them the political and administrative history of half a century. Every change in the policy of the British Government, every leaning to a policy of war or to a policy of peace and retrenchment, has left its impress on the finances of India. And the figures given above are silent witnesses to the administrative reforms effected in India from the time of Cornwallis and Barlow to the time of Bentinck and Metcalfe.

Lord Cornwallis, when he left India in 1793, had so adjusted the finances as to limit the total expenditure to under seven millions, showing a surplus revenue of a million and a half. Within twelve years from this date, the restless and warlike policy of the Marquis of Wellesley had increased the expenditure to fifteen millions, showing a deficit of over two millions. It was this which gave offence to the Court of Directors. That venerable head of a mercantile body looked with indifference on peace or war in India so long as their surplus was safe; the pecuniary returns from their territories was the main standard by which they judged administration; and when the surplus was changed into a deficit they never forgave. They disapproved of the wars of Wellesley because the wars were expensive; and they recalled the great Proconsul from India in disgrace.

All through the fifteen years, from 1795 to 1810, Bengal had showed a surplus, Madras and Bombay had showed deficits. It is not an exaggeration to state that Bengal, with its Permanent Settlement, yielding a steady and unvarying income from the soil, enabled the British nation to build up their Indian Empire. Bengal paid the expenses of ambitious wars and annexations in Northern and Southern India. Madras and Bombay never paid the total cost of their own administration during these years; Great Britain never contributed anything towards the acquisition of India.

On the departure of Lord Wellesley a balance in the finances was restored once more; and between 1810 and 1814 the peaceful administrators of India reduced the annual expenditure to a little above thirteen millions, showing an annual surplus of two to four millions, which delighted the souls of the Directors. But the surplus disappeared under the warlike administration of the Marquis of Hastings; and there was a deficit again in 1818, when the last Mahratta war was concluded. Lord Hastings avoided the wrath of the Directors by showing a surplus of two millions in 1822. Bombay did not yet pay its expenses. It showed a deficit of a million, five years after the dominions of the Peshwa had been annexed; and Bengal showed a surplus of three millions. It may therefore be said with strict truth, that the conquests of Lord Hastings, like the conquests of Lord Wellesley, were made out of resources furnished by Permanently Settled Bengal.

The Burmese war of Lord Amherst once more upset the finances of India, and there was a continuous deficit from 1824 to 1827. The revenues of India had now increased to twenty-two millions, owing to the extension of the Empire and the severity of the Land-Tax; but the expenditure during these years rose to twenty-three or twenty-four millions.

Then were witnessed the striking results of the policy of peace, retrenchment, and reform introduced by Lord William Bentinck. Even as a financial reformer, Lord William Bentinck stands alone among all British administrators ever sent out to India. For financial reforms in India consist, not in hunting after new sources of taxation which do not exist, but in retrenchment. The excessive Land-Tax was reduced everywhere, and fell within six years (1825 to 1831) from thirteen millions to eleven and a half millions; but the reduction in expenditure more than compensated this loss. When Lord William Bentinck arrived in India in 1828, the total expenditure was twenty-four millions, showing a deficit of over a million. When he left India in 1835, the total expenditure was sixteen millions, showing a surplus of four millions.

Happy it were for India if administrators of his type had always succeeded him. But every reduction in expenditure in India affects the privileged classes of that country, and leads to an outcry; and Lord William Bentinck was denounced as no Governor-General under the Company's rule was ever denounced. It is not in human nature that British administrators should brave the wrath of their countrymen to serve the interests of the people of India; and under the present system of government a continuous pressure is exerted for increase in expenditure, while there is none in favour of retrenchment. Expenditure and the public debt have increased by leaps and bounds since the time of Lord William Bentinck; nor is there any possible remedy for this growing evil except to give the people themselves, who are necessarily in favour of retrenchment, some control in the administration of their own concerns. If those who spend have the sole control of the finances, the expenditure necessarily increases; if those who pay the taxes are allowed some control, the expenditure is necessarily restricted. This is the rule all over the world, and India is no exception.

It has been stated above that the whole cost of wars in India and of civil administration was paid out of the resources of India. It is important to note that after paying all these expenses India showed a substantial surplus during the forty-six years ending with the accession of Queen Victoria.

It will be seen from the figures given above, that if there were fourteen years of deficit, there were thirty-two years of surplus; and if the deficit amounted altogether to nearly seventeen millions, the surplus amounted to nearly forty-nine millions. The nett financial results of Indian administration was therefore a surplus of thirty-two millions during forty-six years. But this money was not saved in India, nor devoted to irrigation or other works of improvement. It went as a continuous tribute to England to pay dividends to the Company's shareholders; and as the flow of the money from India was not sufficient to pay the dividends, there was an increasing debt—called the Public Debt of India—adding to the burdens of the taxpayers who had to pay the interest. This is the saddest episode in the sad financial history of India.

In 1792, the Indian Debt, bearing interest, little exceeded seven millions. In 1799, it had risen to ten millions. In consequence of Lord Wellesley's wars, it had risen in 1805 to nearly twenty-one millions, and by 1807 to twenty-seven millions. It remained almost stationary at this figure for many years, but in 1829 it had risen to thirty millions. Lord William Bentinck's beneficent administration had the effect of gradually reducing the debt, and on the 30th April 1836 it amounted to twenty-seven millions.[1]

Under an equable arrangement between the two nations, India should have paid for her own administration, and England should have remunerated the Company for building up an empire so beneficial to her trade and her power, and so advantageous to her sons seeking a career in the East. If both nations benefited by the founding of the British Empire in India, both nations should have contributed to the cost,—India paying for the administration of India, and Great Britain paying the home charges. But a different policy was pursued from the commencement of the British rule in India, and the result was a continuous Economic Drain from India, which has increased in volume with the lapse of years, and has impoverished an industrious, peaceful, and once prosperous nation. These results were foreseen by thoughtful Englishmen in those early years of which we are speaking in the present chapter.

"This annual drain of £3,000,000 on British India," wrote Montgomery Martin in 1838, "amounted in thirty years, at 12 per cent. (the usual Indian rate) compound interest to the enormous sum of £723,997,917 sterling; or, at a low rate, as £2,000,000 for fifty years, to £8,400,000,000 sterling! So constant and accumu-

[1] The exact figure is £26,947,000. Annual Account of the Territorial Revenues and Disbursements of the East India Company, &c. Printed by Order of the House of Commons, 12th August 1842.

lating a drain even on England would soon impoverish her; how severe then must be its effects on India, where the wages of a labourer is from twopence to threepence a day?"

"For half a century we have gone on draining from two to three and sometimes four million pounds sterling a year from India, which has been remitted to Great Britain to meet the deficiencies of commercial speculations, to pay the interest of debts, to support the home establishment, and to invest on England's soil the accumulated wealth of those whose lives have been spent in Hindustan. I do not think it possible for human ingenuity to avert entirely the evil effects of a continued drain of three or four million pounds a year from a distant country like India, and which is never returned to it in any shape."[1]

It would fill a volume to quote all that has been written and said on the subject of this annual Economic Drain, which was increased by the exclusion of the people of India from all the higher services. We shall content ourselves therefore with the views of four distinguished administrators who served in the four great provinces of India—Bengal and Madras, Northern India and Bombay.

The Honourable John Shore, bearing a historic name, was one of the best of the Bengal administrators in the thirties; and he recorded the result of his own observations, fully and clearly, in his thoughtful work on India.

"More than seventeen years have elapsed since I first landed in this country; but on my arrival, and during my residence of about a year in Calcutta, I well recollect the quiet, comfortable, and settled conviction, which in those days existed in the minds of the English population, of the blessings conferred on the

[1] Montgomery Martin's *Eastern India*, London, 1838. Introductions to vols. i. and iii.

natives of India by the establishment of the English rule. Our superiority to the Native Governments which we have supplanted; the excellent system for the administration of justice which we had introduced; our moderation; our anxiety to benefit the people—in short, our virtues of every description, were descanted on as so many established truths which it was heresy to controvert. Occasionally I remember to have heard some hints and assertions of a contrary nature from some one who had spent many years in the interior of the country; but the storm which was immediately raised and thundered on the head of the unfortunate individual who should presume to question the established creed was almost sufficient to appal the boldest."

"I was thus gradually led to an inquiry into the principles and practice of British-Indian administration. Proceeding in this, I soon found myself at no loss to understand the feelings of the people both towards the Government and to ourselves. It would have been astonishing indeed had it been otherwise. The fundamental principle of the English had been to make the whole Indian nation subservient, in every possible way, to the interests and benefits of themselves. They have been taxed to the utmost limit; every successive Province, as it has fallen into our possession, has been made a field for higher exaction; and it has always been our boast how greatly we have raised the revenue above that which the native rulers were able to extort. The Indians have been excluded from every honour, dignity, or office which the lowest Englishman could be prevailed upon to accept." [1]

Elsewhere, in referring to the drain of wealth from India, Shore wrote: "The halcyon days of India are over; she has been drained of a large proportion of the wealth she once possessed; and her energies have

[1] Honourable F. J. Shore's *Notes on Indian Affairs*, London 1837, vol. ii. p. 516.

been cramped by a sordid system of misrule to which the interests of millions have been sacrificed for the benefit of the few."[1]

John Sullivan went out to India as early as 1804, and retired from that country in 1841, after holding responsible posts as Resident at Mysore, as Collector of Coimbatur, as Member of the Madras Board, and as Member of the Madras Council. He was examined on the occasion of the renewal of the Company's charter in 1833, and he spoke feelingly on the exclusion of the people of India from all high appointments in the country.

"503. What are the disadvantages under which the natives at present feel themselves to labour with respect to the British Government?

"Their exclusion from all offices of trust and emolument, and from that position in the administration of the country, civil and military, which they occupied under their own princes."

"509. . . . Does not the system which the natives have always enjoyed under the British Government compensate to them in a very large degree, if not entirely, for their loss of the exclusive possession of offices, to which, under the Native Government, they considered themselves to be entitled?

"I should say that nothing can compensate them under such exclusion."[2]

The same witness was examined again, twenty years after, when the charter of the Company came up for renewal in 1853; and on that occasion he gave his evidence still more emphatically.

"4866. Do you suppose that they [the people of India] have traditions among them which tell them that the economic condition of the population was

[1] Shore's *Notes on Indian Affairs*, vol. ii. p. 28.

[2] Minutes of Evidence taken before the Select Committee, 1832, vol. i. pp. 65 and 66.

better in former times under their native rulers than it is now?

"I think, generally speaking, history tells us that it was; they have been in a state of the greatest prosperity from the earliest time, as far as history tells us."

"4869. How do you account for the superior economic state of the people, and for their ability to lay out the money which they did in canals and irrigation and tanks, if they were wasting more wealth, and sacrificing more lives in wars, than we do now, specially seeing that the wars were carried on very much upon their own territories, instead of being beyond their limits?

"We have an expensive element which they were free from, which is the European element, civil and military, which swallows up so much of the revenue; from that cause our administration is so much more expensive; that, I think, is the great reason."

John Sullivan did not shrink from the logical conclusion of his opinions, when he was asked if he would restore British territory to native rule, keeping the military control of the Empire in British hands.

"4890. You would restore a great deal of territory to native rulers upon principles of justice?

"Yes.

"Because we have become possessed of them by violence or by other means without any just right or title?

"I would do so upon principles of justice and upon principles of financial economy."[1]

Few of John Sullivan's contemporaries went so far as he did, but most of them knew and felt the injustice of the entire exclusion of the people of India from the control of their own affairs.

Holt Mackenzie, whose distinguished work in the

[1] Third Report of the Select Committee, 1853, pp. 19 and 20.

land revenue settlement of Northern India has been referred to in Chapter XI. of this work, recorded the following remarks in his Minute on the Revenue and the Judicial Administration of India in 1830; and this Minute was embodied in the Report of the Select Committee of the House of Commons in 1833.

"Nothing can be more striking than the scorn with which the people have been practically treated at the hands of even those who were actuated by the most benevolent motives; for, since the world began, there is probably no example of a Government carrying the principle of absolutism so completely through the civil administration of the country, if that can be called civil which is in its spirit so military; nay, which sets the people aside in the management of their own concerns much more than the Sepoy in the government of the army. The principle pervades every act, from the highest exercise of legislative power to the appointment of the meanest public officer. . . . It seems to be vain to think that we can by any legislative provision secure the community from extortion and vexation, if we once allow or require the Government officers to interfere perpetually in the minute details of the people's business. We have, unfortunately, acted on an opposite principle, interfering in almost everything, neglecting popular institutions where they exist, and never attempting to create them when wanting."[1]

But the man who spoke with the greatest authority before the Select Committee of the House of Commons in 1832 was Sir John Malcolm, whose name is connected with those of Munro and Elphinstone as builders of the British Indian Empire, and the most able and sympathetic rulers of the people in the first half of the nineteenth century. He had distinguished himself in two Mahratta wars by his success and

[1] Holt Mackenzie's Minute, dated 1st October 1830, para. 67.

valour; he had won the confidence of the Indian soldiery as well as of the civil population by his courtesy and kindness; and after the meritorious service of over a quarter of a century he had succeeded Elphinstone in the high post of Governor of Bombay in 1827. When, therefore, he was examined as a witness before the House of Commons in 1832, he spoke, on the condition of the people of India under British rule, with a knowledge and authority which few Englishmen of his or any later time equalled, and which none ever surpassed.

"278. In your opinion, was the substitution of our government for the misrule of the native princes the cause of greater prosperity to the agricultural and commercial part of the population?

"I cannot answer this in every Province of India, but I shall as far as my experience enables me. I do not think the change has benefited, or could benefit, either the commercial, the monied, or the agricultural classes of many of the native States, though it may be of others. It has not happened to me ever to see countries better cultivated, and so abounding in all produce of the soil, as well as commercial wealth, than the Southern Mahratta Districts, when I accompanied the present Duke of Wellington to that country in the year 1803; I particularly here allude to those large tracts near the borders of the Krishna. Poona, the capital of the Peshwa, was a very wealthy and thriving commercial town, and there was as much cultivation in the Daccan as it was possible so arid and unfruitful a country could admit. . . .

"With respect to Malwa . . . I had ample means afforded me, as the person appointed to occupy that territory and to conduct its civil, military, and political administration, to learn all that the records of the Government could teach, and to obtain from other sources full information of this country; and I certainly entered upon my duties with the complete conviction that commerce would be unknown, and that credit could not exist. . . . I found, to my surprise, that in correspondence with the first commercial and monied men of Rajputana, Bundelkhand, and Hindustan [Northern India], as well as with those of Gujrat, dealings in money to a large amount had continuously taken place at Ujjain and other cities, where Soucars or bankers of character and credit were in a flourishing state, and that goods to a great amount had not only continuously passed through the Province, but that the insurance offices which exist throughout all that part of India, and include the principal monied men, had never stopped their operations, though premiums rose at a period of danger to a high amount. . . . And I do not believe that in that country the introduction of our direct rule could have contributed more, nor indeed so much, to the prosperity of the commercial and agricultural interests as the establishment of the efficient rule of its former princes and chiefs. . . .

"With respect to the Southern Mahratta Districts, of whose prosperity I have before spoken . . . I must unhesitatingly state that the provinces belonging to the family of Putwarden and some other chiefs on the banks of the Krishna present a greater agricultural and commercial prosperity than almost any I know in India. I refer this to the system of administration, which, though there may be at periods exactions, is on the whole mild and paternal; to few changes; to the complete knowledge and almost devotion of Hindus to all agricultural pursuits; to their better understanding, or at least better practice than us in many parts of the administration, particularly in raising towns and villages to prosperity; from the encouragement given to monied men and to the introduction of capital; and above all to the Jaegirdars residing on their estates, and those Provinces being administered by men of rank who live and die on the soil, and are usually succeeded in office by their sons or near relatives. If these men exact money at times in an arbitrary manner, all their expenditure as well as all they receive is limited to their own provinces; but above all causes which promote prosperity is the invariable support given to the village and other native institutions, and to the employment, far beyond what our system admits, of all classes of the population." [1]

The evils which were thus pointed out to the Select Committee by Sir John Malcolm and other eminent witnesses were, principally, the exclusion of the people of India from all the higher services in their own country, and the remittance of a large portion of the Indian revenues out of India year after year. The natural remedies were those which had been suggested by Bishop Heber a few years before, viz., a larger employment of the people in the administration of their own concerns, and the spending of Indian revenues in India. On the first point, Munro, Elphinstone, and Bentinck had already given some relief; and the British Parliament, in renewing the Company's charter in 1833, enacted a famous clause which will be referred to in the next chapter, declaring the people of India to be eligible to all posts without distinction of race or creed. On the second point, Parliament gave no relief to the people of India. On the contrary, although they stopped the Company's trade from April 1834, they provided for the payment of interest on the Company's stock out of the revenues of India at 10½ per cent., as has been stated before. It was an act of injustice to India, against which a strong protest was made once more by another distinguished Englishman, when the Empire passed from the Company to the Crown in 1858.

[1] Minutes of Evidence taken before the Select Committee, &c., 1832, vol. vi. pp. 30 and 31.

Sir George Wingate had distinguished himself in the land revenue settlements of Bombay, as we have seen in Chapter XXI. He had worked under a bad system, but had worked it with his natural kindness and consideration, and had made it a success. He had laboured for some thirty years among the people of India, and had retired to his native country ripe with the knowledge and experience of Indian affairs, honoured by the Government, and recognised popularly as the Father of the Bombay Revenue System. But the financial relations between India and England caused him solicitude and pain; and when the administration of the Empire passed to the Crown, he appealed to his countrymen for a more just and equitable treatment of India under the new arrangements which were then made.

"If, then, we have governed India not merely for the natives of India but for ourselves, we are clearly blamable in the sight of God and man for having contributed nothing towards defraying the cost of that government. Our fair share, represented by the degree in which British interests have decided our Indian policy, be it great or small, should have been duly paid; but this has never been done, and now there is a heavy debt which has been running up against us for many years to be settled. England was powerful and India at her feet, and little chance had the weak of enforcing payment from the strong."

"With reference to its economical effects upon the condition of India, the tribute paid to Great Britain is by far the most objectionable feature in our existing policy. Taxes spent in the country from which they are raised are totally different in their effects from taxes raised in one country and spent in another. In the former case the taxes collected from the population at large are paid away to the portion of the population engaged in the service of Government, through whose expenditure they are again returned to the industrious classes. They occasion a different distribution, but no loss of national income; and hence it is that in countries advanced in civilisation, in which the productive powers of men are augmented by mechanical contrivances and a judicious use of the powers of nature, an enormous taxation may be realised with singularly little pressure upon the community. But the case is wholly different when the taxes are not spent in the country from which they are raised. In this case they constitute no mere transfer of a portion of the national income from one set of citizens to another, but an absolute loss and extinction of the whole amount withdrawn from the taxed country. As regards its effects on national production, the whole amount might as well be thrown into the sea as transferred to another country, for no portion of it will return from the latter to the taxed country in any shape whatsoever. Such is the nature of the tribute we have so long exacted from India."

"The Indian tribute, whether weighed in the scales of justice or viewed in the light of our true interest, will be found to be at variance with humanity, with common sense, and with the received maxims of economical science. It would be true wisdom, then, to provide for the future payment of such of the home charges of the Indian Government as really form the tribute out of the Imperial Exchequer. These charges would probably be found to be the dividends on East India Stock, interest on Home Debt, the salaries of officers and establishments and cost of buildings connected with the Home Department of the Indian Government, furlough and retired pay to members of the Indian Military and Civil Services when at home, charges of all descriptions paid in this country connected with British troops serving in India, and a portion of the cost of transporting British troops to and from India."

"Were India to be relieved of this cruel burden of tribute and the whole of the taxes raised in India to be spent in India, the revenue of that country would soon acquire a degree of elasticity of which we have at present no expectation."[1]

The appeal was made in vain. The home charges, which amounted to three millions when Queen Victoria ascended the throne, had risen to sixteen millions when the Great Empress passed away. So great an Economic Drain out of the resources of a land would impoverish the most prosperous countries on earth; it has reduced India to a land of famines more frequent, more wide-spread, and more fatal, than any known before in the history of India, or of the world.

[1] *Our Financial Relations with India*, by Major Wingate, London, 1859, pp. 56–64.

CHAPTER XXIV

ACCESSION OF QUEEN VICTORIA—FAMINE OF 1837

THE financial arrangements made at the time of the renewal of the East India Company's charter in 1833 have been described in the last chapter; but other important provisions were made by the same Act which also deserve our attention.

The Province of Bengal had increased in territory by the conquests and annexations of Lord Wellesley in Northern India in 1802 and 1803. These northern tracts were now taken out of Bengal and made into a separate Province. From this time, therefore, India had four Provinces instead of three; and in the table of revenue and expenditure given in the last chapter, Northern India has been shown as a separate Province from this date.

The Governor-Generals, from the time of Warren Hastings, were technically *Governor-Generals of Bengal* with power of control over the other Provinces. The person holding the same appointment in 1834 was, by this Act, created *Governor-General of India;* and Lord William Bentinck was thus the first Governor-General of India. Each Province had hitherto made separate *Regulations* for itself; the Governor-General in Council was now empowered to pass *Acts* applicable to all India. The Council, which had hitherto consisted of four members, beside the Governor-General, was now strengthened by the appointment of a fifth member, known as the Legal Member; and Macaulay was sent out to India as the first Legal Member. The Governor-

General was empowered also to appoint Law Commissioners to draft laws for India; and Macaulay, as President of the Law Commissioners, drafted the famous Penal Code of India, which was passed into law twenty-five years later.

All restrictions on the settlement of Europeans in India were removed. Bishoprics of Madras and Bombay were created in addition to the old bishopric of Calcutta; and arrangements were made for the education of candidates for the Indian Civil Service, nominated by the Directors of the Company, at Haileybury College, before their departure for India. The control of the Company's administration of India by Commissioners appointed by the Crown, which had been provided by Pitt's India Act of 1784, was maintained.

The impossibility of administering India properly without the co-operation of the people themselves had been felt by the ablest servants of the Company; and Munro, Elphinstone, and Bentinck had admitted educated Indians to responsible judicial posts, as has been stated in a previous chapter. This liberal policy was now emphatically proclaimed in a famous clause of the Act which runs thus:

"And be it enacted, that no native of the said territories, nor any natural born subject of His Majesty resident therein, shall, by reason only of his religion, place of birth, descent, colour, or any of them, be disabled from holding any place, office, or employment under the Company."

Macaulay was in the House of Commons when this Act was passed, and his famous speech on this clause has often been quoted, and will bear repetition.

"There is, however, one part of the Bill on which, after what has recently passed elsewhere, I feel myself irresistibly impelled to say a few words. I allude to that wise, that benevolent, that noble clause, which enacts that no native of our Indian Empire shall, by reason of his colour, his descent, or his religion, be incapable of holding office. At the risk of being called by that nickname which is regarded as the most opprobrious of all nicknames by men of selfish hearts and contracted minds — at the risk of being called a philosopher—I must say that to the last day of my life I shall be proud of being one of those who assisted in the framing of the Bill which contains that clause. . . .

"It was, as Bernier tells us, the practice of the miserable tyrants whom we found in India, that when they dreaded the capacity and spirit of some distinguished subject, and yet could not venture to murder him, to administer to him a daily dose of the *pousta*, a preparation of opium, the effect of which was in a few months to destroy all the bodily and mental powers of the wretch who was drugged with it, and to turn him into a helpless idiot. That destestable artifice, more horrible than assassination itself, was worthy of those who employed it. It is no model for the English nation. We shall never consent to administer the *pousta* to a whole community, to stupefy and paralyse a great people whom God has committed to our charge for the wretched purpose of rendering them more amenable to our control. What is that power worth which is founded on vice, on ignorance, and on misery—which we can hold only by violating the most sacred duties which, as governors, we owe to the governed—which, as a people blessed with a far more than an ordinary measure of political liberty and of intellectual light, we owe to a race debased by three thousand years of despotism and priestcraft? We are free, we are civilised, to little purpose, if we grudge to any portion of the human race an equal measure of freedom and civilisation. Are we to keep the people of India ignorant in order that we may keep them submissive? Or do we think that we can give them knowledge without awakening ambition? Or do we mean to awaken ambition and to provide it with no legitimate vent? Who will answer any of these questions in the affirmative? Yet one of them must be answered in the affirmative by every person who maintains that we ought permanently to exclude the natives from high office. I have no fears. The path of duty is plain before us, and it is also the path of wisdom, of national prosperity, of national honour.

"The destinies of our Indian Empire are covered with thick darkness. It is difficult to form any conjectures as to the fate reserved for a State which resembles no other in history, and which forms by itself a separate class of political phenomena; the laws which regulate its growth and its decay are still unknown to us. It may be that the public mind of India may expand under our system till it has outgrown the system; that by good government we may educate our subjects into a capacity for better government; that having become instructed in European knowledge, they may in some future age demand European institutions. Whether such a day will ever come I know not. But never will I attempt to avert or to retard it. Whenever it comes, it will be the proudest day in English history. To have found a great people sunk to the lowest depths of slavery and superstition, to have so ruled them as to have made them desirous and capable of all the privileges of citizens, would indeed be a title to glory all our own. The sceptre may pass away from us. Unforeseen accidents may derange our most profound schemes of policy. Victory may be inconstant to our arms. But there are triumphs which are followed by no reverses. There is an empire exempt from all natural causes of decay. Those triumphs are the pacific triumphs of reason over barbarism; that empire is the imperishable empire of our arts and our morals, our literature and our laws." [1]

The lights and shades are laid on somewhat thick in the above speech, as in all Macaulay's utterances and writings, and when he described Moghal emperors as " miserable tyrants," and spoke of " three thousand years of depotism and priestcraft," and of " the lowest depths of slavery and superstition," he only spoke with an Englishman's usual want of appreciation of the customs, institutions, and achievements of nations living outside the narrow limits of England.

There can be no doubt, however, that the new policy, which Macaulay so vigorously advocated, was the policy which England of 1833—which Englishmen who had just passed the Reform Act—wished to see introduced and pursued in India. Monopoly and exclusiveness were distasteful to Englishmen of that day; to shut out a nation from high office in their own country was obnoxious to those who had just extended their franchise; fair play even to a subject nation was the uppermost thought of all earnest reformers, and of the people at large in the British Isles. And the clause we have quoted above was the outcome of the spirit of the times—the embodiment of the policy which the British nation desired for India.

Happy it were for India if that wise and liberal plan had been consistently followed during the seventy years which have since elapsed. The rule of England would have been more popular and more successful to-day, if the people of India had been admitted to a

[1] Macaulay's Speeches. The above speech was made on the 10th July 1833, "in a thin House; a circumstance which may surprise those who are not aware that on a Wednesday, and with an Indian question on the paper, Cicero replying to Hortensius would hardly draw a quorum. Small as it was, the audience contained Lord John Russell, Peel, O'Connel, and other masters of the Parliamentary craft. . . . The Government carried every point by large majorities, and with slight modifications in detail, and none in principle; the measure became law with the almost universal approbation both of Parliament and the country."—Trevelyan's *Life of Lord Macaulay*.

proper share of the administration. And the economic condition of the people would have been better if a large portion of the Indian revenues had flowed back to the people to fructify their trades and industries. But monopoly dies hard in a country where the people have no voice; and during seventy years "that wise, that benevolent, that noble clause," so eloquently praised by Macaulay, has been virtually evaded.

"No sooner was the Act passed," wrote a Viceroy of India half a century later, "than the Government began to devise means for practically evading the fulfilment of it. Under the terms of the Act, which are studied and laid to heart by that increasing class of educated natives whose development the Government encourages without being able to satisfy the aspirations of its existing members, every such native, if once admitted to Government employment in posts previously reserved to the Covenanted Service, is entitled to expect and claim appointment in the fair course of promotion to the highest posts in that service. We all know that these claims and expectations never can or will be fulfilled. We have had to choose between prohibiting them and cheating them, and we have chosen the least straightforward course. The application to natives of the Competitive Examination system as conducted in England, and the recent reduction in the age at which candidates can compete, are all so many deliberate and transparent subterfuges for stultifying the Act, and reducing it to a dead letter. Since I am writing confidentially, I do not hesitate to say that both the Government of England and of India appear to me, up to the present moment, unable to answer satisfactorily the charge of having taken every means in their power of breaking to the heart the words of promise they have uttered to the ear."[1]

[1] Lord Lytton's Confidential Minute of 1878, quoted in Dadabhai Naoroji's *Poverty and un-British Rule in India*, London, 1901, pp.

This evasion of a clause so eloquently praised in the House of Commons, and so emphatically approved of by the British nation, was not foreseen when the Act was passed in 1833. On the contrary, as has been stated before, there was every desire then to promote education in India and to admit educated Indians to an increasing share in the higher services of their own country, without distinction of descent, creed, or colour. Englishmen desired to be just, and the people of India looked forward with a thrill of high expectation to progress and self-government under the Imperial power of a just and righteous nation.

Four years after this, Queen Victoria ascended the throne in 1837. It is not possible to point to any single date in the history of India when the rule of England was more sympathetic and benevolent, and evoked a higher respect and a deeper loyalty among the people. The wars of Lord Wellesley, Lord Hastings, and Lord Amherst were over, and there was peace in the land. The blunders in civil administration had to a great extent been rectified. The people of India had been welcomed to take some share in the administration of their own concerns. Recollections of the rule of Munro in Madras, of Elphinstone in Bombay, and of Bentinck in Bengal, were fresh in men's minds. The policy of spreading English education in India had been decided upon. Wasteful expenditure had been reduced, and the Indian budget showed a surplus. A cruel and

317 and 318. The "stultifying the Act" has been so effectual and complete that the higher services in the Civil, Military, Public Works, Police, Medical, Educational, Postal, Telegraph, Forests, and all other departments in India, are almost as exclusively reserved for Europeans to-day as when the India Act of 1833 was passed. A Parliamentary Return, submitted in 1892, shows that, including all appointments carrying a pay of £100 a year or more (taking ten rupees for a pound), the pay and pensions granted to Europeans annually amount to *fourteen millions*, besides *one million* to Eurasians, while *three and a half millions* only are given to natives of India, generally holding lower posts.

oppressive land-revenue demand had been reduced, and more humane land-settlements for long terms were being made by Bird in Northern India and Wingate in Bombay. The East India Company had ceased to be traders and stood forth as administrators. The British Parliament had given its pledge to the people of India to admit them to the highest posts in their country without distinction of creed or colour. A young Queen had ascended the throne of the British Empire, and awakened in the minds of the people of India all the high hopes and aspirations which a woman's kindly providence inspires in the oriental mind.

And if this was a bright period in administrative reforms, it was no less so in literary culture. Macaulay had introduced into India something of that broad-mindedness which belongs to literature. Horace Hayman Wilson was a distinguished orientalist, and later on became a distinguished historian. Elphinstone was a man of letters, and was on the eve of publishing his famous History of India. Briggs had published his great work on the Indian Land-Tax, and was at work over his famous translation of Ferishta. Colonel Tod was almost a Rajput himself in his sympathies, and wrote that history of Rajasthan which is more thrilling and attractive than any romance. Grant Duff was at work over his great History of the Mahrattas, which will have its value for all time to come. Never did Englishmen of any generation show higher literary culture and talent in India, never did they feel a truer sympathy with the people. It is impossible to read the evidence of some of the great Indian administrators and publicists of the time, given before the Parliamentary Committees of 1831 and 1832, without feeling that they entertained a respect for the people of India in those days, and appreciated their virtues and worth.

"I have always formed a good opinion of the native character generally," said Chaplin, whose revenue work in Bombay we have reviewed in a preceding chapter; "*I think they will bear an advantageous comparison with the natives of any country in the world.*"

"Would you not be disposed to place as much confidence in the natives of India as you would in your own countrymen?" was the question that was put to John Sullivan of the Madras Civil Service. "Yes," he replied, "*if equally well treated.*"

And James Sutherland, who was for some years editor of one of the first English newspapers of Calcutta, the *Bengal Harkara*, spoke of educated Indians that "*they are as trustworthy as any men in the world.*" [1]

This spirit of trust and confidence in the people evoked a warm response. The leaders of the Indian community, the social and religious reformers of India, and the distinguished Indian students who were educated in the Hindu College of Calcutta, felt a warm appreciation for English literature and thought, a deep-seated faith in the British character and the British rule. The most illustrious among them, Raja Ram Mohan Roy, founded the Brahma Somaj or Theistic Church of India, and helped in all social and educational reforms of the day; and his cordial support in abolishing the cruel rite of *Sati* was handsomely acknowledged by Lord William Bentinck. The Raja then came to England, and was present in the House of Commons when a memorial against Lord William's measure was discussed; and he had the satisfaction of seeing the decision of the Indian Government confirmed by the British Parliament. Thousands of younger Indians, fresh from English schools and colleges, imbibed the reforming spirit, the love of Western literature and thought, the faith in British

[1] Evidence of Chaplin, Sullivan, and Sutherland, given in 1831 and 1832. The italics are our own.

rule and British character, which inspired Raja Ram Roy."[1]

Thus, when Queen Victoria ascended the throne of the British Empire, there was a deep, widespread, and devoted loyalty among her Indian subjects, because the policy of England had been generous and trustful. Happy it were, both for England and for India, if that generous and trustful policy had continued to the end of her long reign. For the task of Indian administration is the most momentous and difficult that the British nation has ever undertaken, and that task cannot be performed without the co-operation of the people, and without confidence and trust in the people.

The very year of the Queen's accession revealed the vast difficulties of Indian administration. Famines had followed the wars of Lord Wellesley in Bombay and in Northern India in 1803 and 1804; a fresh

[1] Sir Charles Trevelyan said in his evidence given before the Select Committee of the House of Lords on the 21st June 1853: "I have never heard such pure English, either in construction or pronunciation, spoken as I have heard by the educated natives of Calcutta. They speak purer English than we speak ourselves, for they take it from the purest models; they speak the language of the *Spectator*, such English as is never spoken in England. It is one of the encouraging circumstances of our position in India that the natives have a remarkable facility for acquiring foreign languages."

In my younger days I was brought up among those who had been in school and college in 1837, when the Queen ascended the throne; and I do not exaggerate facts when I state that nothing could exceed the appreciation of English literature, thought, and character, nothing could exceed the loyalty to the British rule which these men felt and expressed in their everyday conversation. They had recollections of the times of Bentinck, Elphinstone, and Munro; they had seen Macaulay, Trevelyan, and Metcalfe; and a faith in English truth was a part of their beliefs. I have lived since with two succeeding generations of Indians—my contemporaries who were in school and college in the Sixties and the younger men who were educated in the Nineties,—and I confess I have marked in them a decadence in this faith. They point to unredeemed British pledges; they exclaim against the continued exclusiveness of British administration; they demand, as Macaulay had foreseen, some degree of self-government, some share in the control of the administration. Are they wrong? Or is the British Government unwise in evading the fulfilment of a generous pledge, and in keeping up an absolute form of government set up by Warren Hastings over a hundred years ago?

famine had occurred in Bombay in 1813; and Madras, with her wretched and oppressive land settlements, had been afflicted by famines in 1807, 1823, and 1833. And now, in the first year of the Queen's reign, Northern India, suffering equally from oppressive land settlements, was desolated by a famine more intense and more widespread than any of the preceding famines of the century. The new settlement of Robert Merttins Bird had not yet been completed; the people were resourceless and in chronic indebtedness, and a failure of rains in 1837 brought on the disastrous famine.

"I have never in my life," wrote John Lawrence, afterwards Lord Lawrence, "seen such utter desolation as that which is now spread over the Perganas of Hodal and Palwal." Deaths were numerous and were never reckoned. In Cawnpur a special establishment patrolled the streets and the river to remove the corpses. In Fatehpur and Agra similar measures were adopted. Hundreds of thousands died in obscure villages, unknown and unheeded. The dead lay on the road-side, unburied and unburnt, till they were devoured by wild animals.

Thus was a signal given at the commencement of a new reign of the difficulties which beset the administration of India, and the gravity of the distress and poverty which prevailed in the country. The reign of Queen Victoria has witnessed many changes in India. It has seen the extension of the Empire by the annexation of Sindh and the Punjab, of Oudh and the Central Provinces, of Burma and Beluchistan. It has seen the wide continent spanned by railways and connected by postal and telegraph lines. It has seen the establishment of High Courts of justice and of Universities in the different Provinces. It has witnessed the enlargement of cities, and the reclamation of great tracts of country for agriculture. It has witnessed the creation of Legislative Councils, of District Boards and Municipalities. It has witnessed the progress of English education in towns, and of vernacular education in villages.

Two essential reforms the reign of Queen Victoria has not witnessed. It has not admitted the people of India to any share in the control and direction of the administration of their own affairs. And it has not improved the material condition of the mass of the people, or protected the country from those frequent, fatal, and widespread famines which have now disappeared from all other lands under civilised administrations. The history of British rule in India repeats the lesson which history has taught us that it is impossible to govern a country in the interests of the people without bestowing on that people some degree of self-government and representation.

INDEX

2 E